Whither the Philippines in the 21st Century?

The **Institute of Southeast Asian Studies (ISEAS)** was established as an autonomous organization in 1968. It is a regional centre dedicated to the study of socio-political, security, and economic trends and developments in Southeast Asia and its wider geostrategic and economic environment.

The Institute's research programmes are the Regional Economic Studies (RES, including ASEAN and APEC), Regional Strategic and Political Studies (RSPS), and Regional Social and Cultural Studies (RSCS).

ISEAS Publishing, an established academic press, has issued more than 2,000 books and journals. It is the largest scholarly publisher of research about Southeast Asia from within the region. ISEAS Publishing works with many other academic and trade publishers and distributors to disseminate important research and analyses from and about Southeast Asia to the rest of the world.

Whither the Philippines in the 21st Century?

Edited by

Rodolfo C. Severino &
Lorraine Carlos Salazar

Konrad Adenauer Stiftung

ISEAS

INSTITUTE OF SOUTHEAST ASIAN STUDIES
Singapore

First published in Singapore in 2007 by
Institute of Southeast Asian Studies
30 Heng Mui Keng Terrace
Pasir Panjang
Singapore 119614

E-mail: publish@iseas.edu.sg
Website: <http://bookshop.iseas.edu.sg>

ISEAS Library Cataloguing-in-Publication Data

Whither the Philippines in the 21st century? / edited by Rodolfo C. Severino and Lorraine Carlos Salazar.
A collection of papers originally presented at a Conference on the Philippines, organized by ISEAS, Singapore, from 13 to 14 July 2006.
1. Philippines—Congresses.
2. Philippines—Politics and government—1986—Congresses.
3. Philippines—Social conditions—1986—Congresses.
4. Philippines—Economic conditions—1986—Congresses.
I. Severino, Rodolfo C.
II. Salazar, Lorraine Carlos.
III. Institute of Southeast Asian Studies.
IV. Title: Whither the Philippines in the twenty-first century?
V. Whither the Philippines in the 21st Century : a Conference on the Philippines (2006 : Singapore)
DS655 W59 2007

ISBN 978-981-230-498-8 (soft cover)
ISBN 978-981-230-499-5 (hard cover)
ISBN 978-981-230-517-6 (PDF)

Typeset by Superskill Graphics Pte Ltd
Printed in Singapore by Utopia Press Pte Ltd

CONTENTS

List of Illustrations vii

Foreword xi
K. KESAVAPANY

Acknowledgements xv

The Contributors xvii

List of Abbreviations xxi

Map of Southeast Asia xxiv

1. The Philippines in Southeast Asia 1
Mely CABALLERO-ANTHONY

2. From Regime Crisis to System Change 18
Joel ROCAMORA

3. Proposed Constitutional Reforms for Good Governance and Nation Building 43
Jose V. ABUEVA

4. The Military in Philippine Politics 78
Carolina HERNANDEZ

5. Religion and Politics 100
Grace JAMON and Mary Grace MIRANDILLA

6. The Philippine Press 127
Melinda DE JESUS

7. Macroeconomic Issues and Challenges 142
Gerardo P. SICAT

8. Investment Climate and Business Opportunities 180
Peter WALLACE

9. Why Does Poverty Persist in the Philippines? 202
Arsenio M. BALISACAN

10. Diaspora, Remittances, and Poverty 222
Ernesto PERNIA

11. The Philippine Development Record 246
Hal HILL and Sharon Faye PIZA

12. Sancho Panza in Buliok Complex 277
Patricio N. ABINALES

13. The Insurgency That Would Not Go Away 313
Alexander R. MAGNO

14. Whither the Philippines in the 21st Century? 330
Rodolfo SEVERINO

Index 347

LIST OF ILLUSTRATIONS

List of Figures

Figure 8.1	Average Gross Domestic Product Growth of the Philippines, 1961–2004	181
Figure 8.2	30-Year GDP Growth of Selected Asian Countries	181
Figure 8.3	Head Office Attitude on Business Operations in RP	187
Figure 8.4	RP vs Rest of ASEAN as Investment Site	189
Figure 8.5	Trend in Investment Since 1990 (US$ Billion)	190
Figure 8.6	RP Infrastructure Spending as % of GDP	190
Figure 8.7	Tourism in the Philippines	198
Figure 9.1	Poverty Reduction in East Asia	205
Figure 9.2	Income Growth and Poverty Reduction, Philippine Provinces, 1985–2003	207
Figure 9.3	Population Growth: Philippines vs Thailand (% per year)	215
Figure 9.4	Per capita Income in the Philippines had the Country Followed Thailand's Population Dynamics	217
Figure 11.1	Annual GDP Growth Rate, 1961–2003 (%)	250
Figure 11.2	Per Capita GDP, 1975–2003 ($PPP)	251
Figure 11.3a	Annual Inflation, 1961–2004 (%)	260
Figure 11.3b	Coefficient of Variation and Average Inflation, 1961–2003 (%)	261
Figure 11.4	Annual Exchange Rate per US$, 1960–2003	262
Figure 11.5	Annual Fiscal and Current Account Balances, 1970–2004	264

List of Tables

Table 2.1	Asian GDP Growth Rates, 2001–2006	35
Table 2.2	Fiscal Performance of the Past Administrations, 1946–2004	36
Table 2.3	Total Debt Service as Percentage of National Government Revenues, 1995–2004	36
Table 2.4	Selected Items of Government Spending	37
Table 5.1	Philippine Catholic Statistics	105
Table 8.1	Some Basic Numbers	183
Table 8.2	RP's Top Investment Barriers	185
Table 8.3	RP's Top Investment Attractions	186
Table 8.4	Net Foreign Direct Investments into Asia (US$B)	188
Table 8.5	Infrastructure Projects of the GMA Administration	191
Table 8.6	Key Bills Critical to Business	192
Table 8.7	CEO Perception of the Philippines as an Investment Site	193
Table 8.8	CEO Perception on Doing Business in RP (June 2006)	194
Table 8.9	RP's 5 Areas of "Natural Advantage"	195
Table 8.10	BPO/Call Centres in RP	197
Table 8.11	The Medium-Term Outlook	200
Table 8.12	Economic Forecast: The Worst and the Best Scenarios	200
Table 9.1	Levels and Growth Rates of GDP per capita, 1980–2005	204
Table 9.2	Poverty Incidence and Income Growth, Philippines Regions, 1988–2003	206
Table 9.3	Average Agriculture Growth (%), 1965–2002	210
Table 9.4	Growth of Total Factor Productivity (TFP) in Agriculture	211
Table 9.5	Indicative Areas for National Government Spending on a Poverty Programme	213
Table 9.6	Why the Philippines Grew So Slowly	216
Table 10.1	Average Annual Reported Remittance Inflows into Asia's Main Labour Exporting Countries	229
Table 10.2	Number of Overseas Workers, 1995–2004	232
Table 10.3	Definitions of the Variables	233

Table 10.4 Average Remittance per OFW, 1995–2004 234
Table 10.5 Three-State Least Squares Regression (Quintile 1) 237
Table 10.6 Three-State Least Squares Regression (Quintile 2) 238

Table 11.1 Key Indicators, 2004 249
Table 11.2 Average Growth of Per Capita GDP (%) 251
Table 11.3 Share of Sectors in GDP, 1965–2004 (%) 253
Table 11.4 Average Shares of Domestic Investment and Government Expenditure in Gross National Expenditure, 1960s–2000 (%) 254
Table 11.5 Poverty and Inequality (%) 255
Table 11.6 Key Social Indicators 256
Table 11.7 Average Inflation (%) 261
Table 11.8 Average Shares of Fiscal and Current Account Balances in GDP (%) 265
Table 11.9 External Debt as a Percentage of GDP, 1970–2004 (%) 265
Table 11.10 Average Shares of Trade and FDI in GDP (%) 266
Table 11.11 World Exports of Parts and Components, 1992–2004 (%) 267

Table 12.1 MILF Affected Barangays (last Quarter 2005) 283
Table 12.2 Preliminary Data on AFP-MNLF Battles and Locations, 1977–2001 288
Table 12.3 Preliminary Data on AFP-MILF Number of Battles and Locations, 1987–2004 290
Table 12.4 Types of Military Encounters, MNLF-AFP, 1972–2002 295
Table 12.5 Types of Military Encounters, MILF-AFP, 1987–2003 295
Table 12.6 Combatants Killed and Injured in Armed Encounters, AFP, MNLF, MILF, by Administration, 1986–2004 296
Table 12.7 Counting the Cost of the Protracted War in Southern Philippines, 1969–1996 297

List of Appendices

Appendix 7 — Selected Macroeconomic Data for the Philippines 172
Appendix 10 — Definition of the Variables and Descriptive Statistics 244

FOREWORD

In 2004 and 2005, the Philippines' gross domestic product grew by 6 and 5.1 per cent, respectively. In the Southeast Asian context, this growth rate places the country behind Singapore and Vietnam, but it compares fairly well with those of Indonesia, Thailand and even Malaysia. Because of this, international credit rating agencies have been upgrading their ratings for the Philippines. Government figures show that, under the administration of President Gloria Macapagal Arroyo, the Philippine economy grew by an average of 4.4 per cent a year, faster than in the three previous presidencies.

Yet, the question in many people's minds is this: why does the Philippines continue to be outside the "radar screens" of most international investors, including those from Singapore and other capital-exporting ASEAN countries? Why has the percentage of the country's population living below the poverty line remained stuck at 30 per cent (in 2003), which, in ASEAN, puts the Philippines in the same league as Cambodia, Laos and Myanmar and worse off than Vietnam (19.5 per cent in 2004)? In spite of the steady macroeconomic growth, why do so many Filipinos have to leave their homeland and their families to seek jobs? If economic growth brings stability and contentment, why do the Philippines' two insurgencies — the communist and the Muslim — so stubbornly persist? Why do Philippine politics appear so volatile? Why do elements of organized religion and the military find it necessary to intervene in the political process?

Is it just a matter of the normal time lag between a macroeconomic surge and its trickle-down effect? Is it a question of unjustified impressions purveyed by media free from undemocratic constraints? Is the problem the country's rapid population growth? Is it the consequence of political decisions? Is it a matter of political will or political institutions? On the other hand, are there niches of progress that are not obvious to many?

To shed light on these questions, the Institute of Southeast Asian Studies, on 13–14 July 2006, convened a gathering of scholars and other observers of the Philippines. They occupy a broad spectrum of political, economic and social viewpoints, approaching the fascinating Philippine conundrum from many angles. All of them are well-known Philippine experts, many of whom are Filipinos — nurturing an abiding interest in Philippine affairs.

As expected, they did not arrive at any kind of unanimity or even consensus; but the discussions sharpened their insights and refined their thinking. In the light of those discussions, they revisited and revised the papers that they had brought to the conference. The revised papers are compiled in this book, which ISEAS is happy to publish. We hope that they will contribute to the continuing debate on the Philippines, a debate often driven by passion, sometimes marked by a measure of bewilderment, always conducted with lively energy. We hope, at the same time, that the papers will enrich the debate's factual grounding and strengthen its analytical rigour.

The Philippine situation is extremely complex, as complex as the situation in any country in the world. This is why the chapters in this volume cover such a variety of subjects from such diverse points of view.

Mely Caballero-Anthony of the S. Rajaratnam School of International Studies of Singapore's Nanyang Technological University offers a sweeping overview of the Philippine situation. Joel Rocamora, a long-time observer, activist, and analyst of the Philippine political scene, shares his insights into the country's political institutions and processes as he interprets them today. José V. Abueva, the highly esteemed political scientist, former president of the University of the Philippines, and foremost advocate of constitutional change, argues the case for a drastic reform of the country's system of governance. Carolina G. Hernandez, a scholar for many seasons and a direct participant in the efforts to reform the Philippine military, and Grace Jamon and Mary Grace Mirandilla, experts on religion in the Philippines, contribute their thoughts on the roles of the military and religion, respectively, in Philippine politics. Melinda de Jesus, a former journalist and an active observer of Southeast Asian media's freedom or lack thereof, examines the state of the Philippine media.

The eminent economist, Gerardo P. Sicat, analyses the Philippines' economic strengths and weaknesses, the political and social factors underlying them, and the economy's prospects for the future. On the other hand, Peter Wallace, a long-time consultant to many multinational companies, views these strengths and weaknesses and their underlying factors from the practical viewpoint of the investor. Ernesto M. Pernia, professor of economics and former economist at the World Bank and the Asian Development Bank, dissects the phenomenon of the Filipino diaspora and the economic, social and political impact of its homeward remittances.

A prominent agricultural economist, Arsenio M. Balisacan of the University of the Philippines examines the distressing picture of poverty in the Philippines, its dimensions, and its causes. Looking at the Philippine development record in comparative perspective, Hal Hill of the Australian National University and Sharon Piza of the Asia Pacific Policy Center contend that one should avoid simplistic generalizations. They argue that while developments are messy, the Philippines is far from a failed state. Patricio N. Abinales, professor of Southeast Asian Studies in Kyoto, and Alexander Magno, former dissident and now professor and newspaper columnist, write about the Muslim and communist insurgencies, respectively, with some unusual insights. The insurgencies are located in the socioeconomic sections of the conference and of this volume because we believe that they are more a socioeconomic than simply a security problem.

The conference ended with a panel discussion among Manu Bhaskaran, an international consultant; Frank Cibulka, a Philippine specialist and professor at Zayed University in Abu Dhabi; Klaus Preschle, country representative of the Konrad Adenauer Stiftung in the Philippines; and Grace Padaca, Governor of the Philippines' Isabela Province. They concluded the conference on an optimistic note, projecting hopeful prospects for the country on the basis of new trends, both national and international, and the unfolding dynamics in the global and regional economy.

Rodolfo C. Severino, visiting senior research fellow at ISEAS, retired Philippine diplomat, and former ASEAN secretary-general, attempts, in the concluding chapter, an analytical summary of the conference papers and proceedings and of the issues that they raise.

The reader will appreciate the wide variety of styles that characterizes the chapters in this volume, a variety that reflects the greatly diverse backgrounds of their authors — from the academically rigorous to the fluidly journalistic to the breezily conversational.

I wish to thank Denis Hew, head of Regional Economic Studies at ISEAS; Mely Caballero-Anthony; Rodolfo Severino; Lorraine Salazar, visiting research fellow at ISEAS; and Karthi Nair of ISEAS for organizing the conference in its many aspects and phases. Severino and Salazar edited this book. I also thank Triena Ong, Head of the Publications Unit of ISEAS, and her staff for seeing this volume through to publication.

Not least, ISEAS and I are profoundly grateful to the Konrad Adenauer Stiftung Singapore for its support of the July conference and to the Konrad Adenauer Stiftung Philippines for its assistance in the publication of this book.

K. KESAVAPANY
Director
Institute of Southeast Asian Studies
Singapore

ACKNOWLEDGEMENTS

Observers of the Philippines are often baffled by what they perceive as the economic malaise and political turmoil that dominate headlines about the country. The news coming out of the Philippines has, for several years, been mostly negative. One scholar has even described the country as being caught in a "developmental bog". Yet, the Philippines continues to hold the potential for improving the lives of its people and being a positive force for the political and economic development of the region.

In 2005, the political noise reached high decibels, making many investors wary and placing yet another obstacle on the country's road to development. At the same time, however, the economy has proved resilient, growing at 4.9 per cent in 2005 and 5.4 per cent in 2006. This underscores the resilience of the economy, at least at the macro level, and reflects Filipinos' tenacity and hard work.

To assess the nature and direction of these seemingly contradictory trends and gain a sense of the country's prospects, ISEAS convened a conference entitled "Whither the Philippines in the 21st Century?" on 13 and 14 July 2006. The conference brought together a high-powered group of experts who provided knowledgeable and provocative assessments of key political, economic, and social issues facing the country. The discussions were interactive and lively, with participants espousing opposing sides on issues and articulating varying ideas and proposals. In order for their analyses to reach a much wider audience, ISEAS has decided to publish the revised papers from the conference, which this volume now comprises.

We wish to thank Denis Hew, head of Regional Economic Studies at ISEAS, and Mely Caballero-Anthony for their insights in designing the conference and Karthi Nair for organizing its many administrative details. We would also like to thank the contributors to this volume for their rigorous analyses in their respective domains. We thank Manu Bhaskaran, Frank

Cibulka, Grace Padaca and Klaus Preschle for the informed thoughts and insights that they shared during the panel discussion that capped the conference.

We wish to thank Triena Ong, Head of the Publications Unit of ISEAS, and her staff for seeing this volume through to publication. Also, we are grateful to the Konrad Adenauer Stiftung (KAS) Singapore for its support of the July conference and KAS Philippines for its financial support in publishing this volume. Finally and not least, we thank Ambassador K. Kesavapany, Director of ISEAS, for his crucial personal interest and support, which made the Philippine conference and this volume a reality.

We hope that this volume will provide readers a deeper insight into and a more balanced appreciation of events in the Philippines as well as a glimpse into its future.

Rodolfo Severino and Lorraine Salazar
Singapore, September 2007

THE CONTRIBUTORS

PATRICIO ABINALES is Professor at the Center for Southeast Asian Studies, Kyoto University, Japan. He is Southeast Asia Editor, *Critical Asian Studies* and Managing Editor, *Kyoto Review of Southeast Asia*.

JOSE V. ABUEVA was the Chairman of the 2005 Consultative Commission created by President Arroyo to study and propose changes to the 1987 Philippine Constitution. Dr Abueva has served as President of the University of the Philippines (UP). He is Professor Emeritus of Political Science and Public Administration at UP and the Founding President of Kalayaan College.

MELY CABALLERO-ANTHONY is Associate Professor at the S. Rajaratnam School of International Studies, Nanyang Technological University, Singapore.

ARSENIO M. BALISACAN is Professor of Economics, University of the Philippines, Diliman, and the Director of the Southeast Asian Regional Center for Graduate Study and Research in Agriculture (SEARCA).

CAROLINA G. HERNANDEZ is Emeritus Professor of Political Science at the University of the Philippines. She is the Founding President of the Institute for Strategic and Development Studies (ISDS Philippines). Until February 2007, she was President Gloria Macapagal-Arroyo's adviser for military reform.

HAL HILL is Convenor of the Division of Economics and the H.W. Arndt Professor of Southeast Asian Economies in the Research School of Pacific and Asian Studies, Australian National University.

GRACE R. GOROSPE–JAMON is Professor of Political Science at the Department of Political Science of the College of Social Sciences and Philosophy (CSSP), University of the Philippines (UP), at Diliman, Quezon City.

MELINDA QUINTOS DE JESUS is the Executive Director of the Manila-based private non-stock, non-profit Center for Media Freedom and Responsibility (CMFR), which she organized in 1989 to address the problems confronting the media in a developing democracy.

ALEXANDER R. MAGNO is a well-known political analyst, a newspaper columnist, and Professor of Political Science at the University of the Philippines.

MARY GRACE P. MIRANDILLA is an Economic Policy Associate at The Asia Foundation – Philippines.

ERNESTO M. PERNIA is Professor of Economics at the University of the Philippines, Diliman. Until recently, Dr Pernia was Lead Economist at the Asian Development Bank, where he also headed the Economics and Research Department's Knowledge Dissemination Unit and was the Managing Editor of the *Asian Development Review*.

SHARON FAYE A. PIZA is Senior Research Associate at the Asia Pacific Policy Center located at the Philippine Social Sciences Center, Diliman, Quezon City.

JOEL ROCAMORA has been working within NGOs and social movements in the Philippines, the United States, and Europe for most of the last forty years. He is also in the leadership of Akbayan (Citizens Action Party), a political party based on social movements.

LORRAINE CARLOS SALAZAR is Visiting Research Fellow at the Institute of Southeast Asian Studies (ISEAS) and an Assistant Professor of Political Science at the University of the Philippines.

RODOLFO C. SEVERINO, a former Philippine diplomat and former ASEAN Secretary-General, is Visiting Senior Research Fellow at the Institute of Southeast Asian Studies in Singapore.

GERARDO P. SICAT is Professor Emeritus of Economics, University of the Philippines, and was Cabinet Minister in charge of the economy and planning in the Philippines from 1970 to 1981.

PETER LESLIE WALLACE has been living in the Philippines since 1975 and is the founder of The Wallace Business Forum, Inc., which provides consulting services to more than 160 multinational corporations and aid agencies, in addition to dealing with successive Philippine governments on foreign investments and policies affecting business.

LIST OF ABBREVIATIONS

ADB	Asian Development Bank
ADC	Asian Developing Countries
AFP	Armed Forces of the Philippines
ARMM	Autonomous Region of Muslim Mindanao
AMRSP	Association of Major Religious Superiors of the Philippines
ASEAN	Association of Southeast Asian Nations
BOT	build-operate-transfer
BPO	business process outsourcing
BSP	Bangko Sentral ng Pilipinas (Central Bank of the Philippines)
CARP	Comprehensive Agrarian Reform Program
CBCP	Catholic Bishops Conference of the Philippines
CCP	Communist Party of the Philippines
CESB	Career Service Executive Board
CESO	Career Executive Service Officer
Chacha	Charter Change
CMFP	Citizens' Movement for a Federal Philippines
CMFR	Center for Media Freedom and Responsibility
Comelec	Commission on Elections
CPP	Communist Party of the Philippines
DECS	Department of Education, Culture, and Sports
DICT	Department of Information and Communication Technologies
DND	Department of National Defence
EDSA	Epifanio de los Santos Avenue
EO	Executive Order
EPF	Employees Provident Fund

EPIRA	Electric Power Industry Reform Act
FDI	foreign direct investment
FIES	Family Income and Expenditure Survey
FPJ	Fernando Po Jr.
FTAA	Financial Technical Assistance Agreement
GCM	General Court-Martial
GDP	gross domestic product
GK	Gawad Kalinga
GNP	gross national product
GRDP	gross regional domestic product
GRP	Government of the Republic of the Philippines
HDI	Human Development Index
IFI	international financial institution
IMF	International Monetary Fund
INC	Iglesia ni Cristo
IPR	intellectual property rights
ISAFP	Intelligence Services of the Armed Forces of the Philippines
IT	information technology
ITES	information technology enabled services
JI	Jemaah Islamiyah
JIL	Jesus is Lord Fellowship
Lakas-NUCD-UMDP	Lakas ng Bansa (Strength of the Nation)–National Union of Christian Democrats–United Muslim Democrats of the Philippines
LFS	Labour Force Survey
LIBOR	London inter-bank rate
MILF	Moro Islamic Liberation Front
MIM	Mindanao Independence Movement
MNLF	Moro National Liberation Front
NCCP	National Council of Churches in the Philippines
NDF	National Democratic Front
NGO	non-governmental organisation
NIE	newly-industrializing economies
NPA	New People's Army
NSCB	National Statistical Coordination Board
NSO	National Statistics Office
OCW	overseas contract worker
ODA	official development assistance

OECD	Organization for Economic Cooperation and Development
OFW	overseas Filipino worker
OIC	Organization of Islamic Conference
OPAIFCR	Office of the Presidential Adviser to Implement the Feliciano Commission Recommendations
OWWA	Overseas Workers Welfare Administration
PCEC	Philippine Council of Evangelical Churches
PCGG	Presidential Commission on Good Governance
PCP-II	Second Plenary Council of the Philippines
PDP-Laban	Partido ng Demokratikong Pilipino–Lakas ng Bayan (Philippines Democratic Party National Struggle)
PMA	Philippine Military Academy
PPCRV	Parish Pastoral Council for Responsible Voting
PROD	Presidential Regional Officers for Development
RA	Republic Act
RAM	Reform the Armed Forces Movement
RPA-ABB	Revolutionary Proletarian Army–Alex Boncayao Brigade
RSBS	Retirement Service and Benefits System
SMS	short messaging service
SNITS	simplified net income taxation system
SOF	Survey of Overseas Filipinos
SSR	Security Sector Reform
SSRI	Security Sector Reform Index
TFP	total factor productivity
Trapo	traditional politician
3SLS	three-stage least squares
ULAP	Union of Local Government Authorities in the Philippines
UP	University of the Philippines
VAT	value-added tax
WTO	World Trade Organisation

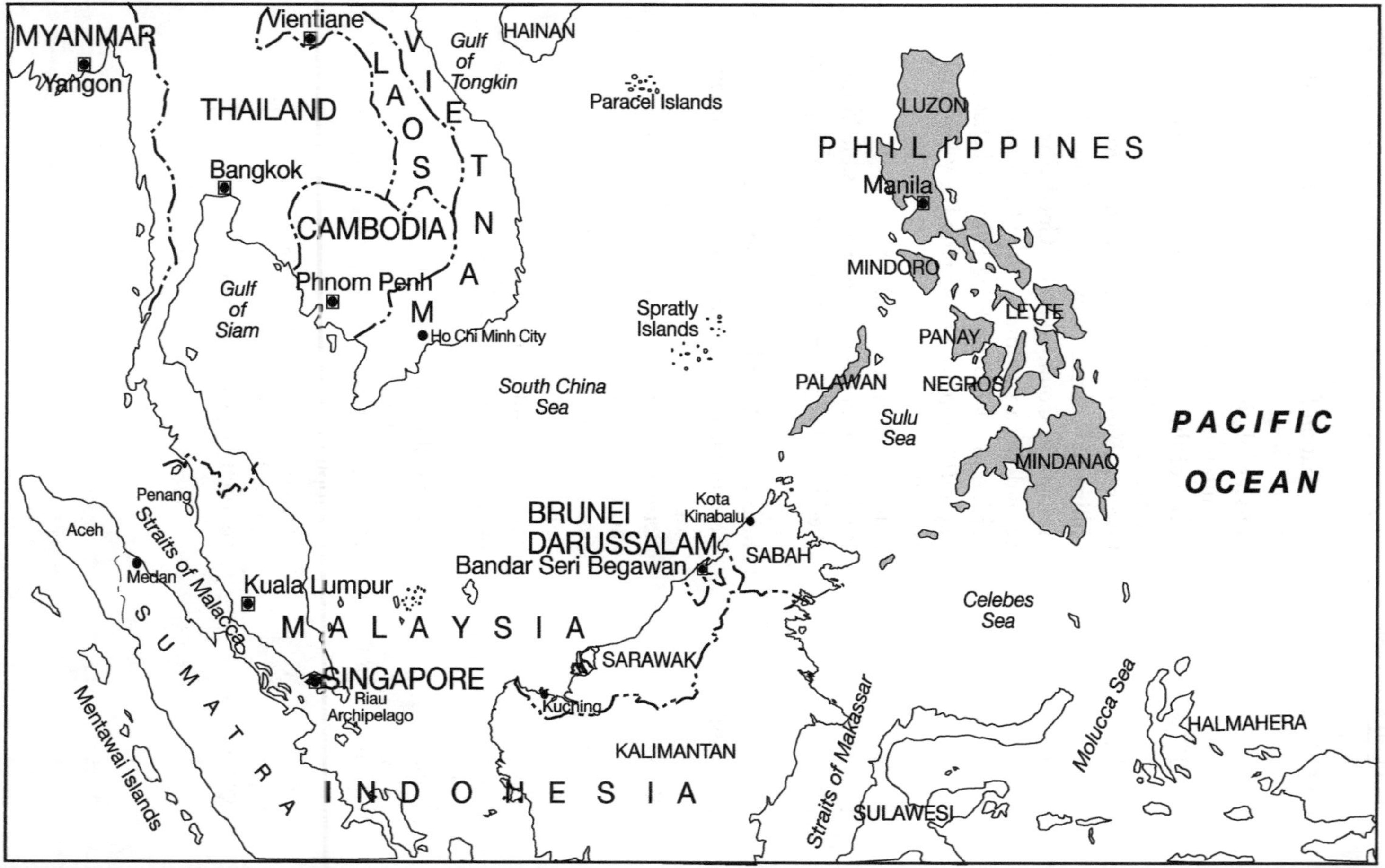
MYANMAR
Yangon
THAILAND
Bangkok
Vientiane
LAOS
VIETNAM
CAMBODIA
Phnom Penh
Ho Chi Minh City
Gulf of Tongkin
HAINAN
Gulf of Siam
Paracel Islands
Spratly Islands
South China Sea
PHILIPPINES
LUZON
Manila
MINDORO
PANAY
LEYTE
NEGROS
PALAWAN
MINDANAO
Sulu Sea
PACIFIC OCEAN
Aceh
Penang
Medan
Straits of Malacca
Kuala Lumpur
MALAYSIA
SINGAPORE
Riau Archipelago
BRUNEI DARUSSALAM
Bandar Seri Begawan
Kota Kinabalu
SABAH
SARAWAK
Kuching
KALIMANTAN
Celebes Sea
Straits of Makassar
SULAWESI
Molucca Sea
HALMAHERA
SUMATRA
Mentawai Islands
INDONESIA

1

THE PHILIPPINES IN SOUTHEAST ASIA: AN OVERVIEW

Mely Caballero-Anthony

INTRODUCTION

The twentieth anniversary of the Philippines' People Power was marred by the sudden declaration of a state of national emergency, a day prior to its scheduled commemoration on 25 February 2006. Reports from Malacañang Palace had cited alleged coup plots by renegade military officers and an apparent "tactical alliance" between right-wing and communist forces to overthrow the government of President Gloria Macapagal-Arroyo.

Notwithstanding security concerns, of significance in the latest coup attempt[1] were the different ways it was viewed depending on one's vantage point. For those who are no strangers to the vicissitudes of Philippine politics, particularly for those who were outside the capital Metro Manila, it was business as usual. To the hardened cynic, it appeared as if the latest coup attempt was just one of the occasional blips that punctuated the country's political landscape, given that in the post-martial law era, the Philippines had already had nine coup attempts, including the seven mounted against the Aquino administration (1986–92).[2] The country's recent political landscape has been starkly defined by the history of two other "people power" movements: EDSA (Epifanio de los Santos Avenue) 2 in 2001, which brought President Arroyo to power, and the lesser known EDSA 3 (also in 2001) which challenged Arroyo's legitimacy. Dramatic twists and turns followed the 2004 elections, which saw the current Arroyo administration besieged by incessant demands for her resignation due to allegations of cheatings in the past elections. These were seen in the street demonstrations that almost culminated in another *Edsa*-like "revolution" in July 2005 and were heard in the cacophony of discourses from a rambunctious Congress mired in political infighting. One may also add to this vista the decades-long problem of communist insurgency and the intractable issue of separatism in the Philippines' Muslim South.

From the outside looking in, the current state of affairs in the Philippines reflects a perplexing paradox in Asia's first democracy. Indeed, the Philippines holds the record of being the first country to establish democracy in Asia, dating back more than one hundred years to the Assembly created by the revolutionary Malolos Republic in 1898 and to the democratic institutions created during the American colonial regime in the early 1900s. Yet, if we fast-forward this narrative to 2006, many would argue that this democracy has been dysfunctional.

If we step out and locate the Philippines within the context of Southeast Asia, we would see a country that offers a very interesting story of the kinds of experiences facing states that go through democratization and development. It is noteworthy that the Philippines has been and continues to be a point of reference for many countries in Southeast Asia that are going through the process of political transition. Against this background, the main objective of this overview chapter is to highlight some of the salient issues that may explain the perplexing narrative of democracy and development in the Philippines. The task of doing so is certainly not easy, given the broadness of the topic. Indeed, how does one adequately capture the dynamics of politics and development in the Philippines?

ISSUES AND CHALLENGES IN THE PHILIPPINES: MORE OF THE SAME?

One of the key questions many Philippine observers raise is: what ails the Philippines? Although it is a value-laden question, implying that something does ail the country, it is not uncommon, nor is it new. In fact, there have been numerous reports, studies, and analyses that ask similar questions, enjoining us to probe deeper and examine the malaise that has seemed to plague one of Asia's gifted under-achievers. At the outset, however, a major challenge I had to face starting this analysis is finding a manageable, yet coherent approach to bringing many of these issues and challenges together. As a political scientist, I have decided to adopt the broad framework of political development in revisiting some of the key themes in the country's development dynamics.

DEMOCRATIC CONSOLIDATION: REVISITING THE 'UNFINISHED REVOLUTION'

From the perspective of political development, the Philippines — despite its long history of democratization — still has a long way to go in consolidating its democracy. It is worth noting that a number of area specialists have already pointed to the unusually long road that the Philippines had been taking to see the benefits of a consolidated democratic system (see for example, Hutchcroft and Rocamora 2003). If we accept the premise that a democratic political system is the best system that allows for the protection of human rights and the promotion of human development and social justice, then the kinds of political, security, and economic challenges we find in the Philippines today are indeed instructive and reflective of the structural weaknesses of its political system.

Against a number of factors cited to explain the country's political malaise, I am reminded of a point made by Fareed Zakaria in his new book, *The Future of Freedom: Illiberal Democracy at Home and Abroad.* He argues that what matters has less to do with democracy than with the rule of law. One could press further Zakaria's point and argue that, without strong institutions, the rule of law cannot be instituted. We could, of course, enumerate a number of factors, which are salient in our reflections and analyses of the Philippine malaise, but I would emphasize the issue of consolidating democracy, particularly for transitioning countries like the Philippines. In order to appreciate the relevance of such a contention to the Philippine case, I will briefly review what democratic consolidation means.

There are two ways of understanding consolidation. First is the minimalist view that looks at democratic consolidation as a process based on the regularity of holding elections or, simply, the procedural angle. The second is the "maximalist view", which regards democratic consolidation as a process that goes beyond popular participation to include the important processes of instituting the rule of law, greater government responsiveness and various and diverse forms of social equity. The other, more definitive view of democratic consolidation is that which is not dependent on electoral tests alone, but leans more towards a stage where all political actors take for granted the fact that democracy is the *only game in town* (Linz and Stephan 1996). However, this stage is arrived at when five interacting criteria are present:

- Strong political society — where citizens and the polity have respect for the democratic institutions that are in place, and any problems are dealt with within the aforementioned institutions;

- Rule of law — where legal guidelines are provided to maintain stability and allow civil and political societies to function;
- Strong state apparatus — where a functioning bureaucracy is present and capable of "commanding, regulating, and extracting tax revenues";
- Strong economic society — to serve as a system to mediate between the state and the market; and
- Flourishing civil society — where citizens organize themselves into social groups and movements such as interest groups and trade unions.

In our assessment of the Philippines, we can examine where the country stands on each of these five criteria. If we focus on the first four criteria — then we might find it instructive to revisit some of the terms and phrases that a number of Philippine and foreign scholars and commentators have used to capture the nature of Philippine politics. Among the more popular ones found in the literature are: *cacique democracy* (Anderson 1998), *bossism* (Sidel 1999), *weak state* (Rivera 2002), *low quality democracy* (Case 2002), *democratic deficit* (Hutchcroft and Rocamora 2003), and *"showbiz democracy"* (*Economist* 2004).

Based on these terms, which have been used to describe the state of Philippine politics, one could argue that the country's consolidation of democracy is its "unfinished revolution". Interestingly, this phrase has been a common refrain. Many Filipino nationalists, from the revolutionary Andres Bonifacio, who in 1896 vowed to continue the colonial war against Spain, to contemporary Filipino scholars like Renato Constantino and Reynaldo Ileto have returned to this idea in their respective works. This notion is also commonly heard in many political discourses across the country at several points in time, even in the inaugural address of President Arroyo in 2001, immediately after she took over from the toppled Estrada.

The salience of this idea can be seen in its various interpretations. To many people, the "unfinished revolution" refers to the long-overdue reforms of the country's political system, long dominated by elites and political clans — hence the term *cacique democracy.* Equally important to the "unfinished revolution" is the fight against poverty. Arroyo in fact used this phrase when she spoke about addressing poverty — the centrepiece of her administration's ten-point agenda. It can be recalled that it was the dire state of the country's economy, rising poverty, and sheer misery that drove the dictatorial Marcos regime out of power. The sense of alienation brought about by poverty pushed many Filipinos to stage its first People Power in 1986. Thus, it is useful to note that in her 2001 inaugural address, Arroyo staked her political legitimacy on improving both the country's politics and its economy.

Arroyo's attention to reforming the structural and systemic problems of the country points to an important element, often overlooked, that impedes the resolution of political crises plaguing developing states like the Philippines. This is the problem of weak institutions.

INSTITUTIONAL CRISIS

One of the major tasks in consolidating democratic gains is the strengthening of political institutions. This remains an important agenda item for the Philippines. Broadly, the process of political institutionalization refers to the "establishment of state authority over society through specifically created political structures and organs". It is through this process that the state-society nexus is strengthened (Kamrava 2001). The extent of a state's institutionalization reflects the capacity of the state to function. It follows, therefore, that the absence and weakness of these political structures weaken the state's relationship with its own people. It is not enough, however, to establish or create these institutions. What is more important is for these institutions to command the respect and trust of the citizenry. Since institutions are the instruments of governance within a state, they facilitate the adoption of a regulatory framework for accommodating varying interests within a polity. These institutions also allow the rule of law to prevail.

Are institutions in the Philippines really that weak? Many scholars and analysts would argue that the answer is yes. Among the weakest institutions that are often cited are the country's political parties. Political parties in the Philippines are often described as "patronage-infested". Through their evolution, many of the characteristics attributed to these parties have remained until today. These include the strong emphasis on personalities rather than credible political platforms, leading to a lack of differentiation between or among parties, and a high degree of *turncoatism* (movement from one party to another), which are inherently destabilizing (Hutchcroft and Rocamora 2003; Montinola 1999; Anderson 1988). Hence, while one may see many political parties in the country, they do not necessarily reflect a diversity of political ideologies. As one commentator aptly described it, "political parties are no more than paper tigers…replete with influential and popular politicians…parties may look powerful on the outside but are ideologically weak and hollow on the inside" (Sambangan 2004).

As observed by many, the kinds of personalities found in many of the political parties emerge mainly from two groups in the country. Making up the first group are the "traditional" politicians or "*trapos*" who come from wealthy and "well-born families" and whose lineage is carefully nurtured through generations and cultivated by inter-marriages among the rich and famous (see for example, Coronel et al. 2004). The second and of more recent vintage are those led by popular movie personalities like Joseph Estrada and Fernando Poe, leading several commentators to brand Philippine democracy as "showbiz democracy" (*Economist*, 2004).

More significantly, political parties are also viewed largely as "elite clubs", vehicles for political and economic elites to perpetuate themselves in power. Families supercede political parties as the main form of political organization. According to a study conducted by the Philippine Center for Investigative Journalism, over 60 per cent of the representatives in the 2001 Congress had relatives in elected office — a trend that has steadily risen since the post-martial law era. Coronel notes, "Regimes come and go but families remain. Political parties are formed and disbanded but the clans that make them up stay on. Families survive wars, dictatorships, and uprisings…some families eventually go into decline after successive electoral defeats or the death of a powerful patriarch, but others, stronger and more resilient, hang on and flourish."

It follows, therefore, that people running for office are elected not because of their political parties' platforms, but more because of who they are. Wealth and celebrity status have become a potent combination in Philippine politics. As a result, twenty years after the first People Power movement in 1986, the Philippines remains mired in this vicious cycle of *cacique democracy*, where the political fiefdoms rule. This dominant characteristic of elite politics perpetuates patronage politics and has been a bane in the Philippines' attempts at consolidating its democracy.

From the developments cited above, one could argue that without credible political institutions — that is, political parties — the Philippines will never grow out of its political culture, which is largely defined by *personalistic* politics. This is one of the major factors that have fed into the patron-client relationship that characterizes the nature of political relations in the country. In fact, it also partly explains why a democratizing state like the Philippines could be turned into an authoritarian state by a strongman like Ferdinand Marcos. As one analyst put it, "the [Philippine] nation's political parties, which were almost exclusively instruments of patronage rather than principle, prove impotent at defending democracy when confronted by a brilliant manipulator of personal and family interest." (Overholt 1986, 1139). Therefore, absent strong institutions, the state would be unable to correct the political system that has been embedded in clientelism. Ideally, strong institutions can reverse the symptoms of a weak state that has been captured by a few oligarchs and has impeded the project of a more participative politics.

Among the consequences of such a political order are the alienation of the masses and the failure to empower the marginalized, which in turn result in various types of so-called People Power demonstrations. Such alienation largely explains the highly contested results of the 2004 elections that plague the Arroyo administration. We recall that, despite the solid backing that Arroyo got from the country's business elites and (tacitly) from the international community, her slim margin of victory over the late Fernando Poe was seen by many as indicative of the widening divide within Philippine society, which was and is increasingly disillusioned with the country's politics. In fact, many (including people in the Arroyo camp), perceive the votes for Poe as a vote against the establishment. To his supporters, Poe was pro-poor — just as the deposed president Joseph Estrada was perceived to be. Both personalities, in fact, had similar backgrounds: Estrada and Poe were very popular movie stars who played the role of a modern-day Robin Hood who stood for the interests of the poor and the marginalized and who defended the oppressed and the abused.

WEAK STATE *VIS-A-VIS* STRONG/DOMINANT INSTITUTIONS?

Given the phenomena of *cacique* democracy and "*bossism*", another term often found in the literature on the Philippine political system, in comparison with other states in Southeast Asia, is the description that it is a weak state. This brings us to the issue of political structure and governance in the country. Where is power — infrastructural and developmental — located and what does this political structure look like? In the post-martial law era, the Philippines has been described as a weak state largely because it has been hampered by its lack of capacity to enforce regulations and policies. More than that, it also lacks autonomy and is constantly acted upon by forces within and outside the state.

But more interesting is the puzzle of a weak state *vis-a-vis* a number of strong or dominant institutions. If we look at Philippine society as a melange of heterogenous social groups and examine the distribution of power and control within the state, we will note that, while there are weak institutions in the Philippines, there are also the all-too-powerful institutions. For our purpose, let us examine the role of the Catholic Church and other religious institutions, the military, and the media, which have a significant influence on politics.

The Catholic Church

The Philippine Catholic Church has always been regarded as highly influential and highly political. Its influence goes as far back as during the Spanish colonial period, when friars were extensively involved in colonial administration, particularly in the rural areas. During that period, religious intervention in political matters was justified under the principle of the union of church and state, which in turn became the rationale of the Spanish *conquistadores* assigned by the Pope's fiat to civilize and Christianize pagan lands (Mendoza 1999; Francisco 2000).

In the country's modern history, the relationship between the state and the Catholic Church has always been ambiguous. While the constitution stipulates the separation of church and state, that principle has not been strictly followed in practice. This ambiguity is best reflected in the way the Catholic Church has exercised its influence on Philippine politics at several points during and after the martial-law period (Youngblood 1987). Much has already been written about the role that the late Jaime Cardinal Sin played in helping to mobilize the first People Power in 1986 with his call for mass prayers and demonstrations to bring an end to the Marcos dictatorship, and in the second People Power, when he once again called on his flock to help oust the Estrada government in 2001.

In the current unresolved crisis of impeaching Arroyo, we almost saw People Power *redux*, in which members of the Catholic clergy were once again seen at the forefront of changing regimes. Some Catholic bishops had joined the opposition and other interest groups in calling for Arroyo's resignation amidst allegations that she cheated in the 2004 elections. Things almost came to a head in July 2005, when ten members of Arroyo's cabinet suddenly resigned, followed by the open call by former President Corazon Aquino for Arroyo "to make the ultimate sacrifice and resign". Were it not for the timely intervention of the Catholic Bishops Conference of the Philippines (CBCP) and the solid support that Arroyo got from the military, she could have been forced out.[3] However, the respite that Arroyo got from the July 2005 crisis was brief. Until now, members of the opposition and other societal forces continue to use every available channel to force her out of office. Incidentally, in the latest round of impeachment cases filed against her in June 2006, the impeachment petition included the signature of a member of the Catholic clergy.

In this continuing saga, one could argue that while the role of the Catholic Church and its religious leaders in bringing democracy back to the Philippines in 1986 may continue to inspire, there is also the more than palpable concern that the clergy's use of mass popular pressure and/or collusion with political elites in forcing out popularly elected leaders is counter-productive. Although the church could continue to frame its political activism in the language of the "moral conscience" of the state, an interventionist church could become a destabilizing agent instead of a moral force for political order, stability, and social justice.

After more than a century of closer co-existence, the challenge for the Catholic Church and other proactive religious bodies in the Philippines is how to find this delicate balance and not overstep its boundaries. More specifically, how the Catholic Church, with its far reach into the Philippine society, would be able to navigate its way through democratic politics, find the proper contours of toleration, and discern the appropriate limits of its role are issues that need to be revisited (Philpott 2004).

Military

The role of the military in politics continues to be of great interest even in post-martial law Philippines. Despite attempts by the Philippine presidents who succeeded Ferdinand Marcos to reform the military and make it "more professional" and apolitical, questions have been raised about its neutrality, given the all too many attempted coups in the post-Marcos era. Indeed, twenty years after People Power, the politicization of the military continues to pose serious challenges to a democratic Philippines.

As one observer put it, the military is "the wild card in Filipino politics" (Meinardus 2005). While one may tend to agree with such an assertion, it may be useful to re-examine this in the light of the dynamics that continue to shape Philippine politics. Although civilian control of the military is the hallmark of a democratic state, one may consider the argument that, for transitioning states (including the Philippines), the nature of this control is often vague and controversial (Alagappa 2001). In a study on military professionalism in Asia, Muthiah Alagappa argued that being professional — meaning having attained a high level of competence in the management of violence — will not prevent the military from expanding its role, including intruding into politics. However, the extent of role expansion is a function of the legitimacy of the civilian government: the weaker the civilian government, the greater the military's role expansion and *vice versa*. Thus, equating the military's professionalism to being apolitical is problematic, especially in situations of domestic conflict or when the government's legitimacy is challenged. Unless the balance of power shifts in favour of democratic forces and institutions, which also entails strengthening the legitimacy, capacity, and role of civilian institutions and sustaining economic development, a politicized military remains a cause for concern (Alagappa 2001, p. 212).

The reality of civil-military relations in the Philippines must, therefore, be fully understood before we can talk about an apolitical and/or professional military. Since 1986, two Philippine presidents, Aquino and Arroyo, rose to power on "the back of the armed forces", which, in moments of great political uncertainty (in 1986 and 2001), threw their weight behind the two leaders and joined the popular uprisings to topple Marcos and Estrada, respectively. With its pivotal role in both uprisings, both Aquino and Arroyo had to pay special attention to the military, leading to the perception that both political leaders have courted the military. Such observations have led one commentator to remark "[one cannot have] professional soldiers in a nation governed by corrupt and incompetent leaders... They [the military] will either try to seize power or become part of the rotten system" (cited in Meinardus 2005).

Such scepticism has been prevalent in a nation torn by many forces that openly compete for power. Despite the drastic changes and reforms being instituted in the armed forces through the "Philippine Defence Reform" and other programmes, serious doubts remain. This is best captured in a comment by Jose Almonte, the national security adviser to the Ramos administration, who was quoted as having said, "Ironically, a reforming AFP could present a mortal danger to a Philippine state which is unable — or unwilling — to reform itself" (Meinardus 2005).

Free-Wheeling Media?

The Philippines prides itself in its free press. Press freedom is a fundamental right guaranteed in the country's constitution. However, while the society is receptive to open debates and discourses facilitated by a vibrant press, concerns have been raised about the country's media. The free press has been criticized as increasingly partisan in its approach and coverage, to the point of fuelling political instability.

This concern led to threats of a media clampdown during the period of state of emergency in February 2006. The response from the media was swift, immediately denouncing the government's intimidation and the infringements on freedom of the press.[4] The move openly pitted the press against the Arroyo administration. Yet, it is interesting to note that, despite the threats, the press remains free — at least on the basis of what is seen on television and newspapers. Nevertheless, questions about the role of the press in a transitioning polity have surfaced as an important issue.

In sum, we see a state where the dynamics of certain weak institutions *vis-a-vis* the emboldened others has tipped the balance against the executive and has weakened the centre. In effect, this "battle of institutions" has significantly destabilized the political system, as seen in the way the current political crisis continues unabated. This brings us to the other crucial question of who controls the Philippines. To answer this question more comprehensively, we need to turn our attention to the socioeconomic challenges that beset the country.

SOCIO-ECONOMIC FAULT LINES

A recent article analysing the economic prospects of the Philippines spoke about the "Philippine conundrum". One of the questions raised was why "a country with so much talent…and such a promising beginning at Independence … run(s) into trouble so frequently" (Hill 2006).

The usual response to such an observation by those who closely follow the development of the country's political economy is that it is (once again) the political rather than the material (Rogers 2004). We find that the phrases used to depict the Philippine state, such as the "weak state" captured by well-entrenched interests, "oligarchic democracy" (Rodman et al. 2001) and "patrimonial state" (Hutchcroft 1998), continue to inform our analysis. If, after sixty years of independence and having gone through several regime changes, the state of the country's political economy remains unchanged — where the overall pattern of elite domination of politics and economics has prevailed, the crucial economic agenda of land reform that was supposed to have addressed the issue of distributive justice remains unrealized, and income inequality continues to widen — then the democratic system of the Philippines has failed in its duty to deliver the basic goods.

Against the seemingly unchanging pattern of power and material distribution within the country, it is not surprising that the annual figures produced by economists on the economic prospects of the Philippines remain lacklustre and uninspiring. Despite posting GDP growth rates of 5 per cent in the last two years, the Philippines continues to register high unemployment rates and poverty levels (World Development Indicators, 2005). Many citizens feel disenfranchised and excluded from the development process, particularly those in the rural areas.

But the extent of the socioeconomic fault lines that beset the country becomes more acute if we compare the conditions of the Philippines with those of its neighbours in ASEAN, such as Indonesia, Thailand, Malaysia, Brunei Darussalam, Singapore, and even Vietnam. Among the ASEAN-6, the Philippines has the highest incidence of poverty, with 15.5 per cent of the population living below US$1 a day, compared to Thailand (1.9 per cent) and Malaysia (less than 2 per cent) (World Development Indicators, 2006).[5] Given the country's fiscal problems, with 40 per cent of revenue going to interest payments and 30 per cent to salaries, the government is resource-strapped and unable to finance key public services or aim for long-term development goals. As a consequence, the country suffers from an acute brain-drain problem and has seen many nurses, doctors, teachers, technicians, and other skilled workers voting with their feet.

These multiple economic woes have also resulted in the declining competitiveness of the Philippines in comparison with its ASEAN neighbours. The World Economic Forum's Growth Competitiveness Index (2005) placed the Philippines in 77th position, behind other ASEAN states (with Singapore 6th, Malaysia 24th, Thailand 36th and Indonesia 74th). In the same assessment, the Philippines has also fared poorly in terms of the quality of its public institutions and macroeconomic environment, even lagging behind Vietnam (cited in Aladdin Rillo, *Regional Outlook*, 2006).

What is more worrying in these trends in economic competitiveness both regionally and globally is the much-vaunted rise of China. China has become the preferred choice for foreign direct investments, and its rapid economic growth has clearly affected even the more competitive ASEAN countries like Singapore, Malaysia, and Thailand. This begs the question of how prepared the Philippine economy is in meeting these enormous challenges. There is also the question of the role that the country can play in ASEAN's efforts to integrate its members' economies to remain competitive *vis-a-vis* China.

As the above demonstrates, the socioeconomic challenges beleaguering the Philippines are symptomatic of the democratic deficit that besets the country. This condition reinforces Hutchcroft and Rocamora's claim about the weakness of the Philippine state having to confront strong demands with weak institutions. According to them, the crisis in the Philippines is "manifested…in a deepening frustration over the inability of the democratic institutions to deliver the goods, specially goods of a public character". Hence, to the ordinary citizens who derive few such benefits, the government "is an abstraction, an alienated entity, whose only palpable dimension is the episodic patronage dispensed by bosses and politicians, which merely reinforces the poor's real condition of dependence" (Hutchcroft and Rocamora 2003, p. 260).

Given the enduring features of the country's political economy, it comes as no surprise that the major security challenges facing the country over the last three decades have remained intractable. Again, compared to its neighbours that had to confront the serious threats of communism and separatism, the Philippines remains to decisively address the problems of insurgency coming from the CPP/NPA and Muslim separatism. It is beyond the scope of this chapter to deal with the nature of the security threats coming from these two groups, but suffice it to say that it is indeed a wonder how the Philippines, beset with multiple challenges from many fronts, has managed to avoid an implosion.

WHITHER THE PHILIPPINES IN THE 21ST CENTURY?

Against the current state of a nation in crisis, we see Philippine democracy demystified. To be sure, consolidating democracy in the country — through the building of strong institutions, political and economic society, and the rule of law — are issues that urgently need to be addressed. Yet, in the rapidly changing regional and global environment, is time on the Philippines' side?

The answer would largely depend on how the Philippine state and its people respond to the many challenges that confront the country. The current political crisis could be a blessing in disguise. It could be a wake-up call for the embattled government of Arroyo (or whoever takes over, depending on how the current crisis unfolds) to work together with the people. Together, they need to put in place a set of institutional innovations that can move the country away from its precarious state of political decay. More importantly, both the leaders and the people must be able to convince themselves that democracy works for them, and that democracy does matter.

In this regard, the move to change the country's charter is an interesting development and has received much attention. To be sure, the move has several implications, which include doing away with an obstructionist Senate, providing for incentives for politicians to stay loyal to party affiliations, and allowing for the streamlining and strengthening of political parties. Questions have been raised on the viability of this proposal, and so far we note that public opinion on this issue is still deeply divided.[6] Whether or not charter change is the way to go, it is clear that the Philippines has reached the point where institutional changes have become critical. The country's institutions have not only proved to be dysfunctional; they have also become disconnected from the country's new realities.

So, whither the Philippines? In looking at the road ahead, I want to go back to Hal Hill's observation on the Philippine "conundrum" and take up some of the points that he and other analysts and commentators have raised in their assessments of the Philippines' prospects. First, despite the structural malaise that has paralysed the country, there are still a number of positive factors that could significantly shift the trends from a perpetual state of crisis to opportunities for change. One of these is the country's vibrant civil society, which is "noisy, but at its best, world class" (Hill 2006). Many would agree that civil society organizations (CSOs) have provided the crucial intervention in the absence of adequate public services. In the process, they have become the cushion that helps absorb the systemic shocks from within and outside the state. Hence, we find that, in the Philippines, the CSOs have already started to make their impact on the political system. Their sustained engagement of the state has seen some pockets of success. Among these is the entry of new actors in the political arena who are starting to pose a challenge to the traditional politicians (Quimpo 2005). The opening of political space to a new breed of political actors who are not necessarily beholden to the clientelist/ patronage system is clearly worth noting. As an important force for change, civil society organizations can help to ensure that, while Philippine democracy may be endangered, it is already deeply embedded and cannot be reversed anymore.

Second is the deep pool of talent still found in the Philippines, in spite of the huge number of Filipinos leaving the country. While it has been said that the country's bane is political rather than material, there are also the many salient ideational facets that the Philippines has. These need to be highlighted to balance negative perceptions about the Philippines. What is often missed is the fact that the country has excellent universities, other academic institutions, and think-tanks. Its service industry is at par with, if not better than, those in some other countries in the region and can easily hold its own in the global environment. The country is not short of entrepreneurs who flourish despite the lack of material resources, while its rich culture and arts continue to draw admiration from abroad. Can the Philippines channel these ideational advantages to bring the country back onto the radar screen of foreign investors and improve its competitiveness in the region?

Finally, we need to remind ourselves of the indomitable spirit of the Filipino people, which, though embattled, has nevertheless been remarkably resilient in the face of huge crises and challenges. This resilience is underpinned by a strong sense of shared values and kinship and could explain why, despite the large Filipino diaspora, these scattered communities have not turned their backs on their beleaguered country. For instance, the remittances of the Filipino diaspora have a tremendous impact on the country's finances and poverty. Remittances in 2004 alone accounted for 13.5 per cent of the GDP; without it the headcount of the country's poor would have increased to 3–10 per cent (World Bank, 2006).

In conclusion, there is perhaps no better time than now for the Philippine state and its people to do some serious soul-searching. In doing so, the leaders need to rethink the Filipino identity and the Philippine state — an identity that is free from the shackles of "caciqueism, bossism, patrimonialism" and a state that not only rules but also governs. These are urgent tasks that cannot be done without the people behind its leaders.

Notes

1 Since Gloria Arroyo assumed the presidency in 2001, she had to face two coup attempts by the military, with the first one staged in July 2003. Also known as the Magdalo affair, the attempted mutiny was led by junior officers in the Armed Forces of the Philippines (AFP).

2 Incidentally, the leaders of those attempts were treated with relative leniency or granted amnesty.

3 Other, equally salient factors were cited to explain why the opposition and others failed to spark another people power. One of them was the support that Arroyo got from former President Fidel V. Ramos and the majority in Congress that was still aligned with the president. The other was the so-called "people-power" fatigue.

4 The media clampdown led one of the country's political commentators to describe the Philippines as the "most endangered democracy"; see Amando Doronila, "RP Most Endangered Democracy in Asia", *Philippine Daily Inquirer*, 20 March 2006.

5 These statistics stand in stark contrast to often-repeated observations that, in the 1950s, the Philippines had the highest per capita income among the Southeast Asian countries.

6 See for example, Solita Collas-Monsod, "Presidential vs Parliamentary System", *Philippine Daily Inquirer*, 27 May 2006; Fr. Joaquin G. Bernas, "Amendment, Revision, Revolution", *Philippine Daily Inquirer*, 5 June 2006; "We Don't Need the Proposed Charter Change", One Voice Position Paper, <http://www.onevoice.org.ph/index.php/page_id=7>; and Paolo Romero, "2007 Polls for Parliament?", *Philippine Star*, 6 June 2006.

Selected References

Alagappa, Muthiah (ed.) *Military Professionalism in Asia: Conceptual and Empirical Perspectives*. Honolulu: East West Center, 2001.

Anderson, Benedict. "Cacique Democracy in the Philippines: Origins and Dreams", *New Left Review* 169 (May/June 1998).

Balisacan, Arsenio and Hal Hill (eds.) *The Philippines Economy, Development, Policies and Challenges*. New York: Oxford University Press, 2003.

Caballero-Anthony, Mely. "The Winds of Change in the Philippines: Whither the Strong Republic?". *Southeast Asian Affairs 2003*, pp. 213–27. Singapore: Institute of Southeast Asian Studies, 2003.

Case, William. "The Philippines: Stable but Low Quality Democracy?". In *Politics in Southeast Asia: Democracy or Less*, pp. 201–44. Richmond, Surrey: Curzon Press, 2002.

Coronel, Sheila L., et al. *The Rulemakers: How the Wealthy and Well-Born Dominate Congress*. Quezon City: Philippine Center for Investigate Journalism, 2004.

"Democracy as Showbiz". *The Economist*, 1 July 2004.

Francisco, Jose Mario, S.J. "The Dynamics Between Catholicism and Philippine Society". *Inter-Religio* 35 (Summer 2000): 21–27.

Hill, Hal. "The Philippine Conundrum". <http://www.aseanfocus.com/asiaanalysis/article.cfm?article ID, 929> March 2006.

Hill, Hal and Peter Warr. "The Trouble with Bangkok and Manila". *Far Eastern Economic Review*, April 2006.

Hutchcroft, Paul. *Booty Capitalism: The Politics of Banking in the Philippines*. Quezon City: Ateneo de Manila Press, 1998.

Hutchcroft, Paul and Joel Rocamora. "Strong Demands and Weak Institutions: The Origins and Evolution of the Democratic Deficit in the Philippines". *Journal of East Asian Studies* 3 (2003): 259–92.

Kamrava, Mehran. *Politics and Society in the Developing World*, 2nd edn. London: Routledge, 2000.

Linz, Juan and Alfred Stephan. "Toward Consolidated Democracies". In *Consolidating Third Word Wave Democracies: Themes and Perspectives*, edited by Larry Diamond et al. Baltimore MD: Johns Hopkins University Press, 1997.

Meinardus, Ronald. "Armed Forces: Wild Card in Filipino Politics". *The Japan Times*, 4 April 2005.

Mendoza, Rene. "Religion and Secularisation in the Philippines and other Asian Countries". <http://www.www.seasite.niu.edu/Module/PhilippineReligions/mendoza>.

Montinola, Gabriella. "Parties and Accountability in the Philippines". *Journal of Democracy* 10 (1999): 126–40.

Overholt, William. "The Rise and Fall of Ferdinand Marcos". *Asian Survey* 26, no. 11 (November 1986).

Philpott, Daniel. "The Catholic Wave". *Journal of Democracy* 15, no. 2 (2004): 32–46.

Quimpo, Nathan Gilbert. "The Left, Elections, and the Political Party System in the Philippines". *Critical Asian Studies* 37, no. 1 (2005): 3–28.

Rillo, Aladdin, "Economic Outlook: Philippines". *Regional Outlook 2006*, pp. 121–28. Singapore: Institute of Southeast Asian Studies, 2006.

Rivera, Temario. "The Philippines". In *Assessing Democratic Evolution in Southeast Asia*, edited by Anthony Smith. Singapore: Institute of Southeast Asian Studies, 2002. <http://www.iseas.edu./52002pdf>.

Rodan, Gary, Kevin Hewison and Richard Robison, eds. *The Political Economy of Southeast Asia*. South Melbourne: Oxford University Press, 2001.

Rogers, Steven. "Philippine Politics and the Rule of Law". *Journal of Democracy* 15, no. 4 (2004): 111–25.

Sambangan, Annie Ruth, "Turncoatism breeds Chameleons". *Manila Times*, 2 February 2004.

Sidel, John Thayer. *Capital, Coercion, and Crime: Bossism in the Philippines*. Stanford: Stanford University Press, 1999.

Steinberg, David J. *The Philippines: A Singular and a Plural Place*. Boulder, Co: Westview Press, 2000.

Velasco, Renato S. "The Philippines". In *Democracy, Governance and Economic Performance*, edited by Ian Marsh, Jean Blondel and Takashi Inoguchi. Tokyo: United Nations University, 1999.

Weekly, Kathleen. "The National or the Social? Problems of Nation-Building in Post-World War II Philippines". *Third World Quarterly* 27, no. 1 (2006): 85–100.

World Bank. *Global Economic Prospects 2006: Economic Implications of Remittance and Migration*. Washington D.C.: World Bank, 2006.

———. *World Development Indicators 2005 and 2006* at <www.worldbank.org/data/wdi>.

Wurfel, David. *Filipino Politics: Development and Decay*. Ithaca: Cornell University Press, 1988.

Youngblood, Robert. "The Corazon Aquino Miracle and the Philippine Churches". *Asian Survey* 27, no. 12 (December 1987): 1240–55.

Zakaria, Fareed. *The Future of Freedom: Illiberal Democracy at Home and Abroad*. New York: WW Norton & Company, 2003.

2

FROM REGIME CRISIS TO SYSTEM CHANGE

Joel Rocamora

The Philippines is in the midst of a deep, systemic crisis. The crisis confronting the Arroyo regime is not just one more instance of the refusal of competing elite factions to accept the legitimacy of elections as a means for mediating elite competition. The crisis of the Arroyo administration manifests the cumulative impact of a long simmering crisis of representation. It is not just President Arroyo who is being challenged, it is the capacity of the whole political system to select leaders capable of responding to the needs of the Philippines in the twenty-first century.

It is precisely the depth of the crisis that prevents a quick and easy resolution. A functioning state resolves conflict through mechanisms that organizes winners and losers. The deeper the crisis the more difficult it is to identify winners and losers. Political players are being forced to think beyond "who gets what, when and how" and to project from the "here and now" to the future, a difficult and uneasy task for most politicians. Put more simply, politicians cannot be sure how changes in the political system will affect them. As a result, even "system change" gets processed in narrow, partisan ways, distorting discourse, and making negotiated outcomes difficult.

Many political leaders, pro-administration and opposition alike, rhetorically acknowledge the depth of the crisis, but continue to behave in the same old ways. The most obvious is President Gloria Macapagal Arroyo. For years she has talked about the crisis in the political system and the need to reform the institutions of government. In September 2005, for example, she said that charter change is one major step the nation must take to achieve peace and stability over the "rapidly degenerating political system".[1] But she has also behaved like an old-style traditional politician, a *trapo.* Worst, since the onset of the crisis only a little more than a year ago, she has undermined the very political institutions she would reform. Abandoned by reformist allies and forced to concentrate on political survival, Arroyo has reduced governance to who is for me and who is not, punishing and rewarding without regard for legality and established procedure.

> In stable societies, political questions like these — that challenge the basic legitimacy of the sitting president — are ultimately resolved by election, or by acts of Congress or Parliament, or they are referred back to the legal and judicial system for further investigation, prosecution, and adjudication. But in young societies like ours — where the institutional spheres are not yet fully differentiated — legal institutions and government agencies tend to be heavily contaminated by partisan politics. This compromises their independence. Instead of being able to put an orderly closure to unresolved political questions, these institutions are dragged into the political arena and lose their credibility. Consequently, legal issues are re-politicized, and the whole process repeats itself, leaving in its wake the debris of institutional wreckage.[2]

REGIME CRISIS

Some of the problems of Gloria Macapagal Arroyo are not of her making. If the government she heads cannot deliver, no government before her has either. She is right, many of the country's problems today derive from its political system. Much of the emotion behind moves to remove her instead comes from the promise of political reform that was the basis of her extra-constitutional ascension to the presidency. She came to power in January 2001 on the crest of a "people power" revolt against the corrupt Estrada government. After a few years of half-hearted reform efforts, Arroyo turned decidedly reactionary in the wake of challenges to her (re-)election as president in June 2004.

Arroyo has faced three separate opposition groups since the Garci tapes (after Commission on Elections Commissioner Virgilio Garcillano) scandal broke in June 2005. The scandal was exposed by opposition politicians linked to losing presidential candidate Fernando Poe Jr., and former president Joseph Estrada. Another group is made up of those who tried to get Arroyo to resign on 8 July 2005: the cabinet ministers who resigned, since then called the Hyatt 10; the reform wing of the Liberal Party; business groups led by the Makati Business Club; the large civil society coalition CODE-NGO; the Roman Catholic Association of Major Religious Superiors; and former President Corazon Aquino. The last is the Left, divided into those linked to the Maoist national democratic movement and the "democratic Left", mainly those in the coalition *Laban ng Masa* (Struggle of the Masses).

Opposition politicians broke the scandal and led large demonstrations together with the Left back in July 2005. But they carry the burden of public judgement against the Estrada regime and the earlier Marcos dictatorship that the older ones among them go back to. They are a small minority of members of Congress, and an even smaller number of local government officials. They have the disadvantage of a particularly debilitating aspect of Philippine party politics, the tendency of politicians to move to the party of the president who controls patronage. Former President Estrada did not pay much attention to building his own party, so the exodus to the party of President Arroyo was easy and the consolidation of pro-Arroyo parties was over by the time the scandal broke four years later. In the House of Representatives, the opposition is minuscule, not even strong enough to secure the one-third vote needed for impeachment. It is in the Senate where the combination of opposition senators with the reform wing of the Liberal Party and the threat of the abolition of the Senate has created an immovable force against the Arroyo administration.

The Left provides the main organized mobilizable force in Metro Manila and other large cities. Because of divisions, mainly between the Maoists and everyone else, and because the Left as a whole has been in decline since the second half of the 1980s, this organized capacity has not been enough to sustain the momentum of mass actions. Without the kind of political momentum that generates spontaneous mobilization, the Left's severe resource limitations come into play. A year ago, this generated debates because some groups wanted to work with the pro-Estrada crowd the better to access Estrada's resources. Similar expectations from the other side of the political spectrum, groups linked to reform business groups, have led to similar disappointments. The Maoists are anxious to bring Arroyo down because she has unleashed the kind of murderous counter-insurgency complete with extra-judicial killings not seen since the Marcos years. The advantage of the democratic Left, as yet not subjected to the same kind of pressure as the Maoists, is that they can locate the anti-Arroyo struggle in a longer-term timeframe and thus relate more easily to a systemic change orientation.

The groups and individuals who called on President Arroyo to resign on 8 July 2005 represent the cutting edge of middle class frustration with the

President. There's a logic to the components of the group. Cory Aquino is the icon of moral rectitude, an important requirement for middle class support. The Makati Business Club represents what might be called the "modernizing bourgeoisie", a segment of the business class most against rent-seeking as business strategy. The economic managers who resigned, ranging from Cesar Purisima to Emy Boncodin, have carried integrity and technocratic competence with them into the bureaucracy. The Liberal Party, minus Manila Mayor Lito Atienza and other LP opportunists, comes closest to being a party of reform. Civil society crossovers provide bridges to civil society, the Association of Major Religious Superiors of the Philippines (AMRSP), and progressive sections of the Catholic Church. These groups and individuals are the political expressions of an upper and middle class political project for a strong, efficient state.

By any measure, together these groups constitute a large and powerful bloc, powerful enough to preoccupy the Arroyo administration and keep it in a destructive survival mode. However, they are not powerful enough to bring the regime down or pry loose the politicians in local governments and the House who are quite adept at smelling changes in the wind. One reason is that the three groups share only the anti-Arroyo goal, not whom to replace her with; certainly not what systemic changes to put in place. They work together well enough considering their differences, but without enough fervour to overcome the advantages of incumbency. Another reason is that anything short of revolutionary change would require the support or at least acquiescence of three key (some would say the only) components of the dominant social bloc in the Philippines: big business, the United States and the Catholic Church. Add to these a fourth, the military.

Business is, in many ways the most crucial. In both EDSA 1 and 2, support of business groups and individuals solved resource problems for the Left, and made it possible for middle class groups to believe that political action would not result in painful sanctions, if nothing else because business support raised the movement's chances of success.[3] A deep crisis that had already led to economic contraction for two years by 1986, and the kind of rogue business behaviour by Estrada and his friends that scared business groups in 2000, resulted in effective business activism. But today business groups including even the Makati Business Club have not yet committed enough resources and open risk-taking to the task of bringing Arroyo down. This is partly because economic activity continues to be shielded from political crisis by overseas Filipino worker remittances and heavy government borrowing. More importantly, it is also because business leaders know that what needs changing is not just a Marcos or an Estrada or an Arroyo, but the political system that spawned them. For many business people, an unsatisfactory *status quo* is better than an uncertain future.

As difficult as it is for Left groups to believe, the Philippines is just not important enough for the United States at this time to intervene actively to resolve the political impasse. Preoccupied with the wars in Afghanistan and Iraq, the United States' main concern in the Philippines at present is having enough room to operate in Mindanao to close down Islamic terrorist training camps. This does not mean that American diplomats and business people are not unhappy about Arroyo's turn away from reform. They privately express sympathy with Arroyo's middle class opponents. But as long as other centres of power, most importantly big business and the Catholic hierarchy, are not actively taking an anti-Arroyo position, and until the crisis reaches a point where there is danger of uncontrolled changes or, more specifically, those that would open the way for the Communist Party of the Philippines (CPP) to come to power, the United States is taking a wait and see attitude.

The Catholic Church is more divided than other centres of power. Religious orders, both those of men and women, have been actively working against the regime. But except for a few vocal bishops, the powerful Catholic Bishops Conference of the Philippines (CBCP) is vacillating between calls for "getting at the truth" and strict interpretations of "separation between church and state". One problem is the absence of a leader of the stature and political activism of the late Cardinal Jaime Sin. The division of the diocese of Manila into several separate dioceses has also made political action in the crucial Manila arena difficult. The new Pope's papal nuncio has reportedly cautioned against political activism. There are indications, however, that some the bishops are moving closer and closer to the kind of mobilizational role that the Church took in EDSA 1 and 2.

The Philippine military is not a centre of power the way the military is in Myanmar, and if in diminished form, still is in Thailand and Indonesia. But under conditions of stalemate between Arroyo and her opponents, many look to the military to break the stalemate. Credible reports of the Arroyo regime's use of the military in the 2004 elections have exacerbated tensions within an officer corps long unhappy with politician interference in the military. Many officers feel that they cannot become professionals with politicians usurping military intelligence capability, intervening in promotions, and corrupting top level officers. An attempt at organizing the military hierarchy's withdrawal of support from Arroyo back in February failed, but resolving the issues raised then has proven to be difficult because punishing top officers from elite military units, the Scout Rangers, Marines and police Special Action Force would be risky and would do damage to these units.[4]

A year after the scandal broke, Arroyo seems to have weathered the storm. She has shown iron will and tactical skill. She resisted calls to resign, bribed and cajoled congressmen into killing impeachment attempts in 2005 and 2006, and countered attempts at extra-constitutional solutions. She instructed police to use force to disperse demonstrations before they could become the focal point for larger, more sustained mass actions similar to EDSA 1, 2, and 3. She came up with an executive order (EO 464) preventing officials from testifying before Senate investigations. She proclaimed a state of emergency (Proclamation No. 1017) in an attempt to justify warrantless arrests of critics, muzzling the media and even threatening to take over public utilities. All these moves have been declared illegal by the Supreme Court, but the regime continues to ratchet up repression, especially against the Left.

In a recent speech, Senator Mar Roxas said:

> Notice that I say crisis of confidence, and not a political crisis, because it goes beyond the simple partisan considerations that turn off so many people regardless of their socio-economic class. The malaise is more pervasive than we know and like an unspoken plague, it threatens to consume us all. It involves the near-total assumption by the governed, that those governing deserve neither confidence nor even token assistance. It becomes every man for himself. Accordingly, the led have near universal disdain for those doing the leading.[5]

Another analyst says, "If we look at the data concerning public opinion and popular will, we are in fact already in a stage of what I call a 'governance vacuum', where people want their political system to provide credible leadership for change but for a combination of reasons this leadership is not forthcoming."[6]

A Pulse Asia survey in July 2006 showed that a "big plurality" of Filipinos remains dissatisfied with the performance of President Gloria Macapagal-Arroyo and also distrusts her. In its *Ulat ng Bayan* (Report of the Nation) survey conducted in July 2006, Pulse Asia said, "44 per cent or about 21 million Filipino adults express disapproval for President Gloria Macapagal-Arroyo's performance while 47 per cent or nearly 22.5 million Filipino adults distrust her." The survey results were practically the same as the March 2006 figures (50 per cent disapproval and 50 per cent distrust). "No president before her has experienced as extended a period of low public esteem," Pulse Asia said. "Whereas public disenchantment in terms of low approval and trust ratings generally improve for Philippine presidents within two to three quarters, President Arroyo's deflated approval and trust ratings have proven less tractable and outright improvements in public assessments of her performance and trustworthiness have been slow in coming."[7]

There is, of course, a difference between "opinion" and willingness to do something about it. Arroyo supporters claim that the unwillingness of the public to support the ouster of Arroyo has to do with the failure of the opposition to present an alternative. The "failure" is not that there is no one in the opposition that the public thinks can do a better job as president than Arroyo. Surveys show many politicians with higher trust levels than Arroyo. The problem is that people believe that even a more honest, more competent president would fail without systemic changes. Placed against intensifying opinion that what is needed is a "change in the system", inaction is a function of being unable to imagine the change required, being nervous about the scale of change associated with "system change" and the type of action demanded.

Arroyo may remain as President but will continue to operate under tenuous conditions within narrow boundaries. The impasse remains because players have different time and space perspectives. Those closest to centres of power want a quick resolution to pre-empt the danger of things getting out of hand and "allowing the Left and the Right" to get stronger. While cloaked in calls for "rule of law" and "following the constitution", these groups want the crisis resolved in small, secure meetings of the powerful. Those on the margins of power, the various Left groups, want the crisis to last long enough for it to spill over into the streets, for the solution to go beyond a new arrangement of powerful individuals and groups towards changes in the political system. In the end, Arroyo remains in power because of what we might call "systemic inertia". Key players understand the need to reform the political system, but uncertainty about how changes in the political system would impact their interests keeps them within the certainties of old ways of doing things.

The resolution of the crisis of the Arroyo regime can only come with her removal.

> If our country were Japan or South Korea, where personal honor is still highly valued, Mrs. Arroyo would have long bowed out of power in shame for disgracing her office. She would have drunk poison, or thrown herself into the murky waters of the Pasig. If this were Germany or Great Britain, where law and politics are taken seriously, the party in power would have instantly and decisively distanced itself from its discredited leader as an act of mortification if not of self-preservation. If this were the United States, she would have been convicted for obstruction of justice on multiple counts, and hounded out of the presidency.[8]

CONSTITUTIONAL REFORM

Whatever the outcome of the current struggle, constitutional reform is likely to be part of the package.

> Somewhere down the reform agenda of all the proposed variations of a transition government is the revision of the 1987 constitution. Most of the groups are amenable to supporting the shift to a parliamentary, federal form of government, an amendment that's a priority among charter-change advocates within the administration... Calling for a shift in the form of government is actually a common ground between the opposition and administration in the face of what both camps acknowledge to be President Arroyo's battered credibility.[9]

Indeed, through most of 2006, pro- and anti-Arroyo contention has mainly been on the issue of charter change.

The discussion on constitutional reform in 2006 was intense but marked by an air of unreality. Political groups pushing constitutional reform most strongly, those identified with beleaguered President Arroyo, are traditional politicians led by House Speaker Jose de Venecia, precisely the groups and individuals who exemplify old-style politics. The groups opposed to constitutional reform at this time, including cabinet secretaries who have resigned and civil society groups who have campaigned on the issue for years, are those who have unquestioned records as political reformers. The intensity of the push for rapid constitutional reform through a constituent assembly is at fever pitch precisely at a time when everyone knows it does not have a ghost of a chance because of Senate opposition.

The reason for this inversion of roles is encapsulated in the slogan "Gloria has to face the music, before we dance the chacha".[10] Longtime proponents of constitutional reform believe that President Arroyo is using "chacha" (or charter change) as a smokescreen, as an issue for distracting public attention away from charges of corruption and election fraud that threaten to get her removed from office.[11] Her propaganda line is that whatever shortcomings she has, she is a victim of a defective political system that now has to be changed. Chacha also serves a practical requirement for Arroyo's survival: getting the support of local officials and Congress persons who are the most avid proponents of chacha. In fact, chacha is impossible under current conditions because everyone is preoccupied with the intense struggle between pro- and anti-Arroyo groups.

While competing proponents of chacha all publicly support a shift from a presidential to a parliamentary form of government and from a unitary to a federal system, there is a deep divide between the two sides. At the root of this division is the difference between one side which wants to transform the political system to ensure the reproduction of the political class which has controlled Philippine politics for most of the last century and the side which wants to transform the distribution of political and social power in the society. In the end, substantive reform happens only when the balance of political power has shifted. This is where the link between the struggle over President Arroyo's continued stay in office and constitutional reform lies. The resignation of reformist members of her cabinet, and her unabashed use of patronage to remain in power have placed her completely on the side of reaction. If she remains in office until the end of her term in 2010, it will mean that the forces of reform have lost. But if she is overthrown, substantive constitutional reform, one that rearranges the balance of political power, will be possible.

The proposals of the "pro-Arroyo chacha camp" and the means for achieving its agenda have become more and more "radical". Faced with Senate intransigence, the House-Malacanang-local government officials combine is pushing ahead with extra-constitutional means. Both the people's initiative and the constituent assembly being pushed by pro-administration groups have questionable legal basis. The proposed amendments have also changed. The House's "shift to parliamentary" agenda has now incorporated the removal of restrictions on foreign participation in the economy, and more ominously, the adoption of authoritarian constitutional formulations. Since the anti-chacha camps roughly coincide with the anti-Arroyo camps, overall polarization precludes negotiation. The pro-Arroyo chacha camp has, as a result, also decided to "go for broke". It is as if the leadership had decided that if you do not have to negotiate chacha outcomes, you might as well "load" your agenda; go from a "minimum" to a "maximum" programme.

Changing discourse on chacha in the past decade has been influenced by deepening crisis. Successive crises have brought out more and more the bankruptcy of the 1935 political system restored by Cory Aquino. The military challenges to that system during the Aquino presidency, then in 2003, and most recently, in February 2006, can be seen as instances of the refusal of a key apparatus of the state to accept the political system. The most important crisis was the extra constitutional ouster of President Joseph Estrada in 2001. The Estrada presidency and its extra constitutional demise, EDSA 2 and EDSA 3, the chaotic May 2001 elections, then the threat of a Poe candidacy converged to heighten a sense of political crisis in the political class. Although inchoate, the crisis is a crisis of representation, a deep and abiding concern about the ability of our political institutions to produce competent and trustworthy leaders.

As more and more people understand that what is at stake is the shaping of a new political system, the implications of the de Venecia chacha agenda have begun to hit home. If the House proposal gets implemented, we will go from the frying pan into the fire. The corrupt, patronage-ridden political system we have had for most of the last seventy or more years will remain and get worse. The link between our personalistic, clan-based, and violent local politics and the central government are congress persons elected in single-member districts. Congressional horse trading was mitigated by having to make deals with a powerful president and the Senate. Under the House proposal, their competitors for power, the senators and the president, would be removed. Political parties would remain weak because members of parliament who depend mainly on their own resources to get elected in single-member districts would not be amenable to the tighter party discipline required in a parliamentary system. As if these were not bad enough, the new regime would have authoritarian powers.

In October 2006, the struggle for constitutional reform moved into the narrow, discreet confines of the Supreme Court. The proponents of peoples' initiative, the association of local government officials, Union of Local Authorities of the Philippines (ULAP), and the coalition of so-called peoples' organizations, *Sigaw ng Bayan* (Demand of the People), petitioned the court to reverse the refusal of the Commission on Elections to call a plebiscite on the amendments some 6.3 million people supposedly support. Another case questioning the insistence of leaders of the House of Representatives that a constituent assembly can vote on amendments without the Senate is waiting in the wings. Meanwhile, most politicians assume that neither mode of constitutional reform is possible and have started preparations for regular midterm elections in May 2007.

ROOTS OF CRISIS

The reason the Philippines has come to this dangerous pass can only be understood by going right to the heart of its political system. It is a system built on networks of local political notables organized in ascending order up to the national level. For most of the last century, these networks negotiated control of patronage among themselves. They retained enough influence on voters to give elections a semblance of democratic reality while retaining control over the allocation of power. Over time this system got eroded by demographic changes. Population growth brought a rapidly expanding electorate. Urbanization and commercialization eroded traditional patron-client ties of deference. The inability of corrupt and incompetent governments to do anything about scandalous poverty eroded trust. Politicians controlled less and less of the vote. Their political parties never developed enough to give people electoral choices. Media — action stars, news anchors, comedians and basketball heroes — took over from politicians in guiding electoral choice.

Marcos had the audacity to pose an authoritarian option. If demographic and political change makes the election of credible national leaders difficult, end elections and make economic performance the basis of your legitimacy. Greed, incompetent would-be captains of industry, lupus, and a powerful anti-dictatorship movement led by the Left closed off the authoritarian option. Instead of dealing with this structural problem, President Aquino simply restored the pre-martial law political system. It is no accident that resurgent populist politics chose to link with Marcos' political option. Erap (Joseph Estrada) and FPJ (Fernando Poe Jr.) shared a bloated, macho sense of their capacity to shape reality with Marcos. Perhaps we should add some leaders of the Left to this cabal of people who believe that their grasp of history and their willingness to use violence and to manipulate popular sentiment add up to a nasty, noxious anti-democratic brew.

Post-Marcos populism creates problems for both the Right and the Left. Karaos captures the character of contemporary populism best by contrasting it to clientilism:

> There are a number of important differences between the clientelism of traditional politics and the relationship between Estrada and his urban poor allies. The first relates to the way the leader views the existing power structure. Populist leaders create and maintain their populist appeal by challenging — at least in rhetoric if not in their actions — the existing power structure and typically portray themselves as the enemy of the elite. Estrada not only cast himself as an enemy of the rich, he even criticized the leaders of the Catholic Church for being elitist. Populist leaders make an effort to blur the class distinction between themselves and their followers. They build their legitimacy on this identification with the masses…
>
> By contrast, the traditional patron never sets out to confront the inequity of the existing power structure. Instead, traditional politicians seek to give legitimacy to the prevailing power structure by ensuring that the poor also get something out of it through their intervention. They act as intermediaries between the poor and the political system. In the eyes of their followers, traditional politicians are seen as effective leaders because of their access to power. A second difference is the articulation of some kind of 'class' or collective interest in a populist relationship. This is absent in clientelism. The latter succeeds in maintaining

> dependency by defining their relationship with their poor constituents in very particularistic terms. By contrast, populist leaders cultivate a class identity by emphasizing how the poor are being victimized by the elite...
>
> Populism and clientelism, however, share an important characteristic: their abhorrence for institutions and institutionalized channels of interest representation. Because of this, both end up reinforcing existing power relations. They do not encourage the formation of independent organizations with stable linkages to political institutions; instead, they cultivate the dependence of subaltern groups on politicians who represent the poor's only access to the political system.[12]

Unlike Latin American populists such as Peron, who mobilized poorer sections of the population into unions and a political party that remains to this day, or nationalist leaders in Asia who led their countries to independence, contemporary Philippine populism is "demobilizing". A distinct feature of the later populist variants is a subtle change in the pattern of mass mobilization. Unlike the first generation of leaders, new populist leaders do not build durable political parties nor labour organizations to carry out their populist project.

The rise of populist leaders has created serious problems for traditional politicians. Decentralization and the changing political economy of more and more local areas have meant new challengers to the political clans who control local politics. But it is not in local politics where *trapos* have the biggest problems. It is at the level of national electoral politics, in particular in the Presidency and the Senate, which have national electoral constituencies. Never been strong, political parties have become even weaker in the post-Marcos period. One attempted solution, setting up political party coalitions, what Abinales calls "big tent politics", does not really work.[13] This was the situation Arroyo confronted in the 2004 election. Facing a very popular movie action star in the mold of Estrada, Arroyo probably felt she had no choice but to use government resources to buy vote banks and organize extensive cheating. For a while it looked like Arroyo would get away with it; then the Garci tapes scandal happened.

Cheating in elections quickly got associated with cheating in other spheres of political life. Extracting rents is what makes the Philippine political system run. The whole political class, to one degree or another, is complicit. But because it "violates" the mythology of the political system, a mythology necessary for sustaining compliance by those who do not benefit from it, one crucial requirement is that anti-corruption is conducted within limits that do not "poison the well" that all politicians drink from. As former President

Estrada cynically put it, "weather weather *lang yan*". That is, politicians take turns at corruption. Limited anti-corruption campaigns form part of the mythological requirement for sustaining this system. It is this consensus in the political class that has been eroded, that underlies the difficulties of Arroyo. It is an underlying part of her message that "it's the system" that is at fault. It is also what sustains her high levels of distrust in opinion polls.

> Politicians like Ms. Arroyo cannot seem to understand why cheating in elections has become so suddenly wrong, or why taking kickbacks from government contracts and pork barrel projects is suddenly frowned upon. They wake up one morning, and they discover to their dismay that our people are demanding better government. I believe that the crisis in our political life arises precisely from the growing refusal of many ordinary Filipinos from all classes to tolerate patronage, fraud, political bossism, corruption, and misgovernance of our public life. The ruling classes of our country — the ones who are used to cynical wheeling and dealing, to corruption, to intimidation, and the exploitation of mass ignorance and dependence — are beginning to discover that they can no longer rule in the old way. Every election year they find that they have to cheat harder in order to get elected.[14]

I would like to agree with Randy David: "our people are demanding better government". But the people will not move on their own, they need leaders. The danger is that

> those most ready with a viable solution to political crisis have often been the vested interests because their goals are clear and their methods decisive. Reform forces with diffused goals and indecisive methods are the first casualties of intensified crisis and their usual palliative resolutions. This recurrent result explains our recurrent cycles of crisis: vested interests capture the solution to a crisis, which postpones but practically guarantees another crisis.[15]

Middle class reform groups "...have squandered our goodwill with every crisis we have participated in resolving that merely led to adopting the best among worst solutions and when crisis once again recurs, our people's trust in our advocacies get weaker until we eventually lose all moral authority to offer solutions altogether".[16]

DAMAGE TO INSTITUTIONS

One of the propaganda lines of the Arroyo administration is that the opposition should stop and let her and the country "move on". This line has resonance among people who do not want to be bothered by political conflict. What these people do not understand is that even if the anti-Arroyo people stop, the country would still not "move on". The country cannot go forward precisely because Arroyo is pushing it backwards by the day. Political institutions which have been painstakingly built over the course of a century are being eroded in Arroyo's desperate effort to remain in power. Some institutions are being damaged because they are being manipulated — the Comelec, the Armed Forces of the Philippines, the House of Representatives, and the Ombudsman, to name a few. Others, especially those providing government services, are being undermined by neglect.

Arroyo's manipulation of the armed forces is particularly dangerous because it is the main source of the kind of unhappiness among junior officers that is fuelling coup plotting. The biggest issue is widespread belief among disgruntled officers that armed forces units were used to cheat in the 2004 elections. Another is the virtual takeover of the Intelligence Services of the Armed Forces of the Philippines (ISAFP) by Malacanang operatives and the unit's use for partisan political purposes. Almost everyone (nobody, not even the ISAFP, denies this) believes the Garci tapes were made by ISAFP. The preferential promotion of officers implicated in the Garci scandal is adding salt to festering wounds. All this on top of the kind of corruption that denies equipment and medical attention to wounded foot soldiers.

If coup attempts remain only a threat, extra-judicial killings and other human rights violations are a reality. Through most of the third quarter of 2006, protests against killings of leaders of the Bayan Muna and other organizations linked to the national democratic movement have been mounting here and abroad. There is, of course, no direct evidence that these killings are organized by the military, but there is widespread belief that they are. These killings are occurring against the backdrop of widely publicized "deadlines" imposed by Arroyo on the military to end the Maoist insurgency. Apart from *pro-forma* condemnations by Arroyo, other key officials provide evasions not explanations, the most often used being that the Left is killing its own. The most ridiculous is Interior Secretary Ronaldo Puno's explanation that the killings continue because of the Leftist groups' refusal to trust the police to protect them. Why should Leftist groups trust the police when they believe they are being killed by military and police?[17]

One core political process, the relationship between the legislative and executive branches, has been bent out of shape. Executive Order (EO) 464 prohibited members of the executive branch from testifying in the Senate, where there were a number of investigations considered threatening by the president. EO 464 was declared illegal by the Supreme Court, the government's appeal denied with finality in July 2006. But in the Senate investigation of the lack of Overseas Workers Welfare Administration (OWWA) funds for repatriating Filipino workers in war-torn Lebanon, the palace again prohibited officials of the Executive Department from attending.[18] Exasperated, the Senate then arrested the Chair of the Presidential Commission on Good Government (PCGG). In retaliation, Malacanang ordered the police to withraw the unit assigned to the Senate. As with other key political issues, the problem has been shifted to the Supreme Court to decide.

A lot more research needs to be done on the damage to a whole range of political institutions. For illustrative purposes, this chapter will focus on the civil service. In contrast to the British who concentrated on building the civil service in their colonial possessions, the Americans left behind a weak, corrupt, and incompetent bureaucracy in the Philippines. Small steps have been taken to build a better civil service, interestingly enough starting at the time of Marcos. Arroyo is undermining these efforts. If we segue from the military and police to reforming the bureaucracy, in a recent speech at a Command Conference of the Philippine National Police, Arroyo expressed support for scrapping the Civil Service Illegibility Exam for promotion to the rank of senior superintendent or higher, undermining a key instrument for professionalizing the police.[19]

What has happened at the Career Service Executive Board (CESB), the government body that oversees the top tiers of the country's bureaucracy, is even more damning. The story starts with the palace buying congressional support to block the impeachment move in the third quarter of 2005. Three postdated cheques worth P15 million from the President's Social Fund for Zambales Congressman Antonio Diaz had to be channelled through the Department of Education, Culture and Sports (DECS). DECS Undersecretary Juan Miguel Luz returned the cheques, citing violations of department rules. For his efforts, he got sacked.[20] But that was not the end of the story.

In a 20 March 2006 resolution (619), the CESB did something unheard of: it accused Malacañang and the Cabinet of "transgressions" of civil-service laws, rules and regulations. It cited the unjust termination of Education Undersecretary Luz and former Pag-Ibig Fund president and chief executive officer Manuel Crisostomo, both career bureaucrats, and the appointment of non-civil service eligible officials. These, the CESB said, "have resulted in growing apprehension and demoralization" in the civil service and threatened to "further erode the institutional foundations of a professional bureaucracy…". In return, Malacañang has reacted with a series of what appear to be punitive and retaliatory moves against the CESB. Within days after the resolution, two of the CESB's eight members lost their seats. Two others, one of whom was reportedly forced to resign, were replaced after a couple of weeks. Insiders at the agency say the resolution also strengthened the resolve of palace officials to replace Civil Service Commission Chair Karina David as CESB chair.[21]

Resolution 619 lists seven categories of personnel actions by the Arroyo administration that affect Career Executive Service Officer (CESO) and third-level eligibles and have "undermined the principles of professionalism and meritocracy". CESB records show that of the 2,583 career executive positions appointed by the president, 42 per cent are currently filled by "non-eligibles", or those who did not have to go through the rigid process undergone by career bureaucrats. Despite repeated pronouncements that it has trimmed the fat in the government service, the bureaucracy under Arroyo is more bloated now than it was under Estrada. Records of the Department of Budget and Management show that Arroyo had 1,150,681 permanent positions in national government agencies in 2005, or 47,555 more than what Estrada had in 2000. Data from the budget department reveal that the Arroyo administration has twenty-two more under-secretaries and eight more assistant secretaries than the previous government.

ECONOMIC IMPERATIVE

One of the reasons why Arroyo remains in power is that "business as usual" conditions paper over deep and dangerous problems in the economy. Business people have become so used to "muddling through" that they hardly ever believe anymore that conditions could be different. Middle class people are busy making ends meet or saving to be able to go abroad. The poor do not have the energy to do more than scrape together enough money for the next meal.

> Official statistics show that poverty incidence (by population) had declined from 49.2 per cent in 1985 to 39.4 per cent in 2000, an average reduction of 0.7 percentage point per year. However, in absolute numbers, the number of poor had increased from 26.5 million to 30.4 million Filipinos. The annual decline in poverty incidence also pales by comparison with the performance of neighboring Asian countries; Indonesia had a reduction of 1.6 per cent per annum between 1985 to 1999, while Thailand, 1.7 per cent per annum between 1986 to 1999.[22]

Pro-administration analysts such as congressman Joey Salceda say that the Philippines is now in a situation where there is a "firewall" between the economy and politics, that this is the reason the economy continues to perform well despite political turmoil. The palace uses a different line. For example, presidential spokesperson Ignacio Bunye said that "...the new impeachment case would be 'counterproductive' given that the country has been achieving 'significant gains' that included a 'respectable' growth, strong stock market and inflation is down, among others... So why rock the boat at this time?".[23] Salceda is partly right in that international markets worry mainly about whether the Philippines can service its debt and FDI earnings. "Respectable" growth, strong stock market and low inflation are the markers of the country's financial capacity. But because these economic indices have little to do with the real economy, much less with poverty, poor people will continue to mistrust Arroyo even if big business remains ambivalent.

Most economists agree that the greatest gains in reducing poverty derive from economic growth. There is also agreement that sustained GNP growth beyond 6 per cent per year is necessary. In the last six years, the Philippines has averaged only 4.4 per cent growth. Even this growth is questionable. Economist Maitet Diokno Pascual says "...the Arroyo government is able to sustain itself, because of two things: OFW remittances and over borrowing." Arroyo is engaging in what economists call the "Ponzi game" of borrowing to repay maturing principal. A recent study of the Asian Development Bank (ADB) said the Ponzi game played by Arroyo is working but is not sustainable. To which Pascual agreed, adding that "the Ponzi game, whose main strategy is to keep treasury bills below market rates, cannot be played indefinitely without squeezing out bank profits".[24] The ADB goes further, "The Bank noted that the largest contributor to the country's GDP growth last year was personal consumption expenditure, buoyed, in turn, by remittances from overseas workers. Remittances pushed up the performance of the banking sector; and remittances were also responsible for reining in the negative impact of a widening trade deficit."[25]

The government's fiscal situation is problematical both at the revenue and the expenditure ends. Even if you factor in the large devaluation in the aftermath of the 1997 Asian financial crisis, the increase from an average annual deficit of P7.2 billion during the Ramos administration (1992–98) to P186.1 billion during the 2001–04 years of Arroyo is massive. On the revenue end, the Arroyo administration performance has been poor. "...revenue effort was on the uptrend from an average of 14 to 16 per cent between 1990 and the Asian crisis in 1997, after which tax effort declined steeply from 15.63 per cent in 1998 to 12.5 per cent in 2003.[26] University of the Philippines economics professor and columnist Solita Collas-Monsod provides more damaging detail. The tax effort ratio (unweighted average tax to GDP ratio) for the thirty-nation OECD for 2003 was 36.1 per cent: Sweden 50.7 in

TABLE 2.1
Asian GDP Growth Rates, 2001–2006

Country	*2001*	*2002*	*2003*	*2004*	*2005**	*2006**
Singapore	–1.8	3.2	1.4	8.4	4.1	4.5
Malaysia	0.3	4.1	5.3	7.1	5.7	5.3
Thailand	2.2	5.3	6.9	6.1	5.6	5.8
Indonesia	3.8	4.3	5.0	5.1	5.5	6.0
Vietnam	5.8	6.4	7.1	7.5	7.6	7.6
Philippines	**1.8**	**4.3**	**4.7**	**6.1**	**5.0**	**5.0**
China	7.5	8.3	9.3	9.5	8.5	8.7
South Korea	3.8	7.0	3.1	4.6	4.1	5.1

*Projected
Source: Asian Development Bank, 2005.

2004, Mexico 18.5, Korea 24.6, United States 25.4. In Southeast Asia, Malaysia recorded 17.6 in 2003, Thailand 16.7, Vietnam 16.4, and the Philippines 12.7 in 2005. Given that the Philippine GDP in 2004 was P5.3 trillion, if we had Vietnam's tax effort, we would have raised an additional P196 billion, enough to wipe out our budget deficit.[27] Promising reforms in revenue administration in the first few years of the Arroyo administration were cut short with the resignation of key members of the team at both the Bureau of Internal Revenue and the Department of Finance in July 2005.

The main source of vulnerability of government finances is debt. "Last year, government spent the equivalent of 81 per cent of its revenues to pay for both interest and principal amortization of its total debt, or more than 4 out of every 5 pesos it made from both tax and non-tax revenues. In 2005, government is allocating the equivalent of over 90 per cent (that is, more than 9 out of every 10 pesos) of projected revenues to interest and principal payments for outstanding debt."[28] Net of interest payments, primary spending of the national government has actually declined significantly since 1999, and is now at its lowest level in a decade. The bulk of the national budget that remains after interest payments is already committed beforehand to salaries, maintenance and operating expenses, and the internal revenue allotment to local governments, leaving very little for infrastructure spending and other development needs.[29]

Massive borrowing as a tactic for dealing with fiscal problems means the government and the economy as a whole are vulnerable to financial shocks from within the country and outside. The damage remains potential as long as there are creditors who are willing to lend. The cost of the

TABLE 2.2
Fiscal Performance of the Past Administrations, 1946–2004

Political Administration	*Average Annual Fiscal Surplus (Deficit) in PhP million*	*Average Annual Fiscal Surplus (Deficit) in US$ million*
Roxas (1946–48)	(30)	(15)
Quirino (1948–53)	(2)	(1)
Magsaysay (1953–57)	(76)	(38)
Garcia (1957–61)	(107)	(53)
Macapagal (1961–65)	(113)	(40)
Marcos (1965–72)	(397)	(85)
Marcos Authoritarian (1972–86)	(6,648)	(537)
Aquino (1986–92)	(24,242)	(1,030)
Ramos (1992–98)	(7,261)	(181)
Estrada (1998–2001)	(111,193)	(2,408)
Macapagal-Arroyo (2001–04)	(186,171)	(3,439)

Note: All figures are rounded. Deficit figures during the Estrada period from 1998–2000 only and for Marcos authoritarian period up to 1985 only.
Source: Batalla 2005.

TABLE 2.3
Total Debt Service as Percentage of National Government Revenues, 1995–2004

Particulars	*1995*	*1996*	*1997*	*1998*	*1999*	*2000*	*2001*	*2002*	*2003*	*2004*
Total Debt Service (%)	**38.0**	**28.7**	**26.7**	**35.6**	**42.9**	**44.3**	**48.7**	**63.1**	**75.0**	**86.2**
Domestic	23.6	17.6	16.2	22.1	28.5	27.0	29.6	35.4	47.1	56.2
Foreign	14.4	11.1	10.5	13.5	14.4	17.3	19.1	27.7	27.9	30.0

Source: Bureau of Treasury.

government's other tactic, cutting back on services, is already being felt. Worse, cutbacks on health and education expenditures compromise future generations. Government primary spending has been steadily declining during the Arroyo years. The 2005 budget mandated a contraction of primary spending by 2.8 per cent in absolute (nominal) terms. The decrease in real terms, of course, is much larger. The cuts would bring primary spending down to only 11.9 per cent of GDP. Since the 2005 budget was re-enacted in 2006, the contraction continues.

The impact of this neglect remains to be measured. Attention was recently focused on education "...when President Gloria Macapagal-Arroyo publicly scolded Acting Education Secretary Fe Hidalgo for suggesting that

TABLE 2.4
Selected Items of Government Spending
(as percentages of nominal GDP)

	1999	*2000*	*2001*	*2002*	*2003*	*2004*
Primary spending[1]	16.25	15.04	14.76	14.95	13.96	12.86
Education	3.39	3.23	3.05	3.03	2.99	2.69
Health	0.44	0.38	0.31	0.33	0.25	0.23
Infrastructure outlays	1.85	1.94	1.77	1.51	1.41	1.06
Memorandum:						
Personal services	7.24	7.01	6.82	6.77	6.42	6.16

[1]Expenditures less interest payments
Source: Department of Budget and Management

there was a shortage of almost 7,000 classrooms with 45 pupils to a room. Arroyo said the shortage was much less — about 1,000 classrooms — but admitted that the government would need to resort to double shifts in which they are used twice a day, with each class having 50 pupils, to overcome the burden."[30] The problem is so bad in some schools that toilets and hallways have to be used to accommodate classes. One report said children have to use umbrellas in class when it rains.

The result is disastrously falling standards. "Only 7 per cent of senior high school students had mastered English; 2 per cent, Science, and 16 per cent Mathematics... The national average score in TIMSS (Trends in Math and Science Survey) in 2003 was 378 in Mathematics — 89 points behind the international average and 227 points away from the highest score notched by Singapore. It will take the Philippines 11 to 12 years to narrow the gap with the world average in achievement tests and 25 to 28 years to reach the Singapore level, says the Department of Education in a presentation to the Cabinet in July 2005."[31] At this rate, a whole generation of children will be sacrificed.

Another social service neglected by government, health, also impacts on education. Former Education Undersecretary Juan Miguel Luz revealed that "30 per cent of all pupils aged 6 to 12 years are 'underweight and under height'. This condition is responsible for 25 per cent of school dropouts before completion of Grade 4 and 35 per cent before the end of Grade 6. The study also says that 65 per cent of pupils aged 6 to 12 are iodine-deficient, while one in every three suffers from iron deficiency anemia. Dental caries affect 87 per cent of the children. No wonder, 32 per cent of absenteeism in Grade 1 is due to mouth-related pain."[32]

SYSTEM CHANGE?

The political situation appears to have settled onto a plateau, one where major developments are unlikely in the short term. This works in favour of Arroyo because the closer the May 2007 elections, the more its political energies will be chanelled towards campaign preparations. While the second impeachment complaint has drawn a lot of media attention, administration resources remain sufficient for scuttling the initiative without getting into the substantive issues. On top of patronage, Congress people who intend to run in the coming elections do not want the administration working against them. The shift in political preoccupations will move the situation away from system change.

There is near universal consensus on the need to make major changes in the Philippines' political system. The pro- and anti-Arroyo camps agree on the need for constitutional reform even if they disagree on the mode and substance of amendment. But since neither people's initiative nor the constituent assembly campaign of the administration is going anywhere, constitutional reform is not likely in the near future. The closest possibility of reviving "chacha" is if Arroyo agrees to the Hyatt 10 call for the election of constitutional convention delegates at the time of the May 2007 elections.[33] Even if this happens, constitutional reform will still be pushed years into the future because newly elected officials, in particular senators, will not be too interested in undoing what they just worked hard for.

As important as constitutional reform is, the kinds of institutional changes contemplated will have to be measured against the need for changes in the socioeconomic distribution of power. "We may be able to get out of the current [economic] crisis by raising enough new revenues and even negotiating for debt relief, but unless we address the long-standing concentration of political, social and economic power to a limited segment of our society and economy, the country will remain weak and constantly subject to recurring crises."[34] At this time, it is Arroyo's desperate obsession with remaining in power that is standing in the way of change. But in the end, it is the oligarchy and its relationship with the state that have to be changed.

> The evidence...points to increased concentration of economic power through the 1990s, as conscious efforts to consolidate market dominance managed to thwart increased competition through market contestability that trade liberalization would have normally provided. This increased monopoly power even in a more liberalized trade regime appeared to make the Philippine experience with liberalization somewhat unique.

> With this trend, it is not surprising that income inequality widened through the 1990s in spite of a generally stronger economy…The problem is that government itself has been largely instrumental in the attainment and perpetuation of such monopoly power. Through a series of policy reversals from the competition-enhancing reforms of the late 1980s and the 1990s, the government has protected a select group of capitalists by preventing other firms from introducing changes that would increase competition and productivity. On top of this, certain regulatory agencies have been 'captured' by the very firms they are supposed to regulate, further contributing to the perpetuation of monopolistic tendencies in key sectors of the economy.[35]

The struggle against the Arroyo regime will continue because effective governance is impossible in a situation where the population does not trust the president, where key segments of business, the church, and civil society are actively working against the regime. As long as Arroyo remains in power, a fiscal policy which sacrifices social services and the health and education of future generations will remain in place. As the Hyatt 10 statement put it recently: "there are no victors in this continuing impasse — only victims. And the biggest victims are our deeply cynical and ever suffering poor themselves and our much-weakened social, economic and political institutions."[36]

Working for system change will be a long and demanding process. It will have to be done in many small and concrete steps. It cannot be done without changes in the perspectives of key anti-Arroyo and pro-reform groups. Middle class groups such as the Black and White Movement will have to develop a will to power.

> We must begin by accepting that this is about the capture and exercise of political power and we need leaders who can gain credibility and following on the basis of what we stand for and who can then become our reliable champions as well as faithful agents in the execution of our agenda for reform. We must also realize that we have tremendous resources available to our cause, as there are many government officials at various levels that share our aspirations, many local government officials that see these things like us and many legislators who could become our allies in the capture of political power and in prosecuting the reform process. These are in addition to our traditional allies in business, academe, professions, Church and non-government sectors. We may also have many fellow travelers in the police and military who will necessarily have to take the backseat in the effort but whose support will be essential to our eventual success.[37]

The second major change in perspective will have to come from the Left. The Maoists are too deliberately set in their ways, but democratic Left groups are already in the process of changing their perspectives. The Left does not have the capacity, at this time, to shape politics to its liking. That will not matter to some who are used to decades of "protracted struggle". What they have to come to terms with is, if the crisis will produce systemic reform in the near future, and they are in no position to shape reform on their own. They will have to ally themselves with other groups in order to have a role in shaping that future. When they see poverty they have to see beyond organizing opportunity to the children's futures lost the longer it takes to win the struggle for reform. Finally, both middle class and Left groups have to see beyond their fear of each other to a joint political project for the Filipino people.

Notes

1 "GMA: Cha-cha to Bring Unity", *The Philippine Star*, 9 September 2005.

2 Randy David, "The National Situation", Manila Polo Club Talk, 7 February 2006.

3 Eva-Lotta E. Hedman, *In the Name of Civil Society* (Honolulu: The University of Hawaii Press, 2006).

4 *Philippine Star*, 4 July 2006.

5 Senator Mar Roxas, AIM Speech, 6 June 2006.

6 Mario Taguiwalo, "*Quo vadis,* Middle Forces?", 16 July 2005, at <http://www.ipd.ph>.

7 "Filipinos Dissatisfied, Distrust Arroyo — Survey", INQ7.net, 23 July 2006.

8 David, ibid.

9 Miriam Grace A. Go and Isagani De Castro, Jr., "Talk About a Revolution", *Newsbreak*, 18 July 2005, p. 27.

10 In acronym-crazy Philippines, "charter change" morphs into "chacha".

11 Amando Doronila, "Analysis: Charter Change a Subterfuge to Keep Arroyo in Power", *Philippine Daily Inquirer*, 19 December 2005.

12 Anna Marie A. Karaos, "Populist Mobilization and Manila's Urban Poor — The Case of SANAPA in the NGC East Side", forthcoming in an Institute for Popular Democracy book on social movements in the Philippines.

13 Patricio Abinales, "Coalition Politics in the Philippines", *Current History* (April 2001).

14 David, ibid.

15 Taguiwalo, ibid.

16 Ibid.

17 Desiree Caluza, Villamor Visaya, Bobby Labalan, Nancy C. Carvajal, "3 Assassinations in a Day, 2 Militant Leaders, Lensman Shot Dead", *Philippine Daily Inquirer*, 1 August 2006.

18 T.J. Burgonio, "Palace Officials Snub Probe of OWWA Funds", *Philippine Daily Inquirer*, 1 August 2006.

19 *Manila Standard*, 1 October 2005.

20 Alcuin Papa, "His Family Genes are too Strong, Especially for Malacanang".

21 Yvonne T. Chua, PCIJ Report on the Career Service Executive Board (CESB).

22 See "Beneath the Fiscal Crisis — Uneven Development Weakens the Republic", Members of the Economics and Political Science Departments (Ateneo de Manila University, Loyola Heights, Quezon City, Philippines, 28 February, 2005).

23 Christine Avendaño and Philip Tubeza, "That's not the Picture we're Getting", *Philippine Daily Inquirer*, 2 August 2006.

24 See Alecks Pabico, INSIDE PCIJ: Stories behind Our Stories, "Unmasking the myth of 'Arrovonomics' ", 26 April 2006.

25 Vinia Datinguinoo, INSIDE PCIJ: Stories behind Our Stories, "RP Growth not Enough to Lick Poverty — ADB", 7 April 2006, <http:/pcij.org/blog>.

26 Marife Lou Bacate et al., "The Bello, et al. Critique: Biased and Economically Unsound".

27 Solita Collas-Monsod, "Is the BIR's Collection Target Achievable?". *Philippine Daily Inquirer*, 10 June 2006, p. 10.

28 Ateneo, 2006: Executive Summary, p. 1.

29 Ibid., p. 11.

30 Lira Dalangin-Fernandez, "School Year Starts amid Lack of Classrooms, Teachers", *Philippine Daily Inquirer*, 5 June 2006.

31 Fernando del Mundo, "Decline in Quality Education Hobbles Job Creation Program".

32 Ibid.

33 Hyatt 10 Statement on the One Year Anniversary of their resignation from the Arroyo cabinet, *Philippine Daily Inquirer*, July 8, 2006.

34 Ateneo 2005, p. 9.

35 Ibid., p. 4.

36 Hyatt 10, 2006.

37 Taguiwalo 2005.

References

Abinales, Patricio. "Coalition Politics in the Philippines". *Current History* (April 2001).

Bacate, Marife Lou, et al. "The Bello, et al. Critique: Biased and Economically Unsound". In "UP 11 Plan: Can It Keep RP Afloat?", *Inquirer News Service*, 19 September 2004.

"Beneath the Fiscal Crisis — Uneven Development Weakens the Republic". Members of the Economics and Political Science Departments, Ateneo de Manila University, Loyola Heights, Quezon City, Philippines, 28 February 2005.

Chua, Yvonne. *INSIDE PCIJ: Stories behind Our Stories*, "Arroyo and ARMM", 22 June 2005, Filed under *In the News, Gloriagate, 2004 Electoral Fraud.*

———. PCIJ Report on the Career Service Executive Board (CESB).

Dalangin-Fernandez, Lira. "School Year Starts amid Lack of Classrooms, Teachers". *Philippine Daily Inquirer*, 5 June 2006.

Datinguinoo, Vinia. INSIDE PCIJ: Stories behind Our Stories, "RP Growth not Enough to Lick Poverty — ADB", 7 April 2006, <http:/pcij.org/blog>.

David, Randy. "The National Situation", Manila Polo Club Talk, 7 February 2006.

de Dios, Emmanuel S. et al. "The Economy on a Cusp, the Proposed VAT Amendments and Their Larger Significance", University of the Philippines School of Economics Discussion Paper 05-05.

Hedman, Eva-Lotta E. *In the Name of Civil Society*. Honolulu: The University of Hawaii Press, 2006.

Hyatt 10 Statement on the One Year Anniversary of their resignation from the Arroyo cabinet, *Philippine Daily Inquirer*, 8 July 2006.

Karaos, Anna Marie A. "Populist Mobilization and Manila's Urban Poor — The Case of SANAPA in the NGC East Side". Forthcoming in an Institute for Popular Democracy book on social movements in the Philippines.

Collas-Monsod, Solita. "Is The BIR's Collection Target Achievable?". *Philippine Daily Inquirer*, 10 June 2006, p. 10.

del Mundo, Fernando. "Decline in Quality Education Hobbles Job Creation Program". *Philippine Daily Inquirer*, 6 June 2006.

Pabico, Alecks. "10 Reasons to Doubt the 2004 Election Results", 5 April 2006, 5:09 p.m. · Filed under i Report Features, Gloriagate, 2004 Electoral Fraud.

———. INSIDE PCIJ: Stories behind Our Stories, "Unmasking the Myth of 'Arrovonomics' ", 26 April 2006.

Papa, Alcuin. "His Family Genes are too Strong, Especially for Malacanang". *Philippine Daily Inquirer*, 2 October 2005, p. 7.

Roxas, Mar. AIM speech, 6 June 2006.

"The Leadership Imperative: Addressing Insufficient Revenues, Ballooning Debts, and 2006 Budget", *Stratbase*, 25 February 2006.

Social Weather Survey, First Quarter 2006. "Options for Toppling GMA: Coup Gets Split Opinions, People Power Gets 48%, Pro-resign Gets 44%".

Taguiwalo, Mario. "*Quo vadis*, Middle Forces?", 16 July 2005, <http://www.ipd.ph>.

3

PROPOSED CONSTITUTIONAL REFORMS FOR GOOD GOVERNANCE AND NATION BUILDING

Jose V. Abueva

In the political struggle over the proposed amendments to the 1987 Constitution from 2004 to 2006, protagonists voiced divergent ideas, perceptions and opinions and their ideological and partisan preferences. The media actively participated not only to report on the events, the protagonists and the issues, but also to take sides in the debates and influence public opinion. The Catholic hierarchy and the largest and most influential media establishments — notably the *Philippine Daily Inquirer* and ABS-CBN radio and television — openly opposed the proposed reforms.

The proposed amendments were effectively opposed as selfishly motivated, unnecessary, defective, untimely, hastily done, and forced on a reluctant people and Senate. In effect the dominant opposition to proposing charter change through either the petition for a people's initiative or by Congress as a constituent assembly favoured the *status quo* in terms of the form, structure and processes of governance and the restrictive economic policies regarding foreign investments. The apparent agenda and vested interests of those who blocked the proposed reforms were largely obscured in the debates.

This chapter focuses at length and in substantive detail on the major proposals for constitutional reform and their stated advantages and justification, as well as summarizes the criticism and opposition of sceptics and opponents. The fierce yet peaceful struggle for and against constitutional reform ended in October to December 2006 in the decisions of the Supreme Court on the petition for a people's initiative and the failure of the majority in the House to push its amendments by a constituent assembly over the Senate's objections.

INTRODUCTION: CHARTER CHANGE FOR GOOD GOVERNANCE

In 2006 the public debate and controversy over proposals for charter change were focused mainly on the lone proposal to replace the presidential government and the bicameral Congress with a unicameral parliamentary government in the same year, or early in 2007.[1] Prominently behind the proposal to amend the 1987 Constitution was the *Sigaw ng Bayan* (Cry of the People) Movement of citizens and local leaders initiated in Manila on 15 February 2006 under the leadership of Manila Mayor Lito Atienza. In no time many non-governmental organizations and labour and business associations joined the movement to propose amendments through a petition for a people's initiative.

As a nationwide alliance, *Sigaw* was supported by the Union of Local Authorities of the Philippines (ULAP), which unites the various leagues of elected local government officials, and by the Charter Change Advocacy Commission, which succeeded the 2005 Consultative Commission, to pursue the proposed revision of the 1987 Constitution. At the national level *Sigaw* enjoyed the backing of President Gloria Arroyo, Speaker Jose C. de Venecia, who co-chairs with the president the Lakas Christian-Muslim Democrats Party, the majority coalition in the House of Representatives, and Secretary Ronaldo Puno of the Department of Interior and Local Governments.

It should be recalled that every endeavour to adopt a new constitution or constitutional amendments had enjoyed the vigorous support of the incumbent national leader: Manuel L. Quezon in 1935 and 1940, Ferdinand E. Marcos in 1973 and succeeding years, and Corazon C. Aquino in 1987. This reminder is needed, because many who were opposed to President Arroyo had been critical of her advocacy of charter change since 2003.

Sigaw ng Bayan and local government leaders gathered the signatures of more than six million qualified voters nationwide, verified by registrars of the Commission on Elections (Comelec), in support of *Sigaw's* petition to the Comelec to hold a national plebiscite on its proposal to establish a unicameral parliamentary government. The movement fulfilled the constitutional requirement that the third mode of amending the constitution, through the people's direct action or people's initiative, should generate the support of at least 12 per cent of the total number of registered voters, including at least 3 per cent of the registered voters in every legislative district.

However, when the proponents of the people's initiative submitted their petition to the Comelec on 25 August 2006, the latter ruled on 31 August that it could not act on the petition because the Supreme Court had enjoined it in 1997 from entertaining any petition for a people's initiative in the absence of an enabling law.[2] The petitioners asked the Supreme Court to compel the Comelec to act on the petition for the initiative and hold the needed plebiscite. At the same time the House of Representatives activated its move for Congress to be the body to propose the amendments to the people.

However, for this review of proposed constitutional reforms in 2005–06, the most comprehensive set of proposed amendments to or revision of the 1987 Constitution was the one recommended by the 2005 Consultative Commission appointed by President Gloria Macapagal-Arroyo.[3] In the view of its chairman, Jose V. Abueva, the proposed reforms sought to bring about good governance, understood as the institutionalized capacity of the government at all levels, with the people's participation, to make policies and decisions and implement them responsively, efficiently, and effectively, and with transparency and accountability to the people. In theory, with sustained good governance and political will, Filipinos can make progress in replacing poverty with prosperity, social inequality with social justice, corruption with effective and ethical government, and under-development with global competitiveness.

But Filipinos need other factors to make their reformed and revitalized institutions succeed. They also need to develop:

- a deeper sense of nationhood, a stronger commitment to the common good and the national interest, spirituality, moral values, and modern ethical behaviour;
- competent, responsible and accountable leaders who have the political will to do what is necessary in terms of policies, decisions and reforms;
- responsible citizens who are empowered economically, socially and politically as members of a growing middle class; and
- a productive, competitive, and responsible private sector and an equitable economy.

By putting these things firmly in place over time, Filipinos everywhere shall be building a global nation worthy of their heroes, a country fit for their children — of which they could all be proud.

But first of all, Filipinos need to reform and revitalize their institutions of governance by amending or revising the 1987 Constitution. For this purpose, in consultation with the people in regional workshops the 2005 Consultative Commission prepared its proposals and submitted them to the President on 16 December 2005. On the same date she submitted them to Congress.

Led by Speaker Jose C. de Venecia and Representative Constantino G. Jaraula, chairman of the House Committee on Constitutional Amendments, the majority coalition in the House of Representatives proposed amendments to the 1987 Constitution that took into account the proposed revision by the 2005 Consultative Commission. Earlier on, the House of Representatives revived its joint resolution for Congress to propose constitutional change in order to abolish the presidential government and bicameral Congress and replace them with a unicameral parliamentary government. The House had proposed to the Senate similar joint resolutions for charter change for several years. As in the past, the Senate did not agree to the House's latest initiative.

It was the repeated inability of Congress to jointly propose any constitutional amendments that precipitated the launching of the people's initiative by *Sigaw ng Bayan* on 15 February 2006. It was originally hoped that the Comelec would hold the plebiscite on the proposition of *Sigaw ng Bayan* and the ULAP in 2006 or early 2007, and a majority of the voters would ratify it. However, because of the refusal of the Comelec to act on the people's petition for an initiative, in the absence of the Supreme Court's favourable ruling on the constitutional issues surrounding the people's initiative, action on the proposed amendments was suspended. The petitioners promptly asked the Supreme Court to order the Comelec to comply with the petition.

THE PROPOSED PARLIAMENTARY GOVERNMENT

In the following sections the major proposals for charter change are presented to flesh out the references to them above. The criticism and preferences of those opposed to the major proposals are tersely summarized below (*in italics*) to afford the reader a fair and balanced view of the intense and heated public debate on charter change.

The proposals of the House of Representatives, led by Speaker Jose C. de Venecia and the majority coalition in the House of Representatives, and the 2005 Consultative Commission to propose the revision of the 1987 Constitution had these features in common.[4]

1. A Parliament that combines legislative and executive powers for efficient, effective and accountable policy-making and implementation.
   Critique: It is better to retain the presidential government that provides separation of powers and checks and balance between the president and Congress, and allows the people to vote for the president as chief executive and head of state.
2. An economical unicameral Parliament that facilitates the legislative function.
   Critique: A bicameral Congress will ensure more judicious deliberation in law-making and in legislative oversight over the executive.
3. The Parliament shall have as many members as may be provided by law. To begin with, it shall have as many elected members as the present 235 congressional district representatives.
4. In addition the members chosen by the political parties shall constitute 20 to 30 per cent of the total members of Parliament (MPs), including those elected to the Parliament. These additional members are to be chosen by "proportional representation" of the political parties, based on their share of the total votes cast nationwide for the individual parties in the previous parliamentary election.
   Critique: The present party list system should be continued to allow representation of marginalized sectors of society, and to exclude the regular political parties.
5. Checks and balance in Parliament are exercised in the competitive and adversarial, as well as cooperative, relations between the majority party or coalition and the opposition parties, including the regular question hour.
   Critique: A strong majority political party can dominate Parliament and remain in power indefinitely.
6. The opposition is represented in the Commission on Appointments. There are also other centres of countervailing power in the Parliament: the business groups, the interest groups, the media, and civil society organizations, not to mention foreign powers and business and international organizations.
7. Members of Parliament shall be elected, or chosen by the political parties, for a term of five years, with no term limits. The electorate shall decide whether incumbents are worthy of re-election. The Consultiative Commission recommends that candidates for MP must have a college degree.
   Critique: Removal of term limits will perpetuate the dominance of political families or dynasties.

8. The prime minister is elected by a majority of all the MPs. He exercises the executive power. He is normally the leader of the majority party in the Parliament.
   Critique: It will be easier to influence the selection of the prime minister than the nomination and national election of the president, by dealing with or buying the support of fewer people — the MPs.
9. As the head of the government, the prime minister is assisted by the cabinet of ministers, at least three-fourths of whom shall be MPs.
10. From among the MPs, the Parliament shall elect the president who is the head of state for a term of five years. The president shall cease to be an MP and a member of any political party.
   Critique: Basically, the Philippines cannot establish a parliamentary government because the political parties are weak and oriented to personalities, not to principles and platforms or programmes of government. The bureaucracy is also inefficient and corrupt. Strong and principled political parties and an efficient and honest bureaucracy are pre-conditions to establishing a parliamentary government. It would be better to just improve the present presidential government and bicameral Congress.

The foregoing critique is refuted in the following sections on the grounds that the present weak and dysfunctional party system and bureaucracy are the long-term consequences of the inefficient, obstructive and ineffective presidential system and bicameral Congress since 1946. Basically, the development of the desired political parties oriented to principles and platforms or programmes of government and the desired efficient and honest bureaucracy will be the outcome of, and not the pre-condition to, the shift to a parliamentary government and its sustained development.

Expected Advantages of the Proposed Parliamentary Government over the Present Presidential Government[5]

1. Because Parliament exercises both legislative power and executive power, it would ensure the coordinated, efficient, and effective making of laws and policies and their implementation, especially because the Parliament shall have only one house or chamber, unlike in the presidential government with its separation of powers between the president and Congress, and in the bicameral Congress where there are two law-making bodies that have to reconcile their separate actions on legislative bills.
2. The prime minister and the government (the cabinet and governing party headed by the prime minister) and their political party or coalition

would assume collective responsibility and accountability for governance to the Parliament and the people. The people would learn whom to reward for good governance and administration, or to punish for failure or corruption. In the presidential government since 1946, the separation of powers between the president and Congress and the diffusion of legislative powers between the Senate and the House of Representatives, without cohesive and responsible political parties to unite them, the citizens cannot hold their one-term president and their individual legislators accountable as their elected leaders.

3. Parliamentary government would be more likely to ensure the election of the head of government — the prime minister — for his leadership and experience in the party and in the public service. He would be known to party members.
4. It would help prevent the election of the head of government on the basis largely of personal popularity and celebrity status or "win-ability", not on proven competence and experience as a political leader. Since 1987 the power of the media has catapulted movie actors and television anchors to the presidency or other high public office at the expense of more qualified and experienced government leaders.
5. It would be easier to change the head of government and the ruling party whenever it becomes necessary, by a vote of no confidence in Parliament, and its dissolution, followed by a new election of MPs. There would be no need for impeachment, people power revolts, and military intervention, which cause political instability, disrupt the economy, discourage foreign investors, and hurt the people, especially the poor.
6. Unlike in the presidential government where the president is both head of government and head of state, the function of head of state would be assigned to a ceremonial president elected by the Parliament. This would lighten the burden on the prime minister, who could then concentrate on governance.
7. At the same time the president, who symbolizes the people's sovereignty and national unity, could be a rallying point as a leader who would be above partisan politics.
8. Parliamentary government and electoral reform would empower the people to choose not only the candidates for the Parliament but also the political party they want to govern the country and the regional and local governments.
9. The practice of parliamentary government would develop a two-party system and political parties that are democratic, disciplined, united, and effective in making and carrying out a programme of government that

can secure popular support. The present political parties are undemocratic, opportunistic, and oriented to personalities and patronage, and not to policy and programme of government.

10. The people would elect the members of Parliament among candidates in parliamentary districts and also by "proportional representation" of the rival political parties in the parliamentary election (a comprehensive party list of all political parties).
11. Parliamentary elections would cost much less than nationwide presidential and senatorial elections that require billions and corrupt the political system.
12. It would be easier and faster and less costly to administer elections and proclaim the winning candidates.
13. It would reduce the high cost of electing the head of government in a national election by having the leader of the majority party (or coalition) in Parliament chosen as prime minister.
14. The selection of additional members of Parliament through "proportional representation" of the political parties would enable the leading political party to select other competent leaders to serve in Parliament and the Cabinet. These would be professionals, business leaders, scholars, and representatives of various sectors of society who could serve in Parliament and the Cabinet, although they are not willing to run for Parliament.
15. Parliamentary government could lead to more continuity in policy and administration if the majority party or coalition governs well and the people are satisfied, because the people would learn to reward or punish the ruling party for its success or failure in governance. The people would know that the ruling party, not just individual leaders, is responsible and accountable for the government's performance.

REFORM OF POLITICAL PARTIES AND ELECTORAL SYSTEM[6]

No Filipino constitution has deliberately promoted political parties as institutions of democratic representation. For this reason, the Draft Constitution of the Citizens' Movement for a Federal Philippines (CMFP) proposed a separate Article on Political Parties in recognition of the importance of political parties in the proposed parliamentary democracy.

In the committee and plenary meetings of the 2005 Consultative Commission, it was finally decided not to have a separate article on political parties. Instead, various provisions were adopted on the reform of political parties and electoral system and the Commission on Elections that would strengthen political parties as institutions of constitutional democracy. These included key ideas proposed by the CMFP and submitted by the author. There are pending bills in Congress to provide state funding of political parties and to penalize legislators for disloyalty to their political party.

Parliamentary government is also called "party government" because of the pivotal role of political parties in parliamentary elections, governance, and public administration. Therefore, reforming political parties in a parliamentary government is basic to good governance.

The Poor State of Political Parties Since Independence in 1946

1. Filipino political parties are personal factions and alliances united mainly for elections and patronage. In the present unitary-presidential system, most political parties are loose personal factions/organizations that exist mainly to elect their candidates and distribute patronage. They are organizations of politicians and have no mass memberships.

2. Political parties have no serious platform or programme of government to offer the people. They do not have a serious programme of government to campaign for and to implement when they are in power.

3. They are largely undemocratic, undisciplined and opportunistic. Their opportunistic members change parties for their personal convenience. They are not bound by party loyalty or democratic rules in selecting the party candidates and building party unity and cohesiveness.

4. They are not responsible and accountable to the people for their performance in or out of office. And the people do not take seriously the statements and promises of party leaders. Not surprisingly, very few leaders and citizens in business or civil society join the political parties.

Proposed Reforms to Strengthen Political Parties and the Electoral System

Above all it is the proposed shift from the present presidential government to a new parliamentary government that will build up and strengthen political parties. In the proposed parliamentary government the majority party or coalition in Parliament would elect the prime minister, who would normally be the leader of the majority party. In the partisan struggle for power, this would put a premium on the strength and unity of each political party and its ability to put up good candidates and offer the people an attractive political platform or programme of government.

Because the ruling majority party or coalition under the prime minister and the Cabinet would exercise both legislative and executive powers, it would assume responsibility and accountability to the Parliament and the people for the success or failure of the government. Under the present presidential government the president does not necessarily command the loyalty and support of the senators and congressmen who belong to his or her political party or coalition. In fact many of these party members may oppose the existing or proposed policies of the president. This weakens the president as head of government and head of state.

Various provisions in the *Proposed Revision of the 1987 Constitution* of the 2005 Consultative Commission would strengthen the political parties in assuming their paramount role in the parliamentary government.

1. "Article XI. Constitutional Commissions. The Commission on Elections. Section (4). Accredit, after sufficient publication, political parties, organizations, or coalitions which, in addition to other requirements, must present their platform or program of government and assume party responsibilities and accountability in governance...."

2. The proposal in "Article VII. Parliament. Section 2 (2)" for the Parliament to select 30 per cent of all its members through proportional representation of the political parties, or based on the voting strength of the political parties in the previous parliamentary election. Again, this would give the political parties a great incentive to be united and disciplined, to put up good candidates, and offer a good, competitive programme of government.

3. The proposal in "Section 12. Any elective official who leaves his party before the end of the term shall forfeit his seat." And he will be replaced by his political party.

4. The proposal in "Section 9. Parliament shall, by law, (1) promote the development of a party system in which various interests and sectors in society shall be represented, including women, labour, the poor, peasants, indigenous peoples, persons with disability, and the youth; (2) encourage the development of two major political parties to ensure that a majority can assume responsibility and accountability in governance; and (3) provide financial assistance to the political parties on the basis of their share of the votes cast for the political parties in the previous parliamentary elections."

5. The proposal in "Section 10. Political parties shall observe fair, honest and democratic processes in the selection of their candidates. They shall ensure the integrity, loyalty, and discipline of their members and publicly account for the sources and use of their funds and for their assets."

6. The proposal in "Section 11. The two dominant political parties shall be represented in the voters' registration boards, boards of election inspectors,

boards of canvassers, and similar bodies. Other political parties shall be entitled to appoint poll watchers in accordance with law."

7. The proposal that voters shall vote not only for their candidates for elective office but also for the political party of their choice. This would make voters conscious of the importance of political parties in politics and governance.

8. The proposal that all members of Parliament and other elective officials shall have a term of five years without term limits.

9. The recommendation that Parliament shall enable absentee voters abroad and those with dual citizenship to vote for members of Parliament, as an amendment to the existing legislation.

10. Other proposals to strengthen the Commission on Elections.

So, what would happen to the political parties in the parliamentary government and the autonomous territories and regions leading to a federal republic, as proposed by the 2005 Consultative Commission?

1. There would be a progressive transformation of political parties. By changing the political system to a federal-parliamentary system, the political parties would be progressively transformed into strong, stable, disciplined, programme-oriented and accountable political organizations.

2. The majority party or coalition in Parliament would have a very important role in that body. The political party or coalition of political parties that obtains a majority of the seats in the Parliament would elect the prime minister and form the cabinet or the government.

3. The majority party or coalition would also have a very important role in the assembly of the autonomous territory or region, which would be the future State Assembly in the federal republic. The political party or coalition of political parties that gets a majority of the seats in the Assembly of the autonomous territory or region would elect its governor and vice-governor and form the cabinet or government at that regional level of governance.

4. The basis of political party representation in Parliament and the Assembly is proposed. Each political party shall be represented in the Parliament and in the Assembly according to the number of its candidates elected in the parliamentary or assembly elections. The political parties shall get additional seats on the basis of "proportional representation" of the competing political parties in relation to their combined electoral votes in the previous election.

5. Electoral reforms would enable the people to vote not only for their candidates but also for the political party of their choice. In electing the members of Parliament and the members of the Assembly, every voter shall vote not only for his/her candidates but also for his/her preferred political party in the Parliament and in the Assembly. The ballots shall provide for this.

6. Political parties would set the direction of government and compete for the support of their candidates and their party. The political parties would compete with each other for the voters' support of their candidates and their political party, in order to obtain more seats in the Parliament and the Assembly; because the majority party or coalition would elect the prime minister in Parliament or the governor and vice-governor of the autonomous territory or region.

7. Voters would become conscious of the importance of political parties in governance and in their lives as citizens. As the people vote for their leaders and for the political parties, they would gradually be more conscious of the important role of the political parties in the governance of the national government and the autonomous territories and regions. The people could hold the ruling party responsible and accountable for the success or failure of its governance and exercise of power. Political parties would become more important in relation to individual politicians and personalities.

8. Political parties would mobilize more political participation. Political parties would be able to mobilize the participation of citizens in the affairs of government at all levels, not only in elections but also in making policies and decisions.

9. The nation shall be building responsible and accountable political parties. Through the reformed political parties, the nation would make the national government, the governments of the autonomous territories or regions, and the local governments effectively responsible and accountable to the people for their conduct and performance in or out of office. The people would become more informed, interested and involved in government and public affairs. Political parties would become more effective as institutions of mobilization, representation, political education, and governance in the country's constitutional democracy.

FROM THE PRESENT UNITARY REPUBLIC TO A NEW FEDERAL REPUBLIC[7]

During the Filipino revolution against Spain, revolutionary leaders in Iloilo established a federal state of the Visayas with the knowledge of General Emilio Aguinaldo. Boholano leaders established the Republic of Bohol. The pro-American Filipino Federalistas in the early years of American colonial rule advocated the annexation of the islands as a state in the United States of America. However, the United States retained the centralized unitary system under Spanish colonial rule, which had been the system embodied in the Malolos Constitution. The Americans also adapted their presidential system in the Islands and governed through their resident governor-general until 1935. To ensure the approval of the 1935 Constitution in Washington, the Filipino framers adopted the familiar unitary and presidential system.

Much later, some leaders in Mindanao, among them Udtog Matalam and Reuben Canoy, would advocate independence from the Republic of the Philippines, or a federation that would grant Mindanao substantial regional autonomy. The Moro National Liberation Front and the Moro Islamic Liberation Front would advocate secession from the republic, later under a referendum supervised by the United Nations or, alternatively, real regional autonomy in a federal republic. In 1981 Salvador Araneta published a draft constitution for a federal republic, which he called the Bayanikasan Constitution. The provisions in the 1987 Constitution for creating the autonomous regions for Muslim Mindanao and the Cordilleras and for strengthening local autonomy responded to the increasing demands against excessive centralization and for federalism.

From its founding by Senator Aquilino Q. Pimentel, the PDP-Laban political party had espoused a federalist platform, and Pimentel has been an ardent champion of local autonomy. Towards the 1992 presidential election, the PDP-Laban, Senator John H. Osmena, and the Lakas-NUCD-UMDP advocated a shift to a federal system.

In the last several years a group of grassroots leaders connected with the NGOs Kusog Mindanao (Mindanao Force) and Lihok Pideral Mindanao (Mindanao Federalist Movement), led by Rey Magno Teves, Lito Lorenzana, Gaudencio Sosmena, Jr. and Michael Mastura among others, spearheaded a federalist movement that spread to the Visayas and Luzon. With research support from the Konrad Adenauer Foundation of Germany, the Citizens' Movement for a Federal Philippines under Teves, with Jose V. Abueva as senior adviser, gained supporters across the country among other NGOs, local leaders, and academics. By joining advocates of parliamentary government, the federalist movement became a broader, nationwide constitutional reform movement whose cause was supported by President Arroyo, Speaker de Venecia, and the Union of Local Authorities of the Philippines.

The Unitary Republic Since 1946

In the unitary Republic, the constitution concentrates political power and authority in the national government: the president, the bicameral Congress (the Senate and the House of Representatives), and the Supreme Court and lower courts. Most national government institutions and officers are based in Metro Manila, the national capital region, far away from many parts of the archipelago.

The president as the head of government is the chief executive and commander-in-chief of the armed forces. S/he has general supervision over local governments (the provinces, cities, municipalities, and *barangays*), which are weak and dependent on the national government, although they are supposed to enjoy some local autonomy.

All major laws and policies are passed by Congress and approved by the president, who is responsible for implementing them through his/her control of the executive departments and agencies and the bureaucracy and his/her general supervision over the local governments.

The Proposed Shift from the Unitary Republic to Autonomous Territories/Regions in Transition to a Federal Republic

As was explained above, the projected parliamentary government would fuse legislative and executive powers in the new Parliament. This would make the national government even more powerful than it has been in relation to the local governments. So it is imperative to have a vertical separation or redistribution of powers that would devolve substantial national government powers and authority to local governments and regions. There are serious weaknesses and disadvantages in the traditional unitary republic that need to be overcome.

1. With very limited powers and authority and inadequate resources, most local governments cannot provide the public services that the people need and expect of their local leaders.

2. National taxes siphon or take away much of the wealth and revenues generated by agriculture and other industries in local communities around the country. Major corporations, including banks, pay their taxes in Metro Manila, whose cities benefit more from their activities than the provinces and other cities in which the branches of the corporations operate and generate their wealth.

3. Local officials have to spend much of their time and energy and their limited funds seeking the assistance and approval of national government officials in Metro Manila.

4. Habits of local dependence on the national government stifle local initiative and resourcefulness, and hamper local business and development.

5. The highly centralized unitary government is not sensitive to the nation's cultural diversity: its many ethno-linguistic and cultural communities and a large Muslim minority, the Moros. The migration of large numbers of people from other parts of the country has led to the loss of their

identity, and of the ancestral domain of the indigenous locals, and to their landlessness and poverty.

6. Decades of unitary rule under the policy of assimilation and national integration have marginalized the Moros and other indigenous peoples in various parts of the country. Meanwhile, many settlers in Mindanao and other regions are becoming prosperous. Deteriorating relations between the Moros and the national government have led to many years of violence and rebellion — the death, displacement and suffering of thousands of people.

7. The efforts to promote local autonomy since the 1950s have reached a dead end because of the reluctance of many national political leaders to decentralize the powers of the national government. The centralization of power enhances their power and control over the local communities.

8. Thus, under the unitary republic since 1946 and the presidential form of government, our government and leaders have generally failed to effectively address our many problems and continuing under-development.

9. For these reasons the federalist movement seeks to change the highly centralized unitary structure to a decentralized structure of autonomous local governments and regions leading to a federal system, in addition to the shift to a parliamentary government.

What is proposed is to change the traditional highly centralized unitary system to a decentralized and devolved structure of autonomous territories (local governments and regions) preparatory to establishing the Federal Republic of the Philippines.

In revising the 1987 Constitution, a participatory process is proposed for extending substantial local and regional autonomy in the transition to the establishment of the Federal Republic of the Philippines. In an act of regional self-determination, contiguous provinces and cities that share common linguistic, cultural and historical features may petition the Parliament to form them into an autonomous territory through an organic act.

The organic act of the autonomous territories to be passed by the Parliament would provide for primary legislative powers of their assemblies over the following: (1) administrative organization, planning, budget, and management; (2) creation of sources of revenue and finance; (3) agriculture and fisheries; (4) natural resources, energy, environment, indigenous appropriate technologies and inventions; (5) trade, industry and tourism; (6) labour and employment; (7) public works and transportation, except railways, shipping and aviation; (8) health and social welfare; (9) education and the development of language, culture and the arts as part of the cultural heritage, science, and technology; (10) ancestral domain and natural resources; (11) housing, land use and development; (12) urban and rural planning and development; (13) such other matters as may be authorized by law for the promotion of the general welfare of the people of the autonomous territory.

The organic act would be subject to approval in a plebiscite in the territory or region concerned. When 60 per cent of the provinces and cities become autonomous territories/regions, they would become federal states of the federal republic. As an alternative, the amended constitution could provide a transition period of ten years before the federal republic is established. As in all federal systems in the world the federal government would provide financial assistance to the various states, especially the less developed ones.

Critique: The unitary structure or system is better suited to the Philippines as an archipelago, because it unites the people in all the regions and local communities into one nation-state. A federal structure would lead to disunity, regionalism, fragmentation, and the secession of the Moros. A federal structure would be very expensive, because it would duplicate functions and expand the bureaucracy. Many poor regions would not be able to survive on their own.

Expected Advantages in Changing the Unitary Republic to a Federal Republic

1. The Federal Republic of the Philippines would build a just and enduring framework for peace through unity in our ethnic, religious, and cultural diversity, especially in relation to Bangsa Moro and our *lumad* (indigenous peoples) everywhere. Responsive federalism would accommodate the legitimate interests of the Moros, end the war in Mindanao, and discourage secessionism.
2. The federal republic would empower the citizens through their participation in the affairs of their autonomous local and regional governments. As the people become more involved in government decisions, they would raise their political awareness and learn to demand better performance and public accountability. Their participation and efficacy in elections and the making of government decisions would enhance the quality of governance. Better policies and implementation would enable the people to raise their standard of living. At the same time, they would be more willing to pay taxes that finance government programmes and services for their direct benefit.
3. The creation of autonomous territories and autonomous regions that would become federal states under a federal system would improve governance by challenging and energizing local and regional leaders, entrepreneurs, and citizens around the country. It would release them

from the costly, time-consuming, stifling, and demoralizing effects of excessive central government controls and regulation in our traditional unitary system.

4. Federalism through autonomous territories would specifically strengthen the powers of the provincial governors, city and municipal mayors, and other elected local government leaders. It will be proposed that the organic acts of Parliament will make key local government executives — governors and mayors of the capital cities — members of the assembly of the autonomous territories and regions that would become federal states in the federal republic. In this way it would not be necessary to elect another set of officials for the regional government, thus saving funds and enhancing local autonomy as well.
5. Federalism, together with parliamentary government, would improve governance by promoting the development of strong, united, disciplined, and programme-oriented political parties that are responsible and accountable to the people for their conduct and performance in or out of power.
6. Federalism would promote equitable regional development by supporting the less endowed and less developed regions and the poor and needy across the land. This is the policy and practice in various federal systems.
7. Thus, federalism would stimulate and hasten the country's political, economic, social, and cultural development and modernization. There would be inter-regional competition in attracting domestic and foreign investments and industries, professionals and skilled workers. A renaissance of regional languages and cultures would enrich the national language and culture and broaden and deepen our democracy.
8. In other words — with political will and sustained effort for the common good — federalism and a parliamentary government would gradually broaden and deepen democracy, enabling it to deliver on the constitutional promise of human rights, a better life for all, a just and humane society, and responsible and accountable political leadership and governance.

LIBERALIZING THE CONSTITUTIONAL PROVISIONS ON NATIONAL PATRIMONY AND ECONOMIC POLICY[8]

The overriding reason for this reform is to attract more foreign investments to enable the Philippines to reduce poverty and social inequality by: (1) creating more jobs for the unemployed and under-employed; (2) raising personal incomes and savings; (3) increasing revenues; (4) improving government services; and thereby (5) promoting development, prosperity and social equality.

The following realities should be considered.

(1) One of every three Filipinos (30.4 per cent of 82 million people) lives in poverty. Indescribably, 2.54 million families (15.5 per cent of 16 million) subsist on only P50 or so (US$1) a day, hardly enough for essential food, basic clothing and shelter, not to mention good health and adequate education.[9]

(2) The main cause of poverty is joblessness and unstable incomes. In the past decade spanning three political administrations, unemployment hovered at 10 to 11 per cent, and under-employment at 25 per cent of the 40 million people in the workforce. Sadly, four million Filipinos of working age were jobless. Another 10 million had only seasonal jobs as construction, trucking or house helpers, tricycle drivers, or scavengers in garbage dumps, or worked below their training or qualifications.

(3) In turn, the main cause of joblessness and unsteady incomes is the lack of investments. The Philippines had only US$1.48 billion in foreign investments in 1995, US$1.35 billion in 2000, and US$319 million in 2003. In contrast, the Philippines' closest neighbour-nations attracted far more.

Foreign Direct Investments in US$ Millions

	1995	*2000*	*2003*
Philippines	1478.0	1345.0	319.0
Indonesia	4346.0	–4550.0	–596.9
Malaysia	4178.2	3787.6	2473.2
Singapore	7123.7	11400.4	5625.5
Thailand	2068.0	2366.0	1949.3

Source: Asian Development Bank, *Key Indicators 2005*.

(4) The main reason for lower investments in the Philippines is the provisions in its constitution that are inhospitable to foreigners. (Other reasons are perennial partisan strife and judicial inconsistency, poor infrastructure, and the lack of peace and order.) By contrast, neighbouring countries' charters welcome foreigners.

(5) Restrictive economic provisions are in Articles XII (National Economy and Patrimony) and XVI (General Provisions), in the areas of:

1. exploration, development, and utilization of natural resources;

2. ownership of industrial, commercial, and residential land;
3. operation of public utilities and ownership of (tertiary) educational institutions;
4. practice of professions (especially high technology);
5. ownership and management of mass media; and
6. ownership and management of advertising.

(6) Filipinos do not have capital for large-scale mining or oil drilling, labour-intensive factories, power and waterworks utilities, advanced colleges and universities, modern engineering, cinema or entertainment, and advertising. This is because of the Philippines' low savings rate of 18 per cent of GDP, only one half of the 35 per cent needed to spur investments.

(7) If restrictions on foreign investments are relaxed, investments will pour into mining and oil production; build-operate-transfer schemes for building roads and ports; electricity and water supply; railways and shipping; specialized schools of higher learning; aircraft and aerospace; movies, media and advertising.

(8) Philippine investments could double in three years from the current 18 per cent to the 35 per cent needed for sustained development. GDP could double in eight years. Per capita income (salaries, etc.) could double in twelve years from the present US$1,100. The Philippines could finally lick poverty and catch up with its neighbour-nations.

GROSS DOMESTIC PRODUCT (Growth rate)

	1999	*2000*	*2004*
Philippines	3.4	4.4	6.1
Indonesia	0.8	4.9	5.1
Malaysia	6.1	8.9	7.1
Singapore	6.8	9.6	8.4
Thailand	4.4	4.8	6.1

Source: Asian Development Bank, *Key Indicators 2005*.

(9) The Philippines needs to protect and sustain its economic gains by shifting from presidential-bicameral Congress, prone to gridlock, to unicameral parliament fusing the executive and legislative powers in a unicameral Parliament.

(10) For good measure, it could ensure more people participation in economic-political activity through greater autonomy in a federal republic.
Critique: Filipinos should protect their national patrimony and economy

from foreign exploitation in the age of globalization, when poor countries are at a disadvantage in global economic competition. It is better to have the safeguards in the constitution than to leave it to the legislature or Parliament to provide them and encourage foreign investments.

A BILL OF DUTIES[10]

In its *Draft Constitution for a Federal Republic of the Philippines with a Parliamentary Government*, the Citizens' Movement for a Federal Philippines (CMFP) proposed a New Bill of Duties and Obligations to complement the Bill of Rights in the 1987 Constitution. It was argued that, together, the Article on the Bill of Rights and the proposed Article on the Bill of Duties and Obligations would be very helpful in civic education and the training of citizens and leaders. While respecting freedom of worship and expression, it was also urged that citizens be encouraged and assisted by concerned leaders and institutions in their voluntary spiritual development — to round out their civic and political education.

The Philippines seems to suffer from an excess of selfish individualism [*Wala akong paki-alam sa inyo. Bahala na kayo*]; materialism [*materialismo, hindi espiritual*]; and secularism [*makamundo, hindi maka-Diyos*]. On the other hand, there are many important reminders regarding the need for nationalistic, responsible and civic spirited citizens to build a strong nation and help govern it effectively. One of them says: "*Bayan muna bago ang sarili!*" (Country before oneself!).

Therefore, as citizens in a developing democracy Filipinos should balance their emphasis on individual rights and privileges with a much stronger sense of collective and communitarian duties and obligations. In this way many more citizens could become patriotic, responsible and effective — in solidarity with our *kapwa Pilipino*. Citizens could build a cohesive national community and a peaceful, just and humane society. Citizens of progressive nations like Japan, Korea, China, Taiwan, Singapore, Israel, the Scandinavian countries, the United Kingdom, the United States, and Germany have a deep sense of their duties and obligations to the community and the nation.

Accordingly, the CMFP Draft Constitution contained Article V. Bill of Duties and Obligations immediately after Article IV. Bill of Rights. The 1935 Constitution and the 1987 Constitution do not have a Bill of Duties and Obligations of citizens. The *CMFP* improved on Article V, Bill of Duties and Obligations in the 1973 Constitution. What the 2005 Consultative Commission finally approved was the following Article on a Bill of Duties:

SECTION 1. It shall be the duty of every citizen to be loyal to the Republic of the Philippines, honor the Philippine Flag, defend the State, contribute to its development and welfare, uphold the Constitution and obey the laws, pay taxes, and cooperate with the duly constituted authorities in the attainment and maintenance of the rule of law and of a peaceful, just, humane and orderly society.
SECTION 2. The rights of the individual impose upon him the correlative duty to exercise them responsibly and with due regard for the rights of others.
SECTION 3. Citizens and the State shall at all times respect the life and dignity of every human person and uphold human rights.
SECTION 4. Citizens shall participate actively in public and civic affairs, and contribute to good governance, honesty and integrity in the public service and the vitality and viability of democracy.

Critique: A constitution defines the powers of the state and government and protects the citizens against the state by guarantees (Bill of Rights) that ensure their political freedom and civil rights. There is no need for a Bill of Duties that cannot be enforced anyway.

IN SUMMARY

It should be emphasized that the proposed constitutional changes are based on studies, discussions and debates that took place over a long period — dating back to the 1971 Constitutional Convention — concerning the nation's own experience in politics, governance and public administration. But the contemporary struggle over charter change began about ten years following the approval of the 1987 Constitution. It has concentrated on the worsening problems of governance, under-development and political instability resulting from the failure of Filipinos to consolidate their restored democracy ten to twenty years after the EDSA "people power" revolution that was supposed to bring about "justice, freedom and democracy". Part of the frustration stems from a comparison of the Filipino experience since the mid-1960s with the experience of progressive neighbours in Asia that have achieved greater economic progress, higher standards of living, political stability, and global competitiveness.

In sum, the constitutional reforms proposed since 2000 have to do with:

1. Changing the form of government, from the old, obsolete and dysfunctional presidential government with a bicameral legislature to a unicameral Parliament;
2. Changing the structure of government, from the highly centralized and debilitating unitary system to a devolved system of autonomous territories in transition to a federal republic;

3. Liberalizing the restrictive economic policies to encourage far greater participation of foreign capital and business in economic and social development;
4. Reforming the electoral system to make it free, efficient, clean, and credible;
5. Reforming political parties to make them more cohesive, disciplined, program and policy oriented, and responsible and accountable;
6. Adding a Bill of Duties to make the citizens far more conscious of their duties and responsibilities in relation to the traditional emphasis on their rights and obligations as members of the national community; and
7. Proposing the reform of the judiciary, the civil service, state principles and policies, and other aspects of the 1987 Constitution.[10]

During 2004 to 2006 the most intensive, extensive and informed consultations, discussions, and debates on charter change in the nation's history involved many more citizens than ever before on the basic issues of form and structure and functions and policies of government that affect their rights and welfare. Such political and citizen participation and education are much needed in a developing nation and democracy. Hopefully, in a changing political culture citizens will be better able to modify their habitual focus on political leaders and personalities and their perceived motives, and to consider the merits of competing ideas for reform and charter change, including institutional or structural and system change, and alternative policies and ideologies of reformed political parties and interest groups.

At best the major proponents of charter change expect the following long-term developments if their proposed reforms are approved by the people in the hoped-for plebiscite and put into force, institutionalized, and sustained in the following decades.

1. Parliamentary government will help bring about good governance.

2. Charter change to a parliamentary government, along with decentralization and devolution of powers to the regional and local governments in a federal structure, will enable the government and the leaders to respond more efficiently and effectively to the country's problems, meet its challenges and achieve its goals, and compete more effectively in the global economy.

3. Charter change to a parliamentary government and a decentralized structure will help to mobilize and sustain "people power" in national, regional and local governance to reduce poverty and corruption.

4. It will in the long term empower the nation to achieve the peace, prosperity, justice and security the people want for themselves and their children.

5. Moreover, with less restriction on foreign investments and participation, the government will be better able to help in attracting far more substantial direct investments that will create more jobs, raise personal incomes, provide better education, health, welfare, and security for our people, and generate badly needed revenues for our government.

6. These will come from building and maintaining many more and better schools, hospitals, waterworks, roads, bridges, seaports and airports.

7. To reiterate, finally, with a great deal of political will, hard work and sacrifice, and with God's grace and blessings, Filipinos will be able to build a global nation worthy of their heroes, a country fit for their children — of which Filipinos can be really proud. Democracy will then be inclusive and egalitarian.

It may be noted that many stable and progressive countries in the world have parliamentary governments. These include Japan, Canada, Australia, United Kingdom, Germany, Italy, Spain, Norway, Sweden, and also India, Singapore, Malaysia and Thailand in Asia. But this does not necessarily mean that the parliamentary form of government, a decentralized structure of governance, and liberal economic policies for foreign investors alone will ensure the stability and prosperity of the Philippines. As acknowledged in this chapter, there are other important factors needed to make this happen.

However, it is believed that the adoption and sustained application of the proposed constitutional reforms will heighten the probability of achieving good governance and an improved political culture. These will help in improving leadership and citizenship, strengthening democracy, promoting the people's welfare, and advancing the country's development.

On the other hand, it is submitted that the existing form, structure, institutions, policies, and styles of governance will continue to be counter-productive and destabilizing. The inability to arrest and surmount the nation's crises will lead to dire consequences for the viability of constitutional democracy and national progress as the nation is already experiencing.

THE OUTCOME OF CHARTER CHANGE BY DECEMBER 2006

The outcome of the struggle for charter change that began intensively in 2005 was decided by the Supreme Court when it struck down the petition for a people's initiative of the *Sigaw ng Bayan*, the alliance of several organizations of civil society, business and labour, and the Union of Local Authorities of the Philippines in October and November 2006.

The unity of diverse factions in the political opposition, the militant left, the urban middle class, the Catholic Church, some business groups, and much of the media doomed the desperate effort of the majority coalition in the House of Representatives, supported by President Gloria Macapagal Arroyo, to force the proposal of amendments through a constituent assembly without the Senate's agreement.

As the congressional and local elections on 14 May 2007 drew near, the prospects for charter change dimmed. The people's initiative failed. Constitutional reforms through Congress as a constituent assembly or by a constitutional convention became as problematic as in the past because some political leaders and their political parties were positioning themselves to run for president, vice-president, senators, and representatives in the 2010 general elections. Defenders of the *status quo* among the political elite are many. Real hope for charter change may still lie in the people at large with the backing of local officials who are closer to the people. The crucial support of an incumbent president for charter change may not come soon after President Arroyo ends her term in 2010.

Supreme Court Rejects People's Initiative Petition

The Supreme Court on 25 October 2006 voted 8–7 to dismiss the petition of *Sigaw ng Bayan* and the Union of Local Authorities of the Philippines (ULAP) for a people's initiative proposing amendments to the constitution that would change the bicameral presidential government into a unicameral-parliamentary government if ratified by the people in a plebiscite, and providing for the transition.

Chief Justice Artemio Panganiban, Associate Justice Antonio Carpio, the *ponente,* and six other associate justices voted to throw out the petition. Their reasons may be summarized as follows:

(1) Flaws in obtaining the signatures of voters "without first showing to the people the full text of the proposed amendments is most likely a deception, and can operate as a gigantic fraud on the people". For their part, the petitioners as proponents of the amendments had asserted before the Supreme Court that they had conducted an intensive and extensive information campaign and had shown the signatories printed copies of their proposed amendments.

(2) The change sought by *Sigaw ng Bayan* and ULAP was a prohibited revision, not only amendments, of the charter. "By any legal test and under any jurisdiction, a shift from a bicameral-presidential to a unicameral-parliamentary system, involving the abolition of the Office

of the President and the abolition of one chamber of Congress, is beyond doubt a revision, not a mere amendment."

(3) There was no need to "revisit" the Santiago vs. Comelec ruling of 1997 because the Comelec's decision to dismiss the petition was "based alone" on *Sigaw*-ULAP's "glaring failure to comply with the basic requirements of the Constitution".
(4) Asserting its role as the guardian of the constitution, the Supreme Court majority said that the court "exists to defend and protect the Constitution".

Seven Justices Dissent

Led by Senior Associate Justice Reynato S. Puno, who penned the dissenting opinion, seven dissenting justices voted to remand the petition of the pro-charter change groups to the Comelec for a re-verification of the 6.3 million signatures they had gathered to push a people's initiative.

The Comelec's rejection of their petition had prompted the *Sigaw ng Bayan* and ULAP to appeal their case before the Supreme Court. They cited the poll body for alleged "grave abuse of discretion" for not giving due course to its petition for Comelec by scheduling a plebiscite for the people's action on the proposed amendments.

The opinion of the dissenting justices may be summarized thus:

(1) The Comelec committed grave abuse of discretion amounting to lack of jurisdiction in denying the *Sigaw*-ULAP petition for a people's initiative and the holding of a plebiscite. Let the Commission on Elections therefore decide on all questions about the *Sigaw*-ULAP petition's compliance with all the requirements provided under the Constitution or Republic Act No. 6735 — the Initiative and Referendum Act. "The issue…involves contentious facts" whose "resolution will require presentation of evidence and their calibration by the Comelec according to its rules". The Supreme Court "is not a trier of facts, it cannot resolve the issue".
(2) RA 6735 is sufficient as enabling law for a people's initiative. The Supreme Court's 1997 ruling on people's initiative in Santiago vs Commission on Elections should therefore be reviewed. It ruled that any initiative for charter amendments could not proceed because of the insufficiency of RA 6735. This ruling was an "intolerable aberration". It did not declare RA 6735 unconstitutional and "actually infringed" on Congress' legislative powers. The court had committed its own "grave abuse of discretion".

(3) As to the allegations that the signatories to the petition failed to understand what they signed or were misled into signing the signature sheets, lower courts had ruled that a person is presumed to have knowledge of the contents of a document he had signed.

(4) The people's sovereignty is paramount and should prevail. As sovereign in a democracy, contrary to the majority ruling, the people can propose and approve substantive changes in the constitution. In the country's history of making constitutions, amendments traditionally meant "change, including complex changes", while revisions pertained to "complete change", including the adoption of an entirely new charter. For example, the 1935 Constitution was changed to convert the legislature from unicameral to bicameral and to shorten the terms of office of the president and vice-president from six to four years with one reelection. These were considered mere amendments. The 1935 Charter was replaced in 1973 and the new fundamental law was considered a revision.

(5) The initiative petition is valid. "The Supreme Court should not be guided with certainty by the 'inconclusive' opinions of the commissioners on the difference between 'simple' and 'substantial' amendments, or whether 'substantial' amendments amounted to revisions… The argument that the people through initiative cannot propose substantial amendments turns sovereignty on its head." The "teaching of the ages" is that constitutional clauses acknowledging the right of the people to exercise initiative and referendum "are liberally and generously construed in favour of the people".

Other Reactions to the Supreme Court Decision

Publicly, President Arroyo and administration leaders in Congress and local officials accepted the decision of the Supreme Court. At the same time they planned their next moves.

In the author's view the majority decision's use of condemnatory language revealed a strong political opinion. It suggested that the people's initiative was a "gigantic fraud" and "a grand deception" and it criticized the ULAP for supporting the political agenda of President Arroyo. The majority justices practically ruled that the support of elected officials of the proposed reform negated and nullified its being a valid and legitimate people's initiative. They further implied that the political opposition's accusations of irregularities in the process had been proved without adequate hearing, with no need of verification by the appropriate constitutional agency: the Comelec.

The majority decision resorted to legalistic distinctions between amendments and revision and to foreign jurisprudence of dubious relevance. By minimizing the primordial principle of the people's sovereignty in constitutional change, the majority decision may be seen as a tragic triumph of technique over purpose, a latent, if not manifest, elitist bias against the people, many of whom are poor and less educated and largely powerless. Unable to hire good lawyers or influence judges, the conventional wisdom goes, the poor are the ones who often suffer from the way the courts dispense justice.

In her column in the *Philippine Star,* Carmen N. Pedrosa said:

> A class bias permeates the entire debate on Charter change, elite vs. *yagit* (masses), plebiscite vs. elections and amendment vs. revision, among others. It is a subtle struggle and not immediately recognizable. Constitutional experts use legalisms and technicalities, protecting the turf of the few. In the end the question remains: who is sovereign in this country? If thousands were able to end a dictatorship at EDSA only to re-install the pre-martial law elite, we now have millions to pursue that initial political awakening to push and continue the still unfinished business of how to democratize this country.
>
> There may be a law [RA 6735] but if the justices decide the people cannot resort to that law, they cannot. So there. And that is final. Well, the fight is not over nor should it be. If we are expounding a Constitution that gives sovereignty to the people then we must fight on. We must never lose sight of what our forefathers sacrificed for what the nation ought to be. We should not allow sophisms about the finality of any judgment that purports to usurp the sovereignty of the people. Although the Supreme Court is respected as an institution, the power given to its members has been misused. Our nation is first a democracy before it is a republic.[11]

Opponents of the People's Initiative Rejoiced

Among those who had prominently opposed the petition of *Sigaw ng Bayan* and ULAP and welcomed the Supreme Court's dismissal of the petition were: the leaders of the political opposition in the Senate and the House of Representatives; the militant Left, former President Corazon Aquino, the Makati Business Club; the One Voice alliance, which includes the Catholic hierarchy, co-authors of the 1987 Constitution, leaders of Ateneo de Manila University, de la Salle University, and Miriam College; businessmen in the Bishops-Businessmen's Conference of the Philippines; and the *Philippine Daily Inquirer* and the Lopez-owned ABS-CBN media.

Senators understandably opposed the abolition of the Senate and the shift to a parliamentary government; a few of them looked forward to their opportunity to run for president or vice-president in 2010. Opposition leaders in Congress also hoped to improve their chances of removing President Arroyo in a third attempt to impeach her, in 2007. Even as they denounced the self-serving motives of the proponents of charter change, the united opposition had their own self-serving agenda in preserving the *status quo*.

"Congratulations to the Supreme Court for standing free and independent despite external and expensive pressures," the CBCP president, Archbishop Angel Lagdameo, said in a statement. He also warned against plans to convene a constituent assembly: "Please pardon the term, but charter change by Congress converted into a constituent assembly will have all the appearance of 'self-service' and '*lutong makao*' [literally, 'a pre-cooked dish']. We will pray against that."

If indeed charter change is needed, along with a shift to the unicameral parliamentary government, the CBCP reiterated its recommendation for a constitutional convention "whose members shall be elected democratically".

A House-Only Constituent Assembly Collapsed

The Supreme Court denied the motions for reconsideration of *Sigaw ng Bayan* and ULAP on 25 October, then on 21 November and on 12 December 2006. The remaining new motion of *Sigaw ng Bayan* was also dismissed.

On 6 December the majority coalition in the House of Representatives led by Speaker Jose de Venecia, with President Arroyo's support, made the final push for a constituent assembly proposal for charter change, without the Senate that adamantly resisted charter change. This was the Speaker's Plan B: to propose the shift to a unicameral Parliament and postpone the elections in May to November 2007 by a vote of 195 members of the House, the equivalent of three-fourths of the total membership of both chambers. But first the majority coalition revised its rules requiring in effect that three-fourths of the members of the House and the Senate should separately approve the proposed amendments or revision of the constitution.

The constitution simply provides that "Any amendment to, or revision of, this Constitution may be proposed by: (1) The Congress, upon a vote of three-fourths of all its members, or (2) a constitutional convention (Article XVII. Section 1)". It does not specifiy that the chambers vote jointly or separately. The House majority expected the Supreme Court to resolve any challenges to its audacious and controversial decisions. The House made these decisions in a marathon televised session that lasted into the early morning of 6 December 2006.

The authors of Plan B had not reckoned with the instant, widespread outrage and condemnation that followed its execution in full view of the anti-chacha media and the television audience nationwide. In the face of a resurgence of urban "people power", Speaker de Venecia and President Arroyo made a quick tactical retreat and offered to pursue charter change through a constitutional convention. The speaker urged the Senate to agree to call a constitutional convention in three days but Senate President Manuel Villar simply ignored it.

Meanwhile, the Catholic Bishops' Conference of the Philippines (CBCP) had called for a massive rally at Rizal Park to protest against charter change through a constituent assembly. At the rally the CBCP called for "a change in character" instead of charter change, indicating its conservative position against constitutional reform and reflecting its view of the public's distrust of the national leadership. The CBCP had earlier said it favoured a constitutional convention after the 2007 elections when the atmosphere for charter change would be more favourable. The church's intervention in the nation's most divisive partisan issue of fundamental change drew strong approval as well as deep resentment from various quarters.

The movement for charter change cannot be stopped by public disagreements on how or when to effect the change or by blocking the people's direct action — it can only be postponed. In denying the motion for reconsideration of the petitioners, ten justices of the Supreme Court finally agreed that RA 6735 was a valid enabling act for a people's initiative. This decision has revived the resolve to push for another people's initiative.

After the 2007 elections a new effort to propose amendments to the constitution may be made through another petition for a people's initiative. For one, a new political party, Unlad Pilipinas — Party of the Global Filipino Nation [*Partido ng Pandaigdigang Bayang Pilipino*] — and other groups may push for charter change. This is only a contingency. The appointment of two new justices to the Supreme Court could tip the balance in favour of fundamental reform of the dysfunctional unitary-presidential system by shifting to parliamentary government and autonomous regions leading to a federal republic.

Meanwhile, in the midst of continuing political, economic and social crises and ineffective governance, the continuing impasse on charter change prolongs the inability of the political system to solve the nation's chronic problems in the face of rapid population growth and accelerating progress of her dynamic neighbours in the region.

Unless political system change takes place, the worsening situation could lead to social unrest on top of the communist and Moro rebellions and embolden those who advocate change through extra-constitutional means or a revolution. Leaders in Mindanao, including the Moro rebels, are disaffected because their hopes for a shift to federalism to free them from the historic grip of Imperial Manila have been dashed.

Notes

1 Amended Petition to the Commission on Elections of Raul L. Lambino and Erico B. Aumentado. In the Matter of Proposing Amendments to the 1987 Constitution through a People's Initiative: A Shift from a Bicameral Presidential to a Unicameral Parliamentary Government by Amending Articles VI and VII; and Providing Transitory Provisions for the Orderly Shift from the Presidential to the Parliamentary System. 29 August 2006.

2 Commission on Elections. Resolution, 31 August 2006. Denying due course to the Petition for Initiative for Amendments to the Constitution.

3 *Proposed Revision of the 1987 Constitution by the Consultative Commission.* Submitted to President Gloria Macapagal Arroyo, 16 December 2005.

4 Jose V. Abueva. "Why Change Our Presidential Government to a Parliamentary Government?: A Primer." In *Proposed Revision of the 1987 Constitution by the Consultative Commission.* Published by KC Institute of Federal-Parliamentary Democracy, Kalayaan College, 2006, pp. 57–83.

5 Op. cit., pp. 57–83.

6 Jose V. Abueva. "Why Reform Our Political Parties and Electoral System?: A Primer." In *Proposed Revision of the 1987 Constitution by the Consultative Commission*, 2006. pp. 74–79.

7 Jose V. Abueva. "Why Establish Autonomous Territories in Transition to a Federal Republic of the Philippines? A Primer." In *Proposed Revision of the 1987 Constitution by the Consultative Commission*, 2006. pp. 64–73.

8 Gonzalo M. Jurado, Jarius Bondoc, and Jose V. Abueva. "Why Liberalize the Charter Provisions on National Patrimony and Economic Policy?: A Primer." Charter Change Advocacy Commission. 26 April 2006.

9 *ADB Key Indicators 2005.*

10 Jose V. Abueva. "Why Have a Bill of Duties to Complement the Bill of Rights?: A Primer." In *Proposed Revision of the 1987 Constitution by the Consultative Commission*, 2006, pp. 80–83.

11 *Philippine Star*, 25 November 2006.

References

Constitutions

Constitutions of: Argentina, Australia, Belgium, Brazil, Canada. Ethiopia, France, Finland, Federal Republic of Germany, India, Japan, Malaysia, Mexico, Nigeria, Norway, Philippines, Puerto Rico, South Africa, South Korea, Spain, Singapore, St. Kitts and Nevis, Sweden, Switzerland, Taiwan, Thailand, United States of America, Venezuela, Yugoslavia.

State constitutions of Alaska, Bangsamoro, California, Hawaii, Ottawa, Queensland (Australia), Sarawak (Malaysia), Washington, Washington, D.C.

Books/Monographs

Abueva, Jose V. "Philippine Democratization and the Consolidation of Democracy Since the 1986 Revolution: An Overview of the Main Issues, Trends and Prospects". In *Democratization: Philippine Perspectives*, edited by Felipe B. Miranda, pp. 1–82. Diliman, Quezon City: University of the Philippines Press, 1997.

——— et al. *The Philippines Into the 21st Century: Future Scenarios for Governance, Democracy and Development (1998–2025)*. Quezon City: UP Press, 1998.

———. *Charter Change for Good Governance: Towards a Republic of the Philippines with a Parliamentary Government.* Citizens' Movement for a Federal Philippines and KC Institute of Federal-Parliamentary Democracy, 2005.

Abueva, Jose V., et al., eds. *Towards a Federal Republic of the Philippines with a Parliamentary Government: A Reader.* A Project of the Citizens' Movement for a Federal Philippines. Center for Social Policy and Governance, Kalayaan College; Local Government Development Foundation; Lihok Pideral-Kusog Mindanao; Konrad Adenauer Stiftung, 2002.

Asian Center for the Study of Democracy. *Christian-Muslim Democracy Towards the New Millennium*. Manila: 1999.

Asian Development Bank. *Key Indicators 2005: Labor Markets in Asia: Promoting Full, Productive, and Decent Employment*. Manila: Asian Development Bank, 2005.

Araneta, Salvador. *The Bayanikasan Constitution for the Federal Republic of the Philippines*. Metro Manila Philippines: Bayanikasan Research Foundation, 1981.

Core-Group of Christian-Muslim Democrat Ideologies and Trainors. *A Christian-Muslim Democratic Ideology*. Manila, Philippines: Institute for Development Research and Studies (IDRS), 1995.

Dejillas, Leopoldo J. and Melissa Mamaclay. *Comparative Political Systems of Selected ASEAN Governments*. Manila: Institute for Development Research and Studies (IDRS), 1995.

Jubair, Salah. *Bangsamoro: A Nation Under Endless Tyranny*, 3rd ed. Kuala Lumpur: IQ Marin Sdn Bhd, 1999.

Kalaw-Tirol, Lorna (ed.) *Edsa: Looking Back, Looking Forward 1996*. Manila: Foundation for Worldwide People Power, Inc., 1995.

Konrad Adenauer Foundation (KAF). *East and Southeast Asia Network for Better Local Governments*. Manila: Local Government Development Foundation (LOGODEF), 1999.

Lakas NUCD-UMDP. *A Christian Democratic Program of Government*. Manila, Philippines: Institute for Development Research and Studies (IDRS), 1992.

Linz, Juan J. and Valenzuela, Arturo, eds. *The Failure of Presidential Democracy: Comparative Perspectives*. Vol. 1, p. 6. Baltimore and London: The Johns Hopkins University Press, 1993.

Lipjhart, Arend, ed. *Parliamentary vs. Presidential Government*, pp. 31–47. Oxford University Press, 1992.

Owens, Jeffrey and Giorgio Panella. *Local Government: An International Perspective.* The Netherlands: Elsevier Science Publishers B.V., 1991.

Santos, Soliman M. Jr. et al. *Shift.* Quezon, City: Ateneo Center for Social Policy and Public Affairs, 1997. In this edited volume are the contributions of: Soliman M. Santos, "History of the Debate", p. 11; Florencio Abad, "Should the Philippines Turn Parliamentary: The Challenge of Democratic Consolidation and Institutional Reform", p. 48; Joel Rocamora, "The Constitutional Amendment Debate: Reforming Political Institutions, Reshaping Political Culture", p. 90; and Chay Florentino-Hofilena, "Tracking the Charter Amendment Debate: 1995–Mid-March 1997", p. 134.

Samson, Laura L. and Ma. Carmen C. Jimenez, eds. *Towards Excellence in Social Science in the Philippines.* Quezon City, Philippines: UP Press, 1984.

Thesing, Josef and Wilhelm Hofmeister, eds. *Political Parties in Democracy*, p. 482. Konrad Adenauer Stiftung, e.V., Sankt Agustin, Germany, Druckerie Franz Paffenholz GmbH, 1995.

Watts, Ronald L. *Comparing Federal Systems.* 2nd ed. Montreal & Kingston: McGill-Queen's University Press, 1999.

(No author). *Proposed Party Act of the Philippines.* Manila: Institute for Development Research and Studies (IDRS).

Journal Articles

Bolongaita, Emil P. Jr. "Presidential vs Parliamentary Democracy". *Philippine Studies* 43 (First Quarter 1995): 105–23.

Buendia, Rizal G. "The Prospects of Federalism in the Philippines: A Challenge to Political Decentralization of the Unitary State". *Philippine Journal of Public Administration* XXXIII, no. 2 (April 1989): 121–41.

Linz, Juan J. "The Perils of Presidentialism". *Journal of Democracy* 1, no. 1 (Winter 1990): 51–69.

———. "The Virtues of Parliamentarism". *Journal of Democracy* 1, no. 4 (Fall 1990): 84–91.

Logarta, Amriano R. "Constitutional Issue: Should We Adopt the Parliamentary System?" *Philippine Graphic*, 15 March 1999, p. 1.

Nerenberg, Karl (ed.) "Federations: What's New in Federalism Worldwide". *Federations* 1, no. 2 (January 2001). Forum of Federations, Canada.

Policy Issues Monitor. "Proposed Amendments to Local Government Code of 1991" (January 2001).

Stepan, Alfred and Cindy Skach. "Constitutional Frameworks and Democratic Consolidation: Parliamentarism vs. Presidentialism". *World Politics* 46 (October 1993): 3.

Torres, Crisline. "The Never Ending Cha-cha Beat: How Should Progressives Dance?" *Political Brief* 9, no. 7 (Nov–Dec 2001): 2–31.

Legislative Bills/Resolutions

13TH CONGRESS

House of Representatives. *House Concurrent Resolution No. 1.* Calling on the Senate and the House of Representatives to Constitute Themselves a Constituent Assembly to Introduce Amendments to the Constitution. First Regular Session. by Rep. Jose C. de Venecia, et al.

Concurrent Resolution No. 05. Concurrent Resolution Calling for a Constitutional Convention to Propose Amendments to, or Revision of, The 1987 Constitution of the Republic of the Philippines. First Regular Session, by Rep. Raul V. del Mar.

Concurrent Resolution No. 07. House Resolution Calling on the Senate and the House of Representatives to be Constituted as a Constituent Assembly for the Purpose of Proposing Amendments to the 1987 Constitution. First Regular Session, by Rep. Roilo Golez.

Concurrent Resolution No. 2. Concurrent Resolution Calling for the Senate and the House of Representatives to Constitute Themselves as a Constituent Assembly to Introduce Amendments to the Constitution. First Regular Session, by Rep. Fred Castro.

Concurrent Resolution No. 3. Concurrent Resolution Calling for the Senate and House of Representatives to Constitute Themselves as Constituent Assembly to Introduce Amendments to the Constitution. First Regular Session. by Rep. Matias V. Defensor, Jr.

Concurrent Resolution No. 4. Concurrent Resolution Calling for the Convening of Congress as a Constituent Assembly to Propose Revision to the 1987 Constitution, Providing for a Unicameral Parliamentary and Federal System of Government as Defined and Specified in the Proposed Amendments Appended Hereto. First Regular Session. by Rep. Constantino G. Jaraula.

Concurrent Resolution No. 10. Concurrent Resolution Constituting the Senate and the House of Representatives into a Constituent Assembly for the Purpose of Drafting and Proposing Revision to the 1987 Constitution to Change the present Presidential Form of Government into the Parliamentary System. First Regular Session. by Rep. Catalino V. Figueroa.

Resolution of Both Houses No. 1. Resolution of Both Houses Calling a Convention to Propose Amendments to, or Revision of, the 1987 Constitution, First Regular Session. by Rep. Antonio V. Cuenco.

Resolution No. 12. Resolution Calling for the House of Representatives and the Philippine Senate to Constitute Themselves as a Constituent Assembly to Introduce Amendments to the Constitution, First Regular Session, by Rep. Alipio Cirilo V. Badelles.

Resolution No. 59. Resolution Calling for the Senate and the House of Representatives to Constitute Themselves as a Constituent Assembly to Introduce Amendments to the Constitution, First Regular Session. by Rep. Douglas R. Cagas.

Resolution No. 89. Resolution Calling for a Constitutional Convention to Propose Amendments to or Revision to the 1987 Constitution of the Republic of the Philippines. First Regular Session. by Rep. Suharto T. Mangudadatu.

Bill No. 564. An Act Constituting a Constitutional Convention to Amend or Revise the Present Constitution, Appropriating Funds Therefor, and Other Purposes, First Regular Session by Rep. Roberto C. Cajes.

Bill No. 685. An Act Calling for a Constitutional Convention for Changing the 1987 Constitution, Appropriating Funds Therefor. First Regular Session, by Rep. Abraham Kahlil B. Mitra.

Proposed Rules of the 13th Congress Acting as Constituent Assembly.

Senate Bill No. 12. An Act Calling for a Constitutional Convention to Study and Approve Proposed Amendments to or Revisions of the 1987 Constitution, Providing for Proportional Representation Therein and other Details Relating to the Holding of the Convention, Setting the Date of Election of Delegates, Appropriating Funds Therefore and Other Purposes. First Regular Session, by Sen. Juan Flavier.

No. 119. An Act Providing for People's Initiative to Amend the Constitution. First Regular Session, by Sen. Luisa P. Ejercito Estrada.

No. 409. An Act Implementing the Provisions of Sections 7 and 8 of Article VII of the Constitution of Presidential Succession, First Regular Session, by Sen. S. R. Osmeña, III.

No. 1051. An Act Strengthening the Political Party System, Appropriating Funds Therefor, and for Other Purposes, First Regular Session, by Sen. Edgardo J. Angara.

No. 329. An Act Instituting Campaign Finance Reform and Strengthening the Political Party System and Providing Funds Therefor, First Regular Session, by Sen. Ralph G. Recto.

No. 1401. An Act Providing for the Establishment of a Presidential Campaign Fund for Payment of the Appropriate and Allowed Expenditures of Political Parties and Political Committees in Presidential and Vice Presidential Elections and Establishing Penalties for Violations Therefor, First Regular Session, Sen. Francis N. Pangilinan.

No. 1818. An Act Prohibiting Political Turncoatism and Providing Penalties for Violations Thereof, First Regular Session, Sen. Jinggoy Ejercito Estrada.

12TH CONGRESS

House of Representatives. *Bill Abstracts* Volume I No. 1-A. First Regular Session.

Bill Abstracts Volume I No. 1-B. First Regular Session,

Bill No. 7845 (An Act Amending RA 7160). Second Regular Session, by Rep. Romeo D.C. Candazo.

Concurrent Resolution No. 02 (Constituent Assembly to Introduce Amendments to the Constitution). First Regular Session, Congress, by Rep. Henry Lanot.

Resolution No. 04 (Constitutional Convention to Propose Amendments to the

Constitution by Adopting A Federal System of Government). First Regular Session, by Rep. Soraya C. Jaafar.

Resolution No. 72 (Constituent Assembly to Introduce Amendments to the Constitution). First Regular Session, by Rep. Conrado M. Estrella III.

Senate Bill No. 06. Constitutional Convention to Propose Amendments to the 1987 Constitution). First Regular Session, by Sen. Juan M. Flavier.

No. 826 (An Act Amending Certain Provisions of RA 7160). First Regular Session, by Sen. Aquilino Q. Pimentel Jr.

11TH CONGRESS

Senate. *Concurrent Resolution No. 26* (Constitutional Convention to Revise the Constitution by Adopting a Federal System of Government). Second Regular Session, 11th Congress, Introduced by Sen. Aquilino Pimentel Jr.

9TH CONGRESS

Senate Resolution No. 1250 (Constituent Assembly to (1) Create a Federal System of Government, and (2) Adopting a Parliamentary Form of Government). Fifth Regular Session, by Sen. Aquilino Q. Pimentel Jr.

4

THE MILITARY IN PHILIPPINE POLITICS: RETROSPECT AND PROSPECTS

Carolina G. Hernandez

INTRODUCTION

Until the imposition of martial law in the Philippines in September 1972, the principles of civilian control and supremacy of civilian authority over the military governed the relationship between the civilian government and the Armed Forces of the Philippines (AFP). As a consequence of the strategy used against the agrarian-based Huk insurgency during the late 1940s to the early 1950s, the role of the military in society slowly expanded beyond the original triad of external defence, internal security, and peace and order to include socio-economic functions.[1] However, the constitutional and institutional framework, including civilian oversight over the military, and a body of civil and political rights that ensured democratic governance, including regular elections, continued to define civil-military relations and the role of the military in Philippine politics.

This changed with Martial Law. The legislature was disbanded, civil and political freedoms were suspended, political parties were outlawed, newspapers and other media outlets were controlled, the private property of Marcos' political opponents was sequestered on the pretext of their outstanding loans from government financial institutions, and the military became a partner of martial law and authoritarian rule. This partnership lasted some fourteen years, and in its wake left civil-military relations in disarray. More disastrously for democracy, it created in the AFP members an "interventionist" tendency.

This chapter focuses on the military in Philippine politics, particularly the implications of martial law for the country's military, civil-military relations, and democratic governance in general. It attempts to explain the emergence of an "interventionist" role for the military by documenting:

- the military's role expansion without civilian oversight institutions and a democratic political system;
- the role the AFP played in the 1986 and 2001 political successions and in providing political stability and regime survival in the 1980s and at present;
- the military's role in countering communist insurgency and Moro separatism; and
- the absence of good governance which helped shape its "interventionist" role.

A discussion on the military and defence reform measures taken as well as the constraints and challenges the country has faced in democratizing civil-military relations since 1986 also addresses the question of whether the military is helping or obstructing peace in Mindanao. A section on what needs to be done precedes a concluding section on the country's future prospects for democratized civilian control of the AFP and democratic governance in general.

MILITARY ROLE EXPANSION, DECAY OF CIVILIAN INSTITUTIONS, AND MILITARY INTERVENTION

Civil-military relations theories stress that to ensure civilian control the role of the military must be clearly defined in the country's constitution and laws. Effective democratic civilian control of the armed forces also requires that civilian oversight institutions function properly. These institutions include legislative oversight committees, for instance, over defence and military budgets, military promotions and appointments at the highest levels of the officer corps, and investigations of allegations of military wrongdoing. Effective civilian control also means military accountability to financial audit and civil service rules and regulations, as well as for violations of human rights and international humanitarian law. It includes openness of the military to public scrutiny through a free press and public opinion.

Beyond these, there has to be institutional and functional separation of the police from the military. The latter normally performs external defence functions and provides policy advice to the civilian political leadership on defence and military security matters. It is subordinated to the civilian government and is politically non-partisan.

In the Philippines, civilian control includes oversight by the deputy ombudsman for the military and the Philippine Human Rights Commission, as well as accountability before the civilian courts for the crime of *coup d'etat*, rebellion, and mutiny. *Coup d'etat* and mutiny were criminalized following the failed coup attempt of December 1989 against the administration of former President Corazon C. Aquino. This means that military offenders are accountable before military and civilian courts.

Military intervention in politics can range from arrogating upon itself the role of making defence and military policy instead of recommending them to the political authorities, withdrawal of support from the commander-in-chief or the chain of command, dissenting from policy decisions made by the commander-in-chief or the chain of command, including on promotions and appointments to top military positions, plotting/conspiring to overthrow the government, unauthorized troop movements, and acts of rebellion, mutiny, and *coup d'etat*.

In short, any act that goes against its constitutionally defined functions and legally-defined mission, intruding into the political arena, is military intervention in politics. In a democratic polity, these are defined by norms and principles of democratic civilian control of the armed forces, including the confinement of the military role to external and internal defence, the separation of the police from the military both in institutional and functional terms, the exercise of civilian institutional oversight powers over the military, and the supremacy of civilian authority over the military at all times.[2]

Decay of Democratic Civil-Military Relations

During the fourteen years following the imposition of martial law in September 1972, these norms and principles governing democratic civilian control of armed forces were seriously breached. The military was made to assume new functions amidst the destruction of civilian oversight institutions in the legislature and the suspension of civil and political rights that helped subordinate the AFP to civilian political authority in the past.[3] In the political realm, members of the high command replaced the politicians as dispensers of political patronage as its top officers became chief executives of local government units and regional peace and order development councils, as well as Presidential Regional Officers for Development with the prerogatives of the Office of the President in implementing programmes including agrarian reform and community development.

The military performed economic functions through the establishment of investment corporations under military control as a reward for their support for martial law, as well as military-run arms production and related development firms as part of the Self-Reliant Military Defence Programme. Several sequestered private firms were put under management boards where active-duty officers sat, and favoured defence and military leaders were allowed to engage in logging and mining activities in private. Moreover, the Retirement Service and Benefits System (RSBS) and savings and loans associations for each of the major services and the AFP were also established, largely, if not entirely, outside the prudential supervision and control of auditing, banking, and other authorities. These were to become sources of military corruption and grievances fuelling recruitment for coup attempts in the post-Marcos period.[4]

The military also performed judicial and administrative functions as well as developmental roles through the management of socioeconomic programmes and projects. With the appointment of the only high-ranking military officer to oppose the imposition of martial law as ambassador to Iran, Marcos started a practice of extending the public service of former military officers through appointments to ambassadorial and other positions in the executive department that lasts to this day. This practice has led to a balance between civilian and former military officers increasingly in favour of retired military officers in the cabinet, for example, as well as in various administrative offices.[5]

For these new or expanded functions, military officers were earlier prepared through a revision of the prescribed military career development pattern that traditionally emphasized military proficiency and values. During the first term of Marcos as president, the new career development pattern required the acquisition of advanced/post-graduate academic training from civilian educational institutions as a criterion for promotion. This new pattern was shaped by the doctrine spread by the United States of training Third World militaries in national development. This doctrine, while useful in the application of huge manpower and other military resources for national development purposes in times of peace, has also accounted for the politicization of armed forces and their intervention in the politics of post-colonial states during the 1960s and 1970s.

Thus, the role of the AFP in national development that started in the counter-insurgency against the Huks, institutionalized since 1965, and deepened without institutionalized civilian oversight between 1972 and

1986, contributed to the politicization of the AFP and the shaping of its "interventionist" role.

The Development of a Military 'Interventionist' Tendency

The "interventionist" tendency in the AFP developed as a consequence of many factors, as discussed above. Prolonged exposure to social ills and the realization that much leaves to be desired in governance politicized the young officers.[6] Moreover, the military played a key role in combating the twin armed conflicts that grew following regime change in 1972, namely, the Maoist communist insurgency of the Communist Party of the Philippines (CPP), its armed wing — the New People's Army (NPA) — and the National Democratic Front (NDF) on the one hand, and ethnic separatism led by the Moro National Liberation Front (MNLF) on the other. The use of coercion in governance[7] was palpable in these conflicts and would sustain the military's political role beyond 1986. Prolonged exposure to domestic conflict where national development is a component of the overall antidote would contribute to the military's politicization and the development of an "interventionist" tendency among its officers.

The combined effects of these political and military developments on governance resulted in the destruction of democratic political institutions, including oversight bodies, military professionalism and cohesion. It also resulted in the personalization of civilian control in Marcos. In combination, these led to the phenomenon of a "fragile democracy",[8] an inevitable result of dictatorship and authoritarian rule where the military was a critical element in governance either as the ruler or its principal support.

It must be noted, however, that the military's entry into political governance as a partner of the martial law regime was upon invitation by its civilian commander-in-chief. Nonetheless, the integrity of the supremacy of civilian authority over the military at all times was thereby compromised, since the military became a partner in governing society during martial law and authoritarian rule. These developments conjoined to create in military officers an "interventionist" tendency, further shaped by the continuing perception among "rebel" officers from 1986 onwards that they were responsible for the successful ouster of Marcos in 1986 (and Estrada in 2001) through "people power".[9] These established their role in political succession, justifying in the minds of some factions within the AFP their interventionist role in politics. Moreover, as the constitutionalist faction of the military suppressed coup attempts in the 1980s and the AFP remained within the chain of command in July 2003 and in February 2006, the military also developed a role as a provider of political stability and regime survival. These are new roles for the military that martial law and its aftermath developed, and they helped nurture military interventionism.

Continuing civilian encouragement and enlistment of military support for ousting incumbents are also powerful shapers of the "interventionist" role of the military. The Reform the Armed Forces of the Philippines Movement (RAM)[10] leaders in testifying before the Davide Commission accused opposition politicians and business leaders of encouraging them to oust Marcos. Similarly, findings of both Davide and Feliciano Commissions document the material and "morale" contribution made by civilians to the coup plotters. During the first decade of the twenty-first century, this enlistment of military support by civilian personalities and groups for political destabilization and other private political agenda continued unabated. In response, government appeared to be more firm in dealing with coup plotters, including those implicated in Oplan Hackle such as former rebel leaders Gregorio "Gringo" Honasan, General Danilo Lim, and Colonel Ariel Querubin.[11]

The first use of "people power" as a method of political succession was in February 1986, leading to the ouster of Marcos. This event also marked the beginning of the restoration of democracy, including democratic civilian control of the armed forces. The new constitution reasserted the principles of civilian control and supremacy of civilian authority over the military at all times. However, it also stressed the role of the armed forces as "protector of the people and the state", a phrase that would raise opposing interpretations and would be used to legitimize military interventionism in the 1980s, as well as in July 2003 and in February 2006.

The framers of the new constitution explained the inclusion of this provision in terms of limiting the armed services' violation of human rights that occurred during counter-insurgency operations.[12] In no way does this provision empower the military to determine issues of political legitimacy, as coup plotters would argue. This particular provision must be interpreted within the context of the proceedings of the constitutional commission that framed the 1987 Constitution and within the context of a democratic constitution where civilian authority is supreme over the military at all times.

An interpretation of this constitutional provision that severs it from the democratic political system in which it is situated abets military interventionism. The irony is that constitutional luminaries repeatedly make this interpretation and some practising lawyers use this provision to justify the withdrawal of support by ranking officers from their commander-in-chief! Such advocates do serious injury to democratic civilian control and good governance of the armed forces. If they happen to be lawyers, they should go back to law school to re-learn constitutional law.

Naturally, this rationale has been lost on coup plotters, among them being the leaders of RAM, Marcos loyalist officers who launched a series of unsuccessful coup attempts in the 1980s, the Magdalo leaders of the 2003 Oakwood Mutiny,[13] and General Lim, Colonel Querubin, and company of the 2006 Oplan Hackle. This rationale has been lost on their civilian co-conspirators and supporters in and out of government. By their interpretation, buttressed by the popular support for the military breakaway against Marcos in February 1986 and from Estrada in 2001, these groups believe that the military had the right to determine the legitimacy of the civilian government. This is a dangerous proposition that has every potential of undermining democratic rule.

Public opinion polls that indicated a decline in the popularity or performance rating of a sitting president coincided with the launch of coup attempts in the 1980s. Coup plotters and their co-conspirators continued to fail to distinguish between decline in the popularity of incumbents on the one hand, and popular support for military intervention on the other. Such decline in public support was usually preceded by an increase in oil prices, rising unemployment or similar bread-and-butter issues that affect the general population. At present, it is fuelled by a wide range of individuals and groups seeking the ouster of President Arroyo for various reasons, including allegations of cheating by the President in the 2004 elections.

There are several other possible explanations for the occurrence of these coup attempts in the 1980s that demonstrate the military's "interventionist" role. The Davide Commission that investigated the failed December 1989 coup against former President Corazon C. Aquino found a mix of causes, including unaddressed military grievances, objections to the inclusion of "left-wing"/anti-military officials in the Aquino administration, opposition to peace negotiations with the communist and the Moro secessionist groups, the perceived loss of power that the coup plotters suffered as a result of the outcome of people power, career dead-end for senior coup plotters, and a "messianic complex" to save Philippine society.[14]

The Feliciano Commission that investigated the Oakwood Mutiny of 2003 endorsed the Davide Commission Report, and in particular concluded that the mutiny had been caused by allegations of anomalies within the AFP involving the RSBS, the military procurement system, particularly the practice of "conversion", the transfer of arms and ammunition to unauthorized parties, and the construction and repair of various facilities at Marine Base in Cavite.[15]

These alleged causes, however, are often used as justification or recruitment vehicles for coup plots. In all the coup attempts investigated by the Davide Commission, the power motive appeared palpable as in the case of the Oakwood Mutiny in 2003. Power grabbers in and out of the military tend to use idealistic officers for their private political agenda to legitimize these actions. In the process, they have destroyed hundreds of military careers and caused broken lives. They have also set back, perhaps irreparably, the political and economic development of the country.

Apart from these causes of coup attempts, "interventionism" is also facilitated by the personalization of civilian control. It is not easy to rebuild the institutions of civilian oversight. Not only would the military have to be subordinated to the civilian political authority as an institution (from Marcos to whoever would be commander-in-chief), but the other oversight institutions in the government, such as in the legislature, the judiciary, the anti-graft and human rights bodies, and outside government, such as media, academe, civil society groups, and political parties, would need to be built and capacitated to discharge oversight functions. Politicians also need to be similarly oriented as oversight actors, a task that could be daunting indeed, given the overall decline in the quality of Philippine legislators.

It did not make it any easier that the new commander-in-chief in 1986, Corazon Aquino, confronted the military on the other side of the barricades during the mass protests against the Marcos regime. Aquino was the wife of the political opposition leader, Benigno Aquino, who was assassinated under military custody. She became the first woman commander-in-chief of a basically male-dominated institution.[16]

Apart from identifying the causes of the coup attempts of the 1980s, the Davide Commission Report also made a detailed analysis of the coup as a political phenomenon, described the string of coup attempts, including their causes, actors, and highlights, and prescribed comprehensive but detailed recommendations, with time-lines, for various government agencies and social sectors (including the church, media, civil society, and academe). Unfortunately, these recommendations were not implemented and, when they were, they were not implemented in the spirit in which they were intended. For instance, no coup plotter of the 1980s has been properly punished as recommended by the Davide Commission, thereby undermining the discipline that is critical to the military as an institution and setting a bad example to other officers who would not learn lessons that could discourage future military interventionism.

Moreover, instead of reopening the investigation of the unlaunched coup of November 1986, which could have unmasked the coup leaders in the defence and military establishments as the Davide Commission recommended, the government chose to let them go by not investigating this coup plot. When Fidel V. Ramos succeeded Aquino as president in 1992, he extended unconditional amnesty to these plotters. Under his administration, two of the known leaders were elected senators, thus giving them a stake in the political system, which obviously they would not rock, but which set a horrific example for future coup plotters.

It is noteworthy that although Ramos was not popular among the military, no coup attempt took place during his watch. But some of the key leaders in the coup plots of the 1980s would resurface in the July 2003 Oakwood Mutiny,[17] the February 2006 Oplan Hackle, and continuing attempts to entice the military to oust the Arroyo government. Honasan surfaced in all of these coup plots. He was captured in November 2006 after months of eluding arrest.

DEMOCRATIZING CIVIL-MILITARY RELATIONS: MEASURES AND CHALLENGES, 1986–2006

Nonetheless, the government adopted significant reforms in the military from 1986 onwards.[18] Institutional and functional reforms dominated the measures adopted during the Aquino administration. The Ramos administration focused on peace talks and amnesty for military rebels and a values reorientation programme to develop a religious, patriotic, and humanistic military. In no other administration since 1986, however, has military and defence reform been taken as seriously as during the present Arroyo administration. Yet, constraints on and challenges to democratic civil-military relations and good governance of the security sector persist.

Military and Defence Reform Measures

The most important reforms affecting the military undertaken by the government during the Aquino administration included:

- the adoption and implementation of a new constitution that restated the principles of civilian control and supremacy of civilian authority at all times;
- the separation of the police (including the Philippine Constabulary that used to be the fourth major service command of the AFP) from the military;
- the confinement of the military role to external defence, while internal

security and peace and order would be with the police, now under a civilian agency;

- the restoration of the civilian oversight institutions in Congress with powers over appropriations (including the defence budget), military promotion and appointments (through the Commission on Appointments), and investigative powers in aid of legislation (including for alleged military anomalies);
- the creation of another constitutional body, the Commission on Human Rights of the Philippines, an oversight agency which certifies that military officers being considered for promotion from the rank of lieutenant colonel and above have undergone training in human rights and international humanitarian law and have no record of human rights violations;
- the restoration of a free press;
- the establishment of the Office of Ethical Standards and Professional Accountability, to address military corruption and unethical or unprofessional conduct, in addition to the General Court-Martial (GCM) and the Inspector-General;
- the grant of a series of increases in military pay and other benefits; and
- the restoration of regular elections, which foreclosed the appointment of active and retired military officers to the post of local chief executives, and other positions.

Thus, despite the coup attempts of the 1980s, there was a general trend towards the restoration of democratic civilian control, differentiation of the structures and functions of the police and the military in which the police was civilianized and placed under the supervision and control of a civilian agency, and the building of an environment of civil and political rights so essential to democratic governance.

Upon assumption to power in January 2001, President Gloria Macapagal Arroyo announced a package of reforms that would affect the military, including:

- a substantial increase in the basic pay of soldiers, to be paid in three tranches from 2002 to 2004;
- the creation of the Presidential Task Force for Military Reform that would address the lack of transparency and accountability in the military procurement and financial systems;
- the establishment of the office of the Undersecretary of Internal Control at the Department of National Defence (DND), the agency with administrative supervision and control over the AFP; and

- a programme, Joint Defence Assessment (JDA), where the Philippines and the United States jointly undertook an assessment of the country's security challenges in the next five-year period, the AFP's current and requisite capability to meet these challenges, and the amount of resources that Congress is likely to appropriate to meet these challenges at a realistic level of capability requirements set by the AFP.

President Arroyo took over the defence portfolio from Angelo Reyes in order to supervise personally the implementation of key elements of this reform package. For all government agencies, the New Procurement Reform Law (Republic Act 9184) and its implementing rules and regulations to promote greater transparency and accountability in the procurement process took effect even prior to the Oakwood Mutiny.

Thus, when the Oakwood Mutiny took place in July 2003, parts of this reform package were already in place. While the Magdalo leaders articulated legitimate military grievances that continued to fester over time, they were also part of a plot to remove President Arroyo, make Estrada president for three days (a period presumably sufficient to dismiss the plunder case against him pending before the country's anti-graft court, and whose maximum penalty at that time was death), and set up a council of which Honasan would be a member to implement his National Recovery Program that purportedly would address the country's multi-dimensional problems.[19]

Subsequent investigations of, and intelligence information regarding, the Oakwood Mutiny indicated that Estrada was the main financier of the plot, not all the Magdalo leaders knew that money had transferred hands, and the implication of key officials in the Arroyo administration in alleged irregularities was probably without basis.

The Feliciano Commission made key recommendations to address the grievances aired by the Magdalo leaders, including:

- reform of the military's procurement and financial systems, including the reduction of the 119 bids and awards committees for DND-AFP, limitation of the tenure of comptrollership, which has been found to be a source of corruption, and reduction of the centrally managed funds at the GHQ and the HQs of the major service commands;
- strict enforcement of the law in which offenders must be punished;
- due diligence among commanders to provide timely information to the troops and to prevent recruitment for coup plots;
- recovery of military land in Fort Bonifacio so the sale proceeds could be used for military modernization;

- increase in the military's share in the proceeds of the land;
- liquidation of major military graft-prone institutions such as the RSBS (one of the Marcos-era rewards to the AFP for its support for martial law whose original purpose of taking over the payment of military pensions from the general appropriations fund is not likely to be realized) and its replacement by a more viable and regulated retirement and pension system;
- appointment of a civilian Secretary of National Defence with no deep ties to the military;
- improvement of the internal grievance mechanism to redress effectively the soldiers' grievances;
- improvement of military equipment, health, housing, and other welfare services; and
- improvement of the capability of the ombudsman to investigate and prosecute military personnel for graft and corruption.[20]

Many of these recommendations echoed those made earlier by the Davide Commission, although the Feliciano Commission's final recommendation was informed by the failure of the government to implement the Davide Commission recommendations. Thus, the Feliciano Commission recommended that the president appoint a person to an office that would monitor the implementation of the Feliciano Commission recommendations, report and make recommendations to the president on measures to improve their implementation, and conduct studies to ensure that coups no longer take place in the future.[21]

In December 2003, President Arroyo created the Office of the Presidential Adviser to Implement the Feliciano Commission Recommendations (OPAIFCR). In the meantime, the prosecution of the Magdalo group began both in the GCM and the civilian court. The bulk of the enlisted personnel had entered into a plea bargain and meted with penalties including imprisonment, forfeiture of salary for varying periods, and demotion of up to two ranks. The cases against the Magdalo leaders remained pending before the GCM and the civilian court.

In August 2004, following her election to a six-year term, President Arroyo appointed a civilian lawyer, Avelino Cruz, Jr. as Defence Secretary. The 119 Bids and Awards Committees were reduced to five — one each for the DND, AFP, and the three major service commands, and biddings were held in public with observers from the OPAIFCR, the church, and civil society present. The office of comptrollership in the GHQ and major service command headquarters was abolished and replaced with a system of checks and balances among a number of offices; the centrally managed funds were drastically reduced and brought down to troop commanders at the operational level.

In May and June 2006, the commanding officers of the Philippine Navy and the Philippine Army caused the eviction of retired high-ranking officers from their quarters in Fort Bonifacio, which they claimed they had purchased.[22] Subsequently, the Supreme Court ruled against one of the claimant groups, the JUSMAG-SHAI (Joint US Military Advisory Group—Southside Homeowners Association, Inc.), saying that in the absence of a presidential proclamation, public land such as that of the contested area, cannot be alienated to private owners. This ruling should lead to the future dismissal of all the claims being made by retired officers on land inside Fort Bonifacio.

Pending the repeal of Presidential Decree No. 361 that established the RSBS and its liquidation, an alternative retirement and pension system for the AFP has been proposed for legislation as recommended by the Feliciano Commission. More importantly, the cases against the RSBS officers allegedly involved in anomalous practices were being prosecuted before the anti-graft court. In October 2006, the DND and the AFP announced the de-activation of the RSBS, the collection of soldiers' contribution to be continued and put in a trust fund at one of the government-owned banks pending the repeal of PD 361, which created the RSBS. A high-ranking officer who served as AFP Comptroller for many years was also tried before the GCM and the anti-graft court and was convicted for violation of a number of provisions in the Articles of War, for crimes including conduct unbecoming an officer, perjury, and plunder.

During the tenure of Secretary Cruz, the DND-AFP adopted the Philippine Defence Reform (PDR) programme implementing the outcome of the JDA as a medium-term defence reform programme whose thrust is military capability upgrading (to communicate, to move, and to shoot) for internal security rather than military modernization, and has drafted a New National Defence Act to institutionalize these reforms and as a replacement for the antiquated Commonwealth Act No. 1 of 1935.[23]

In 2005, the OPAIFCR also undertook the development of a Security Sector Reform Index (SSRI) for the Philippines as part of the programme of the Office of the Presidential Adviser for the Peace Process on conflict prevention and peace building. The SSRI will be used to assess the state of security sector reform in the Philippines over time and includes the core security sector actors (the uniformed and intelligence services), as well as the oversight institutions in government (legislative and other constitutional bodies) and outside of government (academe, civil society groups, political parties, and media). The Institute for Strategic and Development Studies is refining the draft SSRI for pilot testing and validation, after which it will be used to build a baseline on security sector reform in the Philippines. The SSRI is also being eyed, with adjustments and further refinement, as a possible template for a regional, and eventually, a global SSRI.

The list of reform measures goes on.[24] However, all is not well as far as good governance of the security sector is concerned. And this could be among the reasons behind the aborted coup attempt of February 2006, codenamed Oplan Hackle.

Constraints and Challenges

There remain serious constraints preventing the full restoration of democratic civilian control of the armed forces, and for that matter good governance of the security sector. In the Philippines, for example, the separation of police and military security functions suffered a setback as the twin domestic armed conflicts refused to die down, despite the peace agreement reached between the government and the MNLF during Ramos' incumbency. Internal security operations against the communist insurgency and separatism, now led by the Moro Islamic Liberation Front (MILF), the main breakaway faction of the original MNLF, continued to be the military's main function. Legislative oversight institutions, constitutional oversight bodies, political parties, media, and academe continue to mismanage their oversight functions. Many of them solicit or encourage military destabilization against the government. How can the military function properly within a democratic setting with poor security sector governance?

In this regard, the question of whether the military is helping or obstructing peace in Mindanao needs to be addressed. It is always risky to take an entire organization to task, especially on the question at hand. The same question could be asked about the MILF and other groups and organizations, because these organizations do not often act in a coherent and monolithic manner. Factions within these groups are practical realities that tend to complicate analysis. The mainstream MILF, for example, may no longer be harbouring elements of the Jemaah Islamiyah (JI), and may no longer be allowing its camps to be used for terrorist training activities. However, this may not necessarily be the case with some factions of the MILF who reportedly continue to harbour JI elements and allow terrorist activities and training in the camps they control.

What really matters is that the government has to have a coherent policy in Mindanao and an overall counter-insurgency approach. The strategy continues to be divided in four stages: clear, hold, consolidate, and develop. The military is conceptually responsible for clearing and holding areas used to be under the insurgents' control, while the civilian agencies become the principal government actors in the last two stages of the counter-insurgency strategy.

Unfortunately, the military often finds itself holding the bag for the government throughout the four stages. Absenteeism among local government executives is reportedly common, especially in conflict areas in Mindanao. A study of the military's institutional response to domestic conflicts used by the *Philippine Human Development Report 2005* found a lack of coherence in the military's response to these conflicts.[25] There are contradictions among the pacification, military victory, and institutional peace building positions embedded in the military operational plans in countering communist insurgency and Moro separatism. The pacification position seeks to give the insurgents concessions that are just enough to bring them to the negotiating table and return them to civilian life; the military victory position seeks to win the war against the insurgents and return to the *status quo ante bellum* thereafter; and the institutional peace-building position seeks to establish institutions for peace in various spheres over the short, medium, and longer terms through consultative and participatory mechanisms.[26]

On the ground, these three positions have worked at cross-purposes and led to unsustainable peace in Mindanao. Moreover, it has been observed that there is no coherence among the groups that negotiate (the peace panel), those that provide funding (the legislature), and those that implement (various agencies in the executive department, the local government, the military, and the police) the peace agreement.[27] Is the military an obstruction to that peace? If it undermines the government policy to negotiate a lasting peace in Mindanao and conducts military operations contrary to the agreements including on the ceasefire reached between the Government of the Republic of the Philippines (GRP) and the MILF, then it is obstructing peace in Mindanao.

If it does not, then it is helping give peace a chance. The problem, however, is the apparent disconnect between missions given to the troops on the ground, such as to prevent the growth in the size of the MILF, and the commitments of the government under the ceasefire and other agreements with the MILF. When the military obtains firm intelligence information that the MILF is recruiting members while the ceasefire is in effect, the military officers on the ground cannot be expected not to fulfil their mission by taking steps to prevent such recruitment. When troops are being fired upon or ambushed by the MILF, should they not fight back? The bottom line, it seems, is to have as faithful an implementation of the agreements by both sides as feasible, ensured by independent and objective monitoring mechanisms. These mechanisms can include independent external observers with the consent of both sides, who can help determine the state of implementation of agreements, whether on a ceasefire or a peace agreement.

Another challenge to democratic civilian control is the weakness of civilian political institutions established since 1986, while political parties and leaders have remained unable to move beyond personalities to principled structural and behavioural reforms. As already noted, oversight powers are often misused or abused. Some use their office in oversight bodies as rent-seeking avenues exacting tolls from officers being considered for promotion or high-ranking appointments. Politicians and private persons continue to enlist military support for their private agenda. Norms are not observed as a matter of course. For example, meritocracy in appointive positions remains an elusive goal, which when realized is certain to not only increase the efficiency and effectiveness of governance, but also to promote greater transparency and accountability in the public sphere. Together, they are likely to contribute to greater performance legitimacy and political stability and reduce the role of the military in political life.

Instead, however, an increasing number of retired military officers were appointed to civilian government positions by post-1986 presidents from Aquino to Arroyo, a practice that could have serious implications for the consolidation of democratic governance of the armed forces and democratic civil-military relations. While retirement from the military service legally makes an officer a civilian person, the sociological attributes of the military as an institution and as a profession can inhibit the transformation of the military mind whose responses to situations would remain strongly influenced by military orientations. At the end of the day, a trained professional carries with her or him the attributes of the profession beyond retirement from the service.

At the same time, the "ties that bind" developed from cadet days at the Philippine Military Academy (PMA), strengthened during combat experience, last beyond retirement, making officers' relationships with one another "closer than brothers".[28] Hierarchy and subordination to seniors also continue beyond retirement, making it difficult to say no to more senior, even if retired, officers.[29] Thus, we see the phenomenon of retired military officers calling on their juniors still in active service to join anti-government plots and movements. Some even talk to the troops on the ground to entice soldiers to join in plots against the government. It is for this reason that the Feliciano Commission recommended due diligence among commanding officers on the ground to prevent the conduct of these activities.

What More Needs to be Done?

Security sector reform (SSR) could be the framework solution to what ails Philippine civil-military relations. SSR is a fairly recent and highly misunderstood concept. It evolved as a result of the observation that reforming the armed forces would not lead to democratic civil-military relations if the civilian oversight institutions in and out of government do not perform their oversight functions properly. Norms of good governance, such as responsibility, transparency, and accountability, need to be observed in as wide a range of security sector actors (the armed forces, the police, the intelligence community, paramilitary organizations, government oversight institutions in the executive, legislative, judicial, and constitutional offices, "watchdogs" outside government, politicians and political parties) as possible.

In fact, when one reforms only the military and other uniformed and intelligence services (the core security sector actors), the military in particular — having gone through a period of partnership in government with expanded political roles and little civilian oversight — could become "interventionist" out of frustration with abusive, corrupt, and non-performing civilian officials. Thus, security sector governance and reform comes about with reform not only of the uniformed and intelligence services, but also of the civilian oversight institutions.

As already noted, reform of the military has been taking place since 1986. From the ouster of Marcos in 1986 to the present, many reform programmes affecting or targeting the military have been put in place and are ongoing. Constitutional reform through the 1987 constitution reorganized the military and the police. Value reformation programmes, the establishment of the OESPA, and the retirement of overstaying generals are all part of military reform. Addressing poor welfare conditions of the military, particularly salaries and related benefits, has been going on since the Aquino period. Meanwhile, the Arroyo government increased the base pay of soldiers and created the Presidential Task Force for Military Reform even prior to the Oakwood Mutiny.

Good governance of the security sector, particularly its military element, cannot be assured despite the constitutional, legal, and other types of reform measures already put in place by the Philippine government since 1986. Some of the things that still need to be done are the following:

- a reduction in the role of coercion in governance, which includes a resolution of the over three decades-long communist insurgency and Moro separatism;

- a reduction in the dependence of civilian political leaders on the military for political stability;
- the termination of the AFP's role in the electoral process;
- a closure regarding the role of the military in the political succession from Marcos to Aquino and from Estrada to Arroyo;[30]
- effective and well-publicized redress of legitimate military grievances in order to remove a major magnet for recruitment for coup plots;
- an end to differential treatment of academy and non-academy sourced officers both in promotion and assignment as well as in the privileges enjoyed by officers;
- an end to the misuse and abuse of the oversight powers by civilian oversight institutions;
- inhibition on the part of the private sector and other civilian groups and individuals from enlisting the military in their personal and private agendas;
- the prosecution of all erring military personnel, particularly high-ranking officers who have violated military and civilian laws,
- limitation of appointments of retired military officers to high-ranking positions in the executive department and the civilian bureaucracy;[31] and
- full implementation of the military reform programmes, particularly the recommendations of the Davide and Feliciano Commissions.

It bears repeating that security sector reform does not end with military reform, but must include other security sector actors in the uniformed and intelligence services as well as civilian oversight institutions. Congressional oversight committees, constitutional bodies, and others in the civilian government have a particularly critical responsibility in reforming themselves by observing the principles of good governance and to discharge their oversight functions appropriately and effectively.

Future Prospects

Transitions from authoritarianism to democracy are often problematic. The achievement of good governance in the military sector and the entire security sector is not easy, given the challenges suggested in this chapter.

A key challenge that must be addressed is the reduction of the use of coercion in governance as well as the reduction of the civilian government's dependence on the military for political stability or even survival. Here the ball is not only in one court but in the courts of all stakeholders in and out of government. The successful resolution of the armed conflicts requires a comprehensive reexamination of the government's responses to them. Such responses have so far lacked coherence, consistency, and continuity.[32] A long-lasting resolution requires political maturity, civic responsibility, and professional competence among relevant actors to reduce the government's dependence on the military. Constant destabilization only drives the government further into the military's tight embrace.

In the medium to long term, the adoption of security sector reform in the core security sector actors beyond the military, such as the police and other uniformed services, the civilian oversight institutions both in government (executive agencies supervising the uniformed services, congressional oversight committees, the ombudsman and the anti-graft and other courts, the Commission on Human Rights) and outside government (academe, civil society organizations, media, politicians, and political parties) is a necessary and critical factor in achieving good governance in the security sector and in the consolidation of democracy in the Philippines. Only then can good governance of the military and democratic consolidation be assured. In all these, the conversion of citizens towards ethical behaviour in both the private and public spheres is a critical requirement.

The transfer of power from Marcos to Aquino and from Estrada to Arroyo through people power — an extra-constitutional but legitimate method of political succession, according to the Philippine Supreme Court — needs to be re-examined, particularly in terms of its implications for the institutionalization of democracy. As in February 1986, those who joined the demonstration of people power to remove Estrada in January 2001 had a consensus on who should assume the presidency. As in February 1986, the second people power demonstration took place within the context of an ongoing political and constitutional exercise whose outcome was publicly perceived as being manipulated by the incumbent president, prompting largely unorganized people to go to EDSA, the capital city's main thoroughfare.

In the present political context, public appeals to people power have been made by almost everyone that has an axe to grind against the government or an agenda not amenable to constitutional and legal procedures. Icons of past people power movements have fallen out of popular grace as they called on the people to support the call for the resignation of President Arroyo. Public and private monies have been spent to spark people power as in 1986 and in 2001 — all to no avail.

Members of the military continue to be seduced by those who seek to benefit from a political succession out of turn. Referring to Oplan Hackle of February 2006, an investigative journalist wisely wrote: "The new element in this Folly of February is the link of rebel soldiers to some civilian groups which welcome military intervention to oust President Arroyo. The forces who criticize Ms. Arroyo's use and politicization of the military are themselves doing the same thing, eroding the institution that they will be working with — should they be in power."[33]

It needs to be stressed, too, that by abetting military intervention, those whom the military dislikes by training or through personal experience will be the first to fall should it succeed in gaining power. It is therefore in nobody's interest, including the military whose coherence, integrity, and very survival would be seriously compromised, to support or undertake military intervention in politics. Finally, unless warranted by a peculiar set of political circumstances akin to those surrounding people power in 1986 and 2001, resort to people power with or without a military component to remove an unpopular president can lead to political behaviour that imperils democratic governance, particularly in the absence of a broad consensus regarding the likely beneficiary of political succession among those who wish to use it. For to leave the future after the ouster of an incumbent president to chance, or to a process that would sort itself out only after the event itself, would be utterly irresponsible.

Notes

1 The Huk insurgency erupted after independence in 1946 due to agrarian unrest as well as the invalidation of the election of socialist candidates to the House of Representatives of the Philippine legislature. "Land for the landless" was its principal slogan, and it was concentrated largely in the agricultural belt of Central Luzon.

2 Conceptual and theoretical explanations for military intervention in politics are found in Samuel P. Huntington, *The Soldier and the State: The Theory and Politics of Civil-Military Relations* (New York: Vintage Books-Random House, 1957), and S.E. Finer, *The Man on Horseback: The Role of the Military in Politics* (Norwich, UK: Peregrine Books, 1976), among other pioneering works on the subject.

3 The following section is largely drawn from the author's pioneering works on Philippine civil-military relations beginning with her unpublished doctoral dissertation "Civilian Control of the Military in the Philippines: 1946–1976", State University of New York at Buffalo, 1979, followed by numerous subsequent publications from the 1980s onwards.

4 The perpetrators of the Oakwood Mutiny of July 2003 highlighted the anomalies committed by high-ranking officers of RSBS as a major source of grievance. The body that investigated the mutiny documented these anomalies and recommended the prosecution by the ombudsman of the officers who were likely involved in their commission. See *The Report of the Fact Finding Commission* (Pursuant to Administrative Order No. 78 of the President of the Republic of the Philippines

dated 30 July 2003), 17 October 2003, henceforth *The FelCom Report.* This commission was chaired by retired Supreme Court Justice Florentino P. Feliciano and came to be known as the Feliciano Commission or FelCom.

5 See Glenda Gloria, *We Were Soldiers: Military Men in Politics and the Bureaucracy* (Makati City: Friedrich Ebert Stiftung, 2003). Gloria documented the appointments of retired military officers to high-ranking positions in the executive department, including the Cabinet, by former Presidents Corazon C. Aquino, Fidel V. Ramos, and Joseph Ejercito Estrada, as well as by President Gloria Macapagal Arroyo.

6 See *The Final Report of the Fact-Finding Commission that Investigated the Failed Coup of December 1989* (Makati: Bookmark Publishers, 1990), henceforth *The Final Report* on the process of politicization. The commission was headed by Hilario G. Davide, Jr., who later became Chief Justice of the Philippines. The commission came to be known as the Davide Commission.

7 The term is from Muthiah Alagappa, editor, *Coercion in Governance: The Declining Political Role of the Military in Asia* (Stanford: Stanford University Press, 2001).

8 Gretchen Casper, *Fragile Democracies: the Lessons of Authoritarian Rule* (Pittsburgh: University of Pittsburgh Press, 1995).

9 "People power" refers to the extra-constitutional replacement of an incumbent president through massive street demonstrations leading to the erosion or loss of popular legitimacy of the incumbent culminating in his ouster. It is usually non-violent.

10 Reform the Armed Forces of the Philippines Movement (RAM) grew from the disquiet of young officers about the decline of professionalism caused by martial law practices that affected the military.

11 Lim and Querubin were among the leaders of the Young Officers Union (YOU) which took over the Makati business district in December 1989. They were granted unconditional amnesty by Ramos, returned to the AFP, and became respected officers.

12 Joaquin G. Bernas, S.J., *The 1987 Constitution of the Philippines: A Commentary* (Quezon City: Rex Printing Company, Inc., 2003 edition).

13 Magdalo refers to the leaders of the July 2003 Oakwood Mutiny, a term taken from a faction of the *Katipunan* that revolted against Spanish colonial rule in 1896.

14 See *The Final Report.*

15 *The FelCom Report,* p. 15.

16 Carolina G. Hernandez, "Towards Understanding Coups and Civil-Military Relations in the Philippines", *Kasarinlan-Philippine Quarterly of Third World Studies* 3, no. 2 (1987): 19–22.

17 *The FelCom Report.*

18 Carolina G. Hernandez and Cecilia T. Ubarra, *Restoring and Strengthening Civilian Control: Best Practices in Civil-Military Relations in the Philippines* (Quezon City: Institute for Strategic and Development Studies, 1999).

19 Parenthetically, Honasan was one of the two major figures of the breakaway group in February 1986 that got elected to the Senate during the Ramos incumbency. While senator, he did not initiate legislation to effect the elements of his NRP.

20 *The FelCom Report.*

21 Ibid., pp. 146–47.

22 The Fort Bonifacio lands are public lands which cannot be alienated to private persons without a presidential proclamation. Neither of the two contested areas is covered by such a proclamation.

23 For further details, see "Update on the Implementation of the Feliciano Commission Recommendations", 20 November 2006.

24 For a discussion of these reforms, see Carolina G. Hernandez, "The Politics of Defence and Military Reforms in the Philippines", *OSS Digest*, Armed Forces of the Philippines, First Quarter 2005: 4–9.

25 Carolina G. Hernandez, "Institutional Responses to Armed Conflict: The Armed Forces of the Philippines", a background paper for the *Philippine Human Development Report 2005: Peace, Human Security and Human Development in the Philippines* (Manila: Human Development Network, 2005).

26 This framework of the three positions is from Paul Oquist, "Mindanao and Beyond: Competing Policies, Protracted Conflict, and Human Security", Fifth Assessment Mission Report, Multi-Donor Group Support for Peace and Development in Mindanao, 23 September 2002.

27 Ibid.

28 This bonding, earlier explained in the Davide Commission Report is further illustrated in Alfred McCoy, *Closer than Brothers: Manhood at the Philippine Military Academy* (Manila: Anvil Publishing, 1999).

29 One of the comments this author received upon the resignation of Defence Secretary Cruz is a telling commentary of the military mentality. Talking about Cruz, an officer said, "Until he came along we have not had for a long while a defence secretary without an upper-class mentality."

30 Carolina G. Hernandez, "Reflections on the Role of the Military in People Power 2", in Amando Doronila, editor, *Between Fires: Fifteen Perspectives on the Estrada Crisis* (Makati City: Anvil Press and *Philippine Daily Inquirer*, 2001), 67–77.

31 Carolina G. Hernandez, "The Military and Constitutional Change: Problems and Prospects in a Redemocratized Philippines", *Public Policy* 11 (1997): 42–61, and Gloria, *We Were Soldiers.*

32 *Philippine Human Development Report 2005.*

33 Marites D. Vitug, "The Folly of February: It Was Like a Shadow Play", *Newsbreak*, 27 March 2006.

5

RELIGION AND POLITICS: A LOOK AT THE PHILIPPINE EXPERIENCE

Grace Gorospe-Jamon and
Mary Grace P. Mirandilla

In a world where economic growth is an obsession and politics more intractable than ever, the study of religion and its place in the lives of people is both fascinating and challenging. Contrary to the thinking that modernity weakens it, religion remains enmeshed in the complex fabric of human societies. Samuel Huntington, for example, cites a "global religious resurgence" happening during the second half of the twentieth century, involving people returning to, reinvigorating, and giving new meaning to the traditional religions of their communities.[1] This revivalism has created a huge impact on the development of selected nations.

For the past several decades, scholars have been enamored with how religion — its system of beliefs, principles, and doctrines, including norms, values and practices[2] — relates to the modernization of different societies. Robert Bellah, in his discussion of Asian modernization, for instance, examines the influence of cultural traditions, including religion, in building the modern nation-state.[3] This is complemented by Peter Berger's analysis of religion and secularity. Pointing to a phenomenon of Asian religiosity, Berger talks about how culture has contributed to defining and molding Asia's own brand of modernity.[4] The transformation of Confucianism from being an imperial state ideology to an everyday ethic of working people is the most widely celebrated example of this phenomenon. Complementary contrasts also exist within this Asian religiosity. For instance, while Indian Buddhism practices a "concomitant deprecation of all worldly activity, including economic activity", Chinese Buddhism rejects this "world-denying" creed and favours a "world-affirming" doctrine. In contemporary Japanese religions, meanwhile, "pragmatic, even technical, this-worldliness" is emphasized and the individual is encouraged to strive for personal success.[5]

Gilles Kepel, meanwhile, points to the resurgence of the great religions of Islam, Christianity and Judaism in the modern world. In his study, he observes that a new religious approach has taken shape, aimed no longer at adapting to secular values but at recovering a sacred foundation for the organization of society, by changing it if necessary.[6]

Indeed, religion has imprinted its influence on different facets of human society.[7] One of the most relevant discussions looks at religion and its effect on politics. Studies on the multi-dimensional aspect of religion and its impact on political action lend insights into the nature and role of political socialization in a religious context.[8] Kenneth Wald, for instance, considers religion as an important political resource. He regards religiously-based resources as "qualities possessed by religiously motivated people that can prove valuable in political action".[9] Religious motivation may either encourage political activism by fostering personal and group efficacy or stimulate action through morally perceived political issues. This is seen as likely to occur when political issues are articulated in moral terms, mobilizing religiously motivated actors or candidates for or against issues that promote a moral perspective.[10]

In countries all over the world, churches and religious groups have been found to be important instruments or agents of political socialization, as they infuse religious beliefs and values that affect individuals and groups on a daily basis in various aspects of their lives, including political actions as in elections and expressions of public opinion.[11] The Philippines is one illustrative case where religion plays an influential role in politics. One needs only to go back to 1986 when a powerful authoritarian leader, President Ferdinand Marcos, who had ruled the country for nearly twenty years, was toppled by a "people power" revolution waged on EDSA,[12] where Filipinos showed power fused with the Christian notion of altruism … "power not for personal advantage alone, but for the common good."[13]

It is in this milieu that this chapter will discuss religion — its influence and impact on Philippine politics. In the process, it will survey the prominent religious groups and their influence on the country's volatile political life. It will analyse within a religious context the key political events and players who define, motivate, and shape politics in the Philippines. Although recognizing the diversity of religions in the country, the discussion will concentrate on the dominant Christian groups and their role in Philippine politics and society.

RELIGION IN THE PHILIPPINES: SOME HISTORICAL NOTES

History is witness to how religion shapes a nation. This is especially true of a country such as the Philippines. Embedded in the Philippines' history as a nation is the impact of religion in shaping Filipino identity. Over 400 years of Western colonial rule impinged on the full development of an indigenous culture and a burgeoning native spirituality.

Before the arrival of the first Western colonizers in the sixteenth century, the indigenous peoples of the Philippines held belief systems based on "animism" and ancestor worship. The "*babaylan*" (priestess) served as a religious leader. She was believed to have the power to heal and predict good planting and harvest seasons. Religious practices then were closely related to nature, with rituals performed in forests and animal sacrifices made to "*anitos*" (spirits of ancestors) that were thought to be present in both the mortal and spirit worlds. With the powers attributed to her, the babaylan had great influence over community life.[14]

Islam, a religion shared by several Asian countries, made its way to the Philippines through Arab merchants and Islamic missionaries who navigated to the Sulu archipelago, Mindanao and the Visayas sometime in the thirteenth century. The Muslim communities were well established in sultanates, which served as political institutions. However, they considerably weakened towards the close of the nineteenth century due to the intermittent wars these communities fought against the Western colonizers.[15] All throughout the colonial period, Islam struggled to survive.

Christianity, the religion brought by the Western colonizers — first by Spain, then by America — has shaped the modern Filipino identity and is now its major defining element. Recognizing the importance of religion, the Christian missionaries — the Spanish friars (1521 to 1898) and the American Protestant pastors (1898 to 1946) — usurped the role of the *babaylan* and destroyed the sultanates. In this endeavour, the Roman Catholic and Protestant churches helped in legitimizing the political control of the colonizing powers and of the dominant Filipino political elites.[16]

The Spanish colonizers, through the friars, preached and spread the Catholic faith. The foundation of the Spanish *conquista* was the "civilizing and Christianizing of pagan lands". During this period, religious interventions in political matters operated under the principle of the "union of church and state". Encroaching on the jurisdictions of the civil government, and often, inflicting abuse and oppression, the Catholic friars nonetheless provided stability and continuity to Spanish sovereignty in the Philippines. It was during this period that Filipino revolutionaries found a way to use religion and its language, as in millenarian movements and many peasant revolts, to free the country from colonial rule.[17] This experience led to the contrary principle of "separation of church and state" as one of the defining provisions in the constitution of the first Philippine Republic.[18]

Following Spanish rule, the Americans came in 1898 armed with the mission to "Christianize and democratize" the Philippines. The American colonial period introduced another form of Christianity — *Protestantism.*[19] Using education as a socialization tool, the Americans instilled their way of life and faith in Filipinos already formed more or less by over three centuries of Spanish colonization. The first wave of American educators/teachers who arrived in the Philippines was Protestant; in fact, many of them were Protestant ministers. They laid the groundwork for Protestant churches in many lowland barrios while instituting a public education system and exerting a strong influence on the government administration.[20] In 1899, a number of Protestant missions moved into the country with the plan to strategically evangelize the islands. The early missionaries met in Manila in April 1901 to organize the Evangelical Union and to choose a common name for all Protestant churches — Iglesia Evangelica (Evangelical Church).[21]

The colonial period gave rise to a number of indigenous Christian religious groups that thrived amid armed struggles and have survived to this day.

In August 1902, Gregorio Aglipay, an activist priest from Ilocos Norte, and Isabelo de los Reyes, head of the General Council of the Union, formed the Iglesia Filipina Independiente (IFI) or Philippine Independent Church. More popularly known as the Aglipayan Church, it was established as a reaction to Spanish oppression and the desire to free the Catholic Church from friar abuse and corruption.[22] It deposed and arrested Spanish bishops, and sequestered church property as a result. It rejected the spiritual authority of the Pope and abolished the celibacy requirement for its clergy. In the early part of the twentieth century, the number of Aglipayans soared to around 25 to 33 per cent of the population, then significantly declined through the years. They are associated with the Protestant Episcopal Church of the United States.[23]

More than a decade after the IFI was formed, another indigenous church was born — the Iglesia ni Cristo (INC). Established by Felix Manalo in 1914, the INC has to this day remained politically influential because of its growing membership, resources and political clout. In the 1950s, the INC was said to be recruiting from 10,000 to 15,000 converts annually. In the 1990 Census of Population and Housing, INC members were estimated at 1.4 million, three times its size in 1970. The INC continued to grow, with its membership spreading to overseas Filipinos and churches built in sixty-six countries in North America, Asia, Europe, Australia and Oceania, and Africa.[24]

RELIGIOUS INSTITUTIONS: CRITICAL OBSERVERS AND STRATEGIC PLAYERS IN PHILIPPINE POLITICS?

Being a central piece of the country's long colonial history, religion has become an important part of Filipino life. Filipinos consider themselves a religious people.[25] Almost everyone belongs to a religious group, denomination or movement or submits to some form of belief system.

According to the 2000 Census of the National Statistics Office and approximations of other surveys, around 81 per cent of all Filipinos were Roman Catholic. An estimated 5 per cent were Muslims while 3 per cent were Evangelicals. Around 2 per cent were members of INC and another 2 per cent were Aglipayan. Other Christian sects comprised 5 per cent, while the remaining 2 per cent represented other minority religions such as Buddhism, Hinduism and Mormons.[26]

The Roman Catholic Church is the largest religious institution in the Philippines. Precisely because of its size, vast network and resources, the Catholic Church is a potent tool for political socialization and mobilization.

Speaking in 1992, Roman Catholic Bishop Teodoro Bacani pointed to the huge number of parishes, schools, social action and charity networks, and the media as the tools that enable the Church to reach out to its members in every barrio and town of the Philippines.[27]

As of 2005, according to the Catholic Church hierarchy in the Philippines, 69 million or 81 per cent of the country's 85 million estimated total population considered themselves Roman Catholic. In spite of the mushrooming of many Christian sects, the country's Catholic Church is stronger than ever. In Manila alone, there are over 1,700 Catholic parishes, perhaps one of the densest concentrations in the world. And if proximity means anything, there are three major Catholic churches near Malacañang, the country's seat of political power.[28]

Given its pervasiveness in everyday Filipino life, the Catholic Church has consistently earned the trust of Filipinos relative to other institutions. A nationwide survey conducted in 1998 revealed that Filipinos expressed greater confidence in both the church and the schools than in political institutions

TABLE 5.1
Philippine Catholic Statistics

	*1992**	*2005***
Total Population	65 million	85 million
Catholics	55 million (83 per cent of total population)	69 million (81 per cent of total population)
Dioceses	78	85
Parishes	2,200	2,713
Schools	2,300	—
Priests	–	Over 6,700
Manila	–	Over 1,700 parishes

Sources: * Bishop Teodoro Bacani (1992) cited in Alan C. Robles, "The Politics of Sin," *Manila Chronicle*, February 29-March 6, 1992, p. 5.
** <http://www.catholic-hierarchy.org/country/spcph1.html>.

like the courts and Congress.[29] It is no surprise, then, that Filipinos have continued to look to the Church for moral guidance and credibility on a wide range of issues.

Furthermore, the Catholic Church in the Philippines controls a number of organizations and satellite groups under its leadership. Two of the most prominent Church-controlled organizations that have historically been politically influential are the Catholic Bishops Conference of the Philippines (CBCP) and the Association of Major Religious Superiors in the Philippines (AMRSP). These two are widely viewed as "critical observers" of Philippine politics. The Catholic Church opinion is voiced through the position statements and pastoral letters issued by the CBCP and AMRSP on a wide range of issues — human rights violations, population policy, land disputes, constitutional change, environmental degradation — that are disseminated directly to the faithful mostly through Sunday homilies.[30] The CBCP has 95 active member bishops, who serve as moral critics of Philippine society, and 24 honorary members. It manages over 80 ecclesiastical jurisdictions, including 16 archdioceses, 56 dioceses, 7 vicariates, 5 prelatures, and 1 military ordinariate.[31] It also uses various media, including a website and an online magazine. The AMRSP, on the other hand, represents 195 Catholic congregations for religious women and 93 for men, the more prominent being the Dominicans, the Franciscans, the Benedictines, the Jesuits, the Augustinians, the Salesians, the Lasallians and the Marists. It created a special organization, the Justice, Peace and Integrity of Creation Commission, acknowledged for its balanced and objective appraisal of the country's peace and order situation.

The role of religious orders in educational institutions is important not only in making political critique but also in the formation of moral and sociopolitical values in everyday life. The Jesuits, for example, are known for their extensive use of their educational ministry to carry out the mission of the Society of Jesus, a religious order of the Roman Catholic Church founded in the sixteenth century. From over 20,000 members worldwide, 307 are Jesuits in the Philippines (224 priests, 67 scholastics, 16 brothers). The Jesuits run five universities,[32] three major basic-education schools,[33] and several technical and research schools in the direct service of the poor,[34] considered a platform for their social and pastoral apostolates. Through these schools, the Jesuits operate various social ministries and created a network or social organizations that critique society and "conscienticize" and empower people for social change.[35] These schools have afforded the Jesuits a vehicle to preach their ideology as well as the presence and credibility necessary to influence society at large through their alumni. Anecdotal evidence suggests that the alumni of certain Jesuit schools have formed a virtual fraternity in key political institutions that affects policy and political decisions in one way or another.

Another Catholic organization, the Opus Dei (Latin for "God's Work"), is known for its focus on shaping the spiritual values of its members and strictly applying them in their lives. Its origins date back to 1928 when Jose Maria Escriva, a Spanish priest, developed a new vision of Catholic spirituality for a movement of pious laypeople to devote time for prayerful contemplation and to extend holiness to their everyday work lives. The organization gained such strong support from Pope John Paul II that Escriva was canonized less than twenty years after his death. Opus Dei takes an active role in working for church-backed causes. It now has over 84,000 members from every continent,[36] most of them lay people and many well-educated professionals.

However, not much is known about Opus Dei's activities due to its secretive nature. This has caused the group to be painted unflatteringly as a clandestine society. There is a strong impression of the group's involvement in politics, stemming from the participation of some prominent Opus Dei members in Spain's dictatorial regime in the 1950s. Its emphasis on the value of work converted into a "divine occupation" continues to attract many professional and influential members from the government and business sector, a trait that has created for it an elitist reputation. To dispel speculations, U.S. Opus Dei vicar Thomas Bohlin explains that Opus is just a teaching entity, a kind of advanced school for Catholic spiritual formation.[37] In the Philippines, that can be observed in the group's active involvement in running schools, such as the Woodrose School for girls, Southridge School for boys, and the University of Asia and the Pacific. While its influence in Rome is apparent (as it was given the status of "personal prelature", meaning direct access to the Pope), Opus Dei's role in Philippine society and politics can only be attributed indirectly to its members holding important positions in government. One of them, Dr Jesus Estanislao, a noted economist and finance secretary in the Corazon Aquino administration, is credited with bringing Opus Dei into the Philippines and spreading it in Asia.[38]

The Protestant Church is also a key player in Philippine politics by virtue of its size and resources. A recent study showed that there were over 50,000 evangelical and Protestant churches in the country accounting for 9 per cent of the population.[39] Actively involved in the sociopolitical and economic fields through the work of its faith-based organizations, they have become prominent and passionate advocates in the areas of governance and development. Their contributions go down to the community level, some through humanitarian assistance and grassroots community organizing, using their network of local churches as venues for their work.

The Protestant churches are organized under two big umbrella organizations — the National Council of Churches in the Philippines (NCCP) and the Philippine Council of Evangelical Churches (PCEC). The NCCP claims a membership of more than 13 million evangelical churchgoers although national statistics give a much lower figure. The United Church of Christ in the Philippines, the nationalized United Methodist Church, is one of its most prominent members. The PCEC, on the other hand, claims a membership of 20 bishops and more than 500 pastors from Evangelical churches nationwide. It is said to be the largest group of Evangelical churches in the country, counting 65 denominations, 132 mission organizations and over 20,000 local churches among its members.[40] Of these two umbrella organizations, the NCCP assumed historically a more progressive stance on socio-political issues much like the Catholic Church during martial law, while the PCEC took a more conservative position except for a few progressive evangelicals under the leadership of the Institute for Studies in Asian Church and Culture.[41]

The Protestant Church's influence on Philippine politics, however, is not as solid as that of the Catholic Church due to its less hierarchical and more democratic and congregational culture. The current significance and importance accorded to Protestant evangelical groups is manifest in a number of ways, one being their membership in the Presidential Council on Moral

Values of the Arroyo administration, formed in a bid to promote moral values in all sectors of society. Another is the appointment of the Secretary General of the PCEC himself, Bishop Efraim Tendero, as a member of the 2005 Consultative Commission, which is tasked to review and propose amendments to the 1987 Philippine Constitution.

The Catholic and Protestant churches used to be passive observers, conservative in their views of their role in society. But the height of activism during the 1970s and the church's reflection of the Third World's situation awakened an awareness of a "preferential option for the poor", systematized into a "theology of liberation", which has had a profound impact not just on young seminarians, religious, and students, but also on church leadership.[42] This means working with, learning from, and sharing the needs and struggles of the poor.[43]

The Second Vatican Council, or Vatican II, opened the doors of an otherwise rigid Catholic institution as it tried a different approach to both liturgy and theology. The post-Vatican II years saw the growth of non-government organizations, people's organizations, and other movements such as civic groups and religious organizations, a phenomenon intensified by the social, political and economic uncertainties during the martial law period.[44] The emergence of the Roman Catholic Renewal Movement followed by "born again" Protestant groups or new religious movements gave birth to a number of charismatic groups. With their extensive use of prayer rallies, ministries, and new media, these charismatic groups served to strengthen religious institutions in terms of both number and degree of influence.

The past few decades witnessed how the Pentecostal[45] and Evangelical churches flourished in the country, with the Catholic Charismatic groups (the "Pentecostal" Catholics) showing the most striking growth. Two of the biggest Catholic charismatic lay organizations — the El Shaddai Prayer Movement and the Couples for Christ — together claim to have three million registered members each. The Catholic Church has benefited greatly from the development and work of these groups. Not only do they provide the church with more active followers, they enhance its standing as a credible institution to give moral guidance and its influence in society. Because of their populist character, these new organizations have had some significant successes in fostering the growth of Christianity in Asia.[46]

The El Shaddai Movement is a Catholic charismatic group founded in 1984 by Mike Velarde. An otherwise unremarkable man, Velarde as a spiritual leader has the charisma and style that seem to appeal to the religious imagination of the Filipinos. Claiming a constituency of approximately ten million members worldwide to date, El Shaddai is considered a potent tool for political socialization. This it has accomplished in various milieus, mediated by the leadership of Velarde and the movement's powerful use of media such as newsletters, radio programmes, and televised weekly mass and healing rallies attended by an average of 500,000 to a million people.[47] The El Shaddai movement has figured prominently as one of the most important and significant power blocs in Philippine politics today, particularly during elections. Government and politicians — even the Catholic Church itself — actively solicit its support on various advocacies and agendas.

In recognition of El Shaddai's potential, politicians always seek Velarde's approval and support. No less than deposed President Joseph Estrada considered Velarde as "more influential than Cardinal Sin",[48] and, accordingly, named him his spiritual adviser. Velarde in turn, gave his full support to Estrada, using his prayer rallies and radio programmes as occasions to echo Estrada's policies and praise his projects. This support went so far as to mobilize El Shaddai members to join the mass protest launched by Estrada supporters against the newly installed Arroyo administration in January 2001. When violence erupted, Velarde played a key role in pacifying both the crowd and the authorities. In August 2005, in a bid to broker reconciliation, Velarde managed to have Estrada temporarily released from prison so he could attend Velarde's birthday party, to which Arroyo was also invited. The two political opponents accepted his invitation, although they did not come face to face with each other.

El Shaddai has become a truly formidable religious organization. Its members continue to grow exponentially through the years. Concomitant to this, El Shaddai builds its financial resources from the "love offerings" or tithes of its followers. Growing financial strength and membership can only mean independence but the Catholic hierarchy has always kept a check on El Shaddai, requiring Velarde to make public avowals of his loyalty.

The Couples for Christ, on the other hand, is a Catholic organization dedicated to the renewal and strengthening of Christian family life. It is popularly known for *Gawad Kalinga* (to give care), a multi-sectoral partnership project engaged in activities that aim to build integrated, holistic, and sustainable communities starting with depressed areas throughout the Philippines, and to rebuild the nation through faith and patriotism.[49] *Gawad Kalinga* (GK) gained popularity for its efforts to build "communities of homeowners" among the poor. By mobilizing volunteers and partners from the government, business, socio-civic groups, churches and parishes, media, and academe, *Gawad Kalinga* has managed, as of January 2005,[50] to develop over 400 GK communities in Metro Manila and in 50 provinces nationwide, building a total of 1,500 houses. It has also constructed 200 houses for both Christians and Muslims in Mindanao. GK plans to enlarge its vision through GK777, which aims to build 700,000 houses in seven years.

A phenomenon like El Shaddai occurred among Protestant churches. Two prominent charismatic groups — the Jesus is Lord (JIL) Fellowship and the Jesus Miracle Crusade — have both gained prominence over the years due to their growing resources and number of followers.

The JIL is a fellowship movement established in 1978 by Eddie Villanueva. From a handful of students of Villanueva's, the JIL has grown to become the country's biggest "born again" or Pentecostal group. According to the Evangelical Encyclopedia, the JIL is the fourth largest Pentecostal church in the world.[51] Given the size of its membership and its skillful use of media for evangelizing, the JIL has become a serious subject of courting by politicians. The political importance of JIL reached its peak when Villanueva ran for the presidency in the 2004 elections under the *Bangon Pilipinas* ("Rise Philippines") Movement, with the restoration of righteousness and morality in government as his banner agenda.[52] Villanueva's candidacy united an otherwise apolitical and conservative Protestant evangelical community and even gained the support of a number of Muslim groups advocating peace.

The Jesus Miracle Crusade, on the other hand, is one of the largest apostolic churches based in the Philippines. Wilde Almeda, an evangelist pastor, and his wife, Lina Almeda, also a pastor, founded the group. Not new to political campaigning, Almeda's group is also wooed by politicians for support during elections. It is present in forty-five provinces and has chapters in the United States and China. The crusade gained prominence in 2000 when it sent representatives to preach the word of God to the Abu Sayaff, an armed Muslim rebel group that gained prominence by kidnapping twenty-one foreigners in Basilan, an island in Southern Philippines.

RELIGION AS RESOURCE: POTENTIAL FOR POLITICAL MOBILIZATION

Religion can motivate and mobilize the faithful towards a political goal. Some studies on African-American religion, for example, show that the organizational aspect of religion is ideal for mobilizing groups and individuals in shaping political goals. The church provides the leadership base, social interaction and communication networks required by collective action.[53] In a democratic context, studies have also illustrated that certain forms of religious behaviour, church activities and organizational skills can serve as resources for political activism.[54]

With its resources, credibility, and renewed awareness combined, the Catholic Church in the Philippines can easily reach out to its members and mobilize them almost instantaneously, when necessary. It has demonstrated this in regime changes — making or unmaking leaders — for the past two decades. It has also used its influence to shape state policies, political opinion, and decisions on matters of national interest.

The martial law period (1972–86) and the years leading to the overthrow of Marcos heightened the church's awareness of its necessary role and its position of leadership in the sociopolitical field.[55] Although the initial reaction of church leaders to martial rule was generally positive — recognizing the right of civil authorities to protect the state's sovereignty — the CBCP, as well as the NCCP, became critical of Marcos when martial rule turned into a pretext for rampant human rights violations, which included church people as victims.[56] The military repressed and attacked members of the clergy and lay workers assisting poor farmers, minority tribesmen, and wage earners. This was viewed as part of a broader pattern of military actions directed against institutions suspected of engaging in subversive activities. The military harassed and detained church personnel; it staged major armed assaults against Catholic and Protestant church institutions; it destabilized programmes perceived to be inimical to government interests. There were at least twenty-two major military raids between 1972 and 1984,[57] but it was not until the raids conducted against the NCCP and the Sacred Heart Novitiate in 1974 that powerful members of the Catholic hierarchy began to speak out sharply against the Marcos regime.

When Marcos announced snap elections in 1986, the CBCP, in an unprecedented move, issued pastoral statements promoting voting rights while condemning pre-electoral crimes.[58] But the real litmus test for the Catholic Church's political influence came when, in February 1986, the powerful CBCP leader Archbishop of Manila Jaime Cardinal Sin made an appeal over the church-owned Radio Veritas for people to assemble at EDSA and protest against an oppressive government that was slowly losing its allies.[59] Within a few hours, hundreds of thousands of Filipinos had massed at EDSA calling for the overthrow of Marcos. This came to be known as the EDSA 1 "people power" revolution.[60] After days of peaceful protests and prayer vigils, Marcos fled the country. Corazon Aquino, widow of assassinated opposition leader Benigno Aquino, was declared the duly-elected president of the nation.

This new political activism of the Catholic Church was consolidated in the early part of 1991 in the Second Plenary Council of the Philippines (PCP-II).[61] The most important agreement reached in the PCP-II was: the church and state were to be considered "autonomous and independent", but the Catholic Church would assume the position of "critical solidarity" *vis-à-vis* the government, which meant it would continue to judiciously analyse the actions of the state without undermining its power. More concretely, the PCP-II led to the establishment of the Parish Pastoral Council for Responsible Voting (PPCRV) initially in the Archdiocese of Manila and, immediately after this, in all the seventy-six Catholic dioceses in the country. The mission of the PPCRV was to help the electorate assess the worthiness of political candidates and conduct voter education campaigns throughout the country in time for the 1992 presidential elections.[62]

The government itself recognized the strong influence and vast resources of the church, acknowledging, perhaps reluctantly, that only the church had the "stature and organizational muscle that could resist traditional politics".[63] In one instance, the government sought the help of the CBCP, the UCCP, Philippine Independent Church and other churches to use the sermons and regular meetings as opportunities and venues to discuss the "moral necessity of clean, orderly and honest elections" and the "moral duty of voters to use their right to vote responsibly".[64] And knowing that the majority of voters are members of religious institutions who attend church gatherings regularly, the Commission on Elections, the government body charged with the responsibility of conducting clear and orderly elections, also asked the church for assistance in disseminating voter education materials.[65]

The Iglesia ni Cristo (INC) is another religious group that has gained political significance due to its resources and the strong influence that it wields on its two million members. A home-grown Christian sect founded by Felix Manalo in 1914, the INC has a rigid organizational structure and strict policies that oblige members to vote as a bloc during elections.[66] Sensing the potential of the INC to significantly shape election results, Marcos gave his all-out support to the INC, helping expand its membership and paying regular visits to the INC leader. Thus, unlike the Catholic and Protestant churches, the INC supported Marcos throughout his regime. The INC openly endorses candidates for political office during elections — a practice that is also prevalent in Catholic Church organizations and in other religious groups. In the 1998 election, the INC supported Estrada and defended him up until after his ouster, with members even joining the crowd that marched to Malacañang during EDSA 3, in an attempt to emulate the previous people power rebellions. Even then, despite the failure of Estrada to recover his presidency, the INC managed to show that it knew how to pay a debt of gratitude, sticking with Estrada to the bitter end. Recognizing this, current

Philippine president Gloria Macapagal-Arroyo wooed the INC assiduously and won its support during the 2004 elections.[67]

RELIGION'S INFLUENCE IN REGIME CHANGE AND LEGITIMATION

During the country's transition to democracy, the Catholic Church intensified its vigilance and provided guidance to the government, especially during the presidency (1987–92) of Corazon Aquino who owed the Catholic Church her rise to power. During the term (1992–98) of President Fidel Ramos, the Philippines' first Protestant President, however, the country witnessed a more critical church that scrutinized almost all government policies, such as population control and charter change, for their supposed questionable morality. Although careful not to point to the president's religion, the Catholic Church excoriated the Ramos administration for policies contrary to church teachings, often putting on shows of force in church-organized public rallies.

It was this same tactic that was applied by the Catholic Church to rally Catholics in 2001 to support EDSA 2, the people power rebellion that cut short the six-year term of President Estrada to less than three years, 1998 to 2001. An actor-turned-politician and a president with a penchant for demagoguery, Estrada earned the ire of the Catholic Church for what it perceived as a serious character flaw — his continued gambling and womanizing. However, it was the corruption charges and the perceived partiality of his impeachment trial that pushed the Catholic Church to support mass rallies and to call for his resignation. Estrada, according to the Catholic Church, did not have the "moral ascendancy" to lead the nation.

Religious institutions continue to be vigilant observers of Philippine politics and sharp critics of government officials under the current administration of President Arroyo. Their role is again heightened at this critical juncture in the country's politics as Arroyo's administration struggles to maintain its legitimacy. Given recent positions and statements made by the church and other religious institutions on current political issues hounding Arroyo, the current administration is now confronted with increasing pressures to change. This period is witnessing the changing position of church groups towards the Arroyo regime and its policies — from relative caution to increasing militancy.

Beginning with the so-called "Gloriagate" scandal, in which Arroyo was directly implicated in election fraud on the basis of alleged recorded conversations between her and an election commissioner, quite a number of mass protests have been mounted calling for her resignation. While the CBCP does not support extra-constitutional means to oust the president, a position that the Arroyo administration hails as a strategic victory, it issued a pastoral statement in January 2006 calling for the "relentless" pursuit of the truth about the allegations against her.[68] It also criticized the Arroyo administration for blocking efforts to investigate the case when her dominant allies in the House of Representatives dismissed an impeachment motion over charges that she rigged the presidential elections of 2004. The same charges are now being renewed along with additional claims that she had engaged in the systematic killing of journalists and activists.

The issue of the separation of church and state has been raised once again by the government against the church, now that one of CBCP's members, Bishop Deogracias Iñiguez, signed a new impeachment complaint. The government was quick to ask the CBCP to sanction the bishop for his disregard of the principle of separation of church and state. The CBCP, however, issued a two-page statement asserting that the action of the bishop, although based on his personal opinion, was nonetheless valid and in line with the teachings of the church. CBCP President Archbishop Angel Lagdameo further explained: "Concretely, the bishops, clergy and laity must be involved in the area of politics when moral and gospel values are at stake."[69]

But the seemingly staunch support of CBCP's prominent members was not reflected in its much awaited 10 July 2005 Pastoral Letter, which many considered as a defining factor as a new round of impeachment proceedings approached. The letter, some critics observed, was ambiguous and lacked the expected sharp rebuke to the president. Described as "a masterpiece of ecclesiastical hedging and equivocation",[70] the CBCP's decision to take a safer official stand seemed to have dampened hopes of putting the pro-impeachment campaign to a higher level. In contrast to the impeachment case of Estrada, which had the backing of the Catholic Church through Cardinal Sin, it is not surprising if the impeachment campaign against Arroyo would find a less interested audience because of a missing piece — an openly critical influential institution in which Filipinos have the highest confidence and which can provide the critical element in amassing enough enthusiasm and support for a legitimate democratic process.

Related to this, church groups are also wary of Arroyo's efforts to revise the constitution *via* a "people's initiative", a signature campaign for charter change. The current move is pushing for a shift to a parliamentary form of government and the removal of limits to foreign ownership of and investment in certain economic sectors. Using its social action centres to evaluate the "process" being undertaken to push for charter change, the CBCP has warned against the haste with which Malacañang is pursuing the campaign. In a pastoral letter issued in April 2006, the CBCP assailed the initiative's lack of "widespread participation, total transparency, and relative serenity" that it deems necessary for rational discussion and debate. The political mobilization potential of the Catholic Church is so widely recognized that various sectors including the Senate and some activist groups have asked church leaders for help by opening their parishes all over the country for people's organizations conducting an anti-charter change campaign.[71]

There are issues in the proposed constitutional amendments other than the change in the form of government. The Catholic Church is also against the proposed charter change due to its strong opposition to lifting the moratorium on mining, an industry that the government reports to be worth US$840 billion. In a strongly worded statement, the CBCP has called for the repeal of the Philippine Mining Act of 1995 as it undermines the constitutional prohibition on foreign exploitation of mineral resources through financial-technical assistance agreements (FTAA) and destroys life by allowing the interests of big mining corporations to prevail over people's rights.[72] Although opponents of mining successfully lobbied the Supreme Court in 2004 to declare the unconstitutionality of a FTAA with a subsidiary of an Australian mining company, the court reversed itself a year after and upheld the constitutionality of the Mining Act.

Velarde has also boldly committed the entire El Shaddai organization to oppose the signature campaign. He has since been a rallying figure for lay efforts from both Catholic and Protestant communities to oppose the campaign, in response to the CBCP's invitation for creative engagement and principled opposition to the initiative.[73] The INC also quietly supports El Shaddai's position on people's initiative being pushed by the current administration.[74]

More alarming to many religious groups is Arroyo's employment of strong-arm tactics to silence anti-government protests and to destroy leftist movements in the style of Marcos.[75] The Catholic Church and other churches have openly and bitterly criticized the Arroyo administration, expressing grave concern over the spate of recent murders, which included non-combatants and church people as victims. According to the latest statistics, there have been 690 political killings since 2001, almost half the number of recorded killings during the fourteen-year martial law period.[76] This has prompted the Catholic leadership to change its tone, with the CBCP now taking Arroyo to task, calling the "legitimacy question" of her presidency as the root cause or the "original sin" that begets national disunity. The NCCP has likewise demanded that Arroyo step down and assailed her for attacks on civil liberties and intensified political repression.[77]

Despite these calls and as if to taunt her critics, Arroyo allotted P1 billion (about US$20 million) to supplement the budget of the Armed Forces of the Philippines and the Philippine National Police so that they could wage a more effective and efficient war against leftist groups and finally bring down the insurgency movement in the shortest possible time. A disturbing exposé on the Arroyo administration's *Oplan Bantay Laya* (Operation Freedom Watch), the counter-insurgency program of the AFP, revealed that even media groups such as the Philippine Center for Investigative Journalism and religious organizations such as the CBCP and the AMRSP were identified as "sectoral front organizations" and were, therefore, subject to neutralization.[78] This development is seen now by many sectors, including the religious, as a sign of the government's increasing militarization and disregard of human rights.

Recent hostilities against suspected anti-establishment entities have resulted in the gradual radicalization of different church groups in order to protect human rights victims. The AMRSP, for example, has revived its sanctuary programme for real and potential victims of abuse and injustice. According to Max de Mesa, chairman of the Philippine Alliance of Human Rights Advocates (PAHRA), the programme also aims to assist those who are at risk of becoming the next victims of the killings. The AMRSP, a militant religious organization that dates back to the Marcos years, has expressed alarm over the killing of Filipino activists, journalists and church workers, calling the murder clear manifestations of "a culture of fear and death" in Asia's largest Roman Catholic country and at a time when the death penalty law has been abolished. The agreement of the Ecumenical Bishops Forum "to open the doors of the church to those who seek refuge for various political reasons" has also been revived, according to Rev. Fr. Zaldy M. Fababaer of the Cathedral of the Iglesia Filipina Independiente.[79]

The church's heightened activism can be observed in many areas as well. In the fight against illegal gambling, for example, the CBCP has intensified its campaign against "jueteng," a popular numbers game found in many provinces all over the country. Archbishop Oscar Cruz, leader of the *Krusadang Bayan Laban sa Jueteng* (National Crusade Against Jueteng), criticizes the government for dilly-dallying and accuses it of tolerating gambling for its own gains.[80] The Catholic Church is also a strong advocate of protection of the environment, campaigning hard against illegal logging, the cause of periodic massive landslides that have killed thousands in the provinces.

In truth, the current administration, like all previous administrations, does not relish the prospect of a direct confrontation with the church. This predilection underlines how much policy changes depend on the position that the church takes. Thus, for fear of losing the support of the church totally, the Arroyo administration espouses some of the church's position on key issues. Arroyo has constantly upheld the Catholic Church's stand to promote natural family planning methods as opposed to artificial means. When criticized for this retrogressive approach despite a very high annual population growth rate,[81] Arroyo asked the opposition and the international community to "respect the deep Catholicism of the Filipino people".[82] To sweeten the souring relationship with the Catholic Church and at the same time gain points in the international community, Arroyo has strategically pushed for the abolition of capital punishment, earning her a "pat on the back" by Pope Benedict XVI in her recent visit to the Vatican.[83] Arroyo has also been actively seeking the advice of religious leaders like Velarde, regularly paying him visits to solicit affirmation of continuing support. Other politicians — senators, congressmen and key cabinet members — also make frequent visits to Velarde, often in his rest house in Tagaytay.[84]

PROBLEMS AND PROSPECTS

Christianity came to the Philippines in two forms: Iberian and American. Spanish Catholicism first came to the Philippines as a medieval faith that had remained impervious to the upheavals that rocked Europe. It produced a peculiar blend of civil, military and ecclesiastical authority, in which the church played a dominant role in social, political and economic life. This explains why church and state were fused during the Spanish colonial period in the Philippines. This may partly explain the almost *de facto* fusion of church and state in the Philippines even to this day. American Christianity, on the other hand, came as a post-Enlightenment religion with a bias towards secularism, reasoned faith, egalitarianism and the primacy of the individual conscience. The idea of the "separation of church and state", inspired by the above principles, found its way into the 1935 Constitution of the Philippines and succeeding constitutions, and has always been invoked by critics of the church to limit religion's influence in the political sphere.

Despite this, however, the growth of various religious denominations of both Catholic and Protestant varieties, indigenous churches, and charismatic religious communities, their corresponding politicization and increasing sense of political efficacy point to religion's continuing salience in Philippine politics. The experience of EDSA 1 that saw the church assume a crucial role in dismantling the Marcos dictatorship in a nonviolent confrontation was a defining moment — one that exhibited the force of its moral credibility and ascendancy. Thus, it may be safe to hazard the view that when other institutions fail and seriously lose their credibility and legitimacy, Filipinos will always look to the church and their religious leaders for moral direction and guidance.

During the country's critical transition to democracy, the church intensified its vigilance and provided guidance to the government. From the Aquino administration to the succeeding administrations of Ramos, Estrada, and Arroyo, the church has used its ever-growing clout to continue to influence politics. However, how large a role it has to play depends to a large extent on the character of its leadership and its relationship with the government. Thus, the church is seen as taking either a benign position or a very critical stance on issues, depending on its leader. The present political turmoil hounding the Arroyo administration seems to have a unifying effect on the church in upholding its basic mandate of protecting the welfare of its constituents, regardless of denomination or political leaning.

There is a growing convergence of cause as well as moral tenacity among different religious groups to get to the "the bottom of the truth" in regard to Arroyo's election into office and to oppose policy initiatives perceived to be taken to cover up or make up for her lack of political legitimacy. There are those who believe that precisely because of its resources — its moral credibility, infrastructure and mass base — the church may in fact be the tipping point for the current political crisis.[85]

The religious sector's increasing awareness of its political efficacy and influence is reinforced not only by the vast resources, tangible as well as intangible, at its disposal but also by the importance consistently accorded to it by government and its instrumentalities. The church's resources are seen both as a means to support the government and as a threat to its own power. The government's recognition of this capability is evident whenever it asks church groups for assistance in the dissemination of information and services through their parishes, services and religious gatherings. However, the government knows very well that these same resources can be used to overthrow it or to negate its actions that are deemed morally unacceptable.

Its individual leaders and members provide the church a face in Philippine politics either through priests and bishops directly participating in the political process, such as Bishop Deogracias Iñiguez, who signed one of the impeachment cases filed against President Arroyo, or through lay members holding important positions in government, such as health secretary Manuel Dayrit who was vocal about his non-support for contraceptives, a position that reproductive health advocates considered as retrogressive.

A new element in the political landscape is also seen in the increasing influence of religious movements, the sheer number of whose adherents attract the attention of politicians. With their extensive use of prayer rallies, ministries, and new media, these charismatic groups serve to strengthen religious institutions both in size and influence. Mike Velarde of El Shaddai, which claims a following of ten million worldwide, lent support to Estrada. The JIL Fellowship, which claims to have at least three million followers, supported its leader, Eddie Villanueva, when he ran for the presidency in May 2004. In a startling show of force, a crowd of close to three million people attended his final election campaign rally. This served notice that there is a force of highly committed religious elements that, with sufficient motivation, can be tapped and mobilized to fire a political cause or to realize a vision of transformation.[86] The increasing political influence of these religious movements has its greatest impact on governance because of the moral pressure that it carries in forcing those who are in positions of power and authority to be accountable for their actions.

A relatively new development is the use of modern technology — Internet and SMS (short messaging service) or text messaging — by the religious organizations to mobilize their members for political action. On 16 January 2001, for instance, millions of text messages (reportedly exceeding 30 million) were sent out that helped to mobilize people for EDSA 2.[87] The CBCP and JIL use SMS to enable their members to communicate with their leaders. The church also uses the Internet extensively in reaching out to its constituents. The CBCP bishops, for example, have web blogs on its official website that people can visit to read their sermons or opinions on specific issues. Indeed, information and communications technologies can make the potential of the church for mobilization greater than ever.

By virtue of their membership, resources and leadership, religious institutions will continue to be critical observers and strategic players in Philippine politics. As seen in their evolving role, they will not only shed light on morally relevant issues but also actively engage in sociopolitical and economic matters that affect the general welfare of their constituents. And as long as the government looks to the religious sector for support and legitimacy, its influential role will remain deeply entrenched in Philippine politics.

Notes

1. Samuel Huntington, *The Clash of Civilizations and the Remaking of World Order* (New York: Session and Schuster, Rockefeller Center, 1996), p. 95.
2. Glenn Vernon, *Sociology of Religion* (New York: McGraw Hill, 1962) cited in Ma. Lourdes G. Genato Rebullida, "Religion, Church, and Politics in the Philippines", *Philippine Politics and Governance: Challenges to Democratization and Development* (Quezon City: University of the Philippines, unpublished), p. 65.

3 Robert Bellah, "Cultural Identity and Asian Modernization", in *Cultural Identity and Modernization in Asian Countries*, Institute for Japanese Culture and Classics, Kokugakuin University, 1983. <http://www2.kokugakuin.ac.jp/ijcc/wp/cimac/index.html>.

4 Peter L. Berger, "Secularity: West and East", in *Cultural Identity and Modernization in Asian Countries*, Institute for Japanese Culture and Classics, Kokugakuin University, 1983, <http://www2.kokugakuin.ac.jp/ijcc/wp/cimac/index.html>.

5 Ibid.

6 Gilles Kepel, *The Revenge of God: The Resurgence of Islam, Christianity and Judaism in the Modern World* (Pennsylvania: Pennsylvania State University Press, 1994), p. 2.

7 Discussed in Ma. Lourdes Rebullida, "Religion, Church, and Politics in the Philippines", in *Philippine Politics and Governance: Challenges in Democratization and Development* (University of the Philippines: Quezon City, 2006), p. 66.

8 Grace Jamon, "The El Shaddai Prayer Movement: Political Socialization in a Religious Context", *Philippine Political Science Journal* 20 no. 43 (1999): 83–126.

9 ———, "The El Shaddai": 84–85 citing Kenneth Wald, *Religion and Politics in the United States* (New York: St. Martin's Press, 1987), p. 29.

10 ———, "The El Shaddai Movement: A Study of Political Socialization in a Religious Context" (Ph.D. dissertation, University of the Philippines, Diliman, Quezon City, Philippines, 1998).

11 Louis Luzbetak, *The Church and Culture: An Applied Anthropology for the Religious Worker* (Illinois: Divine World Publications, 1963), p. 6.

12 Epifanio de los Santos Avenue is the name of a major highway in Metro Manila where Filipinos staged two peaceful mass revolts that changed the country's president and one that attempted but failed to restore one. EDSA 1 happened in February 1986, a mass rally that overthrew Marcos and catapulted Aquino to power. EDSA 2 occurred in January 2001, which ousted Estrada and made Vice-President Gloria Macapagal-Arroyo his successor. A few months after, Estrada's supporters launched street protests against Arroyo, ending in violent clashes between crowd members and the riot police on 1 May 2001. This became known as EDSA 3.

13 Francisco F. Claver, "People Power and Value Transformation: A Faith Perspective" (mimeographed). Quezon City: Ateneo de Manila University, Institute on Church and Social Issues. 31 January 1987. Cited in Cristina J. Montiel, "Filipino Culture, Religious Symbols and Liberation Politics", in The Council for Research in Values and Philosophy, <http://www.crvp.org/book/Series03/III-7/chapter_x.htm> (accessed 18 July 2007)

14 Jaime B. Veneracion, "Mula Babaylan hanggang Beata (From Babaylan to Beata)", Teresita B. Ohasan (ed.), *Roots of Filipino Spirituality* (Philippines: Manathala, 1998), pp. 31–34. (Original text in Filipino, translated by author.)

15 Prof. Datu Amilusin A. Jumaani, "Muslim-Christian Relations in the Philippines: Redefining the Conflict", 28 October 2000, <http://www.bangsamoro.info/modules/wfsection/article.php?articleid=30>.

16 Robert Youngblood, *Marcos Against the Church: Economic Development and Political Repression in the Philippines* (London: Cornell University Press, 1990), p. 1.

17 See discussion of Reynaldo C. Ileto, *Pasyon and Revolution: Popular Movements in the Philippines, 1840–1910* (Quezon City: Ateneo de Manila University Press, 1979).

18 Article IV Section 8 of the 1935 Philippine Constitution. Discussed in Joaquin G Bernas, S. J., "Church and State", in Vitaliano Gorospe, S. J. ed., *Church and Society: Challenges for Tomorrow*, 1985 Lectures on the occasion of the 125th Anniversary of the Ateneo de Manila University, BUDHI Papers (V), p. 23, and René E. Mendoza, "Religion and Secularization in the Philippines and other Asian Countries", from *Cultural Identity and Modernization in Asian Countries*, Institute for Japanese Culture and Classics, Kokugakuin University, 1983. <http://www2.kokugakuin.ac.jp/ijcc/wp/cimac/index.html>.

19 Ibid.

20 Jack Miller, "Religion in the Philippines", *Ask Asia*, Essay No. 71, <http://www.askasia.org/teachers/essays/essay.php?no=71>.

21 <http://www.acts.edu/oldmissions/philhist1.html>.

22 Rt. Rev. Eustaquio D. Coronados, "Know Some Truths about the Philippine Independent Church in a Question-and-Answer Presentation", <http://www.geocities.com/Athens/Aegean/3083/qanda.htm>.

23 <http://www.acts.edu/oldmissions/philhist1.html>.

24 Malou Mangahas, "INC: A Most Powerful Union", *Philippine Center for Investigative Journalism*, 29–30 April 2002.

25 Ricardo Abad, "Religion in the Philippines", Social Weather Station Occasional Paper, January 2002, p. 18.

26 National Statistics Office (NSO) 2000 Census, also cited in Christl Kessler and Jurgen Ruland, "Responses to Rapid Social Change: Populist Religion in the Philippines", *Pacific Affairs* 79, no. 1 (Spring 2006): 77. Also see World Bank statistics.

27 Cited in Alan C. Robles, "The Politics of Sin", *Manila Chronicle*, 29 February–6 March 1992, p. 5.

28 St. Jude, St. Michael, and San Beda.

29 Ricardo G. Abad, "Religion in the Philippines", *Social Weather Stations (SWS) Occasional Paper*, January 2002, p. 18.

30 Thc CBCP's pastoral Petters are available online at <http://www.cbcponline.net>.

31 CBCP Online, official website of the Catholic Bishops' Conference of the Philippines, <http://www.cbcponline.net/html/statistics.html>.

32 Ateneo de Manila, Ateneo de Naga, Xavier University in Cagayan de Oro, Ateneo de Davao, and Ateneo de Zamboanga.

33 Xavier High School (San Juan, MM), Sacred Heart Jesuit School (Cebu), Sta. Maria High School (Iloilo).

34 Educational Research and Development Assistance Foundation (ERDA) Technical School (Pandacan, Manila) and the SAPAK Experimental Farm (Cebu).

35 The Philippine Jesuit Foundation official website, <http://www.philjesuit.net/min_jesuitsDo.asp>.

36 Jose Maria Escriva website, <http://www.josemariaescriva.info/index.php?id_cat=1434&id_scat=1376>.

37 David Van Biema, "The Ways of Opus Dei", *Time*, 24 April 2006, pp. 42–43.

38 Ma. Ceres P. Doyo, "Opus Dei in RP: It began with 3 Harvard Boys", *Philippine Daily Inquirer*, 18 May 2006.

39 From a study entitled "The Churches in the Philippines" by Dr. Manfred Kohl. Cited in Christian Esguerra, "With so Many Churches, why is RP still Corrupt?" *Philippine Daily Inquirer*, 9 March 2005, <http://news.inq7.net/nation/index.php?index=1&story_id=29882>.

40 Katherine Adraneda, "Evangelical Churches Won't Join Quit Call, But..." *Philippine Star*, 12 July 2005.

41 ISACC is a faith-based non-government organization that led the more progressive thinking evangelicals against the Marcos dictatorship in response to the felt need to reflect on the social-political realities of the period.

42 Bernas, p. 23.

43 Maria Lourdes Genato-Rebullida, "Reconceptualizing Development: The View from Philippine Churches", presented at the Fall Colloquium 1990, Center for Philippine Studies of the University of Hawaii, 7 November 1990.

44 Ma. Cynthia Rose B. Bautista, "The Development of NGOs and the 1992 Elections" in *The Philippine Political and Economic Situation in View of 1992*, edited by Randy S. David and Jonathan Y. Okamura (University of the Philippines Third World Studies Center and the University of Hawaii and Manoa Center for Philippine Studies, 1992, Occasional Paper No. 11), p. 30. Cited in Jamon, "The El Shaddai Prayer Movement" (1999): 83–126.

45 Pentecostalism, which emerged in the United States at the beginning of the twentieth century, aimed to renew the existing "mainline" Protestant churches by concentrating on the individual spiritual experience of believers. When the established denominations reacted hostilely to Pentecostal practices — falling in trance, speaking in tongues, weeping, crying and laughing out loud during services — the renewal movement formed its own churches. Eventually, Pentecostalism spread as a Charismatic movement to mainline Protestant denominations under the leadership of Dennis Bennet in 1959 and to the Roman Catholic Church, beginning in Pennsylvania. Christl Kessler and Jurgen Ruland, "Responses to Rapid Social Change: Populist Religion n the Philippines", *Pacific Affairs* 79, no. 1 (Spring 2006): 77.

46 Ibid., p. 74.

47 Gorospe-Jamon, "The El Shaddai Movement", 1998.
48 Jaime Cardinal Sin was the powerful Archbishop of Manila who was instrumental in rallying Filipinos to join protest rallies in 1987 that eventually overthrew President Ferdinand Marcos. He continued to be a key political observer and critic of Philippine politics until his death in 2005. Christine F. Herrera, "Erap: Velarde more influential than Sin", *Philippine Daily Inquirer*, 20 May 1998, p. 1.
49 Gawad Kalinga official website, <http://gawadkalinga.org/whatisgk.htm>.
50 Gawad Kalinga official website, <http://www.gawadkalinga.org/gk_communities/gk_communities.htm>.
51 Edu Punay, "Only the power of prayer can save RP – JIL Leader", *The Philippine Star*, 3 October 2005.
52 "Bro. Eddie Seeks Righteous Government", *Philippine Daily Inquirer*, 19 February 2004, <http://www.inq7.net/opi/2004/feb/19/text/letter_1-1-p.htm>.
53 Take for example the works of Genoveese, E. (1974) in "Roll, Jordan Roll", Raboteau, A. (1978) "Slave Religion: 'The Invisible Institution' in the Antebellum South", and Wilmore, G. (1983) in "Black Radicalism". Cited in Frederick Harris, "Something Within: Religion as a Mobilizer of African-American Political Activism", *Journal of Politics* 56, no. 1 (February 1994): 45.
54 See works of Hougland, J. and Christenson, J. (1983) in "Religion and Politics: The Relationship of Religious Participation to Political Efficacy and Involvement", Peterson, S. (1992) in "Church Participation and Political Participation", and Verba, et al. (1992) in "Race, Ethnicity as Resources for Participation".
55 Bernas, p. 24.
56 Youngblood, p. 172.
57 Ibid., p. 114.
58 "We Must Obey God Rather than Men", *Joint Pastoral Exhortation of the Catholic Bishops' Conference of the Philippines on the Snap Elections*, 25 January 1986. Also cited in Claver, Francisco F. "The Church and Revolution: The Philippine Solution", *America* (10 May 1986): 376.
59 Two of Marcos' military officers, Minister of Defense Juan Ponce Enrile and Armed Forces Chief of Staff Fidel Ramos, who defected from his government, were detained at the camps on EDSA.
60 Claver, "The Church and Revolution: The Philippine Solution": 383.
61 A historic meeting was held with almost 500 bishops, priests, nuns and lay members participating. The result was a 144-page document that contained the strategic plan that would guide the Philippine Church into the 21st century. Ramon Isberto, "Power of the Cross", in *1992 and Beyond: Forces and Issues in Philippine Elections,* edited by Sheila S. Coronel and Lorna K. Tirol (Philippine Center for Investigative Journalism and the Ateneo Center for Social Policy and Public Affairs, 1992), p. 117.
62 The document entitled "Guidelines for Elections/Appointment of Government

Leaders" had four major categories including personal attributes (40 per cent), service and platform (20 per cent), track record (20 per cent), and disqualifications (20 per cent).

63 Quote from Haydee Yorac, then acting chairperson of the Commission on Elections (Comelec).

64 Commission on Elections Resolution No. 2305, 13 February 1991.

65 Isberto in Coronel and Tirol, p. 106.

66 Malou Mangahas, "Iglesia ni Cristo: Church at the Crossroads", *Philippine Center for Investigative Journalism,* April 2002, <http://www.pcij.org/stories/2002/inc.html>.

67 "Iglesia ni Cristo: the Little Sect is Big Player in RP Politics", *The Philippine Star*, 4 May 2004, <http://www.newsflash.org/2004/02/pe/pe003126.htm>.

68 Catholic Bishops' Conference of the Philippines (CBCP) Pastoral Statament, "Renewing our Public Life through Moral Values", January 2006.

69 "Gil C. Cabacungan, Jr., "Malacanang, Bishops Tangle Anew on Impeachment Case", *The Philippine Daily Inquirer*, 4 July 2006, p. A15.

70 Amando Doronila, "CBCP Letter Masterpiece of Ecclesiastical Hedging", *Philippine Daily Inquirer*, 17 July 2006.

71 Blanche Rivera, "CBCP Asked to Open Parishes for Anti-Chacha Signature Drive", *Philippine Daily Inquirer*, 2 April 2006, <http://news.inq7.net/breaking/index.php?index=1&story_id=71415>.

72 Monica Feria, "Bishops' initiative: No to charter change", *Philippine Graphic* 16, no. 36 (13 February 2006): 16.

73 Two prominent anti-people's initiative groups have since evolved namely "One Voice" — a multi-sectoral movement composed of people from NGOs, academe, and the church, and "*Kapatiran* (or brotherhood)" — a lay Catholic initiated movement that works with other faith-based organizations, both Catholic and Protestant.

74 Based on recent conversations with this author.

75 Amando Doronila, "Arroyo's Hardline Policy vs Reds will crush her", *Philippine Daily Inquirer*, 19 June 2006, <http://news.inq7.net/nation/index.php?index=1&story_id=79646>.

76 Benjie Oliveros, "Oplan Bantay Laya as Arroyo's Inhumane War", *Bulatlat.com* 6, no. 20 (25 June–1 July 2006) < http://www.bulatlat.com/news/6-20/6-20-obl.htm>.

77 Joan Dairo, JP Lopez and Ruelle Albert Castro, "Protestant Churches Join Resign Call", *Malaya,* 7 July 2005, <http://www.malaya.com.ph/jul07/news6.htm>.

78 Oliveros, "Oplan Bantay Laya as Arroyo's Inhumane War".

79 Luis Gorgonio, "Unsolved Murders Revive Church Sanctuary Program", *GMA News TV Special Reports*, 26 June 2006, <http://www.gmanews.tv/specialreports.php?sec=4&id=9422>.

80 CBCP Online, <http://www.cbcponline.net/html/news1-may5.html>.

81 The Philippines has an annual growth rate of two per cent — compared to India's 1.7 per cent and Thailand's 1.3 per cent. Ibid.

82 Ibid.

83 Armand Nocum, " 'Well done,' Pope pats Arroyo on the back", *Philippine Daily Inquirer*, 27 June 2006, p. A1.

84 Based on personal observation of author.

85 Based on this author's conversation with Melba Maggay, President and CEO of the Institute for Studies in Asian Church and Culture (ISAAC), Manila, Philippines, 8 July 2006.

86 Melba Padilla Maggay, "Culture in Politics", *Patmos* 18, no. 1: 4.

87 Cecilia Alessandra S. Uy-Tioco, "The Cell Phone and EDSA 2: The Role of Communication Technology in Ousting a President", *4th Critical Themes in Media Studies Conference* (New School University, 11 October 2003).

Selected References

Abad, Ricardo G. "Religion in the Philippines". *Social Weather Stations (SWS) Occasional Paper*, January 2002.

Bautista, Ma. Cynthia Rose B. "The Development of NGOs and the 1992 Elections". In *The Philippine Political and Economic Situation in View of 1992*, edited by Randy S. David and Jonathan Y. Okamura. University of the Philippines Third World Studies Center and the University of Hawaii and Manoa Center for Philippine Studies, Occasional Paper no. 11, 1992.

Bellah, Robert. "Cultural Identity and Asian Modernization". In *Cultural Identity and Modernization in Asian Countries*. Institute for Japanese Culture and Classics, Kokugakuin University, 1983. <http://www2.kokugakuin.ac.jp/ijcc/wp/cimac/index.html>.

Bernas, Joaquin G., S.J. "Church and State". In *Church and Society: Challenges for Tomorrow*. 1985 Lectures on the occasion of the 125th Anniversary of the Ateneo de Manila University, BUDHI Papers (V), edited by Vitaliano Gorospe, S.J. Quezon City: Ateneo de Manila University, 1985.

Berger, Peter L. "Secularity: West and East". In *Cultural Identity and Modernization in Asian Countries*. Institute for Japanese Culture and Classics, Kokugakuin University, 1983. <http://www2.kokugakuin.ac.jp/ijcc/wp/cimac/index.html>.

Catholic Bishops' Conference of the Philippines (CBCP) Pastoral Statements, 1986–2006.

Claver, Francisco F. "The Church and Revolution: The Philippine Solution", *America* (10 May 1986).

———. "People Power and Value Transformation: A Faith Perspective" (mimeographed). Quezon City: Ateneo de Manila University, Institute on Church and Social Issues, 31 January 1987. Cited in Montiel, Cristina J. "Filipino Culture, Religious Symbols and Liberation Politics", in The Council for Research in Values and Philosophy <http://www.crvp.org/books/Series03/III-7/chapter_x.htm>.

Genato-Rebullida, Maria Lourdes. "Reconceptualizing Development: The View from Philippine Churches". Presented at the *Fall Colloquium 1990*, Center for Philippine Studies of the University of Hawaii, 7 November 1990.

Genato-Rebullida, Ma. Lourdes G. "Religion, Church, and Politics in the Philippines". Philippine Politics and Governance: Challenges to Democratization and Development. Quezon City: University of the Philippines, unpublished.

Gorgonio, Luis. "Unsolved Murders Revive Church Sanctuary Program". *GMA News TV Special Reports*, 26 June 2006. <http://www.gmanews.tv/specialreports.php?sec=4&id=9422>.

Gorospe-Jamon, Grace. "The El Shaddai Movement: A Study of Political Socialization in a Religious Context." Ph.D. diss., University of the Philippines, October 1998.

———. "The El Shaddai Prayer Movement: Political Socialization in a Religious Context". *Philippine Political Science Journal* 20, no. 43 (1999): 83–126.

Huntington, Samuel. *The Clash of Civilizations and the Remaking of World Order*. New York: Session and Schuster, Rockefeller Center, 1996.

Ileto, Reynaldo C. *Pasyon and Revolution: Popular Movements in the Philippines, 1840–1910*. Quezon City: Ateneo de Manila University Press, 1979.

Isberto, Ramon. "Power of the Cross". In *1992 and Beyond: Forces and Issues in Philippine Elections*, edited by Sheila S. Coronel and Lorna K. Tirol. Quezon City: Philippine Center for Investigative Journalism and the Ateneo Center for Social Policy and Public Affairs, 1992.

Jumaani, Amilusin A. (Datu). *"Muslim-Christian Relations in the Philippines: Redefining the Conflict"*. In Bangsamoro.info, 28 October 2000. <http://www.bangsamoro.info/modules/wfsection/article.php?articleid=30>.

Kepel, Gilles. *The Revenge of God: The Resurgence of Islam, Christianity and Judaism in the Modern World*. Pennsylvania: Pennsylvania State University Press, 1994.

Kessler, Christl and Jurgen Ruland. "Responses to Rapid Social Change: Populist Religion in the Philippines". *Pacific Affairs* 79, no. 1 (Spring 2006): 74–96.

Luzbetak, Louis. *The Church and Culture: An Applied Anthropology for the Religious Worker*. Illinois: Divine World Publications, 1963.

Maggay, Melba. "Culture in Politics". *Patmos* 18, no. 1.

Mangahas, Malou. "Iglesia ni Cristo: Church at the Crossroads", Philippine Center for Investigative Journalism, 29–30 April 2002. <http://www.pcij.org/stories/2002/inc.html>.

Miller, Jack. "Religion in the Philippines". *Ask Asia*, Essay no. 71. <http://www.askasia.org/teachers/essays/essay.php?no=71>.

Uy-Tioco, Cecilia Alessandra S. "The Cell Phone and EDSA 2: The Role of Communication Technology in Ousting a President". 4th Critical Themes in Media Studies Conference, New School University, 11 October 2003.

Van Biema, David. "The Ways of Opus Dei". *TIME*, 24 April 2006.

Veneracion, Jaime B. "Mula Babaylan hanggang Beata (From Babaylan to Beata)". In *Roots of Filipino Spirituality*, edited by Teresita B. Ohasan. Philippines: Manathala, 1998.

Youngblood, Robert. *Marcos Against the Church: Economic Development and Political Repression in the Philippines*. London: Cornell University Press, 1990.

6

THE PHILIPPINE PRESS: A STUDY IN CONTRASTS AND CONTRADICTIONS

Melinda Quintos de Jesus

INTRODUCTION

The inclusion of the press in this book may help to better understand some aspects of the political crisis in the Philippines. Basically, it is a crisis of governance, resulting from flawed and failed leadership. The questions of legitimacy and credibility hound the Arroyo administration with consequent loss of public confidence and trust. In this situation, the press has played a role.

The press is a political institution, providing for the public exchange of ideas as well as disseminating news about issues, developments and events. How well or how poorly the press performs these tasks affects the public's ability to understand public affairs and to be engaged in the pursuit of solutions. The press is, therefore, as much part of the problem as, hopefully, it is part of the solution.

Whatever the form of government, the press is always involved in governance and public affairs. In controlled political systems, the press serves as a handmaid of government, a vehicle to transmit official information or propaganda. Such a press assists government to achieve what it sets out to do. It is expected to accept editorial guidance from government so that it can aid and facilitate public acceptance of policy decisions and official programmes.

In political systems based on greater freedom and autonomy, the press plays a different kind of role. The press defines and performs its duty as it sees fit. With varying degrees of independence from owners, the press operates as a private sector endeavour or enterprise. The libertarian model prescribes this freedom from government interference on the premise that the press will uphold public, rather than partisan, interests. To fulfil this mandate, the press must also exercise social responsibility and possess competence and integrity. With these values, the journalists are supposed to provide news and commentary that are truthful and relevant, so as to enable public debate. Because it reports on public affairs and public figures, the press acts as the "watchdog" of those in power. This places it in an adversarial relationship with government.

The press also provides channels of communication for members of the community to share their news and views. It allows a nation to communicate to the world; and consciously or not, to project a national image.

BACKGROUND AND HISTORY

There are several factors that set the Philippines apart from the rest of Southeast Asia. Geographically, it lies on the outer eastern edge of Southeast Asia. Spain's colonization made it the only predominantly Christian country in the region. American rule also left a colonial legacy, the hosting of U.S. military bases, which isolated the country from its neighbours in the region. Its presidential system of government separates the exercise of political power into three separate and co-equal branches of government, a system that breaks away from the pattern of most Southeast Asian governments, which have favoured the more unitary parliamentary system.

Tradition of Free Expression and Press Freedom

The history of the press reflects the nation's history. The country's early commitment to free expression and press freedom had no parallel at the time in all of Asia. The conventional view may credit the establishment of this press tradition to American colonization. But the leaders of the reformist and later revolutionary movements against Spain were familiar with these libertarian values long before America set its imperial sights on the islands across the Pacific. These values were already enshrined in the 1899 Malolos Constitution of the first Philippine Republic, proclaimed before the end of the Spanish-American war, when the United States took over the country from Spain.

Towards the end of the nineteenth century, the struggle against Spain found expression in the paper of revolutionary propaganda, *La Solidaridad.* The writers who filled its pages had travelled to Europe, where they absorbed the libertarian ideals of the French Revolution. Published in Spain by Filipino expatriates, the paper was smuggled into the colony where the native elite had already begun to question many aspects of Spanish rule.

Throughout the country's history, similar publications would give voice to social and political movements pressing for change. Serial colonization set a pattern for government's use of the press to enforce its rule. But anti-government forces have also used the same instrument for the purpose of challenging the incumbent's hold on power. This was true during the periods of colonization by Spain and America, the Japanese Occupation and the homegrown dictatorship of Ferdinand Marcos.

The American Period

Given the American model, the press in the Philippines also saw itself, like its American counterpart, as the "fourth estate", with enough clout to check the abuse of power by government or any other group or institution, such as business or the church.

More specifically, the American model established the press and broadcast media as a commercial enterprise. Financed mainly with advertising and circulation revenues, the operation of media has since been inextricably linked to the selling of products, soap, soup and other merchandise to the public. The viability of the news enterprise, whether print or broadcast, depended on ratings based on circulation or audience. The business objective and the operations of the market shaped the character and conduct of the press.

In the earliest period, those who invested in newspapers and magazines also owned other lucrative businesses. They were part of the establishment community that shared common interests with leaders in politics. Owning a newspaper added political clout to the owners' economic power. But professional editors, who for the most part worked with editorial independence, ran newsrooms.

The adversarial role in relation to those in power made the press also the "champion of the underdog", taking up the cause of people and communities without wealth or power. This dual role has been long embraced by the country's leading journalists and publishers, but as with most ideals, these have not been fulfilled consistently.

During the pre-martial law period, the press was known to take a position of vigorous opposition against every incumbent administration. Only Ferdinand Marcos was able to succeed into a second term; and his declaration of martial law in September 1972 broke the cycle of periodic elections.

We can only speculate about what could have been, if Marcos had not rudely interrupted the political course with fourteen years of authoritarian rule.

Martial Law

While this chapter is not about the country's history, it is helpful to see how Marcos institutionalized his control over the press.

Proclamation 1081 of 1972 effectively closed down the free press, as people knew it. Government secured control over the press, with the aid of the military's coercive force. Leading journalists were picked up and detained. Military censors supervised the newsrooms that were allowed to stay open. Later, those close to Marcos were able to secure licences to publish or operate radio and television stations. In their hands, the press could claim that it was working within a framework of self-regulation.

The period saw news organizations closed down or taken over by new owners. Others were co-opted into the service of government, along with the newly formed media companies owned by friends and relatives of the Marcos couple.

This period also institutionalized wholesale bribery of the press, with various members or organizations assured of perquisites and privileges, as well as access to lucrative deals. Coverage expenses were paid for by government money drawn from department/agency budgets to ensure favourable reporting.

The passing of "envelopes" to journalists during press conferences became common practice. Filipinos coined the term "envelopmental journalism" to describe the phenomenon and to spoof "developmental journalism". Authoritarian governments were then promoting the latter term as an ideal model, but it was seen as government's way to promote itself while pushing so-called development programmes.

From its noble origins, the press in the country was quickly reduced to serving as a mere mouthpiece for government officials, primarily, but not exclusively, in the service of Ferdinand and Imelda Marcos.

These conditions forced journalists into exile abroad or pressed them to make career shifts, moving to advertising, public relations, or information offices in the private sector or government agencies.

Enrolments in journalism schools fell as the press lost its drawing power with young graduates. The rigour of the newsrooms gave way to the dictates of the press release and government prescription.

Critical Voices

In the seventies, a journalist, Jose Burgos, Jr., began publishing critical commentary and reports in *We Forum*. But it had only limited circulation, and government allowed it to publish for some years. "Xerox" and "mimeo" reprints of critical reports from the international press and from the rebel forces were also passed around. These alternative media, however, had little effect on the overall projection of government. The mainstream press, owned by Marcos friends and relatives, reported only positive news about government.

Marcos lifted martial law in 1981, but the military continued to arrest and detain suspected rebels and subversives without proper warrants, especially in remote areas. There were no reports in the media about the disappearances and killings of activists and rebels, and it can be assumed that these included activists in the "underground" media.

Still, the lifting of martial law on paper encouraged more people to test the waters of official tolerance. The *Bulletin Today*, published by a Swiss businessman, Hans Menzi, a Marcos friend who served for some years as the president's *aide-de-camp*, fielded women writers whose critical columns and reports gained popular following. By this time, the business community had begun to question the favours being given to Marcos cronies and welcomed the critical turn in the mainstream press. It was also at this time that reports of Marcos' health and the oil crisis raised questions about the future.

In 1983, a former senator and leading opposition politician, Benigno Aquino Jr., announced that he would return to the country from the United States, where he had stayed after undergoing medical treatment. Knowing about Marcos' failing health, Aquino wanted to talk to him about preparing for a peaceful transition. Before his arrival on 21 August 1983, the *Bulletin* had eased out the political critics in the paper.

Aquino Assasination: A Turning Point

Aquino was assassinated upon arrival at the Manila International Airport and the rest, as they say, is history. Government did not try to stop the massing of the people at Aquino's wake nor the long historic march of sympathizers at his burial. This policy of maximum tolerance on the streets was not matched by open coverage by the controlled press. More than a million people marched with Aquino's funeral cortege. But, following guidelines, newspapers and broadcast media did not report these events.

The killing of Aquino blew the lid off the simmering ferment of discontent with the regime; just as the blackout in media coverage demonstrated to Filipinos the capacity of the media to lie to them. Outraged, the public began a media boycott, which caused the circulation of the Marcos papers to plummet.

A new wave of "alternative" publications quickly filled the media vacuum. Public anger shifted significant readership to a clutch of weekly newspapers, *Veritas Newsweekly, Mr. & Ms. Special Edition, Malaya*, along with the progressive business paper, *Business Day.* The growth of their combined national circulation signalled the decline of Marcos' hold on public loyalty.

POST-MARCOS: OWNERSHIP AND OTHER CURRENT ISSUES

Rising to power, Corazon Aquino declared her policy of opening up democratic space. The press quickly reverted to its traditional position as part of the establishment, with its role as an agent of continuing change diminished. The liberation of the press from the influence of government could have unleashed a powerful force for reform, as the new government drew new faces into politics. A new constitution was ratified in 1987, providing for limits on presidential power. But as in politics, the change in the press was in form only. The press was free from official interference, but working journalists were as vulnerable to pressures, including those of media owners and the owners' friends or allies in high places.

Today, the press reflects the diverse forces of the political class. On the whole, the political class has remained conservative, with little to show for a reformed tax system or more progressive land use. After 1986, the press lost the radical affinities which had joined the "alternative" press with so-called "cause-oriented" groups identified with the Left.

By the early nineties, the political parties in the Philippines had lost even the slightest pretensions at ideology or platform. They all centred on political personalities who would launch a new party for the sole purpose of running for election. And the press generally followed the news agenda as set by the electoral season.

New Conditions of Media Enterprise

The market for media enterprise showed remarkable change. Along with the technological advances, the liberation of the press from government control created a new media environment, which saw the increase of news publications. Congress retained the authority to award franchises for the operation of broadcast media but it was no longer controlled by one dominant party.

The proliferation of newspapers, television and radio stations after 1986 confirmed the commercial character of the press. The market has dictated its own news standards based on popular appeal. The objective is to "rate" — pulling the largest circulation or audience for the sake of advertising revenues. As cheaper tabloids draw on mass readership, some broadsheets have taken the style of the "tabloid press", with its selection of articles for popular appeal and the sensational treatment of news stories.

Ownership

Three journalists were successful in establishing profitable news organizations. Eugenia Apostol founded the *Philippine Daily Inquirer*, Raul Locsin re-organized *Business Day* into *Business World.* Maximo Soliven, Jr., together with Betty Go Belmonte, were partners of Apostol in the *Inquirer*; but broke away to set up the *Philippine Star.*

New owners took over from the big media owners of the past. Apostol sold the *Inquirer* to the Prietos, whose business interests include real estate and paper. After the death of Menzi, Emilio Yap, with business interests in shipping and banking, acquired the majority shares of the *Bulletin.* Dante Ang, a prominent press relations officer who worked for both Presidents Estrada and Arroyo, now owns the *Manila Times. Today,* owned by lawyer turned politician, Teodoro Locsin, Jr., was merged with the *Manila Standard,* owned by Enrique Razon, Jr., whose business is in port management.

After 1986, the Lopezes, a long-established political clan who opposed Marcos, quickly regained their hold over the giant television network, ABS-CBN. GMA-7 took on new owners and is now headed by a lawyer, Atty. Felipe Gozon. Antonio Cojuangco, Jr., whose family sold the Philippine Long Distance Telephone Company, now owns ABC-5.

As with the media owners in the past, the intervention and influence over editorial policy of present owners are evident occasionally. Owner interference varies in degree and from case to case. For the more profitable broadcast media, the dependence on Congress for franchises continues to raise the spectre of political influence over news coverage.

Government controls three television networks. The NBN-4 is a government-owned media company. RPN-9 and IBC-13 were sequestered from previous owners identified with the Marcoses. They continue to be managed by government-appointed officials.

Press Power

Free of government control, the press constitutes a power in itself. As technology intensifies its presence in public life, the projection of its influence has also grown. But the power of the press to turn things around is perhaps exaggerated. It can do this when there is agreement within the press community and when public opinion is focused on the issue. But the press is hardly monolithic. The news organizations are seldom united in their stand on policy or in political orientation. For varying reasons, members of the media have pursued as well as served different, sometimes conflicting, interests in society.

PROBLEMS OF DEVELOPMENT

Question of Quality

The question of quality may actually be a case of quantity getting in the way of quality.

Clearly, the number of trained and seasoned journalists could not meet the demand of the media explosion post-1986. In the new newsrooms, senior "beats" such as Malacanang (the President's residence and office), the Supreme Court and Congress were going to new college graduates. Many newsrooms lost the practice of editorial mentoring and review. The new technology allowed reporters to file their stories from the field through fax and later, e-mail, eliminating editorial discussion and review. Sometime in the early nineties, a group of senior journalists observed that the number of good and experienced journalists in the early nineties would probably ensure only two quality newspapers. But these qualified journalists were spread out among the many newspapers, and the overall quality of reporting and commentary declined.

The 2003 *Philippine Fact Book* counted nine daily national broadsheets based in Manila, which claimed some circulation, however limited, around the country. Its count for provincial newspapers serving local communities was 500. Only a small number of these community newspapers publish daily. The count changes often as publications close down and open for short periods, especially when there is a scheduled election.

Radio's reach remains paramount, reaching the mass audience through national and regional networks. Stations operating on low frequency have also increased. While keeping to its origins as an entertainment medium, radio has increased its news and political coverage.

Television in the Philippines began as a private enterprise and the largest networks are privately owned. Surveys show that while radio enjoys the widest reach, television has become the most important source of political information for Filipinos.

Despite the conditions noted above, the power and influence of the press in the country have not abated since people power toppled the Marcos dictatorship in 1986. The press played a crucial role in bringing the country to that moment of history. It repeated that role to a more limited extent when investigative reports found and revealed crucial evidence about the extravagant lifestyle of President Joseph Estrada in 2002. Investigative reporting has grown in quality and practice and has clearly helped to inform the public about the conduct of government officials, up to the presidency.

But these investigative reports have singular rather than regular impact and effect on the quality of governance. Such reports have caused policy to change or a public official to be fired, or helped to impeach or depose a corrupt president. But not every corrupt official gets exposed and the pattern of corruption remains.

Despite so much free media, the electorate does not receive the kind of information that will help them choose their candidates wisely. The Center for Media Freedom and Responsibility (CMFR) monitor of coverage of the campaign and elections of 2005 showed television and newspapers reporting on the campaigns without forcing the candidates to talk about the issues and their platforms.

Despite so much press freedom, the country cannot boast of a newspaper of record, such as, say, the *New York Times* or the *Washington Post*. Filipinos complain that despite reading several newspapers, they still feel that they do not understand controversial issues, such as the value-added tax or the policy on mining. Despite laws that protect the press from government interference, journalists may be pressured to write only the stories that sell and to suppress stories unfavourable to their owners and patrons. In general, there is little interest in complex issues, and news stories lack the necessary context and perspective.

It is difficult to imagine how such a press can be expected to school a community of citizens. Meanwhile, the decline in the educational system, along with the growth of the entertainment media, has caused the number of newspaper readers to shrink, with only a small audience that is able to read the news critically.

Question of Integrity

With regard to the issue of integrity, unfortunately, corruption of journalists and media practitioners remains quite commonplace. Even after the departure of Marcos and his friends, the "incentive" for favourable coverage continues in many forms, including the adjustment to technology, with payments made through the ATM.

Although many Filipino journalists are untainted by bribery, the perception of corruption has affected the image of the institution. There are also those who, for economic reasons, combine journalistic work with other positions, in business or government, which involves conflicts of interest.

Celebrity Media

Philippine media continue to make up a colourful stage for celebrities where journalists themselves are among the brightest stars. In the political field, editors and columnists exert the kind of influence that has even presidents openly courting their favour. News programs are dependent on the drawing power of anchors and on-camera reporters. Talk shows project pundit columnists as public personalities. Television anchors, reporters and programme hosts become as popular as movie stars.

The current vice-president is a former broadcaster who enjoyed a national following but had no experience in public office. He won against another vice-presidential candidate whose popularity was based also on her career as a news anchor.

TV news programmes place great premium on visual effects and "show business" appeal. On radio, popular talk hosts dish out chitchat, interview public officials and invite listeners to call in their views. This kind of freewheeling exchange enjoys huge audiences. But there is little application of journalistic standards.

In this manner, the press itself has also contributed to the culture of celebrity in politics. Candidates are often chosen from the fields of sports and entertainment.

JOURNALISTS KILLED: VIOLENCE, THE CULTURE OF IMPUNITY

Having a high profile in the community does not always protect journalists. The killing of journalists in a country that boasts of a strong free press tradition is not easy to explain. Of the one hundred slain journalists/media practitioners listed by the CMFR, sixty are classified as having been killed "in the line of duty". The majority of these were working for media in the countryside. A good number of these reported on corruption and questionable deals involving business and government.

A number of those slain were freelance radio broadcasters. Some were "blocktimers", buying airtime and making money on advertisements, and were therefore in business for themselves. Some employed a provocative bombastic style of commentary that is supposed to be favoured by listeners.

But no one deserves to die for offensive speech. The fact that so many have been killed reflects the weakness of the press as an institution. There has been no public outrage expressed over the killings, which also suggests that the public may not really understand and appreciate the role of free speech or press freedom in a democracy.

CMFR first investigated the killings in 1992. It has since kept a database, researching the background of each case. There were journalists killed even as democratic space expanded during the Aquino administration. A variety of motives and causes suggested perpetrators other than the military or police, who were the usual suspects impressed in the mind by the experience of martial law. This writer did not think then that the killings were part of official policy to suppress dissent and to silence critics.

The press community is unusually large in the country. They make a vocal and visible presence and become vulnerable targets. With the failure of the police and the courts to establish the rule of law and to enforce it, the endemic paucity of resources for investigation and prosecution has made a bad situation worse. The killings are part of a systemic failure, another shameful reflection of the national "culture of impunity" as so many cases are left in police files unsolved or languishing or lost in the courts.

The attacks on reporters are symptomatic of the prevailing environment of violence and lawlessness in Philippine society. Journalists are not the only targets. Lawyers, judges, and activists in different fields are among those murdered because of their work. During the Arroyo administration, the killing of both activists and journalists has been reported to be at an all-time high.

GOVERNMENT ACTIONS AGAINST THE PRESS 2006

As the numbers continue to escalate, CMFR has also reviewed the political context of the problem. Ten journalists have been killed "in the line of duty" in the less than two years since 2005. During President Arroyo's watch, twenty-seven journalists have so far been killed because of their work.

Recent statements by the police and justice officials reflect too casual a dismissal of the repeated violation of human rights. The reported number of activists identified with Leftist groups has caused international human rights groups to protest and to call for action. The Philippine Commission on Human Rights has taken the Arroyo government to task for its failure to take action and make arrests.

Decrees issued during the declared state of emergency in February 2006 (General Orders 5 and 6) set out to regulate news coverage. Along with the temporary take-over of a small opposition newspaper, the closure of a radio programme, the surveillance of selected organizations and journalists, and the proposed police guidelines for media reporting, these actions showed that, despite constitutional protection, a government can move to openly intimidate the press, or to regulate and control its conduct.

LOOKING AHEAD

In a world of profound and rapid social and political change, the free press in the Philippines has shown that it is not up to the challenge of nurturing and growing a community of free citizens, which is the way its purpose has been described by exponents of "public" or "civic journalism". It has fallen into the trap of most modern media around the world that had become disconnected from this original purpose: to assist in the construction of democratic society, to provide information and news so that citizens can participate meaningfully in public affairs.

Journalists report the news according to old formulas that limit the scope of news to the breaking stories of the day. The press limits its reports to the most prominent of members and forgets the issues that affect those who are poor and marginalized. Journalists have trouble being engaged by the concerns of the communities, and end up following the "leaders" even when these are the least deserving of public attention.

With the technology of broadcast media overtaking newspapers in this function, the print media continue to focus on "breaking news" when it should give more space for analysis that will help the public to understand the dilemmas of development and controversial policies.

The adversarial role that the press adopts as a matter of course probably needs to give way to more context reporting. The constant flow of bad news has made the public cynical about the prospects of the country as a whole.

The press in the Philippines may need to develop further approaches to engage the masses and create better informed communities. Newspaper readers, estimated at one million and a half, make up only a small percentage of the electorate, 36 million voters in the 2004 elections.

Language of the Press

A press in the local languages brings information more quickly to the masses. While radio and television have shifted to the use of major Philippine languages, the national newspapers continue to publish only in English. The newspapers in English are instruments of the political class. The lack of newspapers in the major national languages reflects the alienation of this critical institution from the masses. Unfortunately, the news programmes in the national languages tend to pander to the audience's taste for news as entertainment.

Need for Independent Public Broadcasting

The Marcos era perfected the government machinery for official propaganda and has all but obliterated the idea of an independent public broadcasting service, as shown in the continuing coverage of government television and radio. These have continued to function as they did during the martial law period — as propaganda offices of the incumbent political administration.

Review of Journalism Education

The review of journalism training in the schools and universities should lead to the development of journalism as a postgraduate certificate course that trains those already schooled in some discipline such as science, medicine, law, business and economics to then enter the media. Such training in another discipline will deepen the knowledge that a journalist brings to the task of reporting and improve the treatment of news.

Initiatives for Reform

The development of a press in a democracy calls for constant attention and review. In the United States, movements for reform and training have spawned new initiatives to help the American press cope with the pressures of commercialism. The cases that have come to public attention indicate that even in more economically developed societies, the press can be part of the problem.

This critique suggests that conventional journalism and the traditional standards of news in general are no longer adequate for current needs. Journalism must help the public understand and cope with complexity and change. In a democracy, the solution of problems involves public engagement.

It must provide information and news that citizens need to be able to make decisions. The role of the press is implicated in the poor choices that the electorate makes and the continuing gridlock that plagues policy-making. The free press in the Philippines must also be blamed for its failure to assist in the building of consensus and peace.

Philippine NGOs working on media issues have started programmes and projects to address the issues of press development, ranging from training in basic to advanced investigative skills.

The CMFR has carved a special niche for itself with its efforts to promote a culture of ethics and self-regulation, along with the advocacy for press freedom. It monitors the press media through the monthly *PJR Reports*. Using content analysis, it has monitored coverage of elections and selected areas of concern, such as the coverage of disasters, women and children, and the conflict in Mindanao. It reports attacks and threats against press freedom to international media watch groups. To encourage good works, it also holds an annual awards programme to recognize the best works in in-depth reporting.

CMFR has also facilitated the formation of citizen press councils in three provinces (Baguio, Palawan and Cebu) to open up venues for the public to air complaints against the press, its errors and abuses. It also organizes forums for the press to discuss problems, such as libel and conflict of interest, and conducts background or content training on issues and developments. But participation in these programmes is voluntary. These programmes have established basic models and have set standards, but the effect on the quality of the practice itself will be in the long term.

The current political crisis brings the Philippine press to another crossroads or turning point in its history. Crisis creates opportunities. Perhaps, the press in the Philippines can take this time to turn a new page and return to its mandate of public trust.

Selected References

De Jesus, Melinda Quintos. "The Media: High on Verve: Low on Substance". In *Duet for EDSA: Looking back, Looking forward 1996*, edited by Lorna Kalaw-Tirol. Manila: Foundation for Worldwide People Power, 1995.

———. "Philippines: The Problem with Freedom". *Development Dialogue: The Journal of The Dag Hammarskjöld Foundation*, no. 2 (1998): 105–19.

De Jesus, Melinda Quintos, Rachel E. Khan, and Nathan J. Lee. "In Search for Solutions: A Study of Journalist Killings in the Philippines, 2000–2005". *PJR Reports* (September–October 2005): 12–15.

Khan, Rachel E. and Nathan J. Lee. "The Danger of Impunity". Unpublished study.

September 2005. *Philippine Fact Book*. Manila: Foreign Service Institute, Department of Foreign Affairs, 2003.

Rosen, Jay. *What Are Journalists For?* (New Haven, CT: Yale University Press, 1999).

Teodoro, Luis V. and Dini Widiastuti. *Freedom of Expression and the Media in the Philippines*. Manila: ARTICLE 19 and Center for Media Freedom and Responsibility, December 2005.

7

PHILIPPINE MACROECONOMIC ISSUES AND CHALLENGES

Gerardo P. Sicat

INTRODUCTION: MACROECONOMIC AND STRUCTURAL PROBLEMS*

This chapter reviews some macroeconomic issues relating to the current Philippine economy. To provide a proper understanding of these issues, their link will be associated with their structural underpinnings. Persistent macroeconomic problems often require a policy adjustment, and inevitably, assessment of the problems boils down to an understanding of what gets done, what gets delayed or what is not possible to do under the circumstances. A further device in presenting the issues is through a comparison with the experience of other East Asian and high-growth countries, which include some ASEAN countries.

The review follows this sequence. First, the recent growth performance of the economy is discussed. Then, the compositions of aggregate demand and of aggregate supply are described, emphasizing the reasons for the observed changes and trends. Next, the economy's saving and investment issues are highlighted, paying notice to the large gap between saving and investment. After that, the spotlight moves to the fiscal front that is a major contributor to the country's low saving rate. The fiscal sector is discussed in terms of dealing with deficit reduction and managing the public debt. Finally, the review expounds on the economy's external trade and payments position.

Current problems and new opportunities are discussed in the context of globalization and the country's open stance.

A major theme that arises from this discussion is that the potentials for development in the Philippines are not fully exploited. A relative measure of this under-performance can be derived from the immense turnaround of economic prospects in 2006 just as soon as the government was able to deal with a reform on the fiscal front. A result of these measures led to higher tax revenues being earned, thereby braking a deteriorating fiscal situation. A lot of other benefits affecting macroeconomic fundamentals were likewise experienced, changing the dynamics of political and economic discourse.

THE RATE OF ECONOMIC GROWTH AND PRODUCTIVITY

Recent growth rates in the Philippine economy have ranged from 3 to 5.7 per cent per year — with the average growth rate from 1999 to 2005 being 4.6 per cent. This is the growth of the GNP, a measure of total national income, not of GDP, or a measure of total output produced in the country. The annual GDP growth rate during the same period was lower, 4.2 per cent. The significance of this discrepancy is explained in detail later.

Philippine economic growth has been on the modest side compared to that of high-growth East Asian economies. During their periods of sustained growth in recent decades, these latter countries achieved annual growth rates of real output ranging from 7 to 10 per cent per annum of real output and income growth. The Philippines is literally surrounded by these countries — Japan (the earliest of the achievers during the 1950s to the 1970s), South Korea, Taiwan, Hong Kong, Singapore and Malaysia. Today, China is repeating the early "economic miracles" of these countries but on a larger scale. Indonesia had done very well in the past four decades, but its performance was reversed after recent political and economic crises.

Philippine economic performance has been characterized by a recurrence of accentuated booms and busts. As soon as macroeconomic fundamentals had gathered momentum to reach a particular environment of encouraging growth, imbalances come back in the form of balance of payments and difficulties on the fiscal front. In part, this problem of recurring imbalances is due to a lack of timely action related to the required economic remedies. Such policy actions are often painful and therefore difficult to push on the political front. The remedies are often in the form of adjusting macroeconomic policies such as dealing with tax reform and expenditure cuts. But often the problems that jolt the economic performance arise from some structural inflexibility that makes the economy very sensitive to political jolts of a domestic origin or from external economic events. Such weakness in flexibility helps to disturb investment confidence.

There is another feature that contrasts the Philippine growth experience with that of the immediate neighbours. Population growth in the Philippines continues to be high at around 2 per cent per year and its rate of growth has not changed much in recent years. This means that per capita growth of income and output is lower because the high population growth absorbs much of the growth of the economy. In comparison, the East Asian high performers have experienced a halving of their rates of population growth from highs of close to 2 per cent per year during the 1960s toward 1 per cent per year by this decade.

The rate of economic growth of output and of productivity in an economy depends on the technical relations with the rate of growth of capital, labour, and other economic resources that enter the production process. A productive and efficient economy displays a high rate of economic growth that helps to eradicate a high level of unemployment. In these relations, the quality of the inputs (amount of knowledge, skills, and learning by experience of the labour force) builds up. It is not surprising that rising incomes and the savings derived from falling birth rates induce a higher investment in education, nutrition, and family welfare. They improve the efficiency of labour even as the economy and rise of inputs help to accelerate the growth of output.

Aggregate studies of growth and productivity have consistently explained that Philippine economic growth is due to growth in the employment of capital and of labour inputs.[1] But total productivity growth has been inconsistent and in fact indicates that during some episodic periods, the growth of productivity has been nil or negative while the growth of capital inputs and labour inputs has been positive. The rate of capital accumulation in the economy has been in general adequate during the years of development. However, even though at the same time such a growth of investment has led to the employment of labour, the total growth of output and productivity has not been adequate to generate a high level of employment and productivity growth.

These studies provide statistical evidence of what was happening in the aggregate. But to understand why this had taken place would require an analysis of the manner in which economic policy evolved in the goods and factor markets. In terms of the goods market, the industries that were promoted for a long time were mainly dependent on protection and high tariffs and government support, with many of them unable to become competitive as the economy was opened to greater competition with international trade.

On the goods side, the gradual evolution of the economy's trade and industrial policy forced a restructuring of the industrial sector. This liberalization of the economy was accompanied by the enlarging role of ASEAN economic cooperation through the preferential trade agreement that arose and, more importantly, the country's accession to the principles of world trading rules in the World Trade Organization. The protectionist policies on the goods side held back the growth of competitive industries in international and domestic trade for decades.

As important to the outcome of the process of economic growth in the Philippines are policies affecting the markets of the factors of production. This refers to the set of policies affecting the employment and attraction of the use of capital, labour, land, and natural resources. A major cause of the underperformance of the Philippine economy is related to the rigidities of the factor markets. As a result, labour and capital have not played as important a role in bringing the economy to to a higher level of growth as found among the East Asian neighbours.

On the labour side, the welfare-oriented approach towards labour introduced labour market rigidities that made it difficult for firms to hire workers. Legislated minimum wages were aggressively set higher than market realities, often guided by welfare considerations using urban-based living standards and often in response to populist tendencies to follow labour welfare standards of advanced industrial nations. This prematurely raised unit costs of labour and introduced antagonistic labour-management relations that were not present in neighbouring countries. This rendered employment creation more difficult. Regional minimum wage setting was introduced during the 1990s that helped to factor in regional competition as a factor in setting minimum wages. Despite this effort, the new policy gets threatened with each new demand for wage revisions.

Such an approach to labour policy would have had benign, or at worst, less harmful effects if the policy on the attraction of foreign capital had been more aggressive and had yielded more than just seemingly good results. On the capital side, however, the restrictions on foreign capital continued in critical sectors that were identified as far back as 1935 when the political constitution was framed.

Even as the country's investment policies have flourished and become more open gradually as a result of the liberalization of many aspects of economic policy, the main restrictions of the constitutional provisions remain in effect with respect to foreign capital in specific sectors, including public utilities and natural resources. Foreign capital is essentially the "free" economic resource, for it is not hampered by the limitation domestic capital faces in the midst of economic opportunities. Attracting capital to flow in more freely would have enhanced the rate of investment and the possibilities of technological growth. Incidentally, this was the pattern of policies in many of the high performing countries of East Asia, including even countries which tried to impose capital controls for other reasons.

Since 1935, the policy pertaining to the attraction of capital was undertaken with major exceptions in several sectors of the economy. These restrictions were specified in the Philippine constitution and they took on the nature of iron laws that reduced the effectiveness of foreign capital attraction. Foreigners are not allowed to buy land, and only companies that are substantially owned by Filipinos (at least 60 per cent majority) are allowed to engage in the operation of public utilities and the exploitation of natural resources.

Over time, these provisions would create a structural problem for the evolution of public utilities and introduce higher costs in the provision of domestic infrastructure because capital — especially risk capital — in these sectors by virtue of restrictions around them would become even scarcer. They also affected the expansion of other sector activities, including agriculture, industry, mineral exploitation and the growth of services like tourism. The more obvious impact of these policies relates to the state of public utilities and the expansion of infrastructure. They suffered in quality as a result of the onslaught of capital inadequacy of local investors who were given the means and opportunity to pursue expansion, modernization, and even rehabilitation of existing facilities.

Under more open access to debt finance in the world's capital markets, these facilities became more dependent on borrowed capital for which there was a high element of risk associated with the interest and foreign exchange rates. The model under which they underwent expansion was mainly through borrowing, but such borrowing was often limited by the amount of domestic equity capital that was put in the undertaking. Local savings and lack of access to foreign direct investments in these facilities due to constitutional regulations prevented rapid solutions to a major problem that had worsened over decades of economic under-performance.

It is widely recognized in the Philippines today that foreign direct investment — its greater participation in the provision of public utilities and in the exploitation of natural resources — would greatly improve the economy's domestic infrastructure and export earning capacity. Some of the actions that permit the participation of foreign direct investment could therefore be undertaken through indirect mechanisms. This was achieved, for instance, through the layering of corporate structures that avoided direct conflict with the constitutional restrictions in these sectors. Others would be through service contract arrangements with state entities that therefore fulfil the equity requirements concerning citizenship without any doubt.

In a recent decision, the Supreme Court helped to make it constitutional to allow fully owned foreign owned companies to engage in mining exploitation within the framework of service contract arrangements with the government. The amendment of the basic document regarding these provisions would be needed to remove the threat of legal challenges that cause delays, discouragement and often uncertainty in the outcome.

The learning process in the Philippines with respect to promoting a liberal foreign investment policy climate was slow for decades because of the restrictions from the constitutional framework and the hang-ups that these restrictions have imparted to the policy milieu. The restrictive posture of investment policies from the constitutional framework had an overwhelming influence on the nation's attitude toward the role of foreign capital. Initially, the policies applied mainly to public utilities and natural resources exploitation. But these gradually expanded into many areas of industry and commerce during the period of economic restrictions that permeated government policy. The infectious pattern of these policies enabled the growth of a highly protective industrial and trade regime that dominated economic policies for many decades.

WIDENING DISPARITY BETWEEN GDP AND GNP

Reference has already been made to the phenomenon of recent times that the rate of growth of GNP has been outstripping that of GDP. As is well known, both concepts measure specific aspects of the output and income definition. The GDP measures output produced within the country's borders by all residents while the GNP measures the output or equivalently income earned by all the country's nationals. When a country's nationals earn a substantial amount of their income outside the nation's boundaries, then these represent incomes derived from work abroad. Hence output produced at home (GDP) has to be corrected by the net contribution of all national labour and capital working abroad (derived from the measure of GNP). In a sense, therefore, the GNP measures the incomes earned by all nationals whether working at home or abroad.

In recent years the GNP has consistently been growing at a faster rate than the GDP. Real GNP grew by 3.7 per cent in 1999 compared to 3.4 per cent for GDP. In 2005, real GNP grew by 5.7 per cent and GDP by 5.2 per cent. The discrepancy in growth rates has been consistent throughout the period in between and even before. Before 1990, GDP and GNP were roughly equal. The phenomenon of GNP being consistently higher than that of GDP says that a large component of Philippine income and output is being accounted for by Philippine factors working in other countries, not at home. The source of output is mainly the out-migration of labour resources to countries of high wages for Philippine labour. In mature economies that export capital to other countries, it is capital that makes up the difference in their GNP and GDP. From 1991, the GNP began to get larger by virtue of the flow of net labour incomes from overseas Filipino workers (OFWs) sending remittances from abroad.

The discrepancy is seen in the ratio of GNP to GDP. This has been consistently higher than one in the 1990s. In 1999, the deviation of GNP was by a factor of 5.6 per cent. By 2005, this deviation was 8.3 per cent. Thus, GNP has outstripped GDP by as much as those levels, assuming the absence of statistical discrepancies. The differences in the total level of output are systematic in their tendency. Suppose, for convenience of illustration alone, that in a given year the initial values of the GDP and the GNP were equal. In 2004, the GDP was P4 trillion in current terms. If GNP grew more by 0.5 per cent of the growth rate of the GDP, the resulting difference in net output would be P20 billion. Cumulate this growth on a year-to-year basis and it is quite a large amount in five years in terms of level of output.

Thus, Philippine labour works abroad in combination with productive foreign capital located in those countries. Viewed from the Philippine side, the phenomenon manifests the relative inadequacy and inefficiency of the domestic capital. Philippine government policy is in control of providing better conditions for domestic capital formation and providing the proper regulation and protection of Filipino labour. Yet, the paradox of the problem is that the promotion of foreign employment by Filipinos is almost in a state of frenzy. But the promotion of inward foreign capital is still full of inconsistent fears and laws that restrict it in important sectors. There is no state frenzy (in spite of the often announced promotion of foreign investments) in removing the real bottlenecks that prevent foreign capital from coming in and participating more fully in the growth of the domestic economy.

COMPOSITION OF AGGREGATE OUTPUT AND DEMAND

A brief overview of aggregate demand and aggregate supply below discusses the pattern of output demand and supply.

Aggregate demand

Aggregate expenditure on output consists of private consumption, domestic investment (both public and private), government expenditure, and net foreign demand (demand for exports minus imports). Ignoring net foreign demand for the moment, we now examine these components of aggregate demand.

Private consumption expenditure is the largest component of aggregate demand, ranging from 72 per cent to 75 per cent of total aggregate demand (GNP). In 2005, this was 72.6 per cent of total demand. Government consumption expenditure has ranged from 5.9 per cent to 7.7 per cent of total demand. The lower demand depends on the level of fiscal disbursements to support government operations. The composition of aggregate demand is based on gross figures of income. Total consumption, combining that of private consumption and that of government spending, takes up close to 80 per cent of total final demand. In general, the remainder is relegated to the combined gross domestic capital formation of the economy.

Gross capital formation in the economy is around 20 per cent of total demand. Part of total demand represents net foreign demand that in recent years has been in favour of relatively more importation of goods and services. As a result, gross capital formation has been a little less than the 20 per cent level of total aggregate demand.

The Philippine economy is highly consumption driven. Poor economic performance at home is partly propped up by the influx of income transfers from OFW remittances, which in recent years have continued to grow. The vibrancy of the retail sector especially in the Metro Manila area and in other cities and towns where air-conditioned retail malls have been established indicates the strength of purchasing power that is powered from the incomes of workers abroad sending dependent families incomes for their consumption needs at home. The presence of a young dependent population arising from the country's high rate of population growth also makes a contribution to this. The persistence of a highly young and dependent population creates a heavy pull of demand for consumption in the economy.

Aggregate Supply of Output

The aggregate supply of output is what the economy produces in the country. In 2005, agriculture supplied 17.8 per cent of GNP; industry (which includes manufacturing) 30.7 per cent of GNP; and services 44 per cent of GNP. This composition is slightly different from that of 2000. Agriculture then was higher in relative composition, 18.5 per cent of GNP; industry 33.2 per cent of GNP; and services 42 per cent of GNP. Such a slow pattern of change in production has been happening over time.[2]

In the normal case, the structural change in output predicts a rising industrial sector in terms of total output until industrial growth has reached some kind of maturity. That is the pattern found in most developed countries today. But these advanced economies experienced in their economic history a process of growth in which industrial expansion played a major role. The relative decline of their industry began when rising costs at home and the effectiveness of competition from other countries resulted in their loss of competitive advantage.

The composition of Philippine output however shows the relative decline of agriculture and industry to total output and the rise of the contribution of services. At the current stage of development, the pattern that is observed for the relative loss of importance of agriculture within a growing economy is not surprising. What is less expected is the relative decline of industry in relation to total output. With an economy that is still highly agricultural in terms of the dependence of the general population on rural and industrial employment, the Philippine economy is actually gradually moving away in relative terms from both agriculture and industry and towards a service-oriented economy without having reached a high degree of industrialization. The expansion of industry and of agriculture does not catch up with the absorption of excess labour and the service sector is expanding more rapidly than the two other sectors.

Some of the promising efforts that were designed to raise the level of industrialization through the development of basic industries failed to grow out of the protective shell of the import substitution framework. When the design for export markets was the target, the heavy dose of government participation in the essentially private sector projects helped to doom the projects. The steel industry, for instance, was initially designed for a small market and the project was heavily borrowed at the start. Perhaps the more critical factor was the poor choice of principal investor. Industrial cronyism was part of the Philippine political economy for large projects. Strong interests backed up highly protected industries. However, such a process was unsustainable over the long term.

Having thrived under heavy protection and governmental patronage in the past but still essentially undercapitalized even with access to government financial support, these early efforts in heavier industrial activity became victims of economic crises or financial collapse once they were exposed to international competition and market forces. These enterprises suffered the pressure of limited markets and the rising cost of credit due to interest rate and foreign exchange depreciation. Their high level of foreign debts, lack of markets abroad, and high costs at home caused them to buckle under greater import competition. However, there are enterprises that were conceived under high levels of protection that survived the shedding of protection and have become more versatile participants in the market place as a result. Through mergers and acquisitions as well as privatization, some of the failing industrial enterprises have thrived under changes in ownership and economic rehabilitation.[3]

Despite these problems, new industries powered by a liberalization of foreign capital inflows did very well and strengthened the country's growth of new exports. These are the new industries that did not depend on tariff protection or market monopolies but which thrive in the open market. Around this framework of industrial growth has sprung the growth of new comparative advantage in international trade. The growth of electronics exports has been propelled by the influx of foreign direct investments in these areas. As a result, the industrial sector has become vibrant and new directions have opened under a more competitive industrial regime.

SAVING-INVESTMENT GAP OR WHY THE LOW INVESTMENT RATE?

Philippine capital formation rates during 1990 and 1995 were 22 per cent and 24 per cent of GDP, respectively. This fell to around 18 per cent of GDP in 2000 (as an after effect of the Asian financial crisis and the political troubles of Joseph Estrada that brought in great uncertainty). In contrast, from 1974 to 1983, the country's capital formation rates ranged from 27 per cent to 33 per cent of GDP. Five of those years involved capital accumulation rates in excess of 30 per cent of GDP. The historic average of capital accumulation before 1974 was an average of 21 per cent of GDP, still a high rate compared to the recent decline of investments. From 2000 to 2005, the rate of investments has fallen to around 20 per cent of GDP. This rate of investment is even lower when measured in terms of a percentage of GNP (because GNP has exceeded consistently that of GDP).

The amount of domestic investment that is financed from the national saving rate can be implied from the ratio of the domestic saving rate to total investment rate (as per cent ratios of GDP), which is also a measure of the saving-investment gap. The high-saving economies finance most of their investment needs; in short, they have almost no saving-investment gap. The gap that arises is essentially the result of short-run imbalances, including some structural problems arising from the immaturity of financial institutions. China, despite its huge inflows of foreign direct investments, is essentially self-financing its domestic investments. South Korea is minimally dependent on foreign saving for its investment needs in recent years.

The Philippine saving rate is low and represents the bottleneck for attaining a higher rate of economic performance. It is deficient in relation to the country's investment needs. It is low in relation to what other East Asian countries have accomplished and continue to achieve. It is low further in relation to what was possible in the country before — from 1974 to 1981, for instance, the investment rate ranged from 27 per cent to 33 per cent of GDP, made possible because the fiscal sector could produce peso counterpart funding for development projects. The national saving rate constrains the possibility of a better and higher level of investments, for it reduces the capacity of the country to take in additional inflows of capital, both new debt and foreign direct investments.

In high-growth countries in the East Asia region, the saving rates were consistently sustained at high levels. During 1985 to 2000, the rates of saving in these countries permitted high rates of domestic capital accumulation. In China, the rates of capital formation were in the order of 36 per cent to 41 per cent of GDP during this period. South Korea had rates ranging from 28 per cent (during the crisis period of 2000 — after-effects of the Asian financial crisis) to highs of 37 per cent of GDP during the 1990s.

Among the five original ASEAN countries during the 1990s, the Philippines had the lowest recorded rate of capital formation. Malaysia and Singapore have had outstanding rates of domestic investment, ranging from 27 per cent to 43 per cent for Malaysia, and Singapore ranging from 31 per cent to 36 per cent of GDP during the 1990s respectively. Thailand's rate of investment of 42 per cent of GDP during the 1990s was almost twice that of the Philippines during the same period. Indonesia consistently had a high rate of investment of around 30 per cent of GDP during the growth years under Suharto. During the crisis years, in 2000, the rate fell to 15 per cent of GDP.

Of the ASEAN countries, Singapore has become a saving surplus country, having essentially more saving than it can invest in the domestic economy. As a result, it has become a capital exporting country. Malaysia is close to achieving self-sufficiency. Of the three other original ASEAN countries, the Philippines today is most dependent on foreign capital for its investment needs. In 1990 and 1995, only around three fourths of its investments were financed from domestic saving. The low level of investment partly arises from the limitations of saving. That limitation also contributes towards providing an upper limit on the inflow of foreign saving. As it is, the level of relatively high dependence on foreign saving makes the country more vulnerable to economic downturns arising from loss of business confidence and to external factors that affect the flows of capital from other countries and to the country specifically.

The capacity of private enterprises to save depends on their ability to earn profits. Profitability depends on the business environment in which they thrive. In general, that environment is made possible by the presence of competitive markets in the goods market. Producers have to face competitive market forces from imported substitutes and from other domestic producers. As a result, producers have to position themselves to produce at low cost in order to thrive. Trade and industrial reforms in the past improved the competitive framework of the goods market. The presence of fiscal and investment incentives further made it possible for some cost disadvantages to be overcome.

Factor markets that the enterprises face are also very important. The contradictory nature of the policies for labour and for capital (as expounded already) has limited the opportunity to make major gains in inducing greater investments in the economy. Without the presence of profitable enterprises, the capacity to generate higher levels of saving in the private sector is also hampered.

Total saving to finance investment comes from three sources: domestic saving of households and enterprises; saving arising from the public sector, including those of government operations; and saving from foreign sources, both foreign direct investment and foreign lending.

The capacity of enterprises and households to save is supplemented by forced saving schemes that are fostered by government programmes. Of the latter, pension funds and retirement funds — the Social Security System, the Government Service Insurance System, and medical and housing funds — are significant sources of institutional saving derived from households and enterprises. In Singapore and Malaysia, the central provident savings of households have brought in enormous resources to help finance investments in housing and other social amenities.

In the Philippines, much needs to be done in mobilizing these financial resources to support private and public investment. These sources of saving have been used to help finance public investment requirements, including support of housing. In addition, they have been used to help in supporting particular private investments, sometimes in the rescue of ailing banking institutions that later were put into rehabilitation. The pension systems based on social security have become significant as generators of financial savings.

Economic policy liberalization has helped to expand the amount of foreign direct investment in the economy. The flow of foreign investments happened in the assembly and manufacture of parts for the electronics industry. Today, much activity is happening in the industries that take advantage of outsourcing of back office operations which is also powered by foreign investments. But in general, total foreign direct investments have not been as large as the flows that have gone into other regions of Southeast Asia and East Asia in general. In part, some restrictive provisions that discouraged substantial foreign capital in natural resource exploitation, investments in land (therefore in agriculture, commerce and property market), and most of all public utilities have played a role in this.

Philippine access to foreign direct investments has been relatively modest compared to the experience of neighbouring East Asian countries. This was not always the case in recent times. In part, the political arena has contributed to the problem. Public debate on economic policies often contains unfavourable political rhetoric that unsettles established consensus on economic issues. In addition, political turbulence arising from perceived threats to social stability due to attempted military coups has heightened tensions. Other factors relate to the litigious nature of the business environment.

FISCAL DEFICIT: TAXES, EXPENDITURE, AND PUBLIC DEBT

For years, government fiscal operations have resulted in deficit. Risks of larger shortfalls in resources when fiscal deficits occur in a persistent manner have higher costs. The financing of the deficit has implications for credit policy, creating a potential trade-off between private use of credit and the government's financing of its fiscal problems. Weak fiscal discipline could stir inflationary expectations and lead to a weakening of the exchange rate. The fiscal position of the government is sensitive to external circumstances because of the economy's openness.

From 2001 to 2004, the fiscal deficit remained on average at around 4 per cent of GDP, peaking at 5.3 per cent of GDP in 2003. As stated in the previous section, improving the fiscal performance of the government is one way of improving the national saving rate, as the persistent fiscal deficit problem of the government contributes to the low saving rate of the economy. Since total savings is the sum of private and public saving, when government revenues are inadequate to cover public expenditure, the deficit contributes to a negative public saving. Therefore national saving is in part reduced.

Fiscal deficits weaken the national saving rate from the government side. This creates pressure for borrowing from the private sector or from external sources. In the latter case, the external public debt rises especially if private savings is inadequate. The financing of the fiscal deficit competes directly with the uses of private credit. The private sector requires its own use of credit for investment and for operations. Its capacity as a generator of its own income surpluses, or savings, is also hampered. This restrains private saving rates. Monetary reform on the other hand has made it more difficult now to borrow from the central bank for purposes of the deficit.

The fiscal performance of the government can be improved *via* a number of routes: improved tax performance; increase of the government's non-tax revenue sources; greater efficiency of tax administration; reduced waste in public spending through the streamlining, focus and reorganization of the government including greater vigilance in stopping corruption. But an indication of the need for tax revenues is that, in recent years, the government has had to cancel quite a lot of projects that were financed by multilateral and bilateral lending institutions for lack of counterpart peso funding support.

Tax Revenues

The ratio of total government revenues to GDP was 17.4 per cent in 1999. This was to be the highest level during the next six years. The ratio fell by 3 percentage points to 14.5 per cent in 2005. The tax effort (total taxes as per cent of GDP) was of course even lower, because total government revenues are the sum of tax revenues and all forms of non-tax revenues — fees, profits of government entities, and revenues derived from the sale of services rendered and property owned by the government. Tax revenue effort in 1999 was 15.6 per cent. Between 2000 and 2006, the tax revenue effort fell from 14.5 per cent in the first year and fell even further to 12.4 per cent by 2005.

Such numbers for revenue and tax efforts are comparable for similar fiscal efforts of governments in East Asia. The Philippine numbers are on the low side of the distribution among these observations. One big reason for the relatively low tax efforts in other countries as well is the prevalence of investment and tax incentives that form a feature of the investment climates everywhere. Competition to offer the most attractive incentives, especially among ASEAN countries, has been a race to the bottom.

Reforming the investment incentives through a reduction of the excessive fiscal grants to private investors is a delicate issue. A streamlining of tax incentives by unifying them under a single system of fiscal incentives for the Board of Investments and the export processing zones investors would improve the setup, reduce some of the excessive incentives, and simplify further the promotion of investments. Such a programme, if planned, should be undertaken with assurance to investors in the country so as not to create any uncertainty for them. There is a great need to inject confidence in the business and investment climate through reassurance that reforms in this area will not affect currently enjoyed fiscal incentives.

The government's low attention to fiscal reform received a jolt from a paper of a group of economics professors at the University of the Philippines (UP) School of Economics that warned of the consequences of the large fiscal deficits. Up until that time, and during the all-important occasion when the president made a post-election speech assessing the nation's future, the official rhetoric continued to be on expenditure programme promises, omitting a warning on the nature of the fiscal problem. The UP paper essentially emphasized that fiscal inaction put the country on the brink of a serious economic and financial crisis.[4] The leadership, Congress, and general public were jolted into action. Publicity of this analysis called for action or the nation would face an economic crisis similar to the macroeconomic collapse of Argentina in 2003.

In early 2006, a substantial set of fiscal measures restored the country's fiscal fortunes. The government raised the 10 per cent Value Added Tax (VAT) to 12 per cent and removed many exemptions and adjusted zero rates. Of the major fiscal measures taken, this one effectively stemmed the decline of the tax effort. At once a number of improvements in the country's macroeconomic outlook were reinforced. Fiscal fundamentals improved, with revenues rising significantly and fiscal constraints being relaxed somewhat more. The economy's outlook in the short run turned positive. The decline of the peso exchange rate stabilized.

The reform of the VAT produced a change in expectations about tax revenue growth and the improvement of the fiscal position. With this, together with other favourable factors concerning payment inflows to the country, the perceptions about the economy's position changed. The peso exchange rate, which had depreciated badly as a result of fiscal woes from 1997 to 2005, began to improve appreciably. This appreciation reached a point that it became a concern for exporters. From a low of 55 pesos to a U.S.

dollar, the rate in October 2006 had improved to 50 pesos to the U.S. dollar. The assessment of sovereign credit rating agencies improved in tone: downgrades that were made because of the worsening fiscal position became less damaging in their later assessments and an improved assessment of future fiscal prospects became a more common theme of their analysis.[5]

In the case of excise taxes, Congress displaced an *ad valorem* tax base for so-called sin taxes — especially cigarettes and tobacco — in favour of specific taxes that were fixed to 1996 prices. Because of inflation and the lack of a flexible inflation rebasing mechanism, the tax take on these objects of taxation had fallen off the pace of economic growth — a desirable feature of tax buoyancy therefore had been lost. The tobacco companies have a strong lobby that successfully checks any attempts of Congress to raise taxes on the sin goods. Obviously, there is need to raise the buoyancy of taxes with respect to changing incomes. Since excise taxes are structured as per unit or specific taxes, they need to get rebased to a higher level of values with price inflation. The Philippines is one of the least taxed countries in terms of cigarettes, tobacco, and alcohol. It is somewhat ironic that the government was able to adjust tax rates on fuel, a very touchy and basic need, but failed to properly rebase those on tobacco!

Tax Administration

Raising the tax effort is often mixed with the problem of the efficiency of tax administration. Both are needed to improve tax collections without changing tax rates and for fiscal stability. In fact, with increased efficiency, further tax rises can be postponed. But somehow, the two go together if the government has to raise its fiscal discipline to a higher level. For one thing, the peso funding for foreign financed public infrastructure projects would need to be made available.

Government efforts to deal with tax administration are focused on improving the administration of the tax collection agencies. Some are linked with administrative changes — personnel changes affecting the collecting agencies at the national and at regional administrative districts, with changes in management practices, including the building of special units of collection for big tax payers, computerization and so on. The most significant change recently is linked to the introduction of pay incentives and targets for personnel. Efforts to pin down widely publicized cases of tax evasion have had difficulty succeeding in the court system.

The last effort is still tied up with a more drastic reordering of incentives and pay of the bureau personnel. The last of these changes still needs to be fully implemented since it was passed almost simultaneously with the VAT reform. Varying degrees of success have been met by the other reforms. In general, it is linked with the effectiveness of the national leadership in dealing with the tax administration issue. It is also tied up with the quality of the appointments at the top of the bureaus. Some of the best bureau directors have not lasted long in their jobs — an indicator of the difficulty of reform in this area.

Public Expenditure Efficiency

Some government expenditure is dissipated through waste and corruption. Corruption in publicly executed projects is widely known to be a problem. It is apparently systemic: the process of bids and contracting is one issue. The other is in the execution of projects. Infrastructure projects that are fully funded by the government tend to be of poor quality. A high degree of accountability in the bidding, construction, and audit system needs to be put in place — an improved governance of public administration. High profile cases have set back the country's international image and practically added higher costs in terms of actual delays and prolonged economic inconveniences for the general community. The landmark case that symbolizes this is the new international airport terminal in Manila, which is now on its third year of inoperation after almost having been finished. This case has been a black mark on the country's investment promotion programme.

Projects funded from international development institutions tend to be of better quality and with reasonable construction periods than those directly funded from peso funds. Internationally funded projects have more steady sources of financing and are therefore likely to get finished on time. Their quality and durability in the end mean lower maintenance and repair costs. This is most evident in the case of road and port projects and irrigation projects. This says a great deal about the quality of supervision and the nature of accountabilities that are observed during the process of construction, audit and post-construction. These examples indicate that governance is a major problem.

Projects undertaken with peso financing should be as good as those funded from loan programmes if proper governance were in place. To strengthen the accountabilities of the present system requires effective leadership from the government. (In contrast, changing the political system or the structure of certain institutions is just a palliative that forces diversionary issues into play.)

Endemic corruption in public works contracts and execution has been a concern for years. The bad reputation of locally constructed projects could be partly aggravated by the pork-barrel system of allocations for members of Congress, a practice that was re-introduced with a vengeance after martial law. Of course, the pork barrel refers to the budgetary allocation to members of Congress and the Senate some amount of money to help out in the financing of their favourite projects, often for their constituencies. The pork barrel is a concession to political expediency.

One example of how this has reduced public use of funds is that invariably the quality of roads produced through this method is generally poor. The mincing of public resources into different small parts has contributed to the ill execution of projects even though these are often good rural projects. An alternative system for the allocation of public money for projects that involve the participation of the legislative branch needs to be instituted to replace the waste of the pork-barrel system.

Public Enterprises and Privatization

Public corporations have added to the fiscal problem because of heavy losses incurred in their operations. The problems of the public financial enterprises were dealt with during the reforms of the 1990s.[6] This included their downsizing and recapitalization, their charter revisions, and some element of privatization. The current problems have to do with those public corporations that deal with the delivery of infrastructure, of public utility services, and with development as well as price stabilization.

There is no reason why government owned corporations delivering public utility services should be losing money. If allowed to maintain a fair rate of return on their operations, profitability of these public corporations could be sustained. The idea behind government ownership and control is that they require large investments and the dearth of private enterprise and capital to provide these major services. Part of the problem is tied up with the restrictions placed on the maximum equity that foreign capital can play in public utilities, a rule that is imposed in the constitution. Public utilities are often natural monopolies and those who obtain the appropriate franchises are often under-capitalized.

Political interference in the control and operations of these enterprises often leads to erratic and ill-timed decisions on the pricing of their services. These interventions often end in large consumer subsidies, hence losses in operations. Another aspect of this interference often causes management to become inefficient through over-employment and inability to move personnel. Sound corporate governance of public corporations is an issue that competes with privatization. Introducing sound corporate governance in the public sector is a delicate operation that needs continuous nurturing. Privatization, however, offers the alternative of closing down the public role, except in the form of regulation.

The reforms undertaken in the public corporate sector have difficulty taking root unless the issue of public control of their services is severed from politics. Without the development of strong public institutions of governance, the same problems of financial indiscipline would keep coming back. Political interference often dissipates the ability of well meaning management to function effectively. The cycles of political change in an electoral democracy contribute to such disruptions.

Public corporations are likely to be more subject to political interference in pricing decisions. The concept of fair rate of return could become a victim of political expediency and populist action.[7] Management that is interfered with often becomes hostage to the decline of sound practices. Rent seeking, if not corruption, could permeate their operations, either through the supply contracting or through the provision of their service.[8]

Privatization therefore appears to be the better alternative. Privatization is permanent in that most if not all the problems would be removed from the public domain. Private sector management is more likely to be stable and efficient than public sector management, especially if public salaries are kept at the low rates that these public enterprises often suffer from.

These considerations have caused the move toward privatization of major public corporations to be a desirable reform direction. In the early 1990s, the government took advantage of privatization. It proved more difficult to sell large government-owned public utilities than to sell the land assets of the government. The privatization of the waterworks system has generally led to better management of the system than under the old regime of a completely public set up.[9]

Privatization of enterprises that sell their services to the general public will become successful if the buyers of privatized assets are well capitalized, have a reputable track record in their running of similar enterprises, and are dedicated to the task of improving the service. Such buyers have access to expertise in the industry in addition to access to the international capital market to augment their capital contribution. Privatization, if the government makes it a credible exercise, could lead to the successful turnover of viable public enterprises into private entities that are better managed and capitalized.

By moving these enterprises to the private domain through privatization, their fiscal burden is removed.

Financing the Public Debt

In recent years, total public sector debt as a result of the fiscal deficits has risen. By 2000, total public debt had reached parity with the level of the GDP, even though about 75 per cent of that is directly due to the national government. From 2001 to 2005 the ratio of public debt to GDP soared to 1.18 (or 118 per cent of GDP). The rise of the public debt is still essentially within reasonable limits taking into account other countries.

The debt service has two faces. The internal debt service burden is linked with the capacity of the government to raise tax money to service the public debt. Of course, the other option is to refinance the debt with debt, a highly popular method of just continually raising the fiscal deficit. When taxes become inadequate, the proportion of the budget that is devoted to debt service naturally rises. An obvious impact of this is to restrain the amount of public resources devoted to the programmes of government that are designed to provide public services, including raising the capacity to raise public capital formation. The complaint that the budget for debt service is the highest expenditure of the government is related to the fact that fiscal deficits have been high and that public tax resources have failed to catch up with wiping out the government's (primary) fiscal deficit.

The second face of the debt service burden refers to the external debt burden. Here, the problem is one of maintaining a high enough level of export and foreign exchange earnings capacity so as to pay for the required debt service. If export earnings and inflows of foreign exchange suffer a downturn, the debt service burden rises (assuming the same level of external debt).

The diversification of the sources of foreign exchange earnings is important for the stabilization of the debt service burden. Those debts that need to be rolled over face interest rate and foreign exchange risks as new terms are sought. Debt consolidations and improvement of long-term debt position is one method of doing this. This requires accessing the capital markets — both domestic and international — in order to float bonds of long-term duration to finance the public debt. In recent years, the government's access to the capital market has improved.

However, access to international credit depends on the perception of the country's fiscal operations. If the fiscal sector suffers from heavy deficits, the country is penalized by higher costs of financing. Pricing is based on LIBOR

(London inter-bank rate), and the poorer the assessment of the credit rating of the country, the higher is the interest rate penalty. Of course, the other problem that would bite in that circumstance is whether the exchange rate depreciates as a result of the deficits. In that case, a double penalty is felt in the matter of foreign borrowing.

The servicing of interest payments from the debt was 4.2 per cent of GDP in 2000. This rose to 5.6 per cent of GDP in 2005. The magnitude of the debt service on long-term resources will be large until the government is able to improve its fiscal position. Reduction of the fiscal deficit can be undertaken through a combination of tax increases, expenditure moderation, privatization of non-essential demands on the government and prudent management of the overall fiscal resources.

The high cost of the interest service of the public debt in the budgetary allocations of the government is troublesome. The risk of exposure to a rise in interest rates has the potential of tilting the economy towards crisis if the rise is sudden and steep. This is because the debt service represents one-fourth of the total resources devoted to the government's public expenditure programme. The politics of the debt then becomes a problem for managing the public debate on how little remaining resources are left to finance other government programmes and priorities. This is where the efforts to raise the level of taxation have paid-off because higher revenues raise the budgetary levels and reduce the relative burden of interest cost as a percentage of the budget.

More important is the effect of relying on extraordinary revenues that can be collected as a result of the programme of privatization if it is done correctly and is undertaken with greater speed so that the nation realizes the fiscal benefits sooner. Privatization revenues reached almost 2 per cent of GDP in the early 1990s for two years when the government sold many public entities. The revenues from privatization are not permanent but their effects on the fiscal budget could be long-lasting.

The scale of the next round of privatization in the energy sector could bring in more resources to the government. This could provide the opportunity to reduce the principal debt and thereby help to extinguish interest cost. But so long as development projects yield productive outputs and are not overpriced, the interest cost of servicing the public debt will yield positive benefits for the economy.

TRADE, BALANCE OF PAYMENTS, AND EXTERNAL DEBT

The Philippine economy has been an open economy for years, even during the period of foreign and exchange controls in the distant past. Today the economy is more open than at any time during the republic's history. Through the policy of economic liberalization of the trade and industrial front, the exchange rate has become flexible and public consciousness already accepts exchange rate variability as a fact of life.

In general, the movement of the exchange rate has caused the path of the economy to take a more realistic and pragmatic course in providing some kind of balance between internal and external prices. The level of the peso exchange rate no longer causes acrimonious public debate. Instead, the peso exchange rate is now taken for granted as changing on a daily basis as a result of the pushes and pulls of the marketplace — domestic and international happenings — that are an integral aspect of the country's daily life.

The liberalization of the economy has helped to strengthen the country's external payments position. The exchange rate of the peso has become a price stimulus for creating export industries and as a brake against imports. The country is geared as never before towards balancing export growth with import restraint. Some structural distortions in industry and agriculture remain, arising from tariff protection despite reforms that have brought down high nominal tariff levels. The major distortions arise from policies regarding resource use. Policies related to factors of production — whether labour or capital — continue to provide a drag on economic performance.

The exchange rate is highly sensitive to short-run changes in expectations. The source of instability is the movement of short-run capital flows often in relation to the volatility of the domestic capital stock exchange. For instance, when the fiscal difficulties during the early part of the decade were pronounced, the peso exchange rate depreciated sharply as a result of withdrawals of funds from the country. This heightens the nature of the domestic shocks. At the beginning of 2006, however, as a result of the anticipated improvement of the fiscal position of the government due to the passage of major fiscal reforms, the peso exchange rate has appreciated. (The peso exchange rate appreciated to the level of 50 pesos to the dollar when only a few months before it was 55 pesos to the dollar.) The volatility of the short-run exchange rate fluctuations has implications for many aspects of the economy, not the least of which are export industries that require a more stable exchange rate framework in order to thrive.

Exports and Industrial Performance

Exports during the early 1990s had spectacular growth, brought in by the foreign direct capital inflows related to the manufacture of semiconductors. This experience had a gestation that began in the late 1970s, something whose acceleration was delayed because of the economic and political volatility of the 1980s. The export boom in this industry established the Philippines as a component of the production base for the revolution in technology and telecommunications in the dynamic economies of East Asia. The great industrial boom in this technological revolution in the production place has found a niche in comparative advantage for Philippine labour skills.

The export sector is gradually changing in character. Even though electronics and semiconductors dominate manufactured exports, there is potential for a deeper expansion of the industry as suppliers and manufacturers agglomerate to form a network of producers. A potential for deeper expansion of the industry could take place if complementary factors and infrastructure continue to improve within the country. Car parts manufacturing exports contribute to the growing sophistication of the ASEAN complementation in this industry, as this is linked primarily within the ASEAN and Asian markets. It is most fully integrated in Thailand, with other countries having become satellites of that network.

Foreign direct investments in shipbuilding represent a new phase in the country's export industrialization. Since the mid-90s, a Japanese shipbuilding company has been expanding its operations in Cebu, and current commitment has led to the entry of a major Korean shipbuilding enterprise in the Subic area. The future of a number of new export industries brought in by world-quality export players guarantees that some growth in this area will be expected.

The country missed the great export boom in labour-intensive skills for industrialization based on garments, textiles and other labour-intensive skills decades before. That was the pattern of industrial growth that propelled the early industrialization of virtually every other East Asian developing country. In the case of the semiconductor industry, the wage rate for the types of high skills of the labour force required for assembly of semiconductors and computers was competitive. And the first flush of industrial manufacturing success for the Philippines helped to win the domestic debate about economic liberalization in the country.

Export performance just before the Asian financial crisis of 1997–2000 had been at spectacular rates, averaging just short of 20 per cent per year. By 1998, export levels had peaked to almost US$40 billion. Seen in relative terms with respect to East Asian counterparts, this expansion of exports is quite modest. By 2000, the level of exports of Malaysia was US$98 billion (more than double the Philippine export level); that of Thailand US$69 billion (more than one-and-a-half times that of the Philippines).

In 1985, the Philippines was in severe economic crisis (that was brought about by internal political events and the third world debt crisis that engulfed it) while Malaysia, Thailand, and Indonesia received massive flows of capital from the Northeast Asian industrial countries that were transferring industries to other countries, mainly to neighbouring Southeast Asia. By 1990, Thailand, Malaysia, and Singapore had at least doubled the level of their exports of goods and services. The Philippine case showed the same doubling but 1985 was the worst year of the economy when the country was in severe crisis. In fact, there was hardly much growth if, for instance, 1980 was used as the base rather than 1985. But the scale of growth of exports between 2000 and 1990 was extraordinary, and the Philippine case showed a very good improvement in scale. From the still low level of exports of 1990 at the time and compared with other East Asian countries, the Philippines had the highest multiple growth in export.

The financial crisis towards the close of the 1990s created a downturn in the export sector affecting a wide range of export products. Otherwise the Philippine export growth of the period would have been even more impressive. By then, semiconductor parts accounted for almost 70 per cent of total export revenues. The effect of the crisis was in part to make the export sector grow somewhat modestly from that point on throughout the first half of 2005. Developments during this period intensified some of the trade competition with East Asian neighbours.

Within ASEAN and as a result of the projected ASEAN Free Trade Area (AFTA) that was by then an agreed programme of future cooperation, the reorganization of industries and exports began to take on a region-wide realignment, with foreign direct investors especially directing mainstream industries (in the consumption based industries especially), reorganizing and rationalizing their market positions. Some trade diversion took place with some Philippine industries moving to other production sites in ASEAN and other countries where overall unit costs were lower. Many formerly import substituting industries shifted production sites from the Philippines to ASEAN competitors and China. Some of the operations in the semiconductor industrial revolution also transferred their production sites to China and Vietnam. But the complementary production of semiconductors in other fields had created new levels of trade. The restructuring of industry has been going on, and part of the transitional move is the relocation of production centres where the least cost of production and comparative advantage in all aspects of the productive trade contributes to the outcome.

In this industrial development, Philippine success has so far been modest. In part, the reason is two-fold. Political uncertainty at home worsened because of the leadership changes at home that were outside of the ordinary constitutional process.[10] The stormy politics of the last six years was therefore not of much help in stabilizing the economy's forward course. The lag in infrastructure services that had accumulated after decades of persistent fiscal deficit problems and poor domestic investment levels in that sector aggravated competitiveness on an international level. The scale of needs has grown more in a larger economy with a bigger population.

Trade and Payments Balance

The growth of trade — of exports and imports — mirrors the open economy. In 2005, export revenues topped the US$40 billion level again, with exports rising modestly from year to year during 2000–05. Imports have become higher because of the growth of energy imports and of raw materials needs of the active semi-conductors assembly sector. The balance of payments of the country has improved over the years. In 2006, despite the pressure of high prices of petroleum imports and their uncertainty in supply because of the volatile situation in the Middle East, the balance of payments improved. The trade balance has been negative but the current accounts balance has been kept solvent. The capital accounts balance has improved somewhat because the country has much more access to international credit. This has permitted an improvement of the country's overall payments position, making international reserves rise.

Several factors account for this improvement of the balance of payments. For one thing, open economic policy has allowed movements of capital and permitted a wider movement of goods and factors so that while exports could be developed, raw materials for exports and capital goods could be made available at home more easily.

The industrial sector, especially the newly rising competitive sector including the burgeoning export sector, has access to international credit. This growing sector is more cost-effective and efficient than the highly import-dependent import-substituting sector which was a high cost for the economy and highly inefficient. The current import-substituting sector that resulted from the restructuring of recent years can avail itself of raw materials from abroad on their own credit. Moreover, the manufacturing sector based on export markets has access to finance from the world capital market through their parent companies or through the financial sector in the

Philippines. The banking and financial reforms of the 1970s and the 1990s helped to strengthen domestic banking and internationalized its outlook.

Capital flows continue to be free, following capital deregulation and liberalization in the previous decades. The current policy rules and regulations have hardened through monitoring across countries as a result of international efforts linked with money laundering arising from hot money movements. But the regulations are formed within a liberal framework.

The market-based peso exchange rate policy allowed the peso to float relatively freely, thereby making it possible for international payments to proceed quite freely and for values on goods and services to seek their proper levels. The economy was made freer from price controls on consumer essentials. Price controls on fuel and other essentials have been removed as a result of the energy sector reform that was put in place during the early 2000s. As a result, energy prices are flexible and are relatively free of public acrimony and protests (compared to the time before the energy reform act was passed). These prices have become like the price of the peso in the foreign exchange market. Price flexibility in the exchange rate, fuel and other items has permitted domestic prices to remain relatively stable under the guidance of monetary policy that has kept inflation in the range of 7 per cent per year.

Foreign direct investment flows have improved. The record is modest in comparison with other countries during critical periods of their development. Foreign direct investments had come in substantially during the 1980s to 2000. Net foreign direct investments in 1999 were US$1,114 million and US$1,477 million in 2002, although in 2001 direct capital inflows fell to US$335 million. The average direct investments inflow for 2003 and 2004 fell to lows of US$188 million and US$109 million. In 2005, the level rose again but was just short of US$970 million. The fall in direct investment flows was due to political volatility and bad publicity about peace and order conditions during the period.

The drop in foreign direct investments during the early 2000s is partly an indication of the poor record of the privatization programme. Any success there would have meant new inflows of foreign direct investment as asset ownership changes took place. Recent adjustments arising from the financial crisis in East Asia at the close of the 1990s were facilitated by the influx of foreign direct investments in South Korea and in Thailand. In the Philippine case, the early episodes of foreign direct investment inflows were linked with major liberalization activities and the effort to bring in new strategic foreign investors in the banking system. Various infrastructure projects were undertaken on the basis of BOT (build-operate-transfer) investment arrangements related to the investments in the electricity generation field when the energy crisis dominated the problems of investments during the early 1990s.

The volumes of foreign direct investments registered during this period were quite modest compared to those that went to ASEAN partners like Indonesia, Malaysia, Singapore and Thailand. They were certainly much lower than the heavy flows that entered China during this period.

OFW Remittances

A new major factor in the balance of payments is the inflow of remittances from Overseas Filipino Workers (OFW). In 1999, remittances were US$6,022 million. From 2000 to 2005, remittances rose from US$6,050 million to US$10,689 million. OFW remittances are likely to reach more than US$12 billion by the end of 2006. The OFW remittances represent a major boon to the country's balance of payments position. The growth in OFW remittances has provided greater international liquidity in spite of the rise in energy imports. The remittances have helped to reduce the burden on the nation of the external debt service. OFW remittances in recent periods have constituted around 25 per cent of the overall receipts from exports and other payments inflows to the country.

External debt service constitutes 13.3 per cent of export receipts in 2005. This is an improvement over the ratio of 17.1 per cent of exports in 2003. Such volatility in debt service burden emphasizes the importance of rising export revenues as the base for shouldering the external debt burden. Translated into debt service as a percentage of total current accounts inflows (which now includes OFW remittances), the debt service burden in 2005 was 12.5 per cent and 15.8 per cent in 2003. In short, the effect of OFW remittances on easing the debt service burden is being felt. Quantitatively, it helps to ease about 7 per cent[11] of the total debt burden based on the capacity to pay through export earnings.

Other new sources of foreign exchange are shaping up and, in the near future, there are likely to be large jumps in new export activities. Call centres and other back-office operations have become a new industry with rising potential. Outsourcing through these new firms has produced a new boom in the employment of young professionals and college graduates with strong qualifications in the English language. The labour market for this group of workers is relatively thin, but the average salary is a large multiple of the minimum wage income for salaried workers. So the net income generation is relatively good. However, the supply of qualified workers is being cornered by the high demand for outsourcing coming from developed countries. The migration of workers exerts a competitive pull, with the problem of retaining workers at home to work in home industries.

Remittances from OFWs have helped to ease the pressure on the balance of payments and consequently on external debt servicing. There is less external indebtedness being incurred, except that maturing obligations are of course still refinanced. External debt finance is constrained by lack of counterpart financing, which is one way of saying that domestic saving is inadequate. The remittances have improved the payments inflows to create greater solvency for the balance of payments. This has obviously given the country more room to service the external debt. It is possible to buy back expensive short-term debts and to foster a sound debt profile that is affordable, which makes it possible to make room for more investments.

CONCLUDING REMARKS: DIRECTION WITHOUT DRIFT?

A forward view of the Philippine economy leaves one with qualified but hopeful possibilities. The macroeconomic fundamentals could be immensely strengthened through the pursuit of economic reforms that have eluded change in the past. From the government sector, fiscal sector reforms are basic to the improvement of the national saving rate. This means, essentially, trying to achieve a fiscal surplus on the operational side in order to provide strong support and finance to the public capital formation. Such an effort includes the need to speed up the stalemated privatization of state assets that have awaited such a programme.

The macroeconomic performance of the economy could be improved significantly through structural policy reforms affecting public utilities and infrastructure as well as land and natural resources. These will have an immense impact on investment performance in the economy. The clearest case of need is to generate a greater flow of capital to the hitherto restricted sectors where there is a great deal of inefficiency and where the need to improve is critical for raising overall economic performance. This reform needs to address the liberalization of foreign capital participation in the country's public utilities and infrastructure. This calls for a move to lift the restrictive provisions of the constitution on foreign capital participation in specific sectors of the economy. The changes in these directions constitute the difference between the present unimpressive economic growth rates that are experienced in the domestic economy and what could be possible — the performance that is characteristic of East Asian rapid growth.

Such measures will make it possible to achieve internal cost reductions. The poor state of public utility services in some regions of the country and of infrastructure services currently keeps costs high. By making possible the enlargement of the capacity and quality of service of Philippine public utilities and infrastructure facilities, domestic costs of production can be reduced. This is accomplished through the economy's increased efficiency resulting from these investments. This will help to make the economy more competitive by reducing internal costs of production for all investors. The country's export industries will be induced to become even more competitive as a result. In this manner, the main beneficiaries will be domestic factors of production because higher incomes and employment will result.

Getting the required economic reforms to work is not an easy job to do. If the economy is to catch up with the rest of high-growth East Asia, the hard economic reform issues have to be faced squarely. Reforms of the critical issues have to be pushed forward.

The scenario described above is hopeful and idealized. Under normal circumstances, governments do not fulfil ideal scenarios. But if leaders in the government stay close to certain ideas of honest economic reforms, the proper forward direction of the economy can be set in motion. The danger is that hesitation in the adoption of the required remedies is always tempting as an alternative. And often, these alternatives produce outcomes that are the basis of political advantage among contestants. Failing to get the reforms done properly contributes to the resistance to the economy's growth.

Notes

* The statistics used throughout the study are derived from Philippine government sources. They may be reviewed from the Philippine Economic Indicators in the Bangko Sentral webpage, <www.bsp.gov.ph>. The international data comparisons are taken and calculated from the Asian Development Bank's *Key Indicators*, an annual publication.

1 Studies of Philippine total factor productivity, pioneered by Richard Hooley and carried out by others, including Caesar Cororaton, have documented the poor record of total factor productivity. Although the findings about the low level of total productivity are consistent, the reasons for this occurrence have evaded consistent explanation. See Richard Hooley, "Productivity Growth in Philippine Manufacturing", Philippine Institute for Development Studies (PIDS); Cesar Cororaton, "Total Productivity in the Philippines", PIDS, Discussion Paper 2002.

2 The discussion of sector output aggregates is based on data calculated as a per cent of contribution to GNP. As a result, the percentage output of all the sectors do not total 100 per cent. This is not a discrepancy but is due to the fact that the GNP includes estimates of output that are called net factor incomes of the nationals living outside the country.

3 The restructuring of the cement industry was achieved essentially through its acquisition mainly by major international players in the cement industry. The steel industry has been resuscitated through privatization of the enterprise. The same is true with large-scale copper smelter plants.

4 The UP Eleven paper, so-nicknamed in public discussion, is written by Emmanuel de Dios, Benjamin E. Diokno, Emmanuel F. Esguerra, Raul V. Fabella, Ma. Socorro Gochoco-Bautista, Felipe M. Medalla, Solita C. Monsod, Ernesto M. Pernia, Renato E. Reside, Jr., Gerardo P. Sicat, and Edita A. Tan, "The Deepening Crisis: The Real Score on Deficits and the Public Debt", UP School of Economics, August 2004. The paper received major notice in the newspapers and suddenly became a focal point in the debate on the fiscal deficit.

5 Tracking down the press statements of the credit rating agencies — Fitch, S&P, Moody's, and others — for instance, in recent months following the passage of the VAT law, would show positive evaluation from them although they still await more positive macroeconomic news.

6 These were discussed in GP Sicat and R. Abdullah, "Public Finance", in *The Philippines: Development, Policies, and Challenges*, edited by A.B. Balisacan and Hal Hill (Oxford University Press, 2003), pp. 106–35. This volume of Balisacan and Hill provides a comprehensive discussion of various sectors of the economy, including recent developments and policy issues. The introductory essay of the two presents a thoughtful discussion of the key issues affecting development.

7 The National Power Corporation, instead of being allowed a return on its costs (in 2003), was made to bear additional losses amidst the public criticism against the rate increase of Meralco electric tariffs. The effect of the decision was to raise the losses borne by the National Power Corporation.

8 In general, corruption is not an issue as much as political interference. Many government corporations are professionally run. The public employees here are often checked by the presence of auditing and other public institutions that are designed to deal with corrupt practices. Often, the issue of public performance is related to protecting the integrity of the professional service against the incursions of political interference.

9 This privatization has done very well in the improvement of the management of the water utility compared to the previous public sector run utility. However, one of the major privatizing companies has encountered problems of insolvency mainly through problems related to its own poor financial structure.

10 Reference here is being made to the people power revolt (EDSA II) which unseated Estrada as President and replaced him by Mrs Macapagal Arroyo, the sitting vice president at that time. Current political problems in the country are focused on the question of legitimacy that arose from the outcome of the presidential election in 2004.

11 The rule of thumb I use for calculating this is by taking the fall of the debt service burden (based on current account receipts) to the debt-service burden as a ratio of export receipts (=0.8 divided by 13.3).

Appendix 7
Selected Macroeconomic Data for the Philippines

TABLE 7A
Output and Expenditure

Item	*1998*	*1999*	*2000*	*2001*	*2002*	*2003*	*2004*	*2005*	*2005*	*2006*
I. OUTPUT, EMPLOYMENT AND WAGES[1]									1st Semester	
A. GNP (Constant 1985 prices, Billion Pesos)	934.50	969.30	1,037.90	1,061.30	1,105.70	1,171.40	1,250.20	1,320.70	633.20	674.60
annual % change	0.40	3.70	4.80	2.30	4.20	6.00	6.70	5.60	5.40	6.50
(constant 1985 prices, US$ B)[2]	50.20	52.10	55.80	57.00	59.40	63.00	67.20	71.00	34.03	36.25
B. GNP (Current Prices, Billion Pesos)	2,802.10	3,136.20	3,566.10	3,876.60	4,218.90	4,631.50	5,235.20	5,876.30	2,749.90	3,094.10
C. GNP by Expenditure Shares (constant 1985 prices)										
1. Personal Consumption (Billion Pesos)	707.90	726.60	752.10	779.01	810.75	853.60	903.10	947.70	451.60	475.90
Percent share to total GNP	75.80	75.00	72.50	73.40	73.32	72.90	72.20	71.80	71.30	70.60
2. Government Consumption (Billion Pesos)	70.30	75.00	79.60	75.41	72.50	74.40	75.50	78.50	41.50	43.10
Percent share to total GNP	7.50	7.70	7.70	7.11	6.60	6.40	6.00	5.90	6.60	6.40
3. Gross Domestic Capital Formation										
(Billion Pesos)	196.80	192.90	239.05	221.60	212.10	218.40	234.10	219.90	112.00	107.70
(nominal as % of GNP)	19.40	17.80	19.90	17.80	16.60	15.70	15.60	14.00	14.70	13.40
Percent share to total GNP	21.10	19.90	23.00	20.90	19.20	18.60	18.70	16.70	17.70	16.00
D. GNP by Industrial Origin (constant 1985 prices)										
1. Agriculture, Fishery, Forestry										
(In Billion Pesos)	173.20	184.50	192.46	199.57	207.50	215.30	226.60	230.80	108.90	114.60

Percent share to total GNP	18.50	19.00	18.50	18.80	18.80	18.40	18.10	17.50	17.20	17.00
2. Industry Sector (In Billion Pesos)	313.90	316.70	345.04	336.50	349.50	363.50	380.50	399.10	190.60	200.40
Percent share to total GNP	33.60	32.67	33.24	31.70	31.60	31.00	30.40	30.20	30.10	29.70
of which:										
Manufacturing (Billion Pesos)	221.15	224.67	237.27	244.08	252.60	263.30	276.70	292.20	136.10	144.80
Construction (Billion Pesos)	51.80	50.99	64.38	49.50	47.50	47.10	48.70	49.10	24.90	24.80
3. Service Sector (In Billion Pesos)	400.92	417.05	435.46	453.98	477.10	506.30	545.00	579.60	279.70	296.70
Percent share to total GNP	42.90	43.03	41.96	42.78	43.20	43.20	43.60	43.90	44.20	44.00
E. GNP to GDP Ratio	1.06	1.07	1.07	1.07	1.08	1.08	1.08			
F. Per Capita GNP (constant 1985 prices; ₱)	12,433.00	12,625.00	13,516.00	13,504.00	13,794.00	14,307.00	14,962.00	15,490.00	7,464.00	7,794.00
G. Savings Rate 3, Note below.	21.46	20.59	22.74	22.95	23.11	26.15	27.46	27.63	..	..
H. Population (in million persons)[4]	73.32	75.04	76.79	78.59	80.16	81.90	83.60	85.30	84.80	86.50
annual % change		2.35	2.33	2.34	2.00	2.17	2.08	2.03	2.00	2.00
I. Unemployment Rate (Average; percent)[5]	10.05	9.80	11.20	11.10	11.40	11.40	11.80	11.40	11.70	11.40[r]

Source of Data: Bangko Sentral; Philippine government statistics

All footnotes (except as noted below) are explained in the Central Bank website on statistics. See <www.BSP.gov.ph>.

GNP to GDP Ratio (Percentage) — Constant 1985 prices.

Note on Savings: These savings data are not reconciled with the income accounts. Discussion of saving levels is based on income accounts framework.

TABLE 7B
Prices and Interest Rates

Item	*1998*	*1999*	*2000*	*2001*	*2002*	*2003*	*2004*	*2005*	*2005*	*2006*
II. PRICES										
A. Headline Inflation (2000=100)									January – September	
1. CPI, Philippines (all items, ave. % change)	9.30	5.90	4.00	6.80	3.00	3.50	6.00	7.60	7.90	6.80
of which: Food, Beverages and Tobacco	8.00	4.60	1.60	4.70	2.30	2.20	6.20	6.40[r]	6.70	5.70
Non-Food	10.50	7.60	6.40	8.80	3.80	4.60	5.80	8.70	9.00	7.70
B. Core Inflation (2000=100)	9.30	6.30	4.00	7.40	3.50	3.40	5.70	7.00	7.40	5.80
III. MONEY AND INTEREST RATES										
A. Money (End-of-Period)									July	
1. Money Supply (M1, P B)	281.51	394.13	386.98	388.00	470.10	510.30	556.40	605.30[p]	553.70	626.00[p]
2. Domestic Liquidity (M3, P B)	1,144.60	1,365.10	1,427.40	1,525.00	1,669.70	1,725.00	1,883.80	2,052.50[p]	1,965.10	2,206.10[p]
(as % of GDP)	42.95	45.86	42.55	41.99	42.12	39.96	38.77	37.88	38.45	38.75
3. Expanded Liquidity (M4, P B)[7]	1,622.49	1,886.76	2,013.38	2,111.10	2,298.10	2,401.50	2,649.30	2,814.30[p]	2,719.90	2,997.50[p]
(as % of GDP)	60.88	63.38	60.02	58.13	57.98	55.64	54.53	51.94[r]	53.26	53.09
4. Base Money (P B)	316.20	357.40	391.70	431.00	458.60	487.30	570.90	637.90	587.80	662.50[p]
B. Interest Rates (% p.a., average)										
Nominal Interest Rates									January – September	
1. Manila Ref. Rates (90 days)[10]	13.70	10.10	8.80	10.13	6.38	9.75	9.50	8.94	8.88	8.25
2. T-bills 91 days[11]	15.30	10.20	9.86	9.86	5.43	6.03	7.34	6.36	6.44	5.37

Source of Data: Bangko Sentral; Philippine government statistics.
All footnotes are explained in the Central Bank website on statistics. See <www.BSP.gov.ph>.

TABLE 7C
External Sector

Item	*1998*	*1999*	*2000*	*2001*	*2002*	*2003*	*2004*	*2005*	*2005*	*2006*
IV. EXTERNAL SECTOR									January – June	
A. Current Account Balance (US$ M)[13]	1,546.00	–2,874.00	–2,225.00	–1,744.00[r]	–279.00[r]	288.00[r]	1,628.00[r]	1,955.00[r]	621.00	2,869.00
(as % of GDP)	2.40	–3.80	–2.90	–2.40[r]	–0.40[r]	0.40	1.90	2.00[r]	1.30	5.30
B. Trade Balance (US$ M)[14]	–28.00	–5,977.00	–5,971.00	–6,265.00	–5,530.00	–5,851.00	–5,684.00	–7,773.00[r]	–3,525.00[a]	–2,342.00[a]
C. Exports (Goods; US$ M)[14]	29,496.00[a]	34,243.00	37,347.00	31,313.00	34,403.00	35,339.00	38,794.00	40,263.00[r]	22,974.00[a*]	26,693.00[ar]
Growth Rate (%)	16.90	n.c.	9.06	–16.16	9.87	2.72	9.78	3.79	4.90	16.20
(as % of GDP)	45.30	44.96	49.20	43.97	44.79	44.40	44.70	40.90[r]	42.20	41.90
D. Imports										
D. Imports (Goods; US$ M)[14]	29,524.00[a]	40,220.00	43,318.00	37,578.00	39,933.00	41,190.00	44,478.00	48,036.00[r]	26,499.00[a]	29,035.00[a]
Growth Rate (%)	–18.80	n.c.	7.70	–13.25	6.27	3.15	7.98	8.00	3.50	9.60
(as % of GDP)	45.30	52.81	57.07	52.77	51.99	51.70	51.30	48.80[r]	49.10	45.30
E. Services, of which OFWs:									January – July	
Remittances (US$M) (coursed through the banking system)	7,367.99	6,022.00[r]	6,050.45	6,031.27	6,886.00	7,578.00	8,550.00	10,689.00	6,049.00	7,006.00[p]
Deployment (in thousand persons)	831.64	837.02	841.63	867.60	891.91	868.00	934.00	982.00	701.00	762.00
F. Investments, Net (US$ M)[13]	187.00	4,022.00	3,225.00	849.00	1,029.00	672.00	–1,647.00	1,621.00[r]	3,888.00	–1,157.00
Growth Rate (%)	119.40	–239.10[b]	–19.80	–73.70[r]	21.20[r]	–34.70[r]	–345.10[r]	–198.40[r]	1,067.60	–129.80
Net Direct Investments	1,592.00	1,114.00	2,115.00	335.00	1,477.00	188.00	109.00	1,222.00[r]	630.00	967.00
Memo items:									January – July	
Net Foreign Direct Investments[15]	1,752.00	1,247.00	2,240.00	195.00	1,542.00	491.00	688.00	1,384.00[r]	720.00	1,154.00[p]
Net Foreign Portfolio Investments[16]	114.00	473.00	–149.00	69.00	212.00	676.00	487.00	2,104.00	2,030.00	1,396.00[p]

continued on next page

TABLE 7C — *continued*

Item	*1998*	*1999*	*2000*	*2001*	*2002*	*2003*	*2004*	*2005*	*2005*	*2006*
H. Overall BOP Position (US$M)[18]	1,359.00	3,591.00	–509.00	–202.00	810.00	115.00	–280.00	2,410.00	2,287.00	2,528.00[p]
I. Net International Reserves, (MA-NIR)									September	
(end-of-period; in US$ M)[19]	8,066.00[r]	11,909.00	11,392.00	11,426.00	13,021.00	14,065.00	14,560.00	17,659.00[r]	17,685.00	21,312.00[p]
J. Total Foreign Assets, BSP-GIR (EOP, US$M)[20]	10,842.00[r]	15,064.00	15,063.00	15,692.00	16,365.00	17,063.00	16,228.00	18,494.00[r]	18,542.00	21,556.00[p]
(in months of imports of goods & payment for services and income)	3.10	3.70[r]	3.50[r]	4.00	4.00	4.10	3.60	3.80	3.90	4.30
K. External Debt (end-of-period; US$ M)[22]	46,146.00	50,997.00	51,206.00	51,900.00	53,645.00	57,395.00	54,846.00	54,186.00	56,047.00	53,908.00
(as % of GDP)	70.80	67.00	67.50	72.90	69.80	72.10[r]	63.30[r]	55.10[r]	60.70	50.70
L. External Debt Service Ratio (in %)									January – June	
(as % of Exports of Goods and Receipts from Services and Income)	11.74	14.63[r]	12.96[r]	15.72[r]	17.08[r]	16.88[r]	13.81[r]	13.51[r]	13.32	11.53[p]
(as % of Current Account Receipts)	11.53	14.18[r]	12.54[r]	14.49[r]	15.81[r]	15.68[r]	12.89[r]	12.63[r]	12.42	10.93[p]
M. External Debt Service Burden (as % of GDP)	7.82	8.64[r]	8.25[r]	9.17[r]	10.10[r]	9.98[r]	8.32[r]	7.75[r]	7.72	6.74[p]
P. World Real GDP Growth (IFS Yearbook)	2.60	3.70[r]	4.90[r]	2.60[r]	3.10[r]	4.10[r]	5.30[r]	4.90		
R. Peso-Dollar Rate (P/US$) (Period average)	40.89[#]	44.19	50.99	51.60	54.20	56.04			55.09	

Source of Data: Bangko Sentral; Philippine government statistics.
All footnotes are explained in the Central Bank website on statistics. See <www.BSP.gov.ph>.

TABLE 7D
Public Finance

Item	*1998*	*1999*	*2000*	*2001*	*2002*	*2003*	*2004*	*2005*	*2005*	*2006*
V. PUBLIC FINANCE										
A. National Government (NG)									January – August	
Revenues, of which:	462.52	478.50	514.76	563.73	567.14	626.60	699.80	795.70	530.20	642.20
(as % of GDP)	17.35	16.07	15.34	15.50	14.30	14.50	14.40	14.70	15.20	16.70
Tax	416.59	431.69	460.03	489.86	496.37	537.40	598.00	685.20	451.90	574.20
(as % of GDP)	15.63	14.50	13.71	13.50	12.50	12.40	12.30	12.60	13.10	14.80
Non-Tax	45.93	46.82	54.73	73.87	70.77	89.30	101.80	110.50	78.30	68.10
Expenditures, of which:	512.50	590.16	648.97	710.76	777.88	826.50	886.80	942.50	611.00	676.40
Surplus/Deficit(–) (P B)	–49.98	–111.66	–134.21	–147.02	–210.74	–199.90	–187.10	–146.80	–80.80	–34.20
(as % of GDP)	–1.90	–3.80	–4.00	–4.00	–5.30	–4.60	–3.80	–2.70	–2.70	–1.10
B. Sources of Financing the NG Deficit										
Borrowings (Net)	88.90	181.70	203.80	175.20	264.20	286.80	242.50	236.00	166.70	109.80
Domestic (Net) (P B)	76.60	98.90	119.50	152.30	155.00	143.00	161.40	143.30	97.30	–15.90
Foreign (Net) (P B)	12.35	82.80	84.36	22.90	109.10	143.90	81.20	92.70	69.40	125.70
Change in Cash (Budgetary)	38.90	70.00	69.60	28.20	53.40	87.00	55.50	89.20	85.90	75.60
C. NG Revenue Effort Ratio (%)[24]	16.51	15.26	14.43	14.54	13.44	13.53	13.37	13.54	14.00	15.20
D. NG Interest Payments as % of GDP	3.74	3.57	4.20	4.80	4.70	5.20	5.40	5.50	5.70	5.50
E. Public Sector Borrowing Requirement (P B)[25]	–111.31	–137.96	–174.58	–189.80	–268.30	–275.00	–280.80	–183.30[r]	–72.90	–66.20
(as % of GDP)	–4.18	–4.63	–5.20	–5.20	–6.80	–6.40	–5.80	–3.40[r]	–6.00	–4.80
F. Consolidated Public Sector Financial Position[25] (CPSFP) Total Surplus/ (Deficit) (P B)	–85.1	–102.1	–155.10	–174.30	–220.20	–221.70	–232.00	–100.70	–51.10	–33.20
(as % of GDP)	–3.2	–3.4	–4.60	–4.80	–5.60	–5.10	–4.80	–1.90	–4.20	–2.40[r]
G. Total Outstanding Debt of the National Government (P B)[26]	1,496.22	1,775.36	2,166.71	2,384.90	2,815.50	3,355.10	3,812.00	3,888.20	June 3,891.00	3,998.50
(as % of GDP)	56.14	59.64	64.59	65.70	71.00	77.70	78.50	71.80	75.90	70.00
VI. STOCK MARKET TRANSACTIONS[28]										
A. Volume (Total, million shares)	287,791.40	948,958.56	659,423.90	164,434.30	99,845.00	85,966.10	284,341.60	317,641.00	282,964.00	434,370.20[P]
B. Value (Total, million pesos)	408,679.40	780,963.48	357,659.90	159,555.30	159,727.30	145,355.30	206,564.60	385,520.00	325,611.00	363,356.40[P]
C. Composite Index (Average)	1,847.00	2,171.60	1,541.70	1,331.90	1,204.90	1,197.20	1,621.70	1,983.10	1,960.20	2,274.30[P]

Source of Data: Bangko Sentral; Philippine government statistics.
All footnotes are explained in the Central Bank website on statistics. See <www.BSP.gov.ph>.

TABLE 7E
Philippines and Other East Asian Countries: Saving, Investment, and Revenue as percentage of GDP

Country	*1985*	*1990*	*1995*	*2000*
Gross Saving-Investment Gap				
China	–1.9	4.3	0.0	1.2
South Korea	–0.4	–0.6	–1.8	3.9
Hong Kong	10.1	0.0	0.0	5.1
Taiwan	15.5	7.4	3.2	3.8
Indonesia	–2.3	–3.0	–4.3	3.4
Malaysia	–2.0	–2.2	–8.6	11.6
Philippines	0.9	–6.0	–5.2	0.0
Singapore	1.2	9.5	0.0	0.0
Thailand	–5.1	–8.3	–6.5	8.6
Gross Domestic Capital Formation				
China	37.8	34.7	40.8	36.1
South Korea	30.0	37.7	37.2	28.2
Hong Kong	23.1	28.5	36.9	29.6
Taiwan	19.1	23.1	25.3	22.9
Indonesia	28.0	30.7	31.9	14.6
Malaysia	27.6	32.4	43.6	26.8
Philippines	14.3	24.2	22.5	18.4
Singapore	42.5	36.6	34.7	31.6
Thailand	28.2	41.4	42.1	22.7
Gross Saving Gap				
China	35.9	39.0	40.8	37.3
South Korea	29.6	37.1	35.4	32.1
Hong Kong	33.2	28.5	36.9	34.7
Taiwan	34.5	30.5	28.6	26.6
Indonesia	25.7	27.7	27.7	18.0
Malaysia	25.6	30.2	35.0	38.4
Philippines	15.2	18.1	17.3	18.4
Singapore	43.7	46.1	34.7	31.6
Thailand	23.1	33.0	35.6	31.4
Total Government Revenue				
China	20.8	17.9	10.3	15.3
South Korea	16.9	17.5	19.0	25.8
Hong Kong	14.4	14.6	14.9	14.5
Taiwan	13.6	16.3	13.3	20.5
Indonesia	19.8	18.8	17.7	16.0
Malaysia	27.3	24.8	22.9	18.2
Philippines	12.0	16.2	17.7	16.9
Singapore	27.7	26.9	26.6	26.1
Thailand	15.2	18.9	18.6	15.2

Tax Revenue				
China	22.8	15.2	9.8	14.1
South Korea	14.9	15.9	16.5	20.6
Hong Kong	10.9	10.9	11.7	10.6
Taiwan	8.5	13.1	10.7	14.1
Indonesia	18.3	17.8	16.0	9.0
Malaysia	21.6	17.8	18.7	13.8
Philippines	10.8	14.1	16.3	13.9
Singapore	16.4	15.4	16.7	15.4
Thailand	13.7	17.7	17.0	13.7

Source: Calculations are derived from key data from Asian Development Bank, Key Economic Indicators 2002.

8

INVESTMENT CLIMATE AND BUSINESS OPPORTUNITIES IN THE PHILIPPINES

Peter Wallace

INTRODUCTION

In the past three decades, the Philippines recorded the lowest growth amongst the major Asian countries, growing at an average of three per cent. What is even more disturbing is that the country's GDP per capita during this period has also been the lowest. To cite a contrast, while China increased its GDP per capita seven times, the Philippines remained at almost the same level. This sorry state reflects the turbulent roller-coaster ride the country has gone through with most of the declines being politically driven, except for the Asian financial crisis. Thus, when trying to understand the Philippine economy, it is imperative to evaluate the political scene.

It is equally important to understand that there are two different kinds of people in the Philippines: politicians and everyone else. The politicians get all the attention, giving the country a bad name. There are, of course, some good politicians, but the rest overshadow them with their high level of self-centredness and too little statesmanship. While this is also true of many other countries, it seems that the level in the Philippines is often exaggerated.

Not surprisingly, the Philippines' inability to attract investments, one of its biggest problems, is the result of the bad press it invariably gets. For instance, the *New York Times* said in an editorial in April 2006:

FIGURE 8.1
Average Gross Domestic Product Growth of the Philippines, 1961–2004

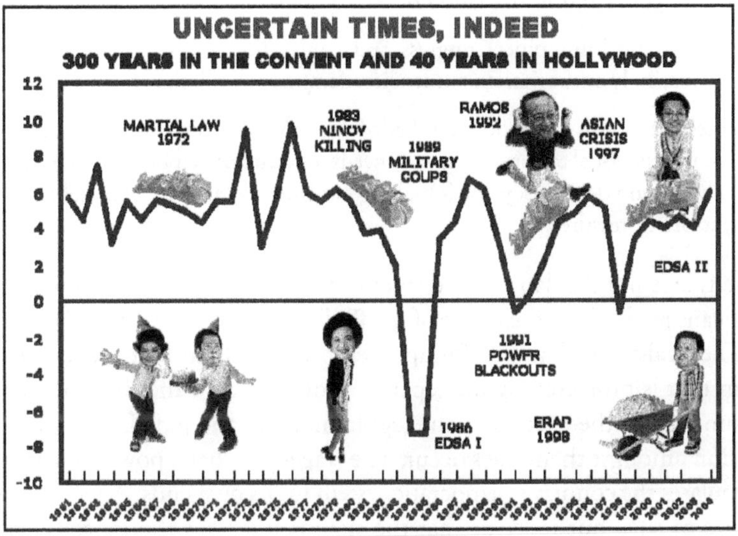

Source: National Statistical Coordination Board (NSCB).

FIGURE 8.2
30-Year Average GDP Growth of Selected Asian Countries

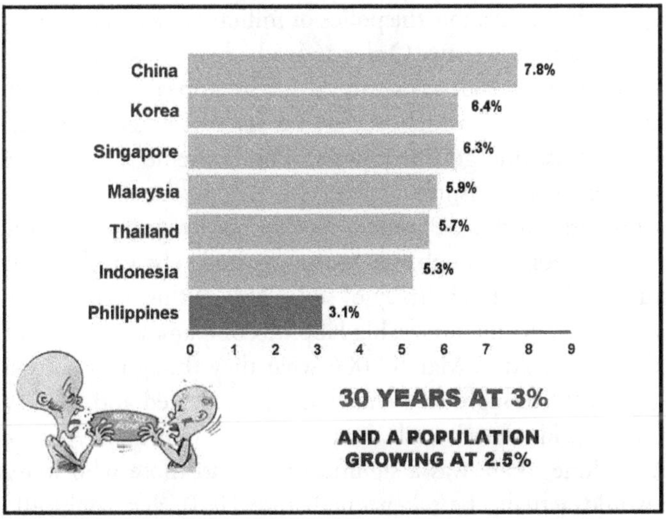

Source: Asian Development Bank.

> Mrs Arroyo is no Ferdinand Marcos, at least not yet. But this one-time reformer is reviving bad memories of crony corruption, presidential vote-rigging and intimidation of critical journalists.
>
> Unless the Philippine Congress and courts find ways to rein in her increasingly authoritarian tendencies, democracy itself may be in danger.
>
> President Bush has repeatedly hailed Mrs. Arroyo as an important ally vs. international terrorism. He now needs to warn her that by undermining a hard-won democracy, she is making her country far more vulnerable to terrorist pressures.[1]

While this is not a balanced assessment of the Philippines, this is what most Americans read. Thus, the image of the Philippines overseas is usually negative.

The reality is that the Philippines has a well-entrenched democratic system that is protected by the separation of powers of the three branches of government — the executive, the legislature, and the judiciary — although collusion amongst them does occur. The tragedy is that a powerful elite often manipulates the country's democratic system for its own ends. Almost everyone is aware of this, but it seems that the state neither has the capacity nor the mandate to address these issues.

However, there are also instances when democracy does work in the Philippines. For instance in May 2006, the Supreme Court cancelled three measures of the Arroyo administration — which were perhaps the reasons for the above *New York Times* editorial. These were: Calibrated Pre-emptive Response, which would allow the police or military to actively break up rallies and demonstrations; Executive Order 464, which required senior government officers to have the president's approval before appearing in Congress; and Proclamation No. 1017, which declared a state of emergency wherein the President could assume greater powers. The Supreme Court unanimously voted down all three measures.

That notwithstanding, President Arroyo has proved to be an incredible survivor. She has gone through attacks that anybody else would not have been able to survive. A quarterly survey of some 160 of this writer's clients (chief executive officers, multinationals, big Filipino companies, ambassadors, World Bank, etc.) were asked in March 2006 what they thought of Gloria Arroyo. About 56 per cent thought that she would be unseated and that civil unrest would continue. However, while civil unrest did continue, Arroyo was not unseated. By June, there was a significant shift to those who were less sure that she would actually be taken out before 2010, with only 40 per cent thinking that was possible. The general perception was that she was doing an average to poor job and making too many populist decisions.

THE ECONOMIC AND POLITICAL SITUATION

What does the situation look like today? When one examines the numbers, it is pretty worrying.

As regards corruption, the country is no better off than when Arroyo started, although corruption was supposedly one of the major policy issues she was going to address. In fact, not only has there been no improvement; it seems that the situation has deteriorated. The latest Transparency International survey ranked the Philippines 117th out of 158 countries.

As Table 8.1 shows, unemployment has gone worse (11.7 per cent in 2005 *vs.* 11.21 per cent in 2000), while the rate of hunger has gone up (16.9 per cent in 2005 *vs.* 10.5 per cent in 2000). Money spent on education (13.9 per cent of the budget in 2005 *vs.* 17.4 per cent in 2000) and infrastructure (2.1 per cent of GDP in 2005 *vs.* 2.7 per cent in 2000) has declined. In fact, the Philippines' infrastructure spending is way below its comparable neighbours: twenty-five years behind Malaysia, thirteen years behind Thailand.

Today, too many people are far below the poverty level. A survey by the Social Weather Stations found that about 60 per cent of the respondents self-rated themselves in poverty. Even former President Estrada did better. Under President Arroyo, foreign investment has declined, and the national government debt has risen (82.2 per cent of GDP *versus* 79 per cent). Competitiveness has not improved to any significant degree. The Philippines is now the thirteenth least competitive economy in a world of sixty-one economies. The political

TABLE 8.1
Some Basic Numbers

	2005	*2000*
Corruption — TI Ranking	117th out of 158	69th out of 90
Unemployment	4.1M, 11.7%*	35M, 11.2%
Degree of hunger	16.9%	10.5%
Education as % of Budget	13.9%	17.4%
Spending on infra	2% of GDP	2.7% of GDP
FDI	$1.1B	$2.2B
Nat'l Govt Debt	83.2% of GDP	79% of GDP
Competitive Banking		
IMD	49th out of 60–82%	40th out of 49–82%
WEF	77th out of 117–66%	36th out of 75–48%
GMA's Net Satisfaction Rating**		
SWS (Social Weather Stations)	–30 (Dec '05)	+27 (Nov '01)

* Based on old definition
** % Satisfied minus dissatisfied

killing of journalists and various activists — with nobody being brought to justice — is at the highest level since the Marcos regime.

However, there are some positive signs too. The international reserves are at their highest level ever and, in terms of months of imports coverage, they have remained quite healthy. This is mainly because of the huge amount of money that Overseas Filipino Workers (OFWs) are bringing into the country. The budget deficit has come down, as has the public sector deficit. Non-performing loans in commercial banks have been lowered dramatically and the foreign debt has been reduced.

Indeed, the Arroyo administration has done very well on the fiscal side — but it has not done better anywhere else. Arguably, the fiscal problem was one of the most important that needed to be addressed. However, it took the government almost five years to get there. When will the administration concentrate on other areas where performance has been so low?

WALLACE BUSINESS FORUM PERCEPTION SURVEY FINDINGS

In 2004, The Wallace Business Forum conducted a comprehensive survey of about 60 companies.

When asked, "What are the top barriers to you investing in the Philippines?", the number one response was corruption, which is perceived to be a major inhibitor to doing business in the Philippines.

The other, equally important, issue is inconsistency in policies. Businessmen will not enter an environment which is unpredictable. While no one knows the future, one must have a reasonable assurance that the environment within which one works will be reasonably foreseeable. This means political stability, security, and economic stability. Other major deterrents cited were the convoluted bureaucratic red-tape and poor infrastructure. All these factors point to the poor performance of the government.

On top of that, while Western business is built around institutions related to the rule of law and other rules-based approaches, in the East, the approach is often based on relationships to get things done. Western business people trust the system, while people elsewhere (including the East) trust their friends. The tragedy of the Philippines is that the "cement" of business — built around human relationships of personal honour, integrity and a long-term approach — is in decline through abuse.

The Philippines' attractions, on the other hand, are English language proficiency (despite its considerable deterioration over the last twenty or so years); availability of labour, its quality, and reliability; adaptability to Western

TABLE 8.2
RP's Top Investment Barriers

Item	*2004*		*Ranking in …*				
	*Score**	*Rank*	*2003*	*2002*	*2001*	*2000*	*1997*
Corruption	102	1	1	2	3	1	4
Inconsistency of policies	74	2	5	5	6	4	–
Political stability	58	3	2	4	1	3	8
Peace and order and security problems	53	4	3	1	5	5	10
Economic instability	47	5	8	8	4	6	11
Bureaucratic red tape/mess	45	6	4	6	7	11	2
Poor infrastructure	42	7	6	3	2	2	1
Currency stability	30	8	9	15	6	16	–
Lack of political will	24	9	10	–	–	9	–
High cost of doing business	22	10	7	12	9	15	–
Local market size, growth and access	22	10	11	7	10	10	–

**5 points for 1st place votes, 4 pts for 2nd, etc.*

THE OTHER TOP BARRIERS IN 1997 WERE:
TAX/INCENTIVES SYSTEM (#3),
SUPREME COURT/JUSTICE SYSTEM (#6),
LABOUR COST/PRODUCTIVITY/UNIONS (#7)

Source: The Wallace Business Forum 2004 Corporate Survey.

culture and management practices; educational attainment of the workers; relatively low cost, particularly of labour; a positive Filipino attitude; and quality of middle management. All these positive attributes relate to the Filipino people. In short, what comes through most clearly is that the Filipino people are good while the government is not.

Our survey found that in order to attract more investments, the quality of governance must be improved. Effective, consistent policies and strong enforcement of laws with no change of rules in midstream are essential to more rapid development. Reducing graft and corruption is also needed. Unfortunately there has been little improvement in these aspects, except on the fiscal side. Some reform of the tax system has taken place, particularly on the value added tax (VAT), which has been raised from 10 per cent to 12 per cent. However, the VAT has a major fault in it, a provision capping at 70 per cent the level of input VAT that can be credited to output VAT. This requirement could put companies out of business. Congress is aware of it but is not moving fast enough to correct the problem. In fact, in recent times,

TABLE 8.3
RP's Top Investment Attractions

Item	*2004*		*Ranking in ...*			
	*Score**	*Rank*	*2003*	*2002*	*2001*	*2000*
English language proficiency	129	1	1	1	1	2
Labour availability, quality & reliability	102	2	2	3	5	
Adaptability to Western culture & practices	57	3	3	4	8	7
Market potential/size/quality	46	4	4	2	2	6
Educational attainment/literacy of workers	39	5	7	5	3	9
Low cost environment, including labour cost	34	6	8	7	6	8
Positive Filipino attitude	26	7	6	8	7	5
Quality/quantity of middle mgt/ technical people	25	8	5	9	4	1
Comfortable lifestyle	23	9	9	10	–	–

**5 points for 1st place votes, 4 pts for 2nd, etc.*

Source: The Wallace Business Forum 2004 Corporate Survey.

almost every law Congress has passed has had a major flaw in it. Another example of a flawed law was the one one granting investment incentives in economic zones. The law was so worded as to cover only Subic Bay, excluding Clark and the other export zones. These other export zones lost their investment incentives status when the Supreme Court undertook a review of the law and upheld its provisions. Thus, the government is now scrambling to get a new law passed.

Improved investment in infrastructure has not happened, nor has liberalization of the business environment. As to the court system, the new chief justice, Artemio Panganiban, has said that the Supreme Court will no longer be involved in business decisions to the extent that it was in the past. It can only be hoped that he keeps his word on this.

The year 2006 saw a mixed business performance. The 5 per cent growth was rather narrowly focused, both in terms of sectors and of companies within those sectors. Eight of the fifty sub-sectors accounted for the bulk of the growth. What was particularly striking, though, was that the enthusiasm one sensed in the community during the Ramos years was lacking amongst businessmen. Then there was optimism for the future; today it is more of resignation — the feeling that "we'll survive, but things are tough".

FIGURE 8.3
Head Office Attitude on Business Operations in RP

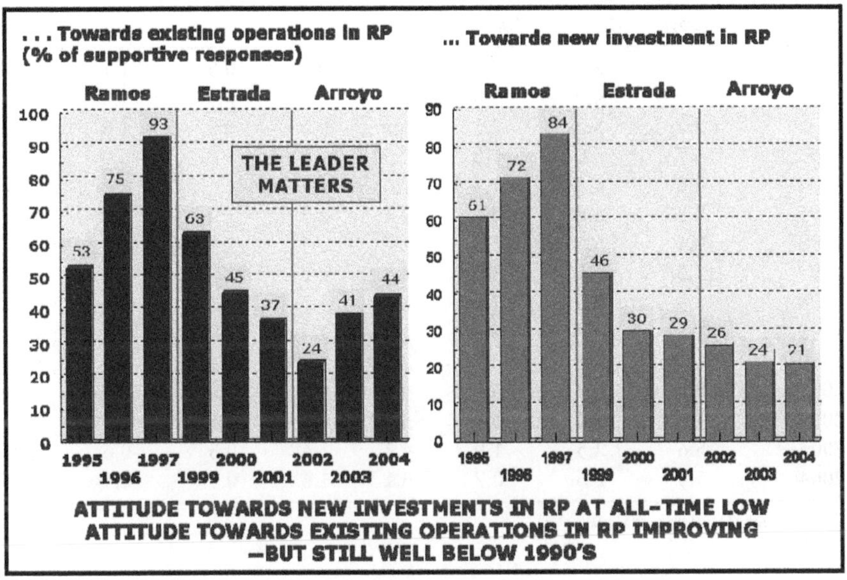

Source: The Wallace Business Forum 2004 Corporate Survey.

For multinationals, the problem extends to their head office. Even if people at the head office receive more balanced assessments of the situations from their Philippine office, reports like the one in the *New York Times* are likely to colour their view. This perception is important, because major investment and expansion decisions are made at the head office.

Very clearly, in all of this, leadership matters. What one thinks of the leader and the performance of that leader has a major impact on what one thinks of the country. What the Philippines has today is a leader who is not showing the kind of attitude necessary to engender business confidence. Although we have seen some improvement in the last couple of years, it is still way below prior administrations.

IMPORTANCE OF INFRASTRUCTURE INVESTMENT

The low levels of investment in recent years further highlight the problem the president faces (see Table 8.4). All this is in contrast with what is happening elsewhere in Asia, where the interest is growing quite significantly from year to year.

TABLE 8.4
Net Foreign Direct Investments into Asia (US$B)

	Singapore	*Malaysia*	*Thailand*	*India*	*Vietnam*	*PHILS*	*Indonesia*	*China*
1990	5.6	2.3	2.4	0.2	0.0	0.5	1.1	3.5
1991	4.9	4.0	2.0	0.1	0.2	0.5	1.5	4.4
1992	2.2	5.2	2.1	0.3	0.4	0.2	1.8	11.2
1993	4.7	5.0	1.8	0.5	1.0	1.2	2.0	27.5
1994	8.6	4.3	1.4	1.0	1.9	1.6	2.1	33.8
1995	8.8	4.2	2.1	2.1	2.3	1.5	4.3	35.8
1996	10.4	5.1	2.3	2.4	2.4	1.5	6.2	40.2
1997	13.0	5.1	3.9	3.6	2.2	1.2	4.7	44.2
1998	6.3	2.2	7.3	2.6	1.7	2.3	–0.4	43.8
1999	8.8	3.9	6.1	2.2	1.4	1.7	–2.7	38.7
2000	11.4	3.8	3.4	2.5	1.3	1.3	–4.5	38.4
2001	–8.6	0.5	3.9	3.8	1.3	1.0	–3.3	44.2
2002	1.7	3.2	0.9	3.7	1.4	1.8	–1.5	49.3
2003	5.6	2.5	1.9	4.3	1.4	0.3	–0.6	53.5
2004	5.4	2.6	0.7	3.1	1.6	0.5	0.9	58.8

Source: Asian Development Bank.

The only country worse than the Philippines is Indonesia. Singapore, Japan, and Australia have substantial investments already — they do not need any more. So the Philippines and Indonesia are the ones that are suffering. How does the Philippines as an investment site compare to elsewhere in ASEAN? In our survey, 73 per cent of firms said the Philippines was the worst place to invest in ASEAN. The low US$1 billion of investment that the Philippines received in 2005 highlights this reality. As Figure 8.5 shows, the low investment trend in the country over the past fifteen years relates to who the leaders of the country were. The figures show that investments rose during Ramos' time, fell during Estrada's time, and is continuing to fall and now beginning to reverse under President Arroyo. While the Philippines experiences a slight recovery, China is just unstoppable with its incredible growth rate.

Expenditure on infrastructure is at the lowest levels since the early part of the Aquino administration. As Figure 8.6 demonstrates, it comes down to the leaders again. Infrastructure expenditure under Aquino was almost nil. It picked up under the Ramos administration when he identified infrastructure as a major priority. However, it started to fall again under the Estrada presidency and has not recovered under Arroyo. She has, in fact, spent less as a percentage of GDP (2 per cent) than any of her predecessors. This rate of

FIGURE 8.4
RP vs Rest of ASEAN as Investment Site
(% of best/better responses)

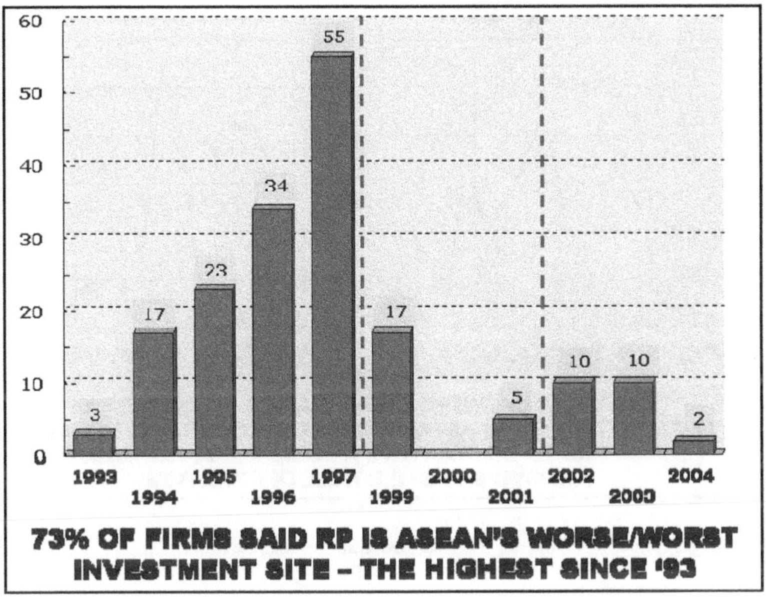

Source: The Wallace Business Forum 2004 Corporate Survey.

infrastructure expenditure is the lowest in the region and is another of the major reasons for low foreign investments in the country. Table 8.5 enumerates some of the projects that have been promised but not yet realized.

The government has to recognize that infrastructure is necessary to attract private investment. Admittedly, the government is showing signs of some recognition of this, with the President demonstrating awareness of the urgency of developing infrastructure, but action is yet to occur.

Because no new power plants are being built, it appears that there are going to be power shortages some time around 2010–11, depending on the country's economic growth rate. I am aware of only one power plant being constructed, KEPCO, which is looking at building a 200-megawatt plant. It takes four or five years to build a power plant. Thus, the country is likely to experience sporadic blackouts, unlike the regular ones it experienced during the Aquino administration, and will experience some power shortages in a few years unless something is done to change this situation. Luzon, the main island, will run short of power in about four or five years. The problem is that

FIGURE 8.5
Trend in Investment Since 1990 (US$ Billion)

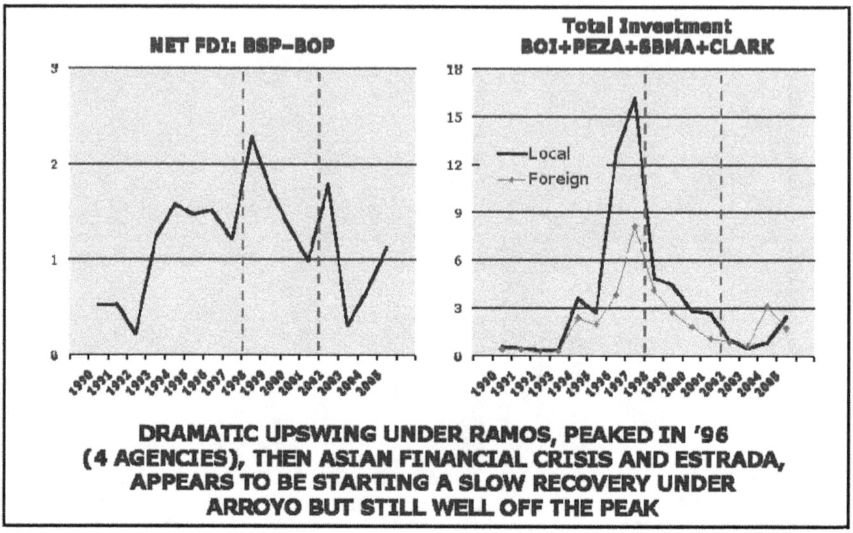

Source: Bangko Sentral ng Philipinas, National Statistical Coordination Board.

FIGURE 8.6
RP Infrastructure Spending as Percentage of GDP

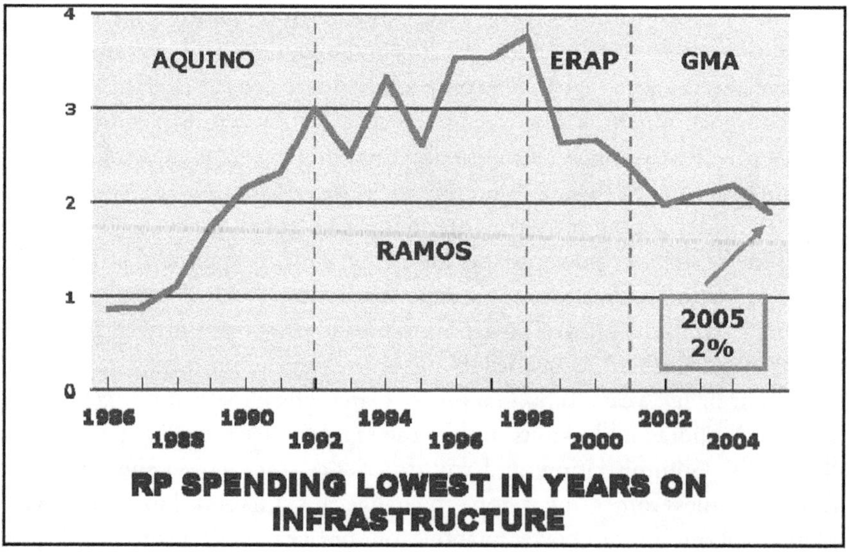

TABLE 8.5
Infrastructure Projects of the GMA Administration

*Completed**	*Promised*
• RORO Ports • NLEX • LRT-2 • C5/Katipunan Interchange	• SLEX Upgrade/Alabang Viaduct • STAR Extension (Batangas Port) • Northrail • Southrail • SCTEP • Skyway Extension • C6 • LRT 3 Extension (ENT) • NLEE • MRT7 • MRT4 • Tarlac-Pangasinan-La-Union Expressway • MRT8 • LRT1 extension

**Only RORO was initiated by GMA*

the government is not prepared to sign purchase contracts, making the risk seem too high for builders, although this risk is perhaps dissipating with the looming shortage. The other problem is that even if there is enough power generation, distributing it will also run into shortages if no new substantial investments in facilities are made. This means that the government must soon privatize Transco, the primary power transmission company.

In fact, companies operating in the country are making contingency plans with regards to power supply. We did a number of studies on this topic and found that the envisaged power shortage is a result of insufficient reserves to handle contingencies. This means that the problem is not as serious as the situation in the early 1990s, when Luzon had eight- to ten-hour blackouts every day. However, sporadic blackouts will be almost inevitable unless additional capacity is soon added.

There are a number of promising road, rail, and airport projects in the pipeline. The availability of government funding depends on the ability of the government to pass an expanded budget rather than a "re-enacted" budget. For privately financed projects (such as through the Build-Operate-Transfer scheme), the key to more investment is the government's ability to guarantee a certain return to investors, which means, for instance, allowing market-determined toll fees. If this is not in place, the government has to pick up the difference between the market fee and the socialized fee.

TABLE 8.6
Key Bills Critical to Business

Bill	*Brief Description*	*Status*
Clarified Clark incentives; one-time tax amnesty for locators	Clarifies the incentive scheme in the Clark ecozone; grants tax amnesty to locators in the interim	Senate Committee; Approved by the House
Simplified net income taxation system (SNITS)	Includes provision lifting 70% cap on input VAT	For Senate 2nd reading; Approved by the House
Rationalization of fiscal incentives	Harmonizes and rationalizes the administration and grant of investment incentives	Senate Committee; Approved by the House
Anti-smuggling	Imposes stringent penalties for persons guilty of smuggling goods worth more than P50M	Senate Committee; Approved by the House
EPIRA amendments	Includes changes to the Electric Power Industry Reform Act (EPIRA)	Senate 2nd reading; House Committee
Creation of DICT	Creates the Department of Information and Communications Technology (DICT)	Senate Committee; House 2nd reading

Another problems is the lack of action on a number of reforms needed to improve the business climate, because the country's leaders have been distracted by the continued intramurals between the President and the various opposition groups.

One of the urgently needed reforms is the rationalization of the numerous, sometimes conflicting, incentives laws. This process is being undertaken, but progress is slow because of political distractions. The Departments of Finance and of Trade and Industry are arguing whether incentives do indeed attract investment or whether they are just a loss of revenues to government. The problem is that the foreign business community — the group that would be most affected — is not included in the discussion.

Despite spending more time on investigations, Congress is now — even though way behind where it should be — relatively more responsive in approving reform bills. The tax enhancement bills, for example, were passed to address a prospective fiscal crisis two or three years down the line. Up to the early 1990s, Congress responded only when a crisis had already occurred.

How do those who do business in the Philippines see the Philippines as an investment site? We asked that question in our survey and the responses we got are summarized in Table 8.7.

TABLE 8.7
CEO Perception of the Philippines as an Investment Site
(Based on 35 criteria)

The Best Features	*The Worst Features*
1. Worker education level	1. Bureaucratic red tape
2. English language capability	2. Economic instability
3. Quality and quantity of middle management/ tech people	3. Stability of policies
	4. Government attitude
4. Comfortable local lifestyle	5. Transport, infrastructure
5. Availability of skilled/semi-skilled people	6. Currency volatility
	7. Political stability

The CEOs we surveyed were of one voice as to what were needed for the Philippines to be considered as an attractive investment site: improving governance with clear and consistent policies, enforcing the rule of law, an even playing field, and honouring and respecting contracts. These reforms are not too difficult to implement if there is the political will to do so.

The other suggestions include imprisonment of high-profile grafters; making the tax incentives system competitive with other Asian countries; spending more on infrastructure, specifically power supply; stopping protectionist policies; getting the government out of business; and minimizing judicial intervention in legitimate business operations.

One of the main worries about the economy's overall growth is that only eight out of its fifty sectors are experiencing economic growth. This means that growth is narrowly defined, and this is also seen in investments, which are concentrated on electronics, water, telecommunications, and infrastructure. Investments are not broad-based or evenly distributed, because the government has been reluctant to provide any kind of guarantee against political intervention. One cannot convince investors to put money into a toll road or a power plant, if there are no guarantees against intervention risk. Thus, there is very low interest in the government's build-operate-transfer (BOT) projects.

Meanwhile, information technology (IT) has become a major investment area. However, it is important to keep in mind that an investment in IT requires far less money to create a job than it does in manufacturing by a ratio of about 6:1. Therefore, in evaluating foreign investments, an adjustment must be made to take account of the fact that less money is now needed to create a job. Hence, we have seen employment continuing to rise despite falling investment. However, the bulk of this is coming from just a dozen or so companies.

TABLE 8.8
CEO Perception on Doing Business in RP (June 2006)

BUSINESS IN '06				
	Generally		*Your Business*	
	1H	*2H*	*1H*	*2H*
Looking much brighter	4	–	13	19
Some improvement	38	38	25	38
Little change	50	54	46	33
Getting worse	8	8	17	10
Much worse	–	–	–	–

Source: The Wallace Business Forum 2006 Quarterly CEO Survey.

In our 2006 survey of businessmen's perceptions, it is interesting to see that there is a significant difference between how they see things generally and how things relate to their businesses. According to the CEOs, their businesses come out better. This basically means that the top companies are doing better than the general economy, as CEOs see it. Yet, a significant percentage — 17 per cent in the first half of 2006 — had a worse performance, and 10 per cent expected the second half of the year to be worse, with a third of them seeing little change. Not many people think that things are looking much brighter. This is particularly worrying for the general economy. Yet surprisingly, the performances of these companies overall are not too bad. However, when you talk to them, they are depressed, even though 62 per cent of them see sales up by 13 per cent and 45 per cent, with profits up by 15 per cent.

One of the interesting developments is that a number of the major consumer companies have downgraded the size of their products. One major multinational recently did a complete revamp of all its products into smaller packs and sachets for the Philippine market. Of course, this makes the product more expensive because the packaging is now a much higher percentage of the product cost. This is not a very economically-efficient way to buy, but it indicates a populace that has less money to buy and is buying on a daily basis rather than weekly or monthly. For instance, shampoo sales in sachets have gone from 45 per to 80 per cent. This is similar to what is called the "one stick economy", where Filipinos buy cigarettes one stick at a time. Thus, it is unfortunate that the Philippine economy is marking time with such a concept. On the positive side, however, it brings the poor into the market.

INVESTMENT OPPORTUNITIES IN THE PHILIPPINES

The Philippines has five sectors of natural advantage — agriculture, mining, IT, tourism, and healthcare.

These sectors are natural advantages, because other countries do not necessarily have these advantages. For instance, Singapore will never be a

TABLE 8.9
RP's 5 Areas of "Natural Advantage"

Advantages	*Why*	*What Needs to be Done*
Agriculture	– Potential for high-value crops – Fertile soil – 1/4 of pop'n engaged in agri; agri is 20% of the economy	– Build more agri infrastructure: AFMA is a good start – Allow investments in large plantations – Liberalize agriculture
Mining	– Rich mineral deposits; copper, gold, nickel, etc. – Strong poverty alleviation impact	– Encourage foreign investors to set up best-practice mines – Be consistent. Arbitrary rules are deterrent.
ICT	– Large pool of educated manpower – Familiarity with US/Western culture	– Stricter intellectual property rights (IPR) laws – Step up quality of IT-related education – Improve access to personal computers/internet
Tourism	– 7,100 islands: beaches, idyllic spots, unique geography – Melting pot of races; expat lifestyle is easy	– Improve security, international image – Provide infrastructure, etc. to get to the key spots
Healthcare	– Unique caring nature of Filipinos, they love and respect old people – Country has established international reputation in this field	– Produce more workers with these skills, more nursing schools, etc. – Sell country as a care-giving haven (will need investment in infrastructure, hospitals; improvement in security)

competitor to the Philippines in agriculture, while Hong Kong will never be a competitor in mining. Therefore, there are areas of advantages that a country should focus on. Mining has a tremendous potential if the Catholic Church and biased non-government organizations (NGOs) will keep their fingers out of it. The church, or at least some of the Catholic clergy, is doing a dreadful service to the Philippine economy and the Filipino people by trying to ban mining. Saudi Arabia is a rich country today because it has oil, takes it out, and sells it. The Philippines, similarly, has huge richness in the soil that can be taken out and sold. And this process can be done responsibly. This is the key thing — to make sure mining is carried out responsibly — and this is where the church can help to ensure that it is done so. For example, GDP per capita in Chile rose four-and-a-half times since mining became a major area of development in the 1980s. The Philippine economy grew at less than twice over the same period. In Australia, agriculture and mining were the two areas that led the growth of the economy.

The Philippines has the fifth richest deposit of gold, the eighth largest of copper and the fourth of chromite in the world. The government is fully committed to supporting mining and helping companies get established. This is an industry that can potentially contribute up to 15 per cent to the country's exports, with export of mined products rising to some US$5–7 billion by 2012 based on investments of US$4-5 billion in already known reserves. Yet, as one mining company found out recently, you need to fully understand the nuances of doing business in the Philippines if you are going to avoid trouble. This company had two minor incidents that were blown out of proportion because of poor handling and not having sound local advice.

There is also tremendous potential in IT. The growth in call centres has been phenomenal. One of the call centres has gone from 0 to 7,000 employees in three years. The call centres and Business Process Outsourcing (BPO) have grown over 100 per cent per annum in the last five years. Although it is now slowing down from its hectic pace in the first half of this decade, the annual growth in the information technology enabled services (ITES) industry in the Philippines will remain high at 30 to 50 per cent over the next five years, with the number of ITES jobs almost tripling from 160,000 in 2005 to 500,000 by 2010. No other industry is growing at this rate. The question is: is this sustainable? The answer rests on the capacity of the government to put English back as the major medium of education. As it now stands, there will be enough people available if the industry growth rates remain at around 35 to 40 per cent, but if the industry grows over 100 per cent annually, there will be shortages of qualified people. Fortunately, the improvement in English can be brought about fairly rapidly. In fact, remedial courses put in place have

TABLE 8.10
BPO/Call Centres in RP

JUST WORK IN THE PHILIPPINES		
HSBC	Teletech	Customer Contact Centre, Inc
IBM Daksh	Sykes Asia	ePerformax Phils
Crescent Services (Citigroup)	eTelecare	Vocative Systems, Inc.
Dell	Chevron	Vision X Phils
Accenture	Hewitt	Sitel Phils
Safeways	Convergys	Pacific Hub
Deutsche Bank	Ambergris Solutions	West Contact Services
Manulife	Advanced Contact Solution	Vertex Solutions
GXS (GE Information Systems)	People Support	RHM Teleserves Asia Pacific
AIG	Clientlogic	Flour Daniel Inc. Phils.
Thomson Corp	Cybercity Teleserves	UPS Asia Consolidated Services Centre
Telus	ICT Group Phils	eData Services Phils.
THERE'S A SHIFT FROM INDIA, PARTICULARLY CALL CENTRES		

improved the hiring rate from about 5 to 6 per cent to as much as 25 per cent. In the longer term, the IT and communications industry requires a much wider improvement in English capability. The record of the Philippine call centres and BPO has been excellent. I have heard no complaint from anybody, whereas in India there are some complaints on the higher cost and the difficulty of comprehending the Indian accent. Thus, we have been seeing some shift from India to the Philippines. Here is a natural advantage of the country, which is the nature of the Filipino people that is not being developed properly by the state.

Tourism is another area of considerable potential. The Philippines, a beautiful country with many lovely places to visit, is one of the more bio-diverse countries in the world. There are no temples or Angkor Wats, but there are magnificent beaches and diving spots, fascinating adventures (such as swimming with seventeen-metre-long whale sharks) and a people that will make you feel right at home immediately. However, getting to the resorts is a nightmare, so tourists do not come. Also the image that the Philippines is not safe has generated travel advisories against visiting the country. Another factor is that not too many people are aware of what there is to see. Also, there are not enough hotels, infrastructure facilities, and transport. All these factors have contributed to the Philippines attracting the lowest levels of tourism in Asia.

Nonetheless, foreign visitor arrivals have increased by about 15 per cent annually in recent years, perhaps not much by Asian standards, but significant for a country where tourism has hardly shown any improvement since the Asian financial crisis.

The expectation of the government and the private sector of 5 million foreign tourists by 2010, a doubling from 2.6 million in 2005, appears to be realistic, and investments in tourist facilities, such as hotels, resorts, and transport, are frantically being put in place, as the existing facilities can accommodate only 3 million.

We are seeing a significant shift from Americans and Europeans to Asian tourists. Facilities and services provided need to adapt to this. Four out of the five top nationalities visiting the Philippines are now Asian. The most phenomenal development is the arrival of the Koreans, now the second largest visitor group after the United States. A large proportion of U.S. arrivals could actually be visiting Filipinos and their descendants who have become U.S. citizens. There are now at least 300,000 Koreans who have made the Philippines their home, and the number is growing. Some even estimate their number to be as high as 500,000. Koreans find low-cost education, especially learning English, many work opportunities, and an ability to make money whilst having time to enjoy life in the Philippines.

FIGURE 8.7
Tourism in the Philippines

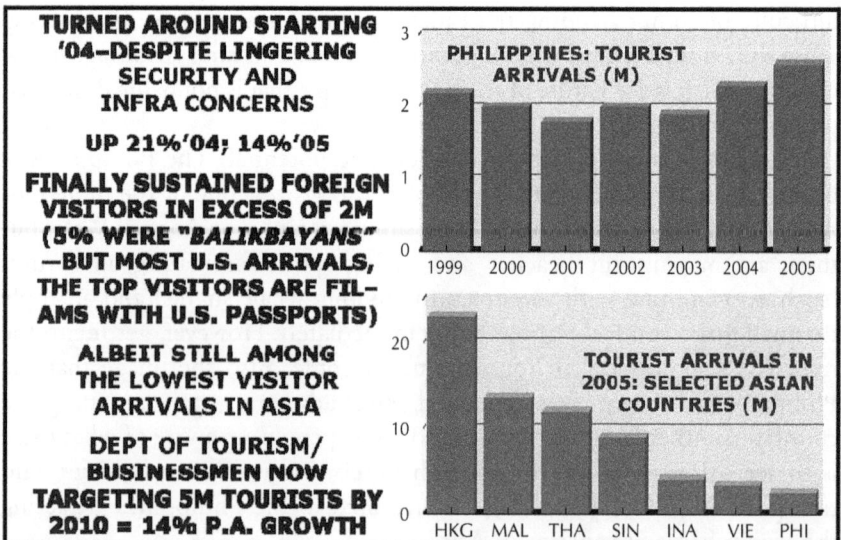

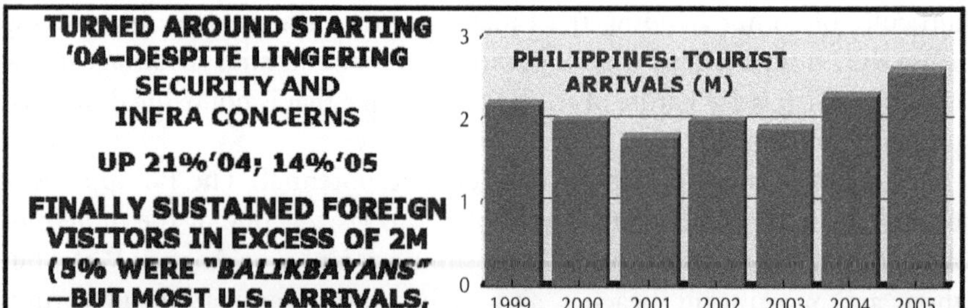

Koreans also share a similar religious fervour as the Filipinos, and it is a little farther away from the vagaries of North Korea.

Retirement homes and healthcare are another two areas with significant potential. Filipinos are gentle, caring, and respectful of the elderly. The Western world wants to get rid of grandpa and grandma. So it is a perfect solution. Send the elderly people to the Philippines to be fully cared for in a warm climate and in beautiful localities. To augment this, there are some excellent hospitals with the latest equipment, and the cost is very reasonable.

Food processing is the one area in manufacturing where there is significant potential. Domestically, the $70-billion consumer market will grow by 30 per cent to $90 billion by 2010. Forty-five per cent of those purchases is for food, with processed food garnering an ever-larger share. Processed food currently accounts for 45 per cent of total food sales and is expected to grow further over the medium to long term. Agricultural products grow well and cheaply in the fertile soil of the Philippines. However, the agrarian reform law misunderstands what agriculture is all about. One needs economies of scale in agriculture in the same way as industry. Yet, the agrarian reform law caps agricultural land to five hectares for each owner, which is a major inhibitor to the growth of the sector. Nonetheless, the established food companies have been very successful. For instance, San Miguel Corporation, one of the biggest food companies in the country and in Asia today, is now going offshore. Also, there are several Filipino multinationals in the food area such as URC, Jollibee, RFM, and others.

CONCLUSION

Given the above context, Table 8.11 shows our forecast for the Philippines in the next few years.

The main thing it shows is a more or less steady rate of growth. The services sector is the area that will lead the economy. The biggest worry is the level of investment, which will remain far too low for a country that needs to grow.

Table 8.12 provides an economic forecast based on the best and worst scenarios — the range the economy could experience based on: "if everything goes wrong" what happens versus "if everything goes right" what happens? On the basis of our computations and as Table 8.12 shows, by 2010 there will be a huge difference between the best and worst scenarios. The economy could grow anywhere between 3 and 7 per cent with the peso somewhere between 53 and 65 to the U.S. dollar, interest rates could double in the worst case, and inflation three times as bad in a worst-case scenario. The potential

TABLE 8.11
The Medium-Term Outlook

	2006	*2007*	*2008*	*2009*	*2010*
% Growth Rate GDP	5.5	5.8	5.8	5.8	6.0
GNP	5.7	5.9	6.0	6.0	6.2
Consumer Spending	5.2	5.5	5.5	5.3	5.3
Fixed Investment	2.9	5.6	7.6	7.5	7.6
Exports	10.0	11.8	9.9	8.7	8.2
Imports	3.8	6.2	7.3	7.1	7.4
Agriculture	4.0	3.3	2.8	1.7	2.3
Industry	5.3	5.6	5.5	5.6	6.1
Services	6.3	7.0	7.1	7.5	7.3
P:$ Rate	52.5	52.5	53.2	54.2	55.3
91-Day TBill (%)	5.7	5.5	5.4	5.2	5.6
Bank Lending Rate	8.5	8.0	7.5	7.1	7.0
Inflation (%)	7.2	6.2	5.7	4.8	4.6

Source: The Wallace Business Forum.

TABLE 8.12
Economic Forecast: The Worst and the Best Scenarios

	2006	*2007*	*2008*	*2009*	*2010*
GDP Growth Rate					
Worst	5.0	4.7	3.7	3.4	3.0
Best	5.8	6.3	6.6	7.0	7.0
P:$ Rate					
Worst	54.0	56.0	58.0	62.0	65.0
Best	52.0	52.0	52.0	52.0	53.0
91-Day T-Bill Rate (%)					
Worst	6.0	6.5	7.0	8.0	10.0
Best	5.0	5.4	4.9	5.0	5.0
Bank Lending Rate (%)					
Worst	10.0	10.6	11.5	12.0	12.6
Best	8.0	7.8	7.0	6.6	6.5
Inflation (%)					
Worst	8.0	7.5	8.2	9.8	11.0
Best	6.9	6.0	4.9	4.3	4.3

Source: The Wallace Business Forum.

is there to grow at the needed 7 per cent, but the economy is not yet on the sustained basis necessary to significantly reduce poverty. More major reform is needed to get there but this does not seem to be happening.

All in all, the Philippines is a country of contradictions. The great opportunity that mining offers and government supports is strongly opposed by the Catholic Church, international NGOs, and some ill-informed local communities. Thus, to realize the potentials in mining, a long and unecessary struggle is in the offing. This is the same story in other sectors. You can win, but you have to fight harder than you need to do elsewhere. That, I think is the fundamental message.

Note

1 *New York Times,* 5 April 2006.

9

WHY DOES POVERTY PERSIST IN THE PHILIPPINES? FACTS, FANCIES, AND POLICIES

Arsenio M. Balisacan

INTRODUCTION

Addressing the widespread poverty problem is the single most important policy challenge facing the Philippines. Not only is poverty high compared with other countries in East Asia, but also its reduction is so slow that the country has become the basket case in the region.

Proposals peddled to address the poverty problem are plenty — and they keep on growing. At one end of the spectrum are proposals contending that the root of the problem is simply the lack of respectable economic growth. Putting the economy on a high-growth path is prescribed as all that is needed to beat the poverty problem. At the other end are proposals asserting that the poverty problem is nothing but a concrete manifestation of gross economic and social inequities. Redistributing wealth and opportunities is viewed as the key to winning the war on poverty. A variant of such proposals holds that economic growth does not at all benefit the poor. Focusing on growth rather than on redistributive reforms is seen to exacerbate inequities, which could lead to the further erosion of peace and social stability. Between these extremes are views that consider economic growth as a necessary condition for poverty reduction and recognize that reform measures have to be put in place to enhance the participation of the poor in growth processes. Most advocates of poverty-reduction ideas, including proponents of the so-called "pro-poor growth", belong to this mold, although not necessarily sharing common ground on what, conceptually and operationally, constitutes pro-poor growth processes.

How do these proposals stand in relation to evidence and policy research? What are facts and what are fancies? Given the country's fiscal bind, what policy levers can be expected to generate high returns in poverty reduction?

This chapter attempts to answer these questions. It does this by examining the Philippine experience in poverty reduction from an "international" perspective. The next two sections characterize the nature, pattern, and proximate determinants of poverty reduction during the past twenty years. The fourth section examines the economy-population-poverty nexus, specifically the quantitative significance of the country's continued rapid population growth for long-term income growth and poverty reduction. Some concluding remarks are given in the final section of the chapter.

THE GROWTH-POVERTY NEXUS

Sustained increases in national income — that is, economic growth — is required for poverty reduction. Claims to the contrary are, however, periodically heard from civil society groups and non-government organizations (NGOs). Recent development experience presents clear evidence: every country that has chalked up significant achievements in poverty reduction and human development has also done quite well in securing long-term economic growth.[1] Indeed, viewed from a medium- to long-term perspective, there is an almost one-for-one correspondence between growth in the incomes of the poor and the country's average income growth. This correlation is not unexpected: economic growth is an essential condition for the generation of resources needed to sustain investments in health, education, infrastructure and good governance (law enforcement, regulation), among other things.

While economic growth in most East and Southeast Asian countries has been remarkably rapid during the past twenty-five years, the same cannot be said of the Philippines. The country's economic growth has been quite anemic, barely exceeding the population growth rate, which has continued to expand rapidly at 2.3 per cent a year for most of the past two decades. Economic growth quickened in the first half of the present decade, but questions about the sustainability of this growth linger. Even at the present pace, it can hardly be argued that the Philippines has come close to the growth trajectories of its neighbours. It is thus not surprising that serious students of Philippine development contend that shifting the economy to a

TABLE 9.1
Levels and Growth Rates of GDP per capita, 1980–2005

	GDP per capita (PPP $, in 2000 prices)		*Annual growth rate (%)*	
	1980	*2005*	*1980–2005*	*2000–2005*
Philippines	4,160	4,381	0.63	2.50
Indonesia	1,462	3,402	3.70	3.25
Malaysia	4,047	9,687	3.65	3.00
Thailand	2,488	7,862	4.59	4.13
Korea, Rep.	4,557	18,316	5.53	4.56
Vietnam*	Na	2,683	4.87	6.10
China	762	5,643	8.49	8.56

* Data start in 1985.
Sources: World Development Indicators 2006; ADB Outlook 2006.

higher growth path — and keeping it there for the long term — should be first and foremost on the development agenda.

The country's dismal economic record shows up even more vividly on the poverty front. Poverty reduction in the Philippines lagged far behind those of its East Asian neighbours, particularly Indonesia, Thailand, Vietnam, and China (Figure 9.1). Both China and Vietnam started with higher levels of poverty incidence than did the Philippines during the early 1980s, but their absolute poverty soon dwindled and became much lower than the Philippines' during the early 2000s. Both Malaysia and Thailand also had virtually eliminated absolute poverty in the past twenty years. Interestingly, while the average income in the Philippines in the mid-2000s (PPP $4,381) was much higher than in Vietnam (PPP $2,683) and Indonesia (PPP $3,402), its absolute poverty was actually much higher than in either of the latter countries.[2]

Clearly, the unenviable performance of the Philippines in poverty reduction has to do largely with its inability to achieve — and sustain — an income growth substantially higher than its population growth. But is this all that can be said about the poverty problem in the Philippines?

The poor performance of the Philippines in economic growth and poverty reduction has often been attributed in part to the relatively large variation in access to infrastructure and social services across regions and island groups. A widely held view, for example, is that development efforts have favoured Luzon and discriminated against the Visayas and (especially) Mindanao. Proponents of this view say that this development pattern has led to substantial regional differences in access to economic opportunities, in rates of poverty

FIGURE 9.1
Poverty Reduction in East Asia

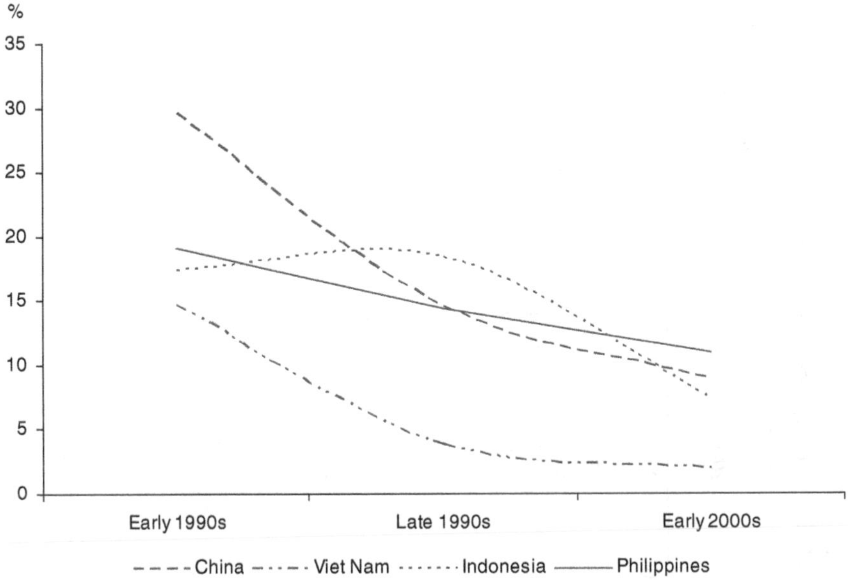

Note: Figures pertain to proportion of population with income per capita below US$1 a day (in PPP).
Sources of data: World Bank and ESCAP.

reduction, and in the incidence of armed conflict. For instance, the *Philippine Human Development Report 2005* shows that measures of deprivation — such as disparities in access to reliable water supply, electricity and especially education — predict well the occurrence of armed encounters.[3]

Table 9.2 shows the patterns of poverty across regions of the Philippines from 1988 to 2003, as well as the contribution of each region to national poverty. As one would expect given the regions' very diverse growth records (see the last column), considerable variations occured. However, Metro Manila consistently had the lowest poverty while Bicol, Western Mindanao, and the Visayas had the highest. In 2003, poverty incidence was roughly ten times higher in Bicol and Western Mindanao than in Metro Manila. Some significant re-rankings also occurred, such as the Autonomous Region of Muslim Mindanao (ARMM) becoming the poorest region in 2003 when it was the third least poor region (out of sixteen regions) in 1988. Even more significant is the differential evolution of poverty over time. In two regions, Western Mindanao and ARMM, poverty — both in incidence and

TABLE 9.2
Poverty Incidence and Income Growth, Philippine Regions, 1988–2003

Region	*1988*	*1991*	*1994*	*1997*	*2000*	*2003*	*Contribution to national poverty, 2003*	*Annual per capita income growth rate, 1988–2003*
Philippines	34.4	34.3	32.1	25.0	27.5	26.1	100.0	2.7
NCR	9.5	5.9	5.6	3.5	5.5	4.8	2.6	2.1
CAR	39.1	46.5	26.6	22.1	19.8	14.8	1.0	2.3
Ilocos	25.5	24.3	26.4	20.8	20.3	16.8	3.4	2.3
Cagayan Valley	39.2	39.1	41.8	30.1	29.9	26.9	3.5	3.3
Central Luzon	15.3	15.4	24.3	13.2	16.1	13.7	5.4	2.2
Southern Tagalog	31.7	22.9	28.6	19.6	19.5	20.9	12.2	3.9
Bicol	60.9	62.2	50.2	45.6	53.3	45.6	10.8	2.9
Western Visayas	34.4	31.6	34.5	21.8	28.1	26.5	8.2	3.6
Central Visayas	55.2	53.2	42.8	35.2	39.4	37.5	10.4	3.3
Eastern Visayas	53.7	54.4	51.5	50.6	46.8	45.6	8.8	4.3
Western Mindanao	47.6	47.1	47.1	35.2	47.0	48.9	7.6	2.0
Northern Mindanao	44.9	55.7	34.4	26.0	27.3	30.3	4.2	1.7
Southern Mindanao	46.9	56.8	30.4	26.7	25.4	27.2	7.4	3.5
Central Mindanao	35.8	46.9	45.2	33.1	38.0	34.0	4.3	2.8
ARMM	23.4	34.0	48.7	50.5	60.7	60.5	6.1	–0.5
Caraga	30.1	45.7	41.0	37.0	33.8	38.4	4.1	2.1

Note: The provincial composition of the regions has changed over the years. For comparability over time, the provinces are grouped consistently according to the 2000 regional classification. Estimates are not comparable with official figures.

Source: Author's estimates based on data from the NSO *Family Income and Expenditure Survey* (various years). Details of the estimation method employed are shown in Balisacan (2003*b*).

in depth — was higher in 2003 than in 1988. This rise also shows up in measures reflecting human development deprivation, particularly in the areas of health and education.[4] Towards the close of the 1990s, these two regions, particularly ARMM, were at the centre of violent confrontations between the military and armed dissidents.

The long-term relationship between Philippine poverty and income growth is even more evident in data on the country's seventy-seven provinces. This is shown in Figure 9.2, which plots the change in poverty incidence between 1985 and 2003 and the corresponding percentage change in real family income per capita, adjusted for provincial cost-of-living differences.[5] Clearly, as noted in the cross-country data above, the pace of poverty reduction at the provincial level is closely linked to local economic performance. However, there are significant departures from the fitted line (that is, provinces not conforming to the "average pattern"), suggesting that factors other than the rate of local economic growth are influencing the evolution of poverty.

Elsewhere, using provincial data covering the country's seventy-seven provinces between the years 1988 and 2003, Balisacan (2007) traced the quantitative significance of the channels by which income growth, together

FIGURE 9.2
Income Growth and Poverty Reduction, Philippine Provinces, 1985–2003

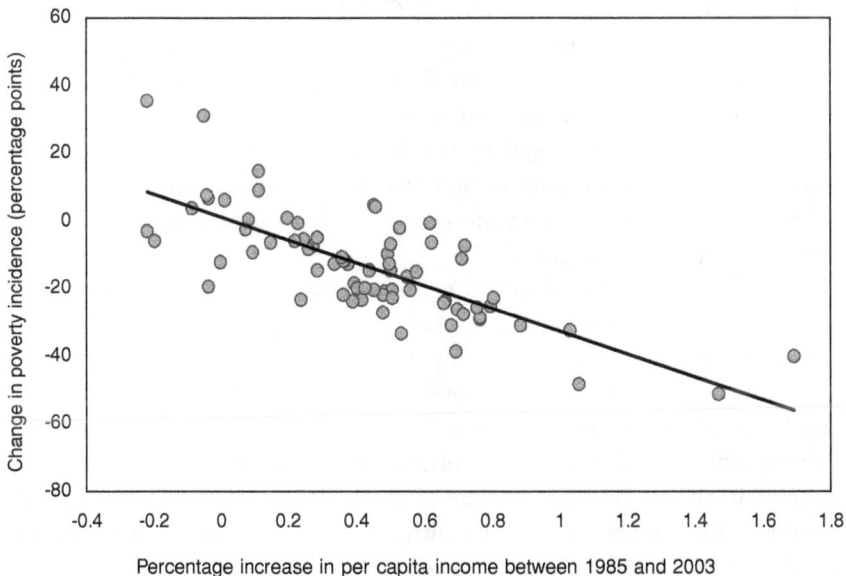

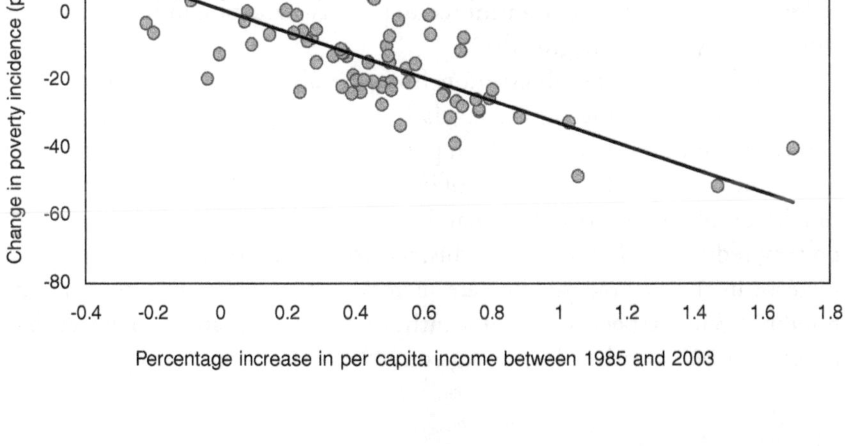

with a host of other factors, influenced poverty reduction. In his model, these other factors affect the speed of poverty reduction directly by changing the distribution of a given economic pie, or indirectly by expanding the economic pie for each person in society (that is, by way of economic growth). These factors can be grouped into two types:

(i) *Initial economic and institutional conditions (in or around 1988).* Initial mean provincial per capita income; initial distribution of per capita income; initial human capital stock; political "dynasty" (as proxy for political competitiveness); and ethno-linguistic fragmentation; and
(ii) *Time-varying policy variables (difference during 1988–2003).* Simple adult literacy rate; agricultural terms of trade (as proxy for economic incentives); access to infrastructure (represented by electricity and good-quality roads); and Comprehensive Agrarian Reform Program (CARP) implementation.

The regression results reveal cracks in poverty reduction efforts. The policy variables and the variables representing initial conditions, except those pertaining to human capital and infrastructure, are found to mainly exert an indirect effect on poverty reduction through their effect on overall income growth. For infrastructure, particularly transport, and initial human capital, both direct and indirect effects are operative and, taken together, have a positive impact on the pace of poverty reduction. Particularly remarkable is the lack of direct response of poverty to CARP. Considering that the agrarian reform programme is touted as an equity tool, this result is not only surprising but also inconsistent with earlier findings.[6] This is not to say that CARP has no effect on the poor. It has, but its effect is mainly through the income growth channel. Taken together, the regression results show very limited direct effects of recent policies and institutions on the speed of poverty reduction; their effects get transmitted to poverty reduction indirectly, mainly through overall income growth.

Another interesting observation from the above study, as well as other studies using the same provincial data (for example, Balisacan and Fuwa 2004), concerns the extent to which poverty responds to overall income, after taking into account the influences of other factors noted above. This response can be aptly summarized by what is referred to as "growth elasticity" of poverty reduction. This elasticity clusters around 1.3 to 1.65 — a 1 per cent increase in the income growth rate increases the poverty reduction rate by roughly 1.3 to 1.6 per cent. Significantly, these estimates are much lower than those reported for other developing countries. For example, using parameter estimates of inequality distribution for each country, Cline (2004) obtained growth elasticities of 2.9 for China, 3.0 for Indonesia and 3.5 for Thailand.[7]

Ravallion (2001) obtained a growth elasticity of 2.5 for 47 developing countries, based on a bivariate regression of the proportionate changes in their poverty rates and mean incomes. A similar bivariate regression of the data employed by Balisacan (2007) gives an elasticity of 1.5. Hence, by all these indications, the growth elasticity in the Philippines is quite low by international standards.

Clearly, the very low income growth achieved in recent years is a key factor in the country's sluggish rate of poverty reduction. Still, even this modest level of income growth could have delivered more poverty reduction than what had been actually realized if the growth elasticity in the Philippines had come close to those in neighbouring countries. Why is this so? What conditions need to change, and what policy responses need to evolve, to make poverty reduction more responsive to economic growth? Put differently, what does it take to improve the quality of growth?

SHARPENING THE RESPONSE OF POVERTY TO LOCAL ECONOMIC GROWTH

Both theory and evidence suggest a strong connection running between agricultural and rural development and poverty reduction. Investments in social services, especially in basic health and education, especially in rural areas, have also high payoffs in terms of poverty reduction. Serious students of Philippine economic development also call attention to the need to address the country's rapid population growth, since there is a strong link between economic performance, on the one hand, and economic growth and poverty reduction, on the other. These channels to poverty reduction are elaborated below.

As in most of Asia's developing countries, poverty in the Philippines is a largely rural phenomenon. Two of every three poor persons in the country are located in rural areas and are dependent predominantly on agricultural employment and incomes (Balisacan 2003*a*). Even poverty in urban areas is largely a consequence of low productivity and slow expansion of employment opportunities in rural areas; that is, extreme deprivation in rural areas induces rural-urban migration.

Recent development experience demonstrates that rural development fuelled by rapid productivity growth in the agricultural sector holds the key to sustained poverty reduction.[8] In developing countries where agricultural growth was rapid, sustained, and broadly based, growth of farm incomes was sustained despite farm price declines in world markets; domestic food prices remained low; rural employment diversification was enhanced; and, consequently, poverty reduction was robust.

Prior to the country's accession to the World Trade Organization (WTO) in 1995, the performance of the agriculture sector was quite poor compared with those in other Asian countries. During the period 1980–94, Philippine agriculture grew at a measly 1.5 per cent a year, the lowest among the major developing Asian countries (Table 9.3). The growth was even less than the rate of population growth then (averaging about 2.4 per cent a year). The mediocre growth mirrored the poor performance of the overall economy.

In the period following the country's accession to the WTO, the country's agricultural growth improved to 2.4 per cent a year, although this still paled in comparison with the averages for China (3.5 per cent) and Vietnam (4.2 per cent), two of the most aggressive globalizers in the Asian region. The figure is surprisingly higher than the averages for Malaysia and Indonesia and comparable with Thailand's. Note, however, that in both Malaysia and Thailand, the relative importance of agriculture in national income had declined substantially during the past two decades of rapid economic growth, while in Indonesia, the Asian financial crisis of 1997–98 left a deep puncture in the economy and the agriculture sector.

What Table 9.3 suggests is that, contrary to popular claims, especially by many NGOs and influence peddlars in government, the country's accession

TABLE 9.3
Average Agriculture Growth (%), 1965–2002

	1980–1994 Pre-WTO Accession	*1995–2003 Post-WTO Accession*
Malaysia	2.44	0.64
Sri Lanka	2.71	1.19
Indonesia	3.51	1.74
India	4.12	1.75
Philippines	1.49	2.40
Thailand	2.87	2.78
Nepal	3.36	2.94
Bangladesh	2.29	3.41
China	5.16	3.50
Pakistan	4.12	3.52
Vietnam	3.24	4.25

Note: Data for Malaysia start only in 1971, Nepal in 1966, Vietnam in 1986.
Source: World Bank, *World Development Indicators 2005*.

to the WTO could not be a compelling reason for the comparatively poor performance of agriculture in recent years. All the other major developing countries in the Asian region operated in a similar global trading environment as the Philippines but had significantly higher agricultural and overall economic growth rates than those achieved by the Philippines.

Production growth could come from either expansion of the cultivated area or from increases in output per unit area. The former is no longer a practical option for the Philippines mainly due to conversion of land to non-agricultural purposes. Hence, output growth would have to come from productivity growth through sustained technological improvements.

A comprehensive measure of productivity growth is total factor productivity (TFP) growth. This measure represents output growth net of the growth in all production inputs. It is thus an appropriate indicator of efficiency (and competitiveness) improvement. The available TFP data for the 1970s suggest that the Philippines at that time fared comparably with Thailand and Indonesia (Table 9.4). However, the succeeding two decades saw productivity stagnating in the Philippines (0.1 per cent a year) but continuing to grow in Thailand (1.0 per cent a year) and Indonesia (1.5 per cent a year). China, on the other hand, enjoyed a very high TFP growth rate of 4.7 per cent per year during this period, although the figures pertain to grains only. At this rate, it is not surprising that China increasingly has become a major producer of cheap agricultural commodities in the world commodity markets. Also, at this rate, China could well afford to reduce tariff protection for its farmers even before it acceded to the WTO, without reducing farmers' net incomes.[9]

Low productivity growth in agriculture, where the bulk of the poor are located and on which they depend for incomes and livelihood, mirrors what would be expected on the evolution of farm incomes, household incomes in

TABLE 9.4
Growth of Total Factor Productivity (TFP) in Agriculture
(% per year)

Period	*China*	*Thailand*	*Indonesia*	*Vietnam*	*Philippines*
1970–1980	Na	1.3	1.6	na	1.0
1980–2000*	4.7	1.0	1.5	2.0	0.1
All Period		1.2	1.5	0.2	

* 1979–95 for China (covering rice, wheat, and corn only), 1981–95 for Thailand, 1981–98 for Indonesia, 1980–98 for the Philippines, and 1985–2000 for Vietnam (rice only).

Source: Mundlak et al. (2004) for Indonesia, Thailand, and Philippines; Jin et al. (2002) for China; ICARD (2004), cited in FAO (2006*b*), for Vietnam.

general, and poverty. As recent experiences in Asia and elsewhere suggest, productivity growth in agriculture exerts a strong direct and indirect influence on poverty and food insecurity.[10]

More importantly, increases in agricultural productivity and farm incomes stimulate the growth of non-farm activities and, hence, employment opportunities. Put differently, while agricultural growth directly reduces rural poverty and food insecurity, the indirect effects on the rural non-farm economy, as well as urban economy, through demand and supply linkages can be even more important sources of food security and rural poverty reduction in the long run.

Drawing on the Asian experience, the response of rural non-farm areas (as well as urban areas) and, hence, of rural poverty to agricultural growth, including export or urban demand expansion, requires a number of things. These include investments in rural infrastructure and human capital, removal of public-spending biases favouring large farmers and agribusiness enterprises, promotion of small-scale enterprises, improved access to land and technology, and macroeconomic and political stability. The Philippine record in virtually all these things is far inferior to those of its East Asian neighbours. Specifically, the country has neglected to invest in what recent economic history has shown as "deep determinants" of rural growth and poverty reduction: market-friendly institutions, rural infrastructure, and health and education.[11]

Besides fostering agricultural and rural development, what else can government do to maximize returns — in terms of poverty reduction — to government expenditures? Given the fiscal bind, what menu of government spending would yield high returns for the poor? Put differently, what programmes would have comparatively high chances of benefiting the poor and therefore should receive comparatively more support in terms of government outlay? Table 9.5 provides such a guide to national government spending. The list is by no means exhaustive, but it includes areas that have been extensively demonstrated — both in the country and elsewhere — as effective vehicles for directly influencing the welfare of the poor, while keeping the fiscal burden of poverty reduction programmes to manageable levels by reducing leakages of the benefits of such programmes to the unintended (non-poor) groups.

THE OTHER BIG BUT NEGLECTED PROBLEM — RAPID POPULATION GROWTH

One particular feature of the Philippine society is its failure to achieve a demographic transition similar to what its Southeast and East Asian neighbours

TABLE 9.5
Indicative Areas for National Government Spending on a Poverty Programme

Areas to spend more	*Areas to spend less*
1. Basic education, especially teaching materials; technical education and skills development esp. in rural areas	Tertiary education: cost-recovery (but with scholarships for the poor)
2. Basic health and family planning services	Tertiary healthcare: impose cost-recovery
3. Rural infrastructure, especially transport and power (but w/ coordination)	Public works equipment programme (except for short-term disaster relief)
4. Targeted supplementary feeding programmes and food stamps	General food price subsidies
5. R&D and small-scale irrigation systems	Post-harvest facilities (private goods)
6. Capacity building for LGUs and microfinance providers	Livelihood programmes (except for short-term disaster relief)
7. Impact monitoring and evaluation	

went through during the past three decades.[12] In all these countries, including the Philippines, mortality rates declined almost at broadly similar rates, but fertility rates declined much more slowly in the Philippines than in its neighbours. Consequently, while population growth rates declined substantially to below 2 per cent a year in such countries as Thailand, Indonesia, and Vietnam, the rate hardly changed from a high level of 2.3 per cent a year in the Philippines. The working-age population of East Asian countries was 57 per cent in 1965 and 65 per cent in 1990, increasing four times compared with the number of dependents. In contrast, the Philippines had a working-age population of below 60 per cent, with 52 per cent in 1980, 55 per cent in 1990, 56 per cent in 1995 and 58 per cent in 2000.

Compelling evidence demonstrates that the demographic dividend has contributed immensely to the rapid economic growth in the so-called "East Asian miracle" countries during the past three decades (World Bank 1993; Bloom et al. 1999; McNicoll 2006). Bloom et al., in particular, estimated this contritbution to be roughly one-third of the observed growth rates of per capita GDP.

In the Philippines, the population issue remains highly contentious. At the centre of the debate is whether population growth has any bearing on economic development and poverty reduction. At one extreme is the Catholic Church's strong opposition to any reference to population growth as a contributory factor to the country's transformation to a basket case. Philippine administrations, particularly that of President Arroyo, have been very sensitive to the Church's stand on the issue, especially concerning population policy and population programmes. Surprisingly, despite its obvious importance in this debate, empirical work examining the quantitative significance of the economy-population-poverty dynamics in the Philippines is quite scarce. Until lately, what exactly the country has missed in terms of economic growth and poverty reduction by way of the demographic dividend has not been known.

In a recent study, Balisacan et al. (forthcoming) attempted to fill this gap by using a combination of estimation techniques and data to "discover" the relationship of population growth and the demographic transition with economic growth and poverty reduction. They used data from eighty developing and developed countries covering twenty-five years. Their focus was on long-run effects, thus the reason for their use of a relatively large time series data. To the extent allowed by available data, their estimation has controlled for the influences of factors other than population growth, including institutions, trade regimes, and income inequality. Some highlights of their findings are:

- Total population growth rate has a negative and significant impact on economic growth.
- Workers' population growth has a positive and significant impact on economic growth.
- Heath status of the population has a positive and significant impact on economic growth.
- Openness to trade has a positive and significant impact on economic growth.
- Quality of public institutions has a positive and significant impact on economic growth.

Of particular interest here is the result of the comparison between Thailand and the Philippines. These two countries are interesting cases because they have many things in common: land area, economic structure, natural resources, and goods traded in the international market. In the mid-1970s, the two countries had roughly the same population: 43 million in the Philippines growing at about 2.6 per cent that year and 41 million in

Thailand growing at about 2.7 per cent. The Philippines was ahead in terms of average income: Per capita GDP in the Philippines was US$1,502 (in PPP), about twice the per capita GDP of Thailand at US$805 (in PPP).[13] During the period 1975–2000, the Philippines' GDP grew at an average of 4.1 per cent only, doubling income after seventeen years. Thailand's GDP, on the other hand, grew at an amazing average rate of 8.8 per cent for the same period (more than twice the growth rate of the Philippines), doubling income after only eight years. In 2000, per capita GDP in the Philippines was US$ 3,971 (in PPP) — about 2.6 times the initial GDP per capita in 1975. Thailand's 2000 per capita GDP was US$ 6,402 — 8 times its 1975 per capita GDP.

While Thailand and the Philippines had also roughly similar population growth rates in 1975, as Figure 9.3 shows, the former was able to manage its population growth during the twenty-five-year period, growing annually at an average of 1.6 per cent only. The Philippines, however, maintained its relatively high population growth rate throughout the period, growing at an average of 2.4 per cent per year in the 1990s. Hence the total population of

FIGURE 9.3
Population Growth: Philippines *vs* Thailand (% per year)

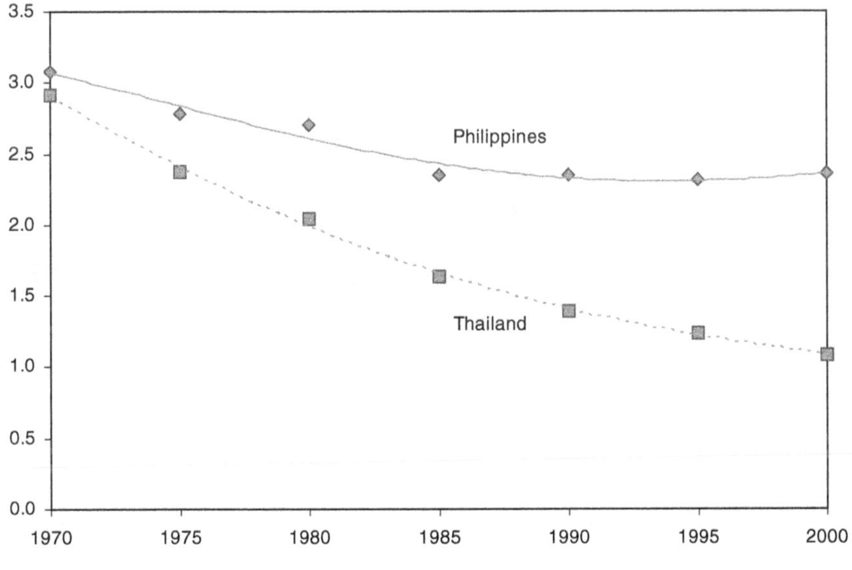

Source: National Statistics Office census for various years (Philippines); International Data Base (Thailand).

the Philippines ballooned to about 76 million in year 2000 while Thailand's was about 61 million only.

To what extent does the difference in population dynamics between the two countries account for the stark difference in their economic performance? Table 9.6 provides the results of a "growth accounting" required to identify this contribution. The first column in the table identifies the relevant variable. The second column corresponds to the actual values of the variables for the Philippines, and the third column reports the values for Thailand. The last column gives the additional growth rate that the Philippines would have enjoyed if it had Thailand's values (column 3) rather than its own values (column 2). Thus, the last column provides the estimate of the foregone economic growth. The results show that differences in the population growth rates between the two countries account for about 0.77 percentage point of foregone growth for the Philippines.[14] This figure implies that had the Philippines followed Thailand's population growth path during the period 1975 to 2000, the country's growth in the average income per person would have been 0.77 percentage point higher every year.

Combining this result with those of previous studies estimating the effects of growth in the income per person on poverty reduction, Balisacan et al. also showed that poverty incidence in 2000, had the Philippines followed Thailand's population growth, would have been lower by 5.3 percentage points. Put differently, given that the population in 2000 was 76.5 million, about 4.05 million would have escaped poverty, if only the Philippines had followed the population growth dynamics of Thailand during the period 1976–2000.

TABLE 9.6
Why the Philippines Grew So Slowly

Variable	*Philippines*	*Thailand*	*Foregone Growth*
Population growth (%)			0.77
Total	2.36	1.58	
Workers	2.85	2.53	
Other included variables* (%)			2.07
Total growth differential accounted by model (%)			2.84
Actual GDP per capita growth rate, average of 1975–2000 (%)	4.10	8.84	4.74

* The other variables included in the model are initial income (GDP per capita in 1975), trade regime, savings rate, health status, education, institutions, and location.
Source: Balisacan et al. (forthcoming).

FIGURE 9.4
Per Capita Income in the Philippines had the Country Followed Thailand's Population Dynamics

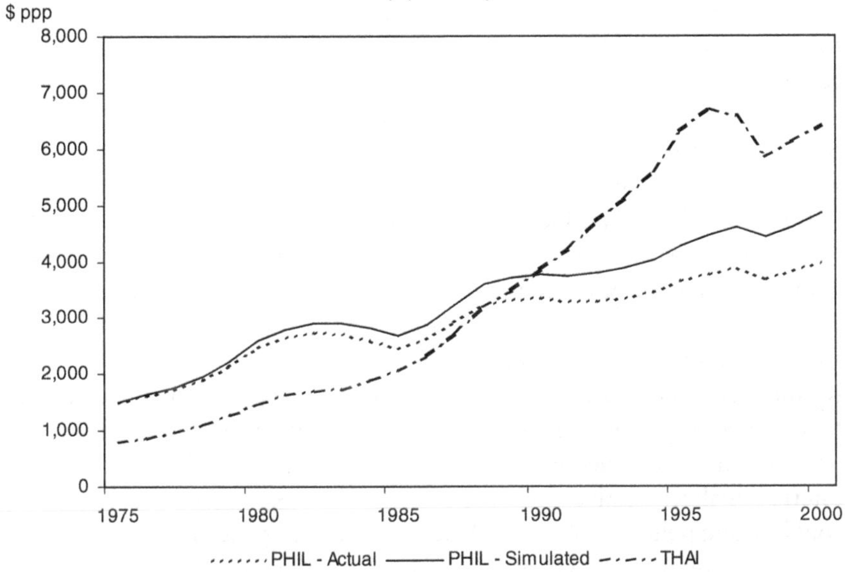

Source: Balisacan et al. (forthcoming).

CONCLUDING REMARKS

The persistence of poverty in the Philippines has to do largely with its inability to achieve — and sustain — an income growth substantially higher than its population growth. Contrary to popular claims, economic growth has been beneficial to the poor — as well as the non-poor.

However, while economic growth is good for the poor, it is not good enough. The response of poverty reduction to income growth in the Philippines has been quite muted by international standards, especially in comparison with the country's neighbours. Hence, the Philippines's unenviable record in poverty reduction in recent years is the outcome not only of its comparatively low per capita GDP growth rate but also of its weakness in transforming any rate of income growth into poverty reduction. The quality of economic growth has to be improved to enhance the benefits of growth to the poor.

Even given the fiscal bind, there are wide avenues for improving the response of poverty to overall income growth. Evidence suggests, for example, a strong connection running between agricultural and rural development and poverty reduction. Investments in social services, such as in basic health and education especially in rural areas, have also high pay-offs in terms of poverty reduction. Serious students of Philippine economic development also call attention to the need to address the country's rapid population growth, since there is a strong link between economic performance, on the one hand, and economic growth and poverty reduction, on the other.

The very high spatial diversity in the Philippines is quite remarkable. Some pockets of the country have human development outcomes comparable with those found in more economically advanced countries; for example, Metro Manila's Human Development Index (HDI) for 2003 is comparable with that of Thailand, and the province of Rizal's with Ukraine's. However, many other areas have outcomes comparable with those found in the poorest countries of the world; for example, the ARMM provinces have HDI scores comparable with those of Sudan, Ghana, and Myanmar. In recent years some regions have done quite well in attaining high per capita income growth and reducing poverty, but others — disturbingly — have experienced falls in their average per capita income and an increase in poverty. Viewed from an international perspective, such disparities could breed regional unrest, armed conflicts, and political upheavals, thereby undermining the progress in securing sustained economic growth and national development.

The good news is that the growth processes in recent years have allowed the lagging regions to catch up with the leading ones. Balisacan (2007) shows that there is a tendency for convergence of provincial mean incomes over the long term. Infrastructure, human capital, economic climate, trade regime, and agricultural relations are the key drivers of provincial income growth. Improvements in access to roads, electricity, and health and schooling have positive effects on provincial income growth rates. Policy regimes that do not unduly reduce the profitability of agriculture relative to non-agriculture also help boost provincial income growth. Likewise, improved access to productive assets and technology by way of CARP is an important source of provincial income growth.

What is disturbing, however, is the finding that certain policy levers that have often been identified as tools for achieving equity objectives — human capital and asset reform through CARP — have no discernible direct effects on poverty reduction; their effects are felt mostly indirectly through the income growth process. In other words, even programmes supposedly targeted at poverty such as CARP have actually been neutral from an income distribution viewpoint. One interpretation of this result is that the implementation of such programmes has actually been poorly targeted. There is evidence to support this proposition as regards many of the country's direct anti-poverty programmes such as food, credit, irrigation and seed subsidies, and housing and schooling subsidies.

Even more disturbing is the government's posture with respect to the rapidly growing population. Policies and programmes concerning population have remained captive to the Catholic Church's stand on the issue. The consequence of such posture on economic growth and poverty reduction has been staggering: it has contributed to the country's transformation to being Southeast Asia's basket case. This stance has to change, if only to improve the country's chances of moving the economy to a higher growth path and winning the war against poverty.

Notes

1 See Deininger and Squire (1998); Sachs (2005); Deaton (2005); Kraay (2006).

2 PPP is the preferred measure when comparing incomes of different countries. It takes into account differences in the prices of goods and services and is used by multilateral institutions such as the World Bank.

3 See HDN 2005.

4 Ibid.

5 Poverty estimates are those used in Balisacan (2007) and Balisacan and Fuwa (2004). These are not comparable with official data released by the National Statistical Coordination Board. As shown in Balisacan (2003*b*), the official estimates are not quite an accurate guide to ascertaining changes in absolute poverty over time or across regions — or provinces, or between rural and urban areas — of the country.

6 See Balisacan (2003) and Deininger and Squire (1998). Balisacan and Fuwa (2004) also found that CARP had a positive direct effect on poverty reduction rate, although the estimate was marginally significant only. It is probably the case that the implementation of the programme evolved quite differently in recent years. There is evidence, for example, that CARP is implemented more vigorously in areas with high growth potentials (Edillon and Velarde 2004).

7 Cline's estimate for the Philippines was 2.2. While higher than the other estimates quoted here, it is still low by Asian standards.

8 Rosegrant and Hazell (1999); Timmer (2005)

9 See FAO 2006*a*.

10 See Rosegrant and Hazell (2000); Timmer (2005); Balisacan and Fuwa (2007).

11 See David (2003) for an analysis of the factors influencing the performance of Philippine agriculture.

12 Demographic transition is a change from a situation of high fertility and high mortality to one of low fertility and low mortality. This change results in sizeable changes in the age distribution of the population. The change can create the "demographic dividend", that is, the increases in per capita income as the bulge

in the age pyramid moves, over time, from young people (infants and children) to prime age for productive work and savings.

[13] Data are drawn from the World Bank's World Development Indicators.

[14] The population factor comes out as the second most important component — after initial income — accounting for the income growth difference between the two countries.

References

Balisacan, A.M. "Poverty and Inequality". In *The Philippine Economy: Development, Policies, and Challenges*, edited by A.M. Balisacan and H. Hill. New York: Oxford University Press, 2003*a*.

———. "Poverty Comparison in the Philippines: Is What We Know about the Poor Robust?". In *Reducing Poverty in Asia: Emerging Issues in Growth, Targeting, and Measurement*, edited by C. Edmonds. Cheltenham, UK: Edward Elgar, 2003*b*.

———. "Local Growth and Poverty Reduction". In *The Dynamics of Regional Development: The Philippines in East Asia*, edited by A.M. Balisacan and H. Hill. Cheltenham, UK: Edward Elgar, 2007.

Balisacan, A.M. and E. Pernia. "The Rural Road to Poverty Reduction: Some Lessons from the Philippine Experience". *Journal of Asian and African Studies* 37, no. 2 (2002): 147–67.

Balisacan, A.M. and N. Fuwa. "Going beyond Cross-country Averages: Growth, Inequality and Poverty Reduction in the Philippines". *World Development* 32, no. 11 (2004): 1,891–907.

Balisacan, A. and N. Fuwa. "Changes in Spatial Income Inequality in the Philippines: An Exploratory Analysis". In *Spatial Disparities in Human Development: Perspectives from Asia*, edited by R. Kanbur, T. Venables, and G. Wan. Tokyo: United Nations University Press, 2006*a*.

———. "Poverty and Vulnerability". In *Reasserting the Rural Development Agenda: Lessons Learned and Emerging Challenges in Asia*. Singapore: Institute of Southeast Asian Studies and Philippines: SEARCA, 2007.

Balisacan, A.M., D. Mapa, C. Tubianosa, and Associates. *The Population-Economy-Poverty Links in the Philippines: A Quantitative Assessment*. Quezon City: University of the Philippines Press, *forthcoming*.

Bloom, D.E., D. Canning and P.N. Malaney. "Demographic Change and Economic Growth in Asia". CID Working Paper, 1999.

Cline, W.R. "Technical Correction". In *Trade Policy and Global Poverty*. Washington D.C.: Institute of International Economics, 2004.

David, C.C. "Agriculture". In *The Philippine Economy: Development, Policies, and Challenges*, edited by A.M. Balisacan and H. Hill. New York: Oxford University Press, 2003.

Deaton, A. "Measuring Poverty in a Growing World (or Measuring Growth in a Poor World)". *Review of Economics and Statistics* 87 (2005): 1–19.

Deininger, K. and L. Squire. "New Ways of Looking at Old Issues: Inequality and Growth". *Journal of Development Economics* 57 (1998): 259–87.

Dollar, D. and A. Kraay. "Growth is Good for the Poor". *Journal of Economic Growth* 7 (2002): 195–225.

Edillon, R. and R. Velarde. "ARC Strategy — Paving the Way from Agrarian Reform to Poverty Reduction: Assessing the Impact of the ARC Strategy on Poverty Using Census, National Housing Surveys, and ALDA". Asia Pacific Policy Center, Quezon City, 2004.

FAO [Food and Agriculture Organization]. *Rapid Growth of Selected Asian Countries — Lessons and Implications for Agriculture and Food Security: China and India*, Policy Assistance Series 1/2, FAO Regional Office for Asia and the Pacific, Bangkok, 2006*a*.

———. *Rapid Growth of Selected Asian Countries — Lessons and Implications for Agriculture and Food Security: Republic of Korea, Thailand and Viet Nam,* Policy Assistance Series 1/3, FAO Regional Office for Asia and the Pacific, Bangkok, 2006*b*.

HDN [Human Development Network]. *Philippine Human Development Report 2005*, Quezon City, 2005.

Kraay, A. "When is Growth Pro-poor? Evidence from a Panel of Countries". *Journal of Development Economics* 80 (2006): 198–227.

McNicoll, G. "Policy Lessons of the East Asian Demographic Transition". *Population and Development Review* 32 (2006): 1–25.

Mundlak, Y., D.F. Larson, and R. Butzer. "Determinants of Agricultural Growth in Thailand, Indonesia, and the Philippines". In *Rural Development and Agricultural Growth in Indonesia, the Philippines, and Thailand*, edited by T. Akiyama and D.F. Larson. Canberra: Asia Pacific Press, 2004.

Ravallion, M. "Growth, Inequality, and Poverty: Looking beyond Averages". *World Development*, 29 (2001): 1803–15.

Rosegrant, M. and P.B.R. Hazell. *Transforming the Rural Asian Economy: The Unfinished Revolution*. Hong Kong: Oxford University Press, 1999.

Sachs, J. *The End of Poverty: How We Can Make It Happen in Our Lifetime*. London: Penguin Books, 2005.

Timmer, C.P. "Agriculture and Pro-Poor Growth: An Asian Perspective". Working Paper No. 62, Center for Global Development, Washington, D.C., 2005.

World Bank. *The East Asian Miracle: Economic Growth and Public Policy*. New York: Oxford University Press for the World Bank, 1993.

10

DIASPORA, REMITTANCES AND POVERTY

Ernesto M. Pernia

INTRODUCTION

Remittances are one of the many dimensions of international migration that of late has attracted a great deal of attention from academics, public officials, and the media. For one thing, the magnitudes have increased sharply, at rates even faster than the departure of migrant workers. For another, in many developing countries, remittances have begun to significantly exceed foreign direct investment (FDI), capital market flows, or official development assistance (ODA). Moreover, remittances provide timely support to otherwise shaky balance of payments and fiscal positions. Further, remittances appear to contribute importantly to lifting households out of poverty, as well as benefit the wider community through the multiplier effects of increased spending.

The Philippines is reputed to be the world's third highest net remittance recipient country after India and Mexico. In 2006, remittances were officially recorded at US$12.8 billion,[1] representing about 10 per cent of GDP. Clearly, remittances resulting from the Filipino diaspora have become a major factor in the economic and social life of the country. This chapter focuses on the home country consequences of remittances, addressing the question whether and to what extent remittances contribute to poverty reduction and regional development in the Philippines.

The next two sections revisit the causes and consequences of international migration, drawing on the more recent literature. The fourth section focuses on remittances in terms of what motivate them and what impact they may have in the labour-sending countries. The chapter then describes the pattern of labour migration and remittances by region in the Philippines. The sixth section carries out an econometric analysis to see if remittances matter to poverty alleviation and regional development. The chapter concludes with the main points and some implications for policy.

CAUSES OF INTERNATIONAL MIGRATION

Given the pronounced economic and social inequalities across the various countries of the world, one would expect floods of migrants from the worse-off to the better-off places. However, actual migration flows are limited by various territorial controls in the destination countries. Still, even these controls have limitations that effectively allow clandestine and irregular migrants, which in some countries are estimated to be as many as half to equal the numbers of legal migrants.

The socioeconomic status of developing countries is typically a critical determinant of the magnitudes and characteristics of international emigration. Economic development, if characterized by tight labour markets, serves to attenuate pressures especially on skilled workers and professionals to migrate. Examples are Malaysia and Thailand — countries with strong economic growth and limited skilled/professional emigration — and India and the Philippines with weak economic growth (especially prior to the 1990s in the case of India) and large educated migrant outflows. In the case of the Philippines, continuing rapid population growth has been a contributory factor as well. South Korea exemplifies a country with a dynamic economy experiencing emigration (mainly to the United States), while Indonesia has shown limited skilled/professional emigration regardless of its economic performance.

It appears that cultural factors (cultural attachment) play a significant role in the cases of Malaysia, Thailand and Indonesia, while India, the Philippines and South Korea illustrate the importance of migrant stocks (family networks and social capital) at destination, resulting in inertial migration (or migration momentum). This migrant stock effect applies as well to Vietnam, following substantial refugee-type migration primarily to the United States after the Vietnam War.

Employing cross-country regressions, Adams and Page (2003) report an inverted U-shaped curve between level of country per capita income and international migration, meaning that migration propensity tends to be weak for low- and high-income countries but peaks among middle-income countries.

They also find no statistical relationship between poverty incidence (headcount ratio) and international migration, implying the considerable costs involved in migration. Other migration determinants found to be significant are distance, income inequality, population density, education, and macroeconomic stability (proxied by credit rating). A variable that the authors did not account for but is likely to have a strong explanatory power is migrant stock. Migrant stock, which represents kinship network and social capital, as mentioned above, appreciably lowers the costs of migration, including distance, and eases the migrant's adjustment pains and woes at destination.

Another factor that is likely to have a significant, if indirect, effect on international migration is greater trade openness in the developed countries. Studies of trade and growth show that economic openness in developing countries contribute to faster economic growth (for example, Krueger and Berg 2002), in turn affecting international migration. Further, one could argue that greater trade openness in the developed countries themselves (e.g., the lifting of agricultural subsidies) would contribute to even faster growth in developing countries and, in turn, dampen the propensity to migrate. Rough estimates of the effects of such greater openness suggest huge global economic gains. However, this issue has hardly been considered in international migration studies.

CONSEQUENCES OF INTERNATIONAL MIGRATION

By and large, international migrants tend to be among the better educated and experienced workers in the community at origin. Most of them would have been previously employed prior to quitting voluntarily or otherwise. This implies that the departure of migrants could result in some disruption of economic activity before the vacancies are filled. And even when these are filled, the situation may not be the same as before.

Lucas (2004) explains how labour market responses would depend on the composition of emigration and the nature of labour markets (flexibility, segmentation, rates of un- and under-employment) as influenced by policy. He further discusses wage effects, cross-market effects, and technology (capital intensity) and output responses. However, the empirical evidence available from country case studies, such as Pakistan, Sri Lanka, the Philippines, and Albania bear out the difficulty of plausible generalization. In any case, Lucas arrives at two categories of cases: (i) where emigrant workers are easily replaced with no discernible loss in output or rise in wages (India, Indonesia, and Sri Lanka); and (ii) where significant upward pressure on wages is palpable (Pakistan, Philippines, Mexico, Malawi, and Mozambique). The outcome in both cases appears to be a happy one, namely, labour market gains for those left behind.

A variation to the foregoing analysis would be to look at two time periods: pre- and post-1985 — the year of the Plaza Accord (resulting in the Japanese yen's dramatic appreciation) — a watershed particularly for Asian developing countries (ADCs). This marked the sharp acceleration of growth in ADCs fueled by exports to and FDIs from Japan. Thus, while prior to the mid-1980s rates of un- and under-employment were high, labour markets actually tightened thereafter. Indeed, some of the higher-income ADCs have become hosts to labour migrants from the lower-income countries.

Another important effect of departing workers is on the quality of goods and services, reflecting the quality of replacement workers. A deterioration in quality would not be unexpected. For example, such deterioration is apparent in the quality of education and health services in the Philippines as a consequence of the departure of skilled or professional workers (teachers and health workers). Of course, one would also have to figure out to what extent the deterioration in service quality is due to diminished real budgets for public services as a result of the country's lacklustre economic growth.

A number of econometric studies, employing cross-country regressions, on the consequences of international migration have also been carried out. Concerning the issue of the brain drain, Adams (2003) finds that international legal migration is largely the movement of educated persons, with the large majority of those moving to the United States and other OECD countries having secondary schooling or higher. However, he claims that although migrants are well educated, international migration does not take away a very large share of a country's best educated (in general, less than 10 per cent of the college-educated or higher). Nonetheless, he admits that for a few labour-sending countries, international migration does result in brain drain.

Indeed, other authors argue that international migration leads to a significant loss of highly educated persons for a wide range of countries (Lucas 2004; Lowell 2003). However, the empirical evidence on the magnitudes and types of costs to labour-exporting developing countries remains scant. An aspect of these costs is the loss of public funds invested in the education of the labour migrants — reinforcing the need to reform the financing of tertiary education. Nevertheless, the brain drain is probably not an unmitigated bane as there are compensating benefits, such as remittances, other beneficial links that the emigrants develop and maintain with the home country, and return migration.[2]

Regarding international migration and poverty in developing countries, Adams and Page (2003) show that international migration (defined as the share of a country's population living abroad) exerts a strong negative effect on poverty. Overall, a 10 per cent rise in the share of international migrants in a country's population is associated with a 1.9 per cent decline in the proportion of the population living below a U.S. dollar-a-day poverty line. They also find that the level of international remittances (defined as the share of remittances in a country's GDP) is significantly associated with poverty reduction. On average, a 10 per cent increase in the share of remittances in a country's GDP is associated with a 1.6 per cent drop in poverty incidence.

Studies of international migration based on regressions of cross-country averages, however, tend to be hobbled by the well-known pitfalls (e.g., considerable inter-country differences in concepts, definitions and measurements of the variables used) and, hence, can offer only broad indications. These need to be complemented or validated by country-specific studies using sub-national (regional, provincial, or district) data.[3]

REMITTANCES

If the data on the number and types of international migrants are imperfect, the data on remittances leave even more to be desired. Obviously, it is easier to hide or store cold cash than warm bodies! It is reported that formal remittance flows to developing countries in 2002 reached an estimated US$88 billion and informal flows are typically estimated to be hugely larger (Ratha 2003). It is plausible to assume that the extent of informal flows varies directly with the proximity of the host country to the home country and/or with the frequency of return home visits by either the remitting migrants themselves or their kin and friends who can serve as trusted couriers. The practice of informal remittance is likely to persist with regulatory systems in both host and home countries that make formal remittance highly cumbersome and costly. Admittedly, governments and international agencies have made some notable progress in helping overcome the hurdles of remitting.[4] But, undoubtedly, a lot more needs to be done.

A notable feature of remittances has been their steady growth over the past several years, compared with FDI whose growth has been erratic and on the downtrend more recently, and ODA, which has been declining. These trends provide strong motivation for improving the remittance system in terms of both making the flows more efficient and broadening and deepening their impact on economic growth and poverty reduction in the sending countries. Indeed, some observers now refer to remittances as the new development finance (Wimaladharma, Pearce, and Stanton 2004).

Determinants

The motivation to remit is often explained in terms of altruism, pure self-interest (target saving), or mutual insurance (Lucas 2004). This view appears somewhat simplistic and, in any case, probably not easily empirically testable. It seems more likely that the motivation to remit is a combination of these and other reasons (such as parental or elder-sibling obligation) that can change over time.[5] It makes more sense to regard remittances as the returns to migration, an investment in human capital of the migrant and his/her family, often to provide a better present and a brighter future for the children or younger siblings. Thus, we often hear the remark: "I'm doing this not so much for myself as for my children and their future."

In terms of macro determinants, apart from the economic conditions in the host country that influence the job opportunities and earnings for the migrants, macroeconomic stability (realistic exchange rate, stable prices and interest rates) in addition to social and political stability in the home country would probably favour the rise of formal remittances and the corresponding fall of informal remittances. While beneficial to the economy's long-term growth, the decline of informal remittances could hurt individual families in the short run (for example, owing to delays, transaction costs). However, in the longer run, as the impact of remittances, working through multiplier effects, deepens and widens throughout the economy, it can contribute to sustained growth and welfare improvement of lower-income households.[6]

Consequences

Since labour migrants tend to come from the not-so-poor households (typically, those above the poverty threshold), it is the lower-middle to middle-income families who directly gain from remittances. The poor and certainly the poorest-of-the-poor could benefit from remittances mainly in subsequent rounds *via* multiplier effects from increased consumption and investment spending. The size of the multiplier effect may hinge on whether remittances are received by rural or urban households, with the former typically consuming more local products, thereby creating a larger multiplier effect (Adelman and Taylor 1990). How much of the remittances will be spent for consumption and how much for investment by the recipient families themselves, or investment by others from the saved remittances, will depend on the investment climate in the locality (Pernia and Salas 2005). The role of policy is to improve such investment environment (macro fundamentals, governance and institutions, and infrastructure). Combined with social and political stability, such an environment could also encourage migrants to remit through formal channels, as pointed out above.

Like the other aspects of international migration, it is precarious to generalize regarding the consequences of remittances. Empirical evidence is called for. Worthwhile evidence can come from country-specific studies. For instance, a trade, growth, and poverty study using sub-national data on Philippine regions indicates a significant relationship between regional trade openness (exports-GRDP ratio) and regional development (increase in gross regional domestic product (GRDP) per capita); further, the regional growth elasticity of poverty is estimated to be 0.2, implying that a 10 per cent rise in regional incomes per capita raises the incomes of the poorest (bottom quintile) by 2 per cent (Pernia and Quising 2003). In other words, as suggested by cross-country studies, economic openness at the sub-national level also influences positively the welfare of the poor through economic growth. With data on international migrant remittances by region, one could incorporate remittances in the equation to gauge their relative impact on regional development and the well-being of the poor. This exercise will be carried out in this chapter.

The economic consequences of remittances can be considered at different levels. At the household level, a substantial portion of migrant workers' earnings is typically remitted to family members in their home communities. Remittances serve to enhance family incomes, although whether they represent a net increase is debatable, given the possibility that family members may reduce their work effort — a moral hazard effect on labour supply. Nonetheless, overall, it seems clear that recipient families are better off with rather than without the remittances.[7]

The extent to which remittances are spent on consumption or investment has been a greatly debated issue, but the discussion seems misdirected. It should be noted that remittances are a fungible resource for the household (Lucas 2004). So, the issue is not really whether the money received is actually invested but whether households whose incomes are increased by remittances save more and such savings become available for investment in the local or macro economy. Moreover, expenditures on education, housing and land are important forms of investment.[8] Further, spending by one household may or may not be an investment for the larger economy depending on how the recipient of these payments spends the income.

At the community level, the distribution of incomes across households would be affected by money flows depending on where the remittance recipients are in the income distribution scale. Income inequality and poverty would diminish to the extent that the poorer households receive the bulk of these income transfers, or the inequality would worsen if the richer families were the main recipients.[9] Nonetheless, creation of jobs and trading opportunities often results from the expanded demand for goods and services, with the beneficiaries in turn spending and generating further spending. These multiplier effects could be concentrated in particular local economies or spread more widely depending on how localized are the migrant networks.

At the macroeconomic level, remittances have become a major source of foreign exchange, especially for developing countries plagued by fiscal deficits, external debts, persistent trade imbalances, and scant foreign direct investment. Foreign exchange inflows, however, tend to put upward pressure on prices, requiring skillful monetary management that often includes sterilization. Moreover, these foreign money inflows may spur a real appreciation of the exchange rate, thereby constraining the development of export-oriented and import-competing industries. This has been likened to the Dutch disease problem of Indonesia brought about by the foreign exchange income from oil exports (Quibria 1986). Further, the remittance windfall may have a moral hazard effect as the urgency for the government to pursue policy reforms or improve governance dissipates while people are lulled into complacency, as appears to be the case in the Philippines.

Table 10.1 shows that while the Philippines' average annual reported remittance inflow during 1995–2001 was next in absolute size only to India's, it was the highest relative to population and GDP among Asia's main labour-exporting countries, and third highest relative to exports after Bangladesh and India. In recent years, exports from Bangladesh and India have been booming, so it is possible that the Philippines' remittances-to-

TABLE 10.1
Average Annual Reported Remittance Inflows into Asia's Main Labour Exporting Countries, 1995–2001

Country	*US$ (millions)*	*$ per capita*	*Remittance/GDP (%)*	*Remittance/exports (%)*
Bangladesh	1,651	13	3.86	32.42
India	9,181	8	2.19	25.68
Indonesia	925	5	0.62	1.71
Pakistan	1,344	10	2.48	16.86
Philippines	**5,942**	**80**	**7.92**	**22.27**
Sri Lanka	993	53	6.57	21.56
Thailand	1,570	26	1.15	2.72

Source: Lucas (2004) based on IMF Balance of Payments Statistics and International Financial Statistics.

exports ratio has overtaken or closed in on those of both countries. In any case, these data indicate how much of a factor remittances have played in the country's macroeconomy.

REGIONAL PATTERNS OF LABOUR MIGRATION

The Data

The data on labour migration and remittances by region are from the annual Survey of Overseas Filipinos (SOF) carried out beginning in the early 1990s. This survey was a rider to the Labour Force Survey (LFS) conducted by the National Statistics Office (NSO). The SOF gathers estimates of the number of Overseas Filipino Workers (OFWs), their socioeconomic characteristics, the amount of remittances in cash and in kind, and the manner of remitting to their families in the Philippines.

OFWs include Overseas Contract Workers (OCWs) who are currently and temporarily out of the country during the reference period (1 April to 30 September of each year) to fulfil a work contract, or who are currently in the country on vacation but still have an existing contract, as well as other Filipino workers abroad with valid work permits. Filipinos currently staying and working full time in other countries even without working visas (tourist, visitor, student, medical, and other types of non-immigrant visas) are also included.[10] OFWs who left for abroad earlier than 1 April of the reference year are also included provided they were working during the reference period.

Overview

In 2004, OCWs accounted for 93 per cent of all OFWs. OFWs were roughly equally divided between females and males, with the former mostly in the 25-29 age group and the latter 45 years or older. Over three-fourths of OFWs were working in Asia in 2004, about 10 per cent in Europe, 8 per cent in North and South America, and the balance in Australia, Africa, and other countries. Of those in Asia, the bulk was in Saudi Arabia, followed by Hong Kong, Japan, and Taiwan. OFWs in Saudi Arabia were mostly males while those in Hong Kong were mostly females. The majority of male OFWs were production and related workers, transport and equipment operators and labourers, while female OFWs were mostly sales and service workers. Only a small minority of OFWs were professional, technical and related workers.

Since the SOF covers remittances only during the reference period (1 April–30 September), the reported amounts would have to be doubled to arrive at yearly estimates. These estimates may miss the additional amounts customarily sent for the Christmas holidays; however, extra amounts are also typically remitted in connection with the opening of the school year in June.

In 2004, total remittances consisted of cash sent (77 per cent), cash hand-carried home (17 per cent), and remittances in kind (4 per cent). The bulk of cash remittances were sent through banks, and the balance was sent through door-to-door delivery, through friends and co-workers or by other means.

Regional Distribution of OFWs and Remittances

The number of OFWs estimated by the SOF was 795,000 in 1995, increasing to 978,000 in 2000, and further to about 1.1 million in 2004, representing an average annual growth rate of 3.7 per cent. The largest share (about one-fifth) has consistently come from Southern Tagalog (Calabarzon and Mimaropa), followed by the National Capital Region (Metro Manila) at 16–18 per cent, then Central Luzon with 13–14 per cent (Table 10.2). Hence, Metro Manila[11] and the adjacent regions of Southern Tagalog and Central Luzon together account for at least half of OFWs. Other significant senders of OFWs are the provinces of Ilocos, Western Visayas, and Cagayan Valley accounting for close to a quarter of the total. By contrast, the poorer regions of Mindanao, Eastern Visayas, and Bicol are responsible for smaller fractions of the total, thus lending support to the hypothesis that the poor are less able to migrate.

Total remittances from OFWs were estimated at P23.2 billion for six months in 1995, thus an annual figure of roughly P46.4 billion. Similarly, total annual remittances can be estimated at P110.2 billion in 2000 and P129.4 billion in 2004. Thus, from 1995 to 2004, remittances grew on average at 12.1 per cent annually in nominal terms, that is, more than thrice faster than the increase in the number of OFWs.

Metro Manila obtained from 18 per cent to 27 per cent of total remittances between 1995 and 2004, Southern Tagalog 18–22 per cent, and Central Luzon 12–15 per cent (Table 10.3). Thus, over 50 per cent of the remittances went to the country's three most developed regions. Another fifth to a quarter of the total was remitted to Western Visayas, Ilocos, and Central Visayas. Predictably, the poorer regions were recipients of much smaller shares.

Average six-month remittance per OFW was P34,207 in 1995, rising to P66,146 in 2000 and further to P72,795 in 2004 for an average yearly

TABLE 10.2
Number of Overseas Workers, 1995–2004
(in thousand persons and percentage shares by region)

		1995	*%*	*2000*	*%*	*2004*	*%*
1	Ilocos Region	105	13.2	99	10.1	86	8.1
2	Cagayan Valley	48	6.0	54	5.5	57	5.4
3	Central Luzon	104	13.1	126	12.9	149	14.0
4	Southern Tagalog (Calabarzon + Mimaropa)	157	19.7	198	20.2	202	19.0
5	Bicol Region	35	4.4	28	2.9	32	3.0
6	Western Visayas	62	7.8	90	9.2	92	8.7
7	Central Visayas	26	3.3	52	5.3	49	4.6
8	Eastern Visayas	15	1.9	19	1.9	24	2.3
9	Western Mindanao/ Zamboanga Peninsula	23	2.9	30	3.1	22	2.1
10	Northern Mindanao	19	2.4	15	1.5	28	2.6
11	Southern Mindanao/Davao	26	3.3	31	3.2	34	3.2
12	Central Mindanao/Soccsksargen	16	2.0	21	2.1	30	2.8
13	National Capital Region	118	14.8	172	17.6	194	18.3
14	Cordillera Administrative Region	25	3.1	25	2.6	24	2.3
15	Autonomous Region in Muslim Mindanao	12	1.5	10	1.0	31	2.9
16	Caraga			8	0.8	10	0.9
	Philippines	**795**	**100**	**978**	**100**	**1,063**	**100**

Notes: Estimates include overseas Filipinos whose departure occurred during the last five years and who are working or had worked abroad during the past six months (April to September) of the survey period.

Source: National Statistics Office, *Survey of Overseas Filipinos*, various years.

increase rate of 8.8 per cent. The data on average remittances by region show a noteworthy pattern (Table 10.4). In 1995, Central Visayas got the highest average remittance per OFW (1.6 times the national average), followed by Metro Manila (1.3 times), then followed closely by Western Visayas (1.2 times), Northern Mindanao, Southern Mindanao, and the Cordillera Autonomous Region, in that order. Southern Tagalog and Central Luzon were only ninth and seventh in the ranking, while Bicol was eighth. In 2000, Eastern Visayas — one of the poorest regions — got the highest average remittance (1.3 times the national average), followed by Metro Manila, then Bicol (also among the poorest regions), Central Visayas, and Southern Mindanao. Southern Tagalog and Central Luzon ranked only sixth and seventh, followed by Northern Mindanao and Ilocos. By 2004, the Autonomous Region of Muslim Mindanao ranked first in average remittance

TABLE 10.3
Definitions of the Variables

		1995		2000		2004	
		Pesos	*%*	*Pesos*	*%*	*Pesos*	*%*
1	Ilocos Region	2,156,642	9.3	5,077,353	9.2	3,623,940	5.6
2	Cagayan Valley	1,072,820	4.6	2,114,517	3.8	2,394,389	3.7
3	Central Luzon	3,479,927	15.0	6,753,929	12.3	8,412,717	13.0
4	Southern Tagalog (Calabarzon + Mimaropa)	4,229,651	18.3	11,449,648	20.8	14,107,479	21.8
5	Bicol Region	1,101,146	4.8	1,523,818	2.8	1,747,257	2.7
6	Western Visayas	2,246,060	9.7	4,964,318	9.0	5,694,762	8.8
7	Central Visayas	1,186,437	5.1	3,358,505	6.1	2,717,955	4.2
8	Eastern Visayas	366,111	1.6	1,415,036	2.6	1,423,691	2.2
9	Western Mindanao/ Zamboanga Peninsula	334,488	1.4	1,245,433	2.3	776,558	1.2
10	Northern Mindanao	590,837	2.6	694,088	1.3	1,488,404	2.3
11	Southern Mindanao/Davao	949,289	4.1	1,880,135	3.4	1,811,970	2.8
12	Central Mindanao/ Soccsksargen	241,376	1.0	810,279	1.5	905,985	1.4
13	National Capital Region	4,225,293	18.2	12,108,006	22.0	17,149,000	26.5
14	Cordillera Administration Region	758,097	3.3	1,236,616	2.2	841,272	1.3
15	Autonomous Region in Muslim Mindanao	223,880	1.0	160,154	0.3	905,985	1.4
16	Caraga		0.0	341,571	0.6	647,132	1.0
	Philippines	**23,161,874**	**100.0**	**55,133,406**	**100.0**	**64,713,207**	**100**

Notes: Estimates cover overseas Filipino whose departure occurred within the last five years and who are working or had worked abroad during the past six months (April to September) of the survey period. For 2004, only total remittances data are available, so the regional shares are computed based on the regional shares for 2002.

Source: National Statistics Office, *Survey of Overseas Filipinos*, various years.

(1.4 times the national average), with Metro Manila second again, followed by Central Visayas, Southern Tagalog, Southern Mindanao, Eastern Visayas, Caraga, Northern Mindanao, Central Luzon, and Bicol, in that order.

The pattern of average remittance per OFW by region is intriguing because it departs from the regional distribution of OFWs and total remittances. Two possible explanations may be advanced here. One is greater altruism on the part of OFWs from the poorer regions, implying the need to send more money to assist their more deprived families. A second is higher positive selectivity of migrant workers from the less developed regions, meaning that OFWs from those regions, though fewer in number, may be more highly

TABLE 10.4
Average Remittance per OFW, 1995–2004
(in pesos and ratio to national average by region)

		1995		2000		2004	
1	Ilocos Region	22,572	0.7	57,703	0.9	47,431	0.7
2	Cagayan Valley	24,803	0.7	44,897	0.7	46,958	0.6
3	Central Luzon	38,074	1.1	60,378	0.9	69,850	1.0
4	Southern Tagalog (Calabarzon + Mimaropa)	31,313	0.9	67,012	1.0	78,306	1.1
5	Bicol Region	37,804	1.1	78,678	1.2	61,798	0.8
6	Western Visayas	41,868	1.2	62,671	0.9	67,066	0.9
7	Central Visayas	54,345	1.6	75,881	1.1	84,115	1.2
8	Eastern Visayas	27,220	0.8	83,946	1.3	71,603	1.0
9	Western Mindanao/ Zamboanga Peninsula	17,121	0.5	56,270	0.9	39,712	0.5
10	Northern Mindanao	41,006	1.2	58,232	0.9	70,364	1.0
11	Southern Mindanao/Davao	40,329	1.2	67,127	1.0	75,809	1.0
12	Central Mindanao/ Soccsksargen	21,216	0.6	55,587	0.8	43,848	0.6
13	National Capital Region	43,753	1.3	83,574	1.3	97,009	1.3
14	Cordillera Administration Region	39,080	1.1	55,385	0.8	58,333	0.8
15	Autonomous Region in Muslim Mindanao	24,982	0.7	30,696	0.5	100,243	1.4
16	Caraga		0.0	49,214	0.7	70,590	1.0
	Philippines	**34,207**	**1.0**	**66,146**	**1.0**	**72,795**	**1.0**

Note: Estimates cover overseas Filipino whose departure occurred within the last five years and who are working or had worked abroad during the past six months (April to September) of the survey period. For 2004, only the national average remittance per OFW is available, so the regional averages are computed based on the regional ratios to the national average for 2002.
Source: National Statistics Office, *Survey of Overseas Filipinos*, various years.

skilled and hence earn higher average incomes. These two hypotheses seem plausible and are not necessarily mutually exclusive.

REMITTANCES, POVERTY ALLEVIATION, AND REGIONAL DEVELOPMENT

The question whether remittances contribute to poverty alleviation and regional development can be probed further through econometric analysis of the available data. This analysis enables us to better appreciate the effect of remittances in the context of several other factors that matter to regional development and improvement in the well-being of the poor.

On the basis of our survey of the literature, we hypothesize that remittances benefit recipient households directly and influence the local economy via increased household spending. Thus, not only the recipient families but also the non-recipient ones are affected indirectly by the initial impact of remittances on the local economy and subsequent multiplier effects.

Regression Equations

There are three main variables — welfare of the poor (or poverty incidence), remittances, and gross regional domestic product (GRDP). These three variables are assumed to be endogenous, hence, requiring three equations:

$$ExPOOR_{rt} = ExPOOR_{rt}(REMIT_{rt}, GRDP_{rt}, LOCAL_{rt}) \quad (1)$$

$$REMIT_{rt} = REMIT_{rt}(GRDP_{rt}, LOCAL_{rt}) \quad (2)$$

$$GRDP_{rt} = GRDP_{rt}(REMIT_{rt}, LOCAL_{rt}) \quad (3)$$

where

$EXPOOR_{rt}$ = per capita expenditure of the poor in region r at time t
$REMIT_{rt}$ = per capita remittance in region r at time t
$GRDP_{rt}$ = per capita income of region r at time t
$LOCAL_{rt}$ = local factors/initial conditions in region r at time t

$LOCAL_{rt}$ is a vector of exogenous local factors or initial conditions that serve as control variables. These include human and physical infrastructures, such as average schooling years of household heads (HHeduc), employment ratio (Employr), dependency ratio (Dep-ratio), initial primary and secondary school participation rates (Elempr0 and Hspr0), initial infant mortality rate (Infmort0), initial road density (roads-to-area ratio, Road0), and initial electricity and water supply coverage (Elect0 and Water0).

Equation 1 shows how the welfare of the poor (proxied by their mean per capita expenditure) is influenced by the region's per capita GRDP, per capita remittance, and local factors or attributes. Equations 2 and 3 take into account the endogeneity of GRDP and remittances as both are affected by each other and by local factors.

Equations 1–3 are estimated using the three-stage least squares (3SLS) method. The 3SLS estimation procedure takes into account not only the endogeneity of the three variables (expenditure of the poor, remittances, and regional income) but also the interaction between equations through the covariance matrix of the equations' disturbances.

To test for dynamic effects, we experiment with current as well as lagged values. Appendix Tables A.1 and A.2 present the definition of the variables and their descriptive statistics, respectively.

For the estimation, we use panel data on fifteen regions for the years 1994, 1997, 2000, and 2003.[12] The data on remittances are from the SOF (as described above), gross regional domestic product (GRDP) from the national income accounts, various socioeconomic data from records of relevant government agencies, and household expenditure data from the Family Income and Expenditure Survey (FIES) conducted by the NSO every three years. We have two indicators for poverty from the FIES: poverty incidence (headcount ratio) — the proportion of population below the poverty line, and mean consumption expenditure of the poorest 40 per cent (quintiles 1 and 2). For theoretical and practical reasons, mean consumption expenditure is deemed superior to mean income as a measure of welfare (Deaton 1997). The theoretical basis is the permanent income hypothesis; at the same time, in practice, current income is more difficult and costly to measure in developing countries, where the majority of the poor are self-employed and engaged in agricultural activities with fluctuating incomes.

Empirical Results

The regression results are mostly in accord with expectations. Table 10.5 shows that remittances have a positive and significant effect on the well-being of poor households, as reflected in higher family spending per capita of the bottom quintile (q1), after controlling for the effects of other variables. To illustrate, an increase of P1,000 in remittance per capita results in P2,543 additional annual family spending per person among the poorest quintile. Roads, education (HHeduc), and health (Infmort0) also appear to be particularly important factors that improve the poor's welfare; by contrast, overall increases in regional incomes (GRDP) do not seem to matter as much. As the third panel of Table 10.5 shows, remittances contribute significantly to regional development through increased spending for consumption, human capital and housing investments, and consequent multiplier effects (Yang 2004; Rago 2005). However, because the more advanced regions tend to get bigger shares of the total, remittances may contribute to regional divergence

TABLE 10.5
Three-Stage Least Squares Regression (Quintile 1)

Variable	*Coefficient*	*t-value*	*P>|t|*	*[95% Conf. Interval]*	
Expoor-q1					
GRDP	–28.00497	–0.88	0.381	–90.99594	34.986
Remit	2543.478	1.92*	0.056	–66.32355	5153.28
Road0	870.0016	5.91*	0.000	579.4172	1160.586
Infmort0	–45.75125	–2.63*	0.009	–80.08043	–11.42206
HHeduc	228.6774	2.65*	0.009	58.50531	398.8495
Employr	–1845.798	–1.09	0.278	–5194.477	1502.88
Elempr0	22.40434	1.13	0.260	–16.7174	61.52607
Hspr0	1.468993	0.15	0.881	–17.94374	20.88173
Cons	511.1144	0.26	0.797	–3411.456	4433.685
Remit					
GRDP	–.0142709	–1.48	0.140	–.0332914	.0047496
Road0	.0715443	1.82*	0.071	–.0061983	.1492869
Infmort0	.0070729	1.49	0.138	–.0023041	.01645
HHeduc	.0090999	0.45	0.655	–.0310341	.049234
Employr	–.8707271	–1.66*	0.098	–1.905436	.1639821
Dep-ratio0	–.0163008	–5.91*	0.000	–.0217518	–.0108499
Cons	1.946634	4.93	0.000	1.165932	2.727335
GRDP					
Remit	12.64628	6.33*	0.000	8.702492	16.59008
Road0	1.68372	3.84*	0.000	.8185789	2.54886
Infmort0	–.3382358	–5.07*	0.000	–.4699202	–.2065515
HHeduc	.5637276	2.02*	0.045	.0115358	1.115919
Employr	5.859465	0.76	0.450	–9.413868	21.1328
Water0	14.9125	7.59*	0.000	11.03354	18.79145
Cons	.0101259	0.00	0.998	–6.865536	6.885788

Equation	*Obs*	*Parms*	*RMSE*	*"R-sq"*	*F-Stat*	*p*
Expoor-q1	60	8	430.999	0.9115	65.27	0.0000
Remit	60	6	.1322012	0.6233	16.64	0.0000
GRDP	60	6	2.033332	0.8772	62.45	0.0000

Note: Asterisked t-values denote significance at 10% level or better.

rather than convergence. As expected, roads, water, education and health infrastructures are critical to regional development.

Table 10.6 shows that the regression results for the next poorest 20 per cent of households (quintile 2) closely resemble those for the poorest quintile. There is a noteworthy difference, however. Not only is the impact of remittances on household welfare more significant, it is also larger (by 30 per

TABLE 10.6
Three-Stage Least Squares Regression (Quintile 2)

Variable	*Coefficient*	*t-value*	*P>|t|*	*[95% Conf. Interval]*	
Expoor-q2					
GRDP	32.77885	0.90	0.369	–39.01094	104.5686
Remit	3317.016	2.20*	0.029	338.739	6295.293
Road0	782.077	4.66*	0.000	450.7938	1113.36
Infmort0	–48.7413	–2.46*	0.015	–87.82006	–9.662534
HHeduc	352.6881	3.59*	0.000	158.7236	546.6525
Employr	–4606.589	–2.39*	0.018	–8418.941	–794.2378
Elempr0	39.42144	1.75*	0.083	–5.188607	84.03149
Hspr0	–9.943257	–0.89	0.377	–32.08834	12.20182
Cons	–130.0807	–0.06	0.954	–4601.875	4341.714
Remit					
GRDP	–.0142709	–1.48	0.140	–.0332914	.0047496
Road0	.0715443	1.82*	0.071	–.0061983	.1492869
Infmort0	.0070729	1.49	0.138	–.0023041	.01645
HHeduc	.0090999	0.45	0.655	–.0310341	.049234
Employr	–.8707271	–1.66*	0.098	–1.905436	.1639821
Dep-ratio0	–.0163008	–5.91*	0.000	–.0217518	–.0108499
Cons	1.946634	4.93	0.000	1.165932	2.727335
GRDP					
Remit	12.64628	6.33*	0.000	8.702492	16.59008
Road0	1.68372	3.84*	0.000	.8185789	2.54886
Infmort0	–.3382358	–5.07*	0.000	–.4699202	–.2065515
HHeduc	.5637276	2.02*	0.045	.0115358	1.115919
Employr	5.859465	0.76	0.450	–9.413868	21.1328
Water0	14.9125	7.59*	0.000	11.03354	18.79145
Cons	.0101259	0.00	0.998	–6.865536	6.885788

Equation	*Obs*	*Parms*	*RMSE*	*"R-sq"*	*F-Stat*	*p*
Expoor-q2	60	8	487.3238	0.9331	86.29	0.0000
Remit	60	6	.1322012	0.6233	16.64	0.0000
GRDP	60	6	2.033332	0.8772	62.45	0.0000

Note: Asterisked t-values denote significance at 10% level or better.

cent), as household expenditure per capita rises to P3, 317 for every P1, 000 incremental per capita remittance. The magnitude of this positive effect on household well-being continues to rise for quintiles 3 and 4, but becomes negative though insignificant for quintile 5.[13] This is not surprising as the richest 20 per cent of families are much less likely to have OFWs or to rely on remittances. It appears, therefore, that remittances are important to at least 80 per cent of households.

Another result worth noting is that while the impact of an increase in regional income (GRDP per capita) on household welfare is negative (though insignificant) for quintile 1, it is positive for quintile 2 and the size of this positive effect increases monotonically through to quintile 5. This suggests that regional development does not benefit low-income households as much as the higher income families, which is consistent with earlier findings based on provincial data (Balisacan and Pernia 2003).

CONCLUSION AND POLICY IMPLICATIONS

Our finding lends support to the conclusion of other studies that remittances help lift households out of poverty. The more developed regions send more OFWs than the less developed ones, resulting in appreciably greater shares of total remittances going to the former. However, OFWs from the poorer regions send home significantly higher average remittance than those from the richer regions. One explanation is greater altruism on the part of migrant workers from poorer regions to send more money to their more deprived families. Another reason — not necessarily at variance with the first — is higher positive selectivity of OFWs from the less developed regions, that is, though fewer in numbers, they may be more highly skilled and, hence, earn higher average incomes. An implication is that while remittances overall may contribute to a widening of the economic disparities across regions, these money flows do improve the well-being of poor households even in the lagging regions.

Econometric analysis provides deeper insights. Remittances contribute significantly to poverty alleviation, as reflected in higher family spending per capita of the bottom 40 per cent of households, while controlling for the effects of other variables including physical infrastructure and human capital in the regions. This beneficial effect rises monotonically up to quintile 4, then peters out for quintile 5, which is not surprising given that the richest 20 per cent of families are unlikely to have OFWs or need remittances.

Remittances also matter importantly to regional development through increased spending for consumption as well as investments in human capital and housing, and consequent multiplier effects. However, overall regional development does not seem to benefit low-income households as much as the upper income ones.

The government seems right in calling OFWs the country's "modern-day heroes". However, instead of lip service *ad nauseam*, the government should provide genuine service to OFWs, and there are several ways this could be done. For example, the government could do a much better job in shielding

OFWs from unscrupulous recruiters and agents and helping them forge fair contracts with their overseas employers. The accounts one often gathers either directly from or about OFWs on how they have been short-changed and maltreated are heart-rending.

Channelling remittance flows also requires more improvement, such as minimizing the inconvenience and financial costs of remitting. The fact that a large share of total remittances continues to be sent informally suggests the transaction costs OFWs have to bear in accessing the more formal channels. Further, the government should improve the climate for investing remittances in the regions.

Finally, while the country has certainly benefited from the diaspora, the remittance bonanza has not been totally an unmixed blessing, not only for the households but also for the macroeconomy. It has allowed the government to skirt the difficult task of policy reform that would have improved the performance of the domestic economy and reduced the need for overseas employment. The government would probably be well advised to rethink its policy on labour export — a phenomenon subject to all kinds of vicissitudes, regard it as transitory (following the examples of South Korea and Thailand), and just buckle down to doing its long overdue homework.

Notes

1. Total remittances are often estimated to be much more if those sent through non-bank and other informal channels — also known as "unbanked" remittances — are included.
2. Good examples are the Chinese and Indian diasporas that are playing an important role in the continuing rise of FDIs into China and India. Likewise, both countries are experiencing return migration, either permanent or circular.
3. For instance, while Dollar and Kraay (2001) find, based on cross-country averages, a one-to-one correspondence between economic growth and increase in incomes of the poor, sub-national regressions reveal much smaller elasticities between growth and welfare of the poor, ranging from 0.55 for the Philippines to 0.7 for Indonesia and close to 1.0 for Vietnam (Balisacan and Pernia 2003; Balisacan, Pernia, and Asra 2003; Balisacan, Pernia, and Estrada 2003).
4. This is probably a significant factor in the marked rise in recorded remittance flows into home countries.
5. In the Asian context, and probably also in other developing counties with strong familial ties, caring and giving (including remittance) among family members are typically not considered "altruism" but a natural gesture of concern. "Altruism" is essentially an individualistic concept that probably applies more to Western societies.

[6] However, Burgess and Haksar (2005) argue that the longer term economic effects of remittances are ambiguous.

[7] Latapi and Janssen (2006) present empirical evidence on the poverty-alleviation effect of remittances in Mexico. Burgess and Haksar (2005), however, find no clear empirical support for the purported short-term stabilizing effect of remittances on consumption in the Philippines.

[8] These investments reflect a rational behaviour on the part of the family particularly when the investment climate is unfavourable. Yang (2004) examines the exchange rate shocks due to the 1997–98 Asian financial crisis and finds that households whose overseas workers experienced favourable shocks were able to reduce child labour, increase educational spending, improve child schooling, and afford higher ownership of durable goods.

[9] However, as noted earlier, even families that receive no remittances at all could benefit indirectly from the remittance flows through the multiplier effects of increased spending in the community.

[10] Filipinos in other countries with immigrant visas are not included in the SOF's definition of OFWs. Hence, their remittances are not included in the SOF remittance data.

[11] It is possible that although some OFWs may originate in the other regions, Metro Manila is given as the residential address (of relatives) while prospective OFWs are still processing their departure papers and making other preparations to leave.

[12] The regions are as classified in 2004 and this regional classification is used consistently throughout the period.

[13] In Mexico, the greatest impact relative to household income is reported to occur to the first quintile, diminishing monotonically till quintile 5 (Latapi and Janssen 2006). The regression results for quintiles 3–5 for the Philippines are not presented here due to space constraints. To test for robustness of the remittance effect on the poor's welfare, we also carried out 3SLS regressions substituting poverty incidence for household expenditure per capita as the dependent variable and the results are consistent, that is, negative and significant effect of remittances on poverty incidence. Likewise, ordinary least squares (OLS) regressions (random-effects GLS) for both measures of poverty indicate a strong effect of remittances. These results are not shown here but are available from the author.

References

Adams, Richard H. "International Migration, Remittances and the Brain Drain: A Study of 24 Labour-Exporting Countries". World Bank Policy Research Working Paper 3069, Washington, D.C., 2003.

Adams, Richard H. and John Page. "International Migration, Remittances and Poverty in Developing Countries". World Bank Policy Research Working Paper 3179, Washington, D.C., 2003.

Balisacan, Arsenio M. and Ernesto M. Pernia. "Poverty, Inequality, and Growth in the Philippines". In *Poverty, Growth, and Institutions in Developing Asia*, edited by E.M. Pernia and A.B. Deolalikar, pp. 219–46. London: Palgrave Macmillan, 2003.

Balisacan, Arsenio M., Ernesto M. Pernia and Abuzar Asra. "Revisiting Growth and Poverty Reduction in Indonesia". In *Poverty, Growth, and Institutions in Developing Asia*, edited by E.M. Pernia and A.B. Deolalikar, pp. 191–218. London: Palgrave Macmillan, 2003.

Balisacan, Arsenio M., Ernesto M. Pernia and Gemma Estrada. "Economic Growth and Poverty Reduction in Viet Nam". In *Poverty, Growth, and Institutions in Developing Asia*, edited by E.M. Pernia and A.B. Deolalikar, pp. 273–91. London: Palgrave Macmillan, 2003.

Burgess, Robert and Vikram Haksar. "Migration and Foreign Remittances in the Philippines". IMF Working Paper 05/111, Washington, D.C., 2005.

Deaton, Angus. *The Analysis of Household Surveys: A Microeconomic Approach to Development Policy*. Baltimore: Johns Hopkins University Press, 1997.

Dollar, D., Kraay, A. "Growth is Good for the Poor". World Bank Policy Research Paper No. 2587, The World Bank, Washington, D.C., 2001.

Krueger, Anne and A. Berg. "Trade, Growth, and Poverty: A Selective Survey". Paper presented at the World Bank's Annual Bank Conference on Development Economics, Washington, D.C., 29–30 April 2002.

Latapi, Agustin Escobar and Eric Janssen. "Migration, the Diaspora and Development: The Case of Mexico". *International Institute for Labour Studies Discussion Paper 167/2006*, Geneva, 2006.

Lowell, B. Lindsay. "Skilled Labour Migration from Developing Countries: Annotated Bibliography". International Migration Papers, International Labour Office, Geneva, 2002.

Lucas, Robert E.B. "International Migration Regimes and Economic Development". Paper prepared for the Expert Group Meeting on Development Issues, Stockholm, 13 May 2004.

Pernia, Ernesto M. and Pilipinas F. Quising. "Trade Openness and Regional Development in a Developing Country". *Annals of Regional Science* 37 (2003): 391–406.

Pernia, Ernesto M. and J.M. Ian S. Salas. "Investment Climate, Productivity, and Regional Development in RP". Discussion Paper no. 0501. U.P. School of Economics, Diliman, Quezon City, 2005.

Quibria, M.G. "Migrant Workers and Remittances: Issues for Asian Developing Countries". *Asian Development Review* 4, no. 1 (1986): 78–99.

Rago, Raquel D. "The Effect of Remittances on Household Welfare and Expenditure Pattern". Paper submitted to the U.P. School of Economics in partial fulfilment of the requirements for the Master's in Development Economics, 2005.

Ratha, D. "Workers' Remittances: An Important and Stable Source of International

Development Finance". *Global Development Finance 2003*. Washington, D.C.: World Bank, 2003.

Wimaladharma, Jan, Douglas Pearce and David Stanton. "Remittances: the New Development Finance?". *Small Enterprise Development* 15 (2004): 12–19.

Yang, Dean. "International Migration, Human Capital, and Entrepreneurship: Evidence from Philippine Migrants' Exchange Rate Shocks". Gerald R. Ford School of Public Policy and Department of Economics, University of Michigan, Ann Arbor, 2004.

Appendix 10
Definition of the Variables and Descriptive Statistics

TABLE A.1
Definitions of the Variables

Variable	*Definition*	*Source*
Expoor-q*i*	real expenditure per capita, quintile i = 1 (poorest) … 5 (richest)	FIES
Povinc	proportion of families with per capita income below poverty line	FIES
Remit	real remittances per capita (remittances/regional HH pop)	SOF; FIES
GRDP	gross regional domestic product per capita (1985 prices)	NIA; FIES
Road0	lagged road density (concrete or asphalt roads/land area)	DPWH
Elect0	lagged proportion of households with electricity	FIES
Water0	lagged proportion households with potable water from faucets	FIES
HHeduc	average number of years of education of households heads	FIES
Hspr0	lagged high school participation rate of pop 13–16 yrs old	DECS
Elempr0	lagged elementary school participation rate of pop 7–12 yrs old	DECS
Infmort0	lagged infant mortality rate	NSO
Dep-ratio0	lagged dependency ratio (pop 0–15/pop 15+)	FIES
Employr	ratio of employed persons (old def.) to total HH population	LFS/FIES

Note: Expoor-q*i*, Remit, and GRDP are in constant (1985) prices.

TABLE A.2
Descriptive Statistics

Variable	*Obs*	*Mean*	*Std Dev*	*Minimum*	*Maximum*
povinc	60	0.3666	0.1373	0.0509	0.6599
Expoor-q1	60	3405.9990	1347.3150	1862.6660	8366.5780
Expoor-q2	60	4125.3440	1752.1010	2488.0450	10325.9800
Expoor-q3	60	5121.2380	2182.8530	3038.7010	12453.6900
Expoor-q4	60	6957.6430	2843.7310	3389.0330	16105.2700
Expoor-q5	60	13960.6000	6352.2200	5578.5810	41787.0900
GRDP_pc	60	10.7057	5.4989	3.9900	30.2580
Remit_pc	60	0.3323	0.2042	0.0422	0.8864
HHeduc	60	6.0952	1.2803	3.6200	9.8300
Elect0	60	0.6197	0.1806	0.2143	0.9957
Water0	60	0.3813	0.1805	0.0858	0.8209
Road0	60	0.3671	1.0079	0.0256	4.1863
Infmort0	60	16.3002	5.1471	4.6700	25.2900
Elempr0	60	89.6250	7.8542	71.5000	99.9800
Hspr0	60	59.5830	14.8476	18.0200	92.5700
Dep-ratio0	60	81.0957	10.0407	60.7100	103.7400
Employr	60	0.3866	0.0367	0.3216	0.4902

11

THE PHILIPPINE DEVELOPMENT RECORD: A COMPARATIVE ASSESSMENT

Hal Hill and Sharon Faye Piza

INTRODUCTION

The development economics literature has not been kind to the Philippines. It has been variously described as the "East Asian exception", "East Asia's Stray Cat" (Vos and Yap 1996), and a "Latin American country in East Asia". Harvard's Lant Pritchett (2003) was even less complimentary, characterizing the country as a "democratic dud".

This literature is struggling with the central development puzzle of the Philippines: why has a country with favourable initial conditions — at least relative to its neighbours — grown much slower than almost all of East Asia, particularly since 1980? In particular, the country commenced with a decisive advantage in educational spread and quality. It also inherited a set of functioning public institutions and a constitution, without the trauma of a protracted independence struggle or civil war. Moreover, although this observation is unpopular in certain circles, the Philippines had what many countries are now queuing up for — a free trade agreement with the United States.

The East Asian context is at once both central to the story and somewhat misleading. It is central in the sense that other countries, mainly in the neighbourhood, and some quite similar, have managed to grow very fast. The comparison with Thailand is particularly pertinent. The two countries share much in common — similar population size, land area, resource base, economic structure, movements in their terms of trade, and of course location. Yet Thailand, which was significantly poorer in the 1950s, overtook the Philippines in the early 1980s, and just prior to the recent Asian crisis its per capita income was almost twice higher. If ever there were a case of non-identical twins, this would be it. Thus, more generally, the international environment cannot hold the key to the puzzle, unless (implausibly in our view) one wants to argue that there are aspects of this environment specifically inimical to Philippine economic development interests.

Conversely, it might be argued that these countries are all "exceptions", and that the Philippine record looks deficient partly because of the company it keeps. In fact, as Felipe Medalla often reminds us, the country's performance is broadly similar to that of the developing world as a whole. Outside East Asia, there are no obvious comparators. One has to consider middle-sized countries which had promising early potential, but where growth has subsequently stalled. But the differences here are too great to generate significant insights. In passing, while the Latin American caricature may offer some understanding of the Philippine record, it has its limitations. There are some obvious similarities, especially in the colonial legacy of deep agrarian inequality. But the Philippines has never experienced Latin American-style hyper-inflation (except very briefly in the mid 1980s). The plantation sector was never quite so dominant. The labour market has generally been more flexible. And there have been powerful positive "neighbourhood effects" flowing from Philippine proximity to high-growth economies.

This chapter examines the Philippine development record in comparative perspective, principally with reference to that of its Southeast Asian neighbours. It commences with the growth record in section 2, followed by social dimensions. Section 4 shifts attention to the variables, which are argued to be important long-term growth explanators, including macroeconomic management and openness. Section 5 extends this analysis with reference to the literature, which has attempted to explain the record more formally.

GROWTH AND STRUCTURAL CHANGE

The Philippine development story is well-known. Since the 1950s, the Philippines has grown more slowly than most of its neighbours. In 1950, when most developing countries' national accounts were admittedly rudimentary, the country's per capita GDP, in PPP (purchasing power parity) terms, was midway between the richer city states and the poorest in the sample, China. By the mid 1970s, it had slipped behind Taiwan and Korea, and was similar to Thailand. By the mid 1990s, China and Indonesia had overtaken it, though since the 1997–98 economic crisis it has moved ahead of Indonesia.

Table 11.1 provides a set of summary socioeconomic indicators for the six largest ASEAN economies (the original five members plus Vietnam). In per capita income terms, the Philippines ranks fourth, while its economy is the second smallest (at official exchange rates). Perhaps the most telling statistic is the comparison between per capita incomes in 2004 and 1960 (1984 for Vietnam). Whereas all the other original ASEAN member countries had increased their per capita incomes at least five-fold, and in Singapore's case a remarkable eleven-fold increase, Philippine per capita income had not quite doubled. This is obviously the central issue in any comparative assessment of the Philippine development record.

Table 11.1 also highlights the country's well-known record on social indicators and inequality. In human capital, it continues to lead the region. Inequality is high, though a little below Malaysia. Life expectancy and poverty incidence are about on par with the country's income ranking. One puzzle with the US$1 poverty estimates is that the Philippine incidence is considerably higher than that of both Indonesia and Vietnam. Presumably this reflects the effects of the country's higher inequality (see Balisacan, Chapter 9 in this volume).

Figures 11.1 and 11.2 and Table 11.2 document the comparative growth record in more detail. Viewed over the long term, the country really began to part company with its neighbours in the late 1970s. In the 1950s, it was reportedly the fastest growing Southeast Asian economy, averaging 3 per cent for the decade, and driven by the post-war catch-up and the first round of import-substituting growth. Growth was respectable in the 1960s, at nearly 2 per cent (per capita), although this was a period when both Singapore and Thailand began to grow very fast. Its growth of almost 3 per cent in the 1970s was the slowest among the ASEAN five, but still quite strong, and similar to the middle-income average. It was in the 1980s when the most pronounced differences emerged, with its negative growth compared to the average for the rest of the five of about 5 per cent. Although growth returned in the 1990s, it was only weakly positive for the decade as a whole, and by far the lowest among the ASEAN six (now that Vietnam had joined the growth league), even with the sharp contractions in Indonesia, Malaysia, and Thailand in 1998.

Growth is typically episodic, especially in countries more prone to political disturbance, exogenous terms of trade and other shocks, and fiscal fragility.

TABLE 11.1
Key Indicators, 2004

	Per capita GDP, $[a]	*Per capita GDP, $PPP*[b]	*Per capita GDP ratio*[c]	*GDP, $ millions*[a]	*Population, millions*	*Average years of schooling*[d]	*Life expectancy at birth*	*Gini*[e]	*Population below $1 a day,*[e] *%*	*Population below $2 a day,*[e] *%*
Indonesia	906	3,609	5.1	176,323	214.7	5.0	66.9	34.3	7.5	52.4
Malaysia	4,290	10,276	5.5	106,474	24.8	6.8	73.3	49.2	<2	9.3
Philippines	1,085	4,614	1.8	90,481	81.5	8.2	70.5	46.1	15.5	47.5
Singapore	24,164	28,077	11.0	101,091	4.3	7.1	79.0	42.5	–	–
Thailand	2,356	8,090	7.1	149,859	62.0	6.5	70.1	43.2	<2	32.5
Vietnam	502	2,745	2.5	41,194	81.3	–	70.0	37.0	<2	33.4

[a] in 2000 US$ prices
[b] in current US$ prices
[c] ratio of 2004 to 1960 per capita GDP figures, both in 2000 US$ prices, except for Vietnam - ratio of 2004 to 1984
[d] formal schooling of adults ages 15 and above in 2000
[e] reference year differs: Indonesia — 2002, Malaysia — 1997, Philippines, Thailand and Vietnam — 2000, and Singapore — 1998.
Source: World Development Indicators, World Bank Poverty Net, Barro and Lee (2000).

FIGURE 11.1
Annual GDP Growth Rate, 1961–2003 (%)

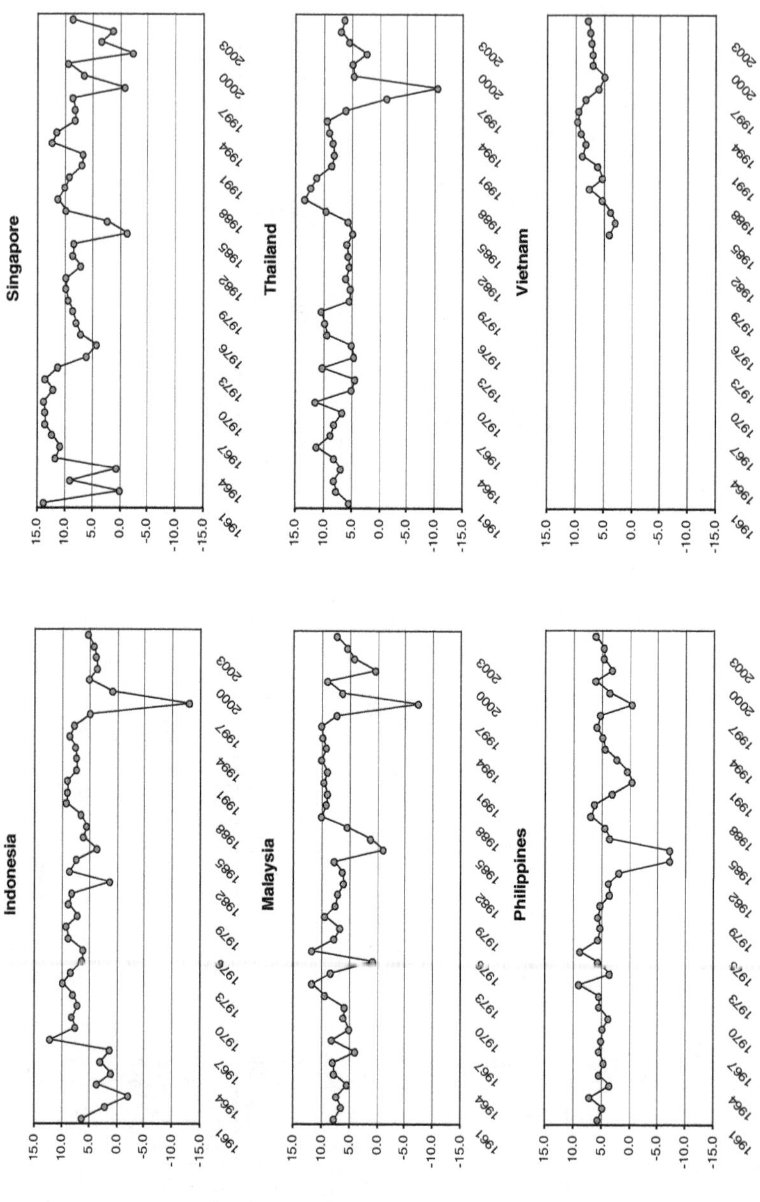

Source: World Development Indicators.

FIGURE 11.2
Per Capita GDP, 1975–2003 ($ PPP)

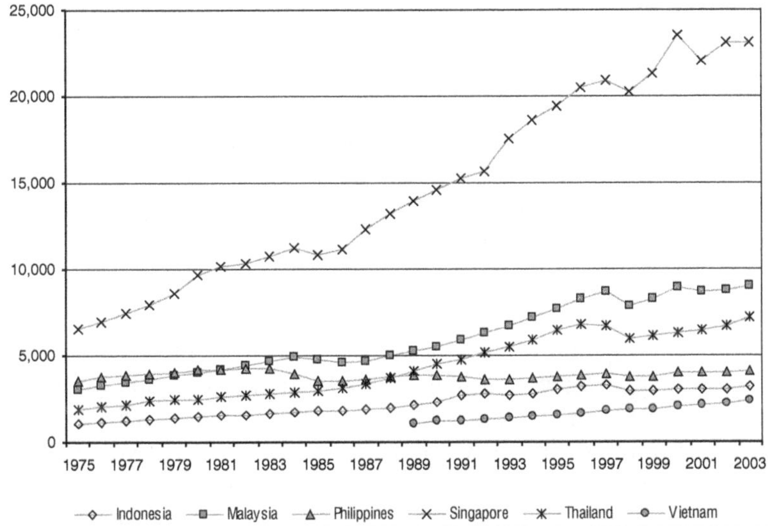

Source: World Development Indicators.

TABLE 11.2
Average Growth of Per Capita GDP (%)

	1960s	*1970s*	*1980s*	*1990s*	*2000s*
Indonesia	1.42	5.32	5.46	3.26	3.24
Malaysia	3.49	5.18	3.19	4.52	3.10
Philippines	1.92	2.92	-0.44	0.56	2.40
Singapore	6.86	7.64	5.29	4.47	2.79
Thailand	4.59	4.58	5.56	3.99	4.13
Vietnam	–	–	2.14	5.51	5.92
Low income	1.67	0.68	1.85	2.24	3.19
Middle income	4.66	3.05	0.91	1.98	3.96
High income	4.26	2.83	2.20	1.82	1.59

Authors' estimates.
Income grouping is based on the World Bank income classification of countries.
Source: World Development Indicators.

All three factors have been at work in the Philippines. Since 1970, for example, we witnessed the debt-driven growth over the period 1970–83, followed by stagnation, then deep crisis, 1984–86. An erratic recovery occurred in 1987–91, followed by a mild crisis in 1992–93. Thereafter, another recovery took place, with growth in the mid 1990s returning to levels not seen since the 1980s. This growth was again nipped in the bud, this time owing to external factors, principally the Asian economic crisis. But the economy weathered the crisis quite well, and has since returned to what seems to be a trend growth rate of about 4–5 per cent, or 2–3 per cent in per capita terms.

Thus the Philippine economy has not grown as fast, or as consistently, as its neighbours. Its growth has rarely exceeded the 7 per cent figure commonly recorded by the NIEs earlier on, China currently, and its higher-growth Southeast Asian neighbours quite regularly. Its growth limit seems to be lower, a point to which we return shortly. And even when it occasionally grows quite strongly, it is rarely durable growth. In fact, over the period 1980–2000, the country never experienced more than four consecutive years of positive growth in GDP per capita. That its growth has tended to be more volatile is illustrated by the fact that the coefficient of variation (of GDP growth per capita) since 1960 is the highest among the six, at 79.[1]

Section 5 returns to explanations of the long-term record, and discusses briefly why the country was not deeply affected by the 1997–98 crisis. It passes over the deep crisis of 1985–86, except to note that it was not unlike Indonesia in 1997–98.[2] The contraction was similar, in the range of 12–14 per cent, although in the Philippines spread over two years. There was an exodus of short-term capital beforehand which triggered the crisis, followed by political turbulence which led to a generalized regime collapse. In both countries, too, these twin crises, economic and political, led to major changes in the political and institutional landscape, protracted negotiations with the IMF and donors, a collapse in investment, and a halting recovery. One key difference, however, was that the Indonesian crisis was completely unanticipated, and was preceded by buoyant economic growth and fiscal prudence.

The Philippine growth record by sector is not examined here in any detail, except to note three general points. First, growth among the principal sectors has generally followed the aggregate picture, once account is taken of sector-specific factors. If there has been a sectoral success story, the closest thing would be services. Second, the process of structural change has differed from its neighbours. It has been slower, as would be expected since the principal driver of change — growth — has also been slower. Third, and an unusual feature of the country, unique in East Asia, is that the resources shifting out of agriculture have gone not to manufacturing but to services. In fact, the share of manufacturing in GDP has actually shrunk since 1980, in contrast to the doubling observed elsewhere. As shown in Table 11.3, the Philippines has by far the highest services share among the ASEAN Six, apart from the special case of Singapore, and the lowest industry share. This high service sector share seems to have become particularly prominent since the 1990s.

This unusual pattern reflects the interplay of several factors. There has been a major dismantling of the protection for manufactures, which has both discouraged investment in the formerly protected sectors and reduced the measured value added, in prices now more closely resembling those in international markets. The country seemed to have greater difficulty managing the transition from import substitution to export orientation, with the result that some of the formerly protected "infants" have not grown up, particularly

TABLE 11.3
Share of Sectors in GDP, 1965–2004 (%)

	1965	*1975*	*1985*	*1995*	*2004*
Agriculture					
Indonesia	53.2	30.3	23.4	17.0	15.7
Malaysia	29.6	29.0	19.9	12.8	9.6
Philippines	25.6	30.2	24.4	21.4	13.3
Singapore	–	–	–	0.2	0.1
Thailand	32.0	26.9	16.3	9.4	10.2
Vietnam	–	–	39.1	27.5	22.2
Industry					
Indonesia	14.0	33.9	36.2	42.0	43.7
Malaysia	27.4	34.2	38.5	41.7	49.5
Philippines	27.4	34.9	35.9	32.2	32.5
Singapore	–	–	–	32.9	34.5
Thailand	22.4	26.7	32.3	40.7	43.5
Vietnam	–	–	28.1	29.1	39.8
Services					
Indonesia	32.8	35.8	40.4	41.0	40.7
Malaysia	43.1	36.7	41.6	45.6	40.9
Philippines	47.0	34.9	39.7	46.4	54.1
Singapore	–	–	–	66.9	65.4
Thailand	45.7	46.5	51.4	49.9	46.3
Vietnam	–	–	32.8	43.4	38.1

Note: Figures are three-year averages of years indicated, previous year, and succeeding year.
Source: World Development Indicators.

in the auto and heavy industries. There has been some notable success in export-oriented electronics, which accounts for virtually all of the increment to exports since 1990.

The country's slow growth is also reflected in the expenditure accounts. Since the 1980s, the share of investment has been well below that of the 1970s, and around 10 percentage points below the high-growth East Asian norms (Table 11.4). This is the result of two factors. First, the country has been a low saver since around 1980, with rates more akin to OECD levels than East Asia. Second, owing to its political and macroeconomic history, the Philippines has been unable to run a current account deficit of much more than 3–4 per cent of GDP. Hence investment rates are rarely much above 20 per cent of GDP, on any reasonable capital-output ratios, implying a growth ceiling of about 6 per cent.[3]

It is beyond the scope of this chapter to delve into the reasons for the country's low savings rate. The general conclusion from the savings literature

TABLE 11.4
Average Shares of Domestic Investment and Government Expenditure in Gross National Expenditure, 1960s–2000 (%)

	1960s	*1970s*	*1980s*	*1990s*	*2000s*
Gross domestic investment, % of gross national expenditure					
Indonesia	9.6	22.4	29.4	28.1	17.7
Malaysia	18.1	24.0	28.3	37.7	29.9
Philippines	19.3	26.3	22.0	21.0	19.8
Singapore	16.7	36.2	41.9	40.4	29.3
Thailand	20.1	24.9	28.6	35.5	25.8
Vietnam	–	–	13.7	21.9	30.9
Cambodia	–	–	9.5	11.1	18.9
Lao PDR	–	–	8.0	22.7	20.2
Myanmar	–	–	15.5	13.1	12.4
Government expenditure, % of gross national expenditure					
Indonesia	7.2	9.3	10.6	8.0	8.7
Malaysia	14.1	16.5	15.9	12.6	15.8
Philippines	8.6	9.8	8.3	10.7	12.1
Singapore	8.7	9.9	11.2	10.9	15.5
Thailand	9.6	10.4	11.8	10.1	11.9
Vietnam	–	–	7.1	7.5	6.2
Cambodia	–	–	6.1	5.6	5.3
Lao PDR	–	–	7.9	5.6	4.6
Myanmar	–	–	–	–	–

Source: World Development Indicators.

is that there is a "virtuous circle" involving growth and savings. In all the fast-growing East Asian economies, savings rates have lifted once high and durable growth has been achieved. Hence, savings in the Philippines may be expected to rise once growth rates are durably elevated. Other factors are probably also relevant to the Philippine story. Public sector savings have been at best minimal, owing to the general pattern of fiscal deficits discussed below. Political instability and a lack of personal and property rights security (especially among the ethnic Chinese community) have no doubt contributed at the margin. It should be noted of course that savings rates may be underestimated in the presence of huge remittances from abroad.

SOCIAL DIMENSIONS

Five inter-related features dominate the Philippine social record in comparative perspective. Each is considered in turn. Tables 11.5 and 11.6 summarize a range of relevant indicators over recent decades. See also chapters 9 and 10 by Balisacan and Pernia respectively, in this volume.

TABLE 11.5
Poverty and Inequality (%)

	1980s	*1990s*	*2000s*
Population below $1 a day			
Indonesia	28.2	17.4	7.5
Malaysia	2.0	1.0	0.2
Philippines	22.8	18.4	15.5
Thailand	21.6	2.2	1.9
Vietnam	–	3.8	2.2
Population below $2 a day			
Indonesia	75.8	59.3	52.4
Malaysia	15.0	14.0	9.3
Philippines	61.3	53.1	47.5
Thailand	55.0	28.3	32.5
Vietnam	–	58.2	33.4
Gini			
Indonesia	33.1	36.5	34.3
Malaysia	48.6	48.5	49.2
Philippines	41.0	42.9	46.1
Thailand	45.2	43.4	42.0
Vietnam	–	58.2	33.4

Source: World Bank PovcalNet.

TABLE 11.6
Key Social Indicators

	1970s	*1980s*	*1990s*	*2000s*
Human development index				
Indonesia	0.468	0.583	0.663	0.697
Malaysia	0.615	0.695	0.76	0.796
Philippines	0.654	0.693	0.736	0.758
Singapore	0.725	0.784	0.861	0.907
Thailand	0.614	0.678	0.749	0.778
Vietnam	–	–	0.660	0.704
Average years of adult schooling[a]				
Indonesia	3.0	4.0	4.6	5.0
Malaysia	4.4	5.5	6.5	6.8
Philippines	6.0	6.7	7.9	8.2
Singapore	5.5	6.1	6.7	7.1
Thailand	4.0	5.2	6.1	6.5
Vietnam	–	–	3.8	–
Life expectancy at birth				
Indonesia	52.7	60.2	65.1	66.9
Malaysia	65.3	69.5	71.9	73.3
Philippines	60.1	64.3	68.6	70.5
Singapore	70.8	73.6	77.1	79.0
Thailand	61.2	66.3	68.3	70.1
Vietnam	58.3	63.4	68.1	70.0

[a] Adults ages 15 and above

Source: UNDP Human Development Reports, World Development Indicators, Barro and Lee (2000).

High Inequality

Philippine inequality is high by international norms, and it exceeds that observed in most of East Asia (Balisacan 2003). Over time there has been little change in these levels. This is as would be expected. Inequality indicators are slow to change, unless there is a radical change in socio-economic conditions. And successive Philippine governments, while officially subscribing to various redistributive measures, have done little to address the issue, *via* vigorous and progressive tax collections, expenditure targeting or distributive measures.[4]

Slower Poverty Reduction

The combination of slower growth and high inequality has meant that poverty reduction has been significantly slower in the Philippines than in its neighbours. Reflecting this high inequality, the country's poverty elasticity (with respect to growth) has been slower (see Balisacan, chapter 9). The comparisons with Indonesia and Thailand in the US$1 per day poverty incidence measures are quite striking. The percentages were broadly similar in the 1980s, with Indonesia the highest of the three. By the early 2000s, this form of poverty had almost disappeared in Thailand, while the Indonesian figure was about half that of the Philippines. If the data can be believed, the incidence in Vietnam is also much lower than in the Philippines. As noted above, presumably these figures reflect higher inequality in the Philippines, as the differences in the "below US$2" category are not as pronounced.

It would, however, be a mistake to assert, as is done by some, that there has been no progress. The incidence of poverty fell significantly from the depth of the recession (1985) to the peak of the boom (1997), by about one-third, from 41 per cent to 25 per cent (Balisacan 2003). Moreover, Balisacan shows that poverty declined the fastest in the sub-periods of higher growth, 1985–88 and 1994–97.

Educational Strengths

The country has retained its educational advantage, although other countries are catching up, an increasing proportion of the talent is finding work abroad, and in comparative educational quality indicators the country appears to be lagging behind (see Pernia, chapter 10).

The Philippine education achievement rates above most countries with similar per capita incomes, with the additional advantage of widespread English-language fluency (Herrin and Pernia 2003). It still records the highest number of average years of schooling in ASEAN, a position it has always occupied. By the late 1990s, about 95 per cent of the population had "simple" literacy skills, while about 84 per cent may be said to be functionally literate. There is no gender bias, and in fact female participation is slightly ahead of males. The country has some of the finest tertiary educational institutions in ASEAN, and is internationally competitive in the provision of these services. However, the country's lead is slipping, and other countries are catching up. Moreover, in (the admittedly problematic) international quality comparisons the country ranks poorly. For example, it ranked 39 out of 43 in a recent testing of maths/science competence.

In life expectancy, generally regarded as the best general indicator of health standards, the Philippines is very close to the ex-Singapore ASEAN average, with levels very similar to those of Thailand and Vietnam. As a composite summary, its HDI more or less accords with its per capita income ranking, although in general it scores better on this criterion. One notable feature is the slower improvement in its HDI since the 1970s. For example, it was above both Malaysia and Thailand in the 1970s, and a long way ahead of Indonesia. However, the former two overtook the Philippines in the 1990s, a reflection presumably of their faster decline in poverty.

Demographic Outlier

Philippine population growth rates are high even by developing country standards. The rate is declining, but slowly, and more slowly than most of East Asia, with the exception of Malaysia, whose growth is driven by its high-fertility Malay population. Moreover, survey findings report that actual family sizes exceed the desired size, with serious implications for women's health.

Employment Growth — Slow at Home, Rapid Abroad

Employment growth has been sluggish. This too is linked to the slower growth, combined with somewhat restrictive labour market policies. Meanwhile, as international labour markets become more open, increasing numbers of Filipinos are finding work abroad. This is testimony to the quality and "employability" of Philippine workers, and is illustrative of what could be achieved at home with the right mix of policies. Based on official data, the Philippines is the third largest recipient of remittances in the developing world, behind only India and Mexico (Burgess and Haksar 2005). There are estimated to be about eight million Filipinos residing abroad, equivalent to almost one-quarter of the domestic labour force, while remittances are estimated unofficially to be equivalent to almost half of merchandise exports.

PROXIMATE DRIVERS OF GROWTH: MACROECONOMICS, OPENNESS, AND INSTITUTIONS

As noted, the Philippines historically tended to lag in its macroeconomic management and openness, and this was central to its longer-term under-performance. However, its record has improved considerably in both areas since around 1990. Indeed, one of the puzzles is why the country has not received a larger growth dividend from such significant reforms.

On comparative institutional quality, we lack readily comparable and objective long-term data series, and instead have to rely on a range of variable-quality, business-oriented and subjective surveys. For what they are worth, these surveys generally place the Philippines at about the same level as its per capita income ranking. We put this question to one side, pending the availability of more reliable institutional quality indicators over time.[5]

Philippine macroeconomic outcomes have traditionally lagged behind its high-growth East Asian neighbours, although by general developing country standards they have not been disastrous. Macroeconomic management began to improve in the wake of the crisis, from the late 1980s, and especially during the Ramos administration (Sicat and Abdula 2003; Gochoco-Bautista and Canlas 2003). An independent central bank was able to focus more clearly on inflation objectives. At the same time, its task was facilitated by significant progress in fiscal policy, again from the late 1980s. The deficit, narrowly defined, peaked at 8.5 per cent of GDP in 1986. The position then improved steadily, and for three years — 1994–96 — a slim surplus was recorded. With the onset of the crisis, however, there was a quick return to deficits. In the early 2000s, the fiscal situation again became very serious, until 2005 and 2006 when decisive — although not permanent — steps were taken to address the problem.

Figures 11.3*a* and 11.3*b* and Table 11.7 summarize comparative inflation outcomes. They illustrate three key features of Philippine macroeconomic performance. First, the government has rarely lost control of inflation — in modern times, only once, and briefly, as former president Marcos tried to spend his way into another term in Malacañang in the mid 1980s. Second, the country has rarely been able to match the exemplary low inflation records of Malaysia, Singapore and Thailand. In almost all decades, its average inflation has been more than double that of these three. Perhaps paradoxically, the coefficient of variation for Philippine inflation has been the lowest of all five economies (and six since Vietnam joined the group). A visual inspection of the annual data reveals the explanation. The Philippine inflation record has been a reasonably consistent one, albeit at consistent higher levels. There have been only two significant spikes, in the mid-1970s oil boom and the mid-1980s recession. By comparison, the average for the other three countries has been consistently lower but, being such open economies, occasional exogenous shocks produce shortlived spikes.

The third feature of the Philippine inflation record is that moderately low inflation now appears to be a permanent feature of economic policy. That is, it has been present for over a decade, during a period of massive turbulence, external and internal, economic and political. The decision to establish an independent central bank, the Bangko Sentral ng Pilipinas (BSP), and its subsequent performance, must surely be counted a major policy success in the long sweep of Philippine economic policy-making.

FIGURE 11.3a
Annual Inflation, 1961–2004 (%)

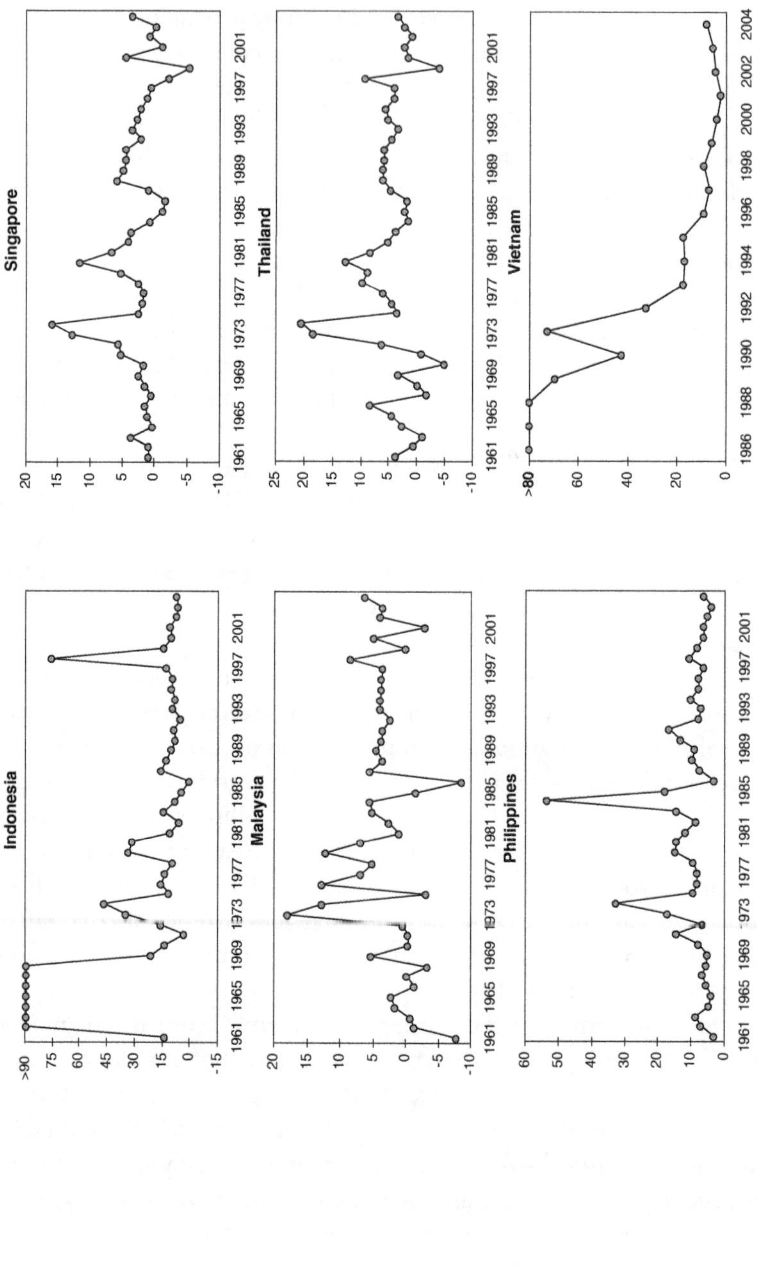

Source: World Development Indicators.

FIGURE 11.3*b*
Coefficient of Variation and Average Inflation, 1961–2003 (%)

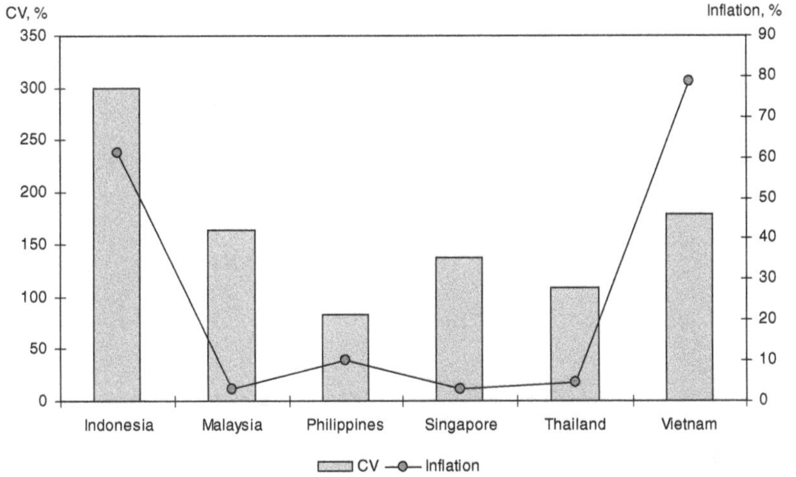

Source: World Development Indicators.

TABLE 11.7
Average Inflation (%)

	1960s	*1970s*	*1980s*	*1990s*	*2000s*	*CV*
Indonesia	242.7	19.6	11.2	15.9	8.2	299.0
Malaysia	–0.6	6.4	2.5	3.7	3.1	164.0
Philippines	5.5	12.8	14.9	9.4	5.5	82.9
Singapore	1.4	5.5	3.5	1.3	1.4	136.8
Thailand	2.2	7.2	5.2	4.3	1.9	107.8
Vietnam	–	–	310.3	22.9	4.5	179.0

Source: World Development Indicators.

These inflation outcomes, combined with volatile capital flows, are reflected also in long-term exchange rate movements (Figure 11.4). Here the difference between Indonesia and the Philippines on the one hand, and the three low-inflation economies on the other, is stark. Singapore's dollar has displayed a long-term propensity to appreciate against the U.S. dollar. This was also evident in Malaysia, at least until the 1997–98 crisis, after which its currency depreciated sharply. Then one year later, the ringgit was pegged to the U.S. dollar. Thailand has also had a long history of remarkable exchange

FIGURE 11.4
Annual Exchange Rate per US$, 1960–2003

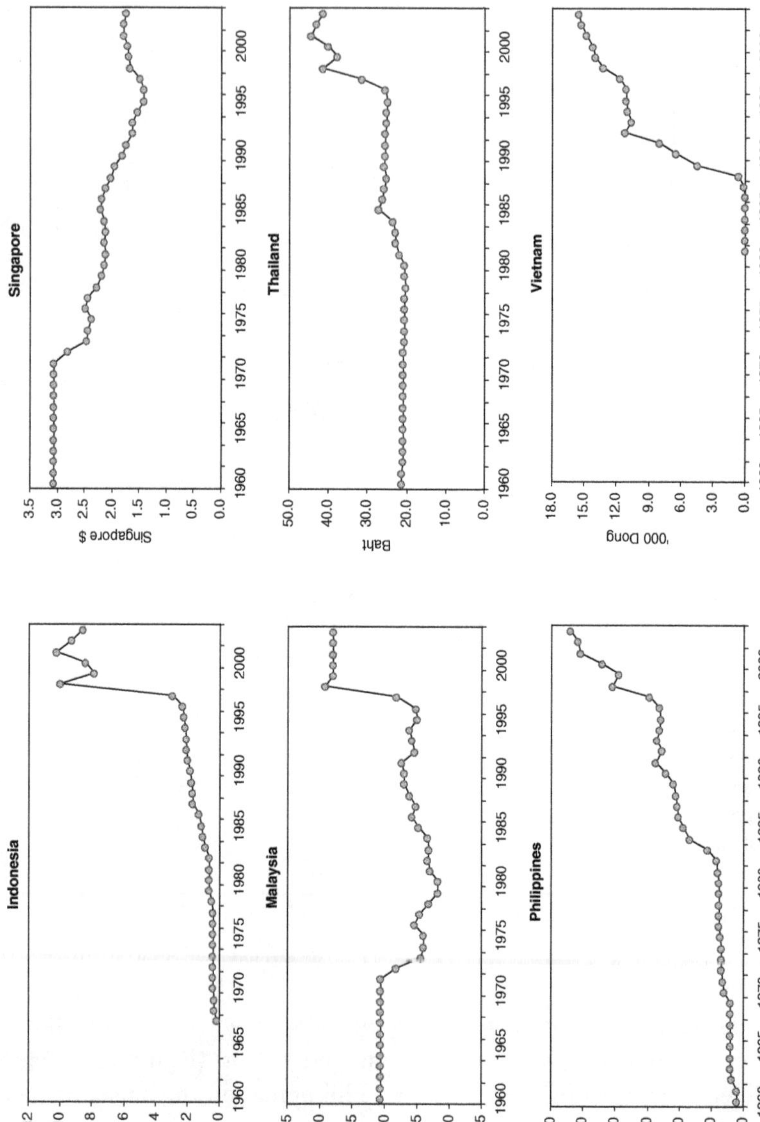

Source: World Development Indicators.

rate stability. By contrast, the Philippine peso has depreciated almost continuously since it broke with the 2:1 peg in the early 1960s, except briefly during the mid-1990s when it was buoyed by capital inflows and more recently, by remittances. These depreciations were formerly administrative and discrete, frequently dictated by near payments crises. More recently, they have occurred under the (generally effective) managed float system.

With regard to long-term macro balances, the Philippines does not emerge as an outlier (Figure 11.5 and Table 11.8). With the exception of the early 2000s, by decades its fiscal deficits have not been unusually large, and generally close to or even below the ex-Singapore average. The largest deficits have been recorded in the 1980s, as a result of the economic crisis, and in the early 2000s, owing to the political and budgetary log-jams. Similarly, the current account deficits have been around the ASEAN average, again ex-Singapore. In fact, in all three decades from 1970 to 2000, the Philippine deficit has been slightly lower than Thailand's. There is moreover no strong case to be made that these are necessarily "bad" deficits. That is, they have tended to be larger when the economy has been growing more strongly and attracted foreign savings. By contrast, surpluses have been recorded at times of contraction or political instability, when foreign investors have largely shunned the country.

Of course, these aggregate figures conceal a good deal of the story. The fiscal accounts need to take account of contingent liabilities, private debts and arrears being passed on to the public sector (for example, much of the 1980s' "crony debt"), spending programmes being pushed through the banking system (especially during the Marcos era), and a variety of off-budget government activity. The deficits also need to be seen in the context of private sector savings. For example, Malaysia has been able occasionally to run quite large fiscal deficits owing in part to much healthier private sector savings, including the compulsory Employees Provident Fund (EPF) programme.

For these reasons, and also owing to the slower overall growth, the Philippine external debt problem has been serious since the 1970s. The country already had a sizeable external debt in 1970, by the standards of the day, and it had the greatest percentage point increase in debt/GDP through the 1970s (Table 11.9). The increase was driven by a combination of factors: a sharp decline in terms of trade, the international financial institutions' concern to recycle petro dollars to countries seen as bankable (as the country was then regarded), coinciding neatly with the political and business ambitions of Marcos and his "entrepreneurial" supporters. Thus by 1980 the Philippines had the highest debt/GDP ratio of the ASEAN Four. The situation deteriorated further with the 1980s crisis and debt work-outs, and the country remained

FIGURE 11.5
Annual Fiscal and Current Account Balances, 1970–2004

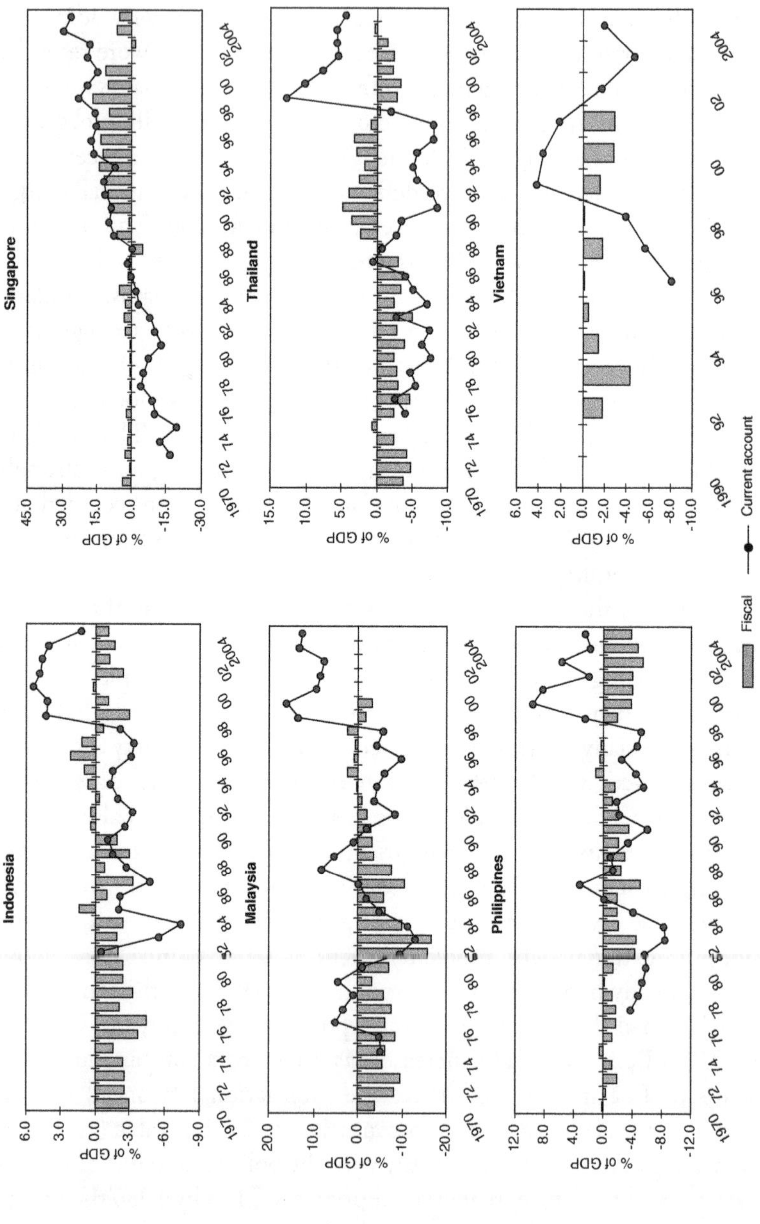

Source: World Development Indicators.

TABLE 11.8
Average Shares of Fiscal and Current Account Balances in GDP (%)

	1970s	*1980s*	*1990s*	*2000s*
Fiscal balance				
Indonesia	–2.8	–1.7	0.1	–1.3
Malaysia	–6.5	–8.6	–0.4	–
Philippines	–0.9	–2.9	–1.2	–4.4
Singapore	1.3	2.0	12.2	4.3
Thailand	–2.9	–1.9	1.4	–1.4
Vietnam	–	–	–1.5	–2.9
Current account balance				
Indonesia	–	–3.1	–0.3	3.6
Malaysia	0.3	–2.9	–0.4	10.3
Philippines	–5.0	–3.6	–0.7	2.9
Singapore	–11.2	0.3	15.1	23.1
Thailand	–5.2	–4.1	–1.2	5.2
Vietnam	–	–	–2.0	–1.6

Source: World Development Indicators and International Financial Statistics.

TABLE 11.9
External Debt as a Percentage of GDP, 1970–2004 (%)

	1970	*1980*	*1990*	*2000*	*2004*
Indonesia	48.7	28.4	60.6	92.4	55.5
Malaysia	13.6	28.5	37.2	50.0	45.6
Philippines	32.6	53.4	69.2	79.2	76.1
Thailand	14.4	27.0	34.6	67.4	34.0
Vietnam	–	–	310.6	53.5	39.6

Note: Figures are three year averages centered at the year indicated.
Source: World Development Indicators.

the most indebted at the end of the 1980s.[6] The ratio continued to rise during the 1990s, as the current account deficits also increased. But the country recorded the smallest percentage point increase among the Four, for two main reasons. First, as noted, it was only mildly affected by the crisis. Secondly, although the numerator (that is, external debt) rose, the denominator (that is, growth) also began to increase faster.

In trade and investment policy, the country has been slow to engage the international economy. As Power and Sicat (1971) demonstrated in a landmark contribution to the comparative OECD project, and to thinking about trade and industrialization more generally, the country was one of the first to embark on import substitution in East Asia. In consequence, the Philippines has had a history of perverse trade policy interventions, which have been extensively documented. Here too there has been significant progress since the late 1980s, to the point where openness appears to be quite deeply rooted in the polity and community at large, and the country now has a reasonably open trade policy regime. Average rates of protection have fallen, the dispersion in these rates is lower, and there is less reliance on non-tariff barriers.

Table 11.10 provides a partial indication of this opening up, as measured by trade/GDP ratios. The Philippines and Thailand have been very similar since the 1960s, with Thailand being somewhat more open, but not by a large margin. The two fall between the much more open Malaysian economy and the traditionally more inward-looking Indonesia. It needs to be emphasized, of course, that these ratios are a very crude indicator of openness to trade. They are unreliable for economies whose exports are dominated by commodities.[7] They also need to be qualified for economies where, as in the Philippines, electronics dominate exports. (As Table 11.11 shows, the country has the highest share of electronics in East Asia, and probably the world.) This is because this industry is characterized by extensive intra-industry and intra-firm trade, in which parts and components frequently cross national boundaries within vertically integrated global factories. Hence there is likely

TABLE 11.10
Average Shares of Trade and FDI in GDP (%)

	1960s	*1970s*	*1980s*	*1990s*	*2000s*
Trade					
Indonesia	22.6	41.4	47.8	57.6	66.7
Malaysia	80.6	84.1	112.0	178.1	216.6
Philippines	30.9	45.1	51.0	82.4	101.7
Singapore	–	–	–	–	–
Thailand	34.5	41.6	54.7	87.1	126.6
Vietnam	–	–	30.2	82.7	121.2
Foreign direct investment					
Indonesia	–	–	0.4	1.0	–1.0
Malaysia	–	3.5	3.2	5.6	2.9
Philippines	–	0.5	0.6	1.6	1.3
Singapore	–	4.9	8.9	5.9	13.3
Thailand	–	0.4	0.9	2.3	1.8
Vietnam	–	–	–	7.3	3.9

Source: World Development Indicators.

TABLE 11.11
World Exports of Parts and Components, 1992–2004 (%)

Country/Region	*Country/regional Composition*			*Share of P&C in manufacturing exports*			*Growth of manufacturing exports*	*Growth of P&C exports*	*Contrib of P&C to growth of mfg exports*
	1992	1996	2004	1992	1996	2004	1992–04	1992–04	1992–04
APEC	52.9	61.6	62.3	25.8	31.0	32.5	3.9	4.8	36.1
East Asia	29.6	36.4	43.6	23.3	30.5	33.5	4.3	5.7	38.2
Japan	15.6	15.1	11.7	28.9	36.8	37.5	2.1	3.1	48.4
Developing East Asia	14.0	21.3	31.9	19.1	27.2	32.2	5.3	7.3	36.3
China	1.0	2.3	8.3	4.8	8.8	18.8	7.1	12.6	21.2
Hong Kong SAR	2.1	1.5	1.1	21.1	27.0	32.9	0.1	1.7	645.1
Taiwan	3.2	4.2	6.2	22.2	32.1	46.3	3.9	6.7	59.2
Korea, RP	1.9	4.0	4.9	19.7	37.0	35.6	5.5	7.8	40.3
AFTA	5.9	9.5	11.6	31.9	41.0	47.8	5.2	6.8	52.9
Indonesia	0.1	0.2	0.3	2.6	6.9	14.2	4.2	10.9	19.6
Philippines	0.5	1.2	2.3	34.1	55.1	74.8	7.2	10.3	81.7
Malaysia	2.0	3.5	4.3	38.3	46.6	58.1	5.5	7.1	63.9
Singapore	2.6	3.5	3.1	43.9	56.2	53.2	4.1	4.8	57.8
Thailand	0.7	1.1	1.5	21.5	28.0	32.6	5.4	7.0	36.0
Vietnam	0.0	0.0	0.1	1.0	3.5	6.0	13.2	20.9	6.2
Oceania	0.2	0.3	0.3	13.3	15.2	16.5	3.6	4.4	18.6
Australia	0.2	0.2	0.2	14.7	17.1	18.3	3.5	4.3	20.5
New Zealand	0.0	0.0	0.0	9.1	9.5	11.7	3.7	4.6	13.2
NAFTA	22.9	24.7	18.3	30.4	32.0	30.7	3.3	3.4	30.9
USA	17.4	19.8	13.4	30.7	33.8	32.3	3.0	3.2	33.5
Canada	3.6	3.2	2.3	28.5	27.1	23.9	3.2	2.6	20.6
Mexico	1.8	1.8	2.5	31.2	25.1	30.7	5.5	5.4	30.5
Other APEC	0.0	0.0	0.0	5.6	11.6	3.8	4.3	2.9	3.1
Chile	0.0	0.0	0.0	7.2	14.5	4.5	4.7	2.9	3.4
Peru	0.0	0.0	0.0	2.2	2.7	1.9	3.4	2.9	1.8
European Union 15	41.1	32.6	29.0	18.8	20.0	20.9	2.5	2.9	22.9
Other	6.0	5.8	8.7	12.4	12.7	17.3	4.3	5.6	19.5
World	100.0	100.0	100.0	21.2	24.5	26.3	3.4	4.2	29.6
US$ billion[1]	403.8	709.5	1,257.8						

Source: Athukorala (2006) based on the UN Comtrade database.

to be extensive "double-counting" of trade. For this reason, alternative trade regime indicators suggest that the Philippines is somewhat less open.[8]

This more open economy has generated quite an impressive export performance (see Athukorala (2006*a*) which is the source of the figures in this paragraph). Over the period 1989–96, Philippine total and manufactured exports grew by 18.3 per cent and 26.4 per cent respectively, faster than both those of the ASEAN Five (13.6 per cent and 14.8 per cent), and those of Thailand (11.9 per cent and 12.8 per cent). Over the crisis and its immediate aftermath, 1997–2000, the Philippines' manufactured export growth was by far the fastest (19.8 per cent versus 7.8 per cent for the ASEAN Five), presumably owing to the beneficial effects of the peso depreciation but without the major financial and corporate debt crises in the other three ASEANs. However, worryingly, manufactured exports have stagnated since 2001. The decline in export-oriented foreign direct investment (FDI) flows, in part a response to increased political instability, has been a factor here.

The Philippines has also done quite well in electronics, the fastest growing sector of global merchandise trade, owing to its effective liberalization of trade and FDI, albeit in the second-best context *via* export processing zones. As Athukorala (2006*b*) demonstrates, its electronics exports have grown rapidly since 1990, and these products now dominate the country's exports. From a slow start, the Philippines recorded one of the fast growth rates among developing countries over the period 1992–2004, not far below that of China. There are some caveats that need to be attached to this record. The fiscal incentives, which attracted multinational enterprises (MNEs) to the country, are probably not sustainable. And the partial nature of the reforms has resulted in a dual policy regime, thin domestic value added, and export-oriented enclaves with limited backward linkages to local suppliers, especially those located outside the zones. Upgrading has reportedly proceeded slowly, although it has commenced.[9] Moreover, there is an historical irony in the sense that Philippine export patterns are now more concentrated than ever before, even though one of the original justifications for import substitution was export diversification. Nevertheless, the achievements are notable, certainly on balance desirable, and they have enabled the country to get its foot in the door to this key global industry.

The Philippines has also been a comparatively minor recipient of FDI, owing to both a historically restrictive policy regime and an unwelcoming commercial environment. But it is certainly not an outlier. As Table 11.10 indicates, it has attracted much less FDI than Malaysia and Singapore, but these are exceptionally large recipients. Traditionally, it received amounts similar to Thailand, although the latter pulled away during its decade of hyper growth prior to the crisis. FDI inflows have been maintained since the 1997–98 slowdown, albeit at lower rates, and in contrast to its other frequent comparator, Indonesia, which has experienced an FDI exodus since 1998. As important as these magnitudes is the change in the commercial policy environment into which this FDI has flowed. Once again, the major break occurred around the late 1980s, when FDI policy became more open (Bautista and Tecson 2003). Moreover, and significantly, the more open FDI stance was accompanied by trade liberalization, with the result that the nature of FDI inflows shifted, from the old rent-seeking import substitution model to efficiency-seeking export-oriented projects, with electronics as noted the key recipient.

EXPLANATIONS[10]

The explanations for the Philippines' indifferent performance are complex, inter-related, and not easily amenable to quantitative analysis. No simple or single theory suffices. We need to develop a coherent story relating outcomes to an array of external and internal factors, some narrowly economic, others broader and embedded in political, historical and institutional factors.

Surviving the Crisis

This is the more easily answered of the two questions. Unlike its neighbours, the Philippines suffered only a mild recession in 1997–98 for two main reasons.[11] First, during the 1990s it did not receive the exceptionally large private, short-term capital flows which went into neighbouring high-growth economies. The country was effectively excluded from international capital markets until 1992, except for inflows associated with the debt workouts. Even as the capital account was opened, foreign investors who lost out in the 1980s approached the country with caution. By the mid-1990s, these flows began to increase rapidly. However, the boom was so shortlived that the magnitudes were quite modest. Thus, no (or limited) boom also meant no bust.

Secondly, the Philippine financial sector was in better shape than its neighbours. The banks were comparatively prudent and cautious, and the Central Bank's regulatory/supervisory framework had been strengthened since the early 1990s. The strength of the finance sector is indicated by the fact that banks were able to endure a sharp depreciation of the peso in the second half of 1997, a factor which was central to the financial crisis in neighbouring countries. Hence, the combination of a sharp peso depreciation and a banking system intact contributed to rapid export growth recorded in the immediate aftermath of the crisis. Moreover, the economy was then, as always, connected to the strong U.S. economy more than any other in East Asia, and therefore less affected by the East Asian decline of 1997–98 and by Japan's long-term recession.

Slower Long-term Growth

Here we briefly evaluate, and integrate where possible, the various explanatory hypotheses.

'Conventional' growth explanations. There is a large literature, which attempts to explain international variations in long-term rates of economic growth. The key explanatory variables include, but are not restricted to, proxies which summarize macroeconomic outcomes, trade policy, human capital, institutional quality, social "inclusiveness", geography and initial levels of per capita income (the latter to capture the "catch-up" phenomenon).

Such a framework has intuitive appeal for the Philippines. For example, its economy was traditionally somewhat more inward looking than most high growth economies, and macroeconomic outcomes have not been as good. It does not typically score well on various (albeit crude) indicators of institutional quality.

Attempts to explain the slower growth rates using such a framework have been at best moderately successful.

Pritchett (2003) reviews a range of possible explanations, within the context of modern growth theory and empirics. He discounts some of the standard factors, notably excessive appreciation of the exchange rate (as an indicator of macroeconomic disequilibria) and budget deficits. A number of adverse exogenous shocks are noted, but generally discarded as key explanators. Factor accumulation appears not to be relevant, as the decline in investment was arguably a consequence not a cause of the growth slowdown, and human capital levels as noted remain high. He is therefore left to conjecture that "institutions" may be the central factor. The argument — or at least hypothesis — here is that some institutions may have improved in the transition to democracy, but "institutional uncertainty" has also increased. This invokes the Shleifer-Vishny notion that corruption has become more "disorganized", in contrast to the more predictable form under Marcos. (A very similar argument can be advanced for Indonesia in its transition from Soeharto to democracy.) Faced with this more unpredictable policy regime, investors are likely to eschew longer-term investments, and prefer instead more liquid options such as real estate, the stock market and shopping malls.

Hill and Hill (2005) employed the usual range of explanatory variables in their quantitative examination of growth in the ASEAN Five over the period 1970–2000. Their four main equations, from the parsimonious to the more elaborate, generated estimates which were quite close to the observed per capita growth rate over this period of 1.3 per cent. The predicted rates ranged from 1.6 per cent to 2.1 per cent, presumably exceeding the actual rate because growth models cannot typically incorporate the effects of deep economic contractions. One obvious limitation of these growth studies is that they develop a "general model" of the relationship between economic growth and the explanatory variables presumed to be important. As a result, they are not necessarily able to accommodate country-specific factors and nuances. For example, as is generally the case with such estimations, Hill and Hill did not find the human capital and inequality variables to be significant explanators, and thus they were excluded from the predicting equations. Their inclusion may have increased the difference, that is, the "unexplained residual", still further.

While it has its uses, such a methodology raises as many questions as it answers. The Philippines has diverged from the "stars" in its macroeconomic outcomes and openness, but it has not trailed all that far behind the pack, and on both these key indicators, outcomes have improved markedly since the late 1980s. Its human capital continues to be superior to that of any comparable country, while a range of other variables[12] are either irrelevant or would make little difference to the story. Moreover, this framework is useful particularly in explaining long-term growth differentials, and is therefore less relevant in coming to grips with the episodic nature of Philippine growth. That is, until about 1980, its growth was slower but not markedly inferior to that of most of its neighbours. It was the "lost decade" of the 1980s that really separated it from East Asia.

Can other theories and explanations help? The country has unfortunately received more than its fair share of natural disasters, but so too have other, faster-growing economies (Indonesia and Taiwan readily come to mind), and thus this argument is hardly convincing. Similarly, while at crucial periods the international economic environment has been unfavourable,[13] high-growth economies have invariably experienced similarly adverse impacts and been able to maintain their growth trajectory.

Institutional/political barriers to good policy. It is sometimes argued that highly unequal social structures — the "oligarchs" — have infected the political process to the point where serious policy reform, especially that which challenges this group's vested interests, is impossible. As shown earlier, the country's distributional outcomes are more unequal than most of its neighbours, and perhaps that renders the country more susceptible to political and social instability born out of this inequality. But one would hesitate to give this argument top billing as an explanation. First, the empirical cross-country evidence on the relationship between inequality and growth is not clear-cut.[14] One can readily think of countries which have grown rapidly in spite of continuing high inequality. Botswana (at least pre-AIDS), Chile, and Malaysia come to mind. Second, the Philippines has grown at respectable rates when reform has proceeded. The Ramos presidency is the obvious recent example, and its record does clearly illustrate that the sociopolitical structures are not so ossified as to be incapable of reform and growth.

In the post-Marcos period, and consistent with Pritchett's (2003) thesis above, it might be argued that the political system is now not able to provide longer term economic policy predictability. Owing to the U.S.-style strong legislature and weak bureaucracy, and highly personalistic politics, regime changes every six years introduce much commercial uncertainty. Thus, each new administration results in significant turnover at the upper echelons of the bureaucracy, percolating down even to the middle levels. It therefore becomes very difficult to establish "insulated" technocratic policy-making capacities, together with policy continuity and predictability. In consequence, investors do not think much beyond a six-year time horizon, and probably even less. However, it is a moot point whether shifting to a Westminster style of government would make much difference. Indeed, our impression of the political science literature is that there is a predilection towards presidential-style systems for low-income countries on the grounds that they are more likely to be able to deliver stronger, more purposeful governance.

Harberger (1984, p. 427) once concluded that "... there is no magic formula [for economic growth] — no combination of one or two or even ten or twelve policy buttons that, once pushed in the right order, will guarantee economic growth." The search for explanations for the Philippine puzzle certainly endorses such an approach. A number of inter-related factors are relevant. The country failed to grow as quickly as several of its neighbours in the 1960s and 1970s in part for conventional economic reasons. Then, in the second Marcos decade, it grew into trouble, owing to a combination of reckless investments, ever-increasing cronyism and corruption, increasing instability and disaffection with the regime, and external misfortune. It then experienced a deep economic and political crisis from which — unlike Mexico in the early 1990s — it has found great difficulty growing out of. In seeking explanations for under-development, one cannot blame history (Marcos, colonial rule, etc.) forever. But the country's complicated political history is certainly relevant to contemporary challenges.

SUMMING UP

The Philippine development record must surely be judged a disappointment, in light of its relatively favourable initial conditions and compared to almost all its East Asian neighbours. Especially since 1980, it has grown much more slowly than the regional norms, and it has consequently delivered significantly inferior social outcomes. It has in fact performed at about the developing world average: that is, well behind East Asia (and now India), better than practically all of Africa, and about on a par with Latin America ex-Chile.

But it would be a mistake to characterize it as a "failed state". Perhaps a "messy state" is a more accurate description. Living standards have been rising, albeit slowly. Economic policy reform is an arduous, complex process, but there have been notable achievements, especially during the Ramos administration. Since the Asian economic crisis, from which the country escaped largely unscathed, growth appears to have settled on what may be termed a "Southeast Asian archipelagic growth rate" of around 5–5.5 per cent. (That is, about the same as Indonesia, and for similar reasons.) This translates into per capita growth of 2.5 per cent, and a doubling of incomes every 25–30 years.

The key development challenge is to achieve East Asian norms of growth and poverty reduction. In turn, this raises the question of how to achieve "good policy" in the face of complex and unpredictable politics, in which the key actors have short time horizons and lack the clear-headed commitment to rapid growth evident in much of the neighbourhood. In this context, the discussion concerning the establishment of a so-called "firewall" between economics and politics has much to commend it. Countries can do well in spite of unpredictable politics, as Thailand demonstrated for the three decades prior to the 1997–98 economic crisis. The key element is to embed economic policy predictability in such an environment. In fact, steps have already been taken in this direction. A notable achievement has been the operation of an independent central bank. The BSP has stuck to its increasingly well-defined objective of inflation targeting and a floating exchange rate in spite of an exceptionally challenging political environment. The trade regime has remained largely open, bolstered by (admittedly second best) arrangements which place exporters on a free-trade footing and connected to just adequate infrastructure. Competitive structures are gradually being put in place for much of the business sector, including some non-tradables.

Thus, there is a possible way forward: maintaining the hard-won fiscal reform measures, continuing the microeconomic reforms, addressing the social inequities, resolving the deep-seated Mindanao insurrections, and avoiding debilitating coup attempts and military disaffection. A decade of accelerating growth would lift living standards substantially and develop a constituency for further, deeper reform. The next few years will determine whether the current political leadership is up to the challenge.

Notes

1 The coefficients of variation for the other countries are Indonesia 74, Malaysia 53, Singapore 55, Thailand 57, Vietnam (since 1984 only) 30.

2 For excellent accounts of the 1980s Philippine crisis, see Dohner and Intal (1989) and Remolona et al. (1986). The seminal political economy analysis of the Marcos period is provided by Sicat (1985).

3 Table 11.4 also illustrates that the size of the Philippine public sector has been at about the ASEAN average, and quite similar to that of Thailand. Of course, this is simply an aggregate figure, and it reveals little about the composition of these expenditures, nor the regulatory reach of the government. For example, both Malaysia and Singapore have larger public sectors, but more "light-handed" governments.

4 The latter observation includes the agrarian reform programme, which has had little distributive impact in aggregate, although of course individual recipients have benefitted from it.

5 The major limitation of the various institutional quality indicators is that very few of them reliably extend back over more than a decade. One indicator which does, and is therefore widely used, is the variable "contract-intensive money". This refers to the proportion of M2, which is held in forms other than currency. It is intended to reflect the extent to which property rights are sufficiently secure for agents to make use of financial intermediaries. On this indicator, the Philippines ranks quite close to both Malaysia and Thailand (see Hill and Hill, p. 322).

6 Among the four, Indonesia's debt rose the most sharply during this decade, as oil prices collapsed. But owing to prompt and effective reform, and a supportive donor response, the growth momentum was quickly restored.

7 For example, Indonesia became significantly more open in the 1980s, but the ratio rose only moderately owing to the very sharp decline in oil exports.

8 For example, among seventy-two countries in the Hill and Hill (2005) sample, the Philippines ranked 29th on the trade/GDP measure but 37th according to

the widely used Sachs-Warner indicator of openness. The latter refers to the proportion of years a country is deemed to be "open" according to six main indicators.

9 See Tecson (2006) for a detailed study of Philippine industrial upgrading prospects in comparative perspective. For example, according to Intel, the world's largest semi-conductor producer, its Philippine plant has been in operation since 1974 and employs 65,000 workers. It is the centre for "flash memory" production in the company's global network. (We are most grateful to Prema-Chandra Athukorala for drawing our attention to this fact.)

10 We draw here in particular on Balisacan and Hill (2003), Hill and Hill (2005), and Sicat (2003).

11 Noland (2000) and Sicat (1999) provide cogent analyses of the crisis episode and its impact on the Philippines.

12 For example, proximity to major economies, length of coastline, the incidence of political disturbances, and ethnolinguistic fragmentation.

13 For example, there was a sharp deterioration in the country's terms of trade in the 1970s (on both the export and import side), just as it was embarking on increased foreign borrowings, partly it should be noted with the active encouragement of the IFIs. Similarly, as growth faltered in the early 1980s, and these debts had to be repaid, world interest rates began to rise significantly.

14 See for example Forbes (2000), whose cross-country analysis consistently finds a positive correlation between inequality and growth.

References

Athukorala, P.-C. "Post-Crisis Export Performance: The Indonesian Experience in Regional Perspective". *Bulletin of Indonesian Economic Studies* 42, no. 2 (2006*a*): 177–211.

Athukorala, P.-C. "Multinational Production Networks and the New Geo-economic Division of Labour in the Pacific Rim". Paper presented to the 31st Pacific Trade and Development Conference, Guadalajara, Mexico, June 2006*b*.

Balisacan, A.M. and H. Hill (eds.). *The Philippine Economy: Development, Policies and Challenges*. New York: Oxford University Press and Manila: Ateneo de Manila University Press, 2003.

Balisacan, A.M. and H. Hill. "An Introduction to the Key Issues". In Balisacan and Hill (eds.), pp. 3–44.

Balisacan, A.M. "Poverty and Inequality". In Balisacan and Hill (eds.), pp. 311–41.

Barro, R., Lee, J.-W. International data on educational attainment updates and implications. NBER Working Paper 7911 (2000).

Bautista, R.M. and G. Tecson. "International Dimensions". In Balisacan and Hill (eds.), pp. 136–71.

Burgess, R. and V. Haksar. "Migration and Foreign Remittances in the Philippines". IMF Working Paper, WP/05/111, Washington D.C., 2005.

Dohner, R.S. and P. Intal Jr. "The Marcos Legacy: Economic Policy and Foreign Debt in the Philippines". In *Developing Country Debt and Economic Performance*, vol. 3, edited by J.D. Sachs and S.M. Collins, pp. 371–614. Chicago: University of Chicago Press, for the NBER, 1989.

Forbes, K.J. "A Reassessment of the Relationship Between Inequality and Growth". *American Economic Review* 90, no. 4 (2000): 869–87.

Gochoco-Bautista, M.S. and D. Canlas. "Monetary and Exchange Rate Policy". In Balisacan and Hill (eds.), pp. 77–105.

Harberger, A.C. (ed.) *World Economic Growth*. San Francisco: Institute for Contemporary Studies, 1984.

Herrin, A. and E. Pernia. "Population, Human Resources and Employment". In Balisacan and Hill (eds.), pp. 283–310.

Hill, H. and S. Hill. "Growth Econometrics in the Tropics: What Insights for Southeast Asian Economic Development?". *Singapore Economic Review* 50 (2005): 313–43.

Noland, M. "The Philippines in the Asian Financial Crisis: How the Sick Man Avoided Pneumonia". *Asian Survey* 40, no. 3 (2000): 401–12.

Power, J.H. and G.P. Sicat. *The Philippines: Industrialization and Trade Policies*. London: Oxford University Press, 1971.

Pritchett, L. "A Toy Collection, a Socialist Star and a Democratic Dud? Growth Theory, Vietnam, and the Philippines". In *In Search of Prosperity: Analytical Narratives on Economic Growth*, edited by D. Rodrik, pp. 123–51. Princeton: Princeton University Press, 2003.

Remolona, E.M., M. Mangahas, and F. Pante, Jr. "Foreign Debt, Balance of Payments, and the Economic Crisis of the Philippines in 1983–84". *World Development* 14, no. 8 (1986): 993–1018.

Sicat, G. "A Historical and Current Perspective of Philippine Economic Problems". *Philippine Economic Journal* 24, no. 1 (1985): 24–63.

Sicat, G.P. "The Philippines". In H.W. Arndt and H. Hill *Southeast Asia in Crisis* (Singapore: Institute of Southeast Asian Studies, 1999), pp. 41–50.

———. *Philippine Economic and Development Issues*. Manila: Anvil, 2003.

Sicat, G.P. and R.M. Abdula. "Public Finance". In Balisacan and Hill (eds.), pp. 106–35.

Tecson, G. "High-Tech Industry Development in the Philippines: At a dangerous Crossroad?". In *The East Asian High-Tech Drive*, edited by Y.-P. Chu and H. Hill (Cheltenham: Edward Elgar, 2006), pp. 225–58.

Vos, R. and J.T. Yap. *The Philippine Economy: East Asia's Stray Cat?* London: Macmillan, 1996.

12

SANCHO PANZA IN BULIOK COMPLEX: THE PARADOX OF MUSLIM SEPARATISM

Patricio N. Abinales

> We are all Islam, but we are different. I cannot understand them." (Maguindanao merchant)[1]
>
> They don't have a message about the future. You can't simply say Islam is the only solution. You have to deal with problems of electricity, water, the environment, transportation. Those can't be Islamic." (Edward Said on Hamas)[2]

If we read past the rhetoric and examine more closely the political dynamics of Muslim-Filipino separatism, the following peculiarities become apparent. First, despite repeated declarations by the Moro National Liberation Front (MNLF) and the Moro Islamic Liberation Front (MILF), their rebellions are better understood as modern mobilizations against the intrusive reach of the nation state than as the latest edition of an epic Moro struggle against various colonialisms. The fighting is also portrayed as a principled act in pursuit of a sovereign *Bangsamoro* (Moro nation); but this is a slant that downplays ethnic, class, gender, and linguistic cleavages within the *umma* (community) itself. Second, while we should not deny the intensity of the separatist war, we also must be aware of its limited geography and the brevity of its major battles. Almost 95 per cent of the MNLF's and the MILF's clashes with the Armed Forces of the Philippines (AFP) occurred within a circumscribed area, and efforts by both groups to expand their military operations have failed. Third, the radicalism of their message is often belied by their political pragmatism. The MNLF was forced by Libya, the Organization of Islamic Conference (OIC), and Malaysia to negotiate with the Philippine government, with disastrous results. The MILF has called for an Islamic revolution but has asked the United States and Malaysia, and most recently Japan, to broker the peace talks with the government.[3]

This chapter examines these issues to explain why, despite having taken a toll on the weak, corrupt and inefficient Philippine state, Muslim separatists are still unsuccessful in reaching their goal.[4] The *Bangsamoro Republik* is nowhere in sight, the MNLF has been integrated into the state it once fought, and the MILF is having second thoughts about the viability of armed struggle. The chapter takes a second look at the myth of the eternal Moro resistance, in which the MNLF and the MILF anchor their revolutions. It revisits the question of the Muslim elite, the different responses of the Muslim community *as a whole* to the separatist movement, and the failure of the MNLF and the MILF to reach out to non-Muslim groups. It then discusses the limited geography of the wars and its implications for the separatist project. It closes with an overview of revolutionaries as state managers, recalling the fate of the MNLF since it accepted the government's offer to run a regional body, and laying out problems the MILF may face after signing the peace pact.

THE INVENTION OF (A) TRADITION

Today, everyone accepts the mantra that Muslim separatism has a history longer than that of the nation-state. The Philippine government acknowledges it and the compromises and concessions it granted Muslim groups since the time of President Ferdinand Marcos were made in recognition of separatism's supposed popularity. Filipino communists and social democrats have added their voices, expressing solidarity with the Moro struggle and recognizing that under a repressive Manila regime, Muslims have a right to secede.[5] International groups have also joined the chorus. The OIC has taken up the cause of the MNLF, after accepting Nur Misuari's contention that Marcos ordered a wholesale massacre of Muslims. But less likely associations have also chimed in.[6] The British Broadcasting Company's "Guide to the Philippine Conflict" states that the "southern Philippines has a long history of conflict, stretching back to the arrival of Islam in the 14th Century", while the United States Institute of Peace, the leading American institution involved in the peace negotiations, prefaced an announcement of a forum it sponsored with this line: "Going back to the colonial era, one of the longest-running internal conflicts in Asia is the struggle by the Muslims of the southern Philippines for greater autonomy or even independence."[7]

This remarkable propaganda success is made possible by a number of reasons. First, the MNLF's rebellion was the first major conventional war ever in the history of the republic. Its intensity, not to mention the possibility that it could break up the nation, has profoundly affected Filipinos. That it happened under martial law, similarly a radically different condition that altered the shape and direction of Philippine politics, further reinforced separatism's significance.[8] Second, the OIC's recognition of the MNLF as the representative of the Moro people ensured that the war has an international hearing. The legitimacy of separatism was only boosted by the decision of the Marcos dictatorship to expand diplomatic ties with the Middle East to counteract the MNLF's overseas political campaigns and lift the embargo that the oil-producing countries of the OIC had placed on the Philippines.[9] Third, because of the dominating presence of nationalist historiography and its dogged emphasis on the perpetual "state of struggle" as locus of the Philippines' national narrative, scholars and activists supportive of, or sympathetic to, separatism know their explanations will always have a receptive audience.[10] Finally, with the rise of political Islam worldwide, separatism has received fresh and far more militant support from abroad. Al Qaeda and Jemaah Islamiyah have replaced the OIC, and while there is still little evidence that the MILF has been won over to the cause of Osama bin Laden, these supposed links have upgraded its political capital immensely.

Separatism also draws its resilience from the elisions and ahistorical slants that inform its discourse. Principally, the portrait of an interminable struggle fails to recognize the differing contexts in which Muslim communities engaged hostile external forces. Neither does it devote equal time or passion to explaining actions other than resistance. The battles waged by the great Maguindanao Sultan Kudarat against the Spaniards are therefore seen as no different from the revolts of Datu Ali of Kudarangan in the early years of American rule, of Hadji Kamlon of Sulu in the 1950s, and of the Mindanao Independence Movement (MIM) of Cotabato strongman Datu Udtog Matalam in the late 1960s. All were commitments to defend the Moro homeland.[11]

This portrait does not withstand closer scrutiny. Sultan Kudarat (1581–1671) did fight the Spaniards never in defence of a "Moroland". For the so-called "Moro wars" were mainly sallies against the Spanish colonial state, not the other way around. Religious zeal may have been a reason for Kudarat's attacks on the central and northern Philippines, but equally important to him were the economics. He was concerned about his kingdom's competitiveness in the vibrant trade in maritime Southeast Asia, and the raids up north were designed to maintain access to an important source of slaves.[12] Muslim resistance only took on an "anti-colonial" hue much later when Spanish gunboats and better-trained Visayan and Tagalog troops forced the sultans and datus of Sulu and Maguindanao to sign peace agreements. The stance of Datu Uto of Buayan (1860–88) symbolized this shift, but even his conflict with the Spaniards was less driven by nationalist sentiment than by a pragmatic need to preserve his declining power.[13]

Southeast Asia scholars have pointed out that these actions were not unique to Muslim Mindanao but common to a region in which port cities and towns controlled by strongmen [*orang besar*] competed and collaborated in the exchange of goods and slaves.[14] The *orang besar's* frames of reference included his port town in relation to other port towns, larger markets like China and India, and the surrounding areas where forest products and humans were tapped for the regional trade. In short, there was no "Moroland", only a hinterland. The separatist movement is arguing a concept whose ancestry is relatively new.[15]

More recently, Matalam's MIM has been described as the precursor of the MNLF. What is less often recalled is that Matalam's call for separatism came after a long history of collaboration with Manila, during which he worked closely with its representatives (mainly his brother-in-law Salipada Pendatun) to keep the peace between Magiundanaos and Christian settlers. He was no different from other provincial warlords and "discovered" separatism only after consistently larger voter turnout in the settler zones shifted local power away from him (and Pendatun) to aspiring Christian strongmen. But even this was only a ruse to gain concessions from Manila; and while the student allies who helped Matalam form the MIM decided to push for armed struggle, the old *datu* made peace with Marcos.[16]

REBELS, RULERS, AND MASSES

Muslim "collaboration" is rarely treated on its own terms, and in the past, separatists generally eschewed the issue. The MNLF played down its criticism of Muslim politicians in the name of a fragile unity against Marcos. But it was a shortlived coalition as Misuari was abandoned by his politician allies.[17] The MILF has been more circumspect in dealing with traditional politicians, having learned from the MNLF's negative experience.[18] But it has also gone out of its way to incorporate Muslim elite politics into the separatist narrative, arguing that elites did try "to secure Mindanao and

Sulu from the control of the outsiders but failed miserably" because their actions did not match their promises. The MILF ideologue Salah Jubair wrote that these "politicians or high government officials" had "become too preoccupied with the present", exhibiting a "lackluster mentality" that "ultimately led to surrender or what we may mildly term as 'subservience' ". Moreover, their inability "to shed off their traditional privileges" had "contributed a lot to this unfortunate frame of mind".[19]

The problem with this amended portrait is that it cannot easily pursue the critique to its logical conclusion. That conclusion would have to trace the backwardness, poverty and misery of the *umma* to the compromises traditional leaders made with the Philippine state in defence of their own political and economic interests. This is a position leftwing analysts have consistently taken. Saturnino Borras, Jr. and Eric Gutierrez, for example, argue that widespread poverty and war in Mindanao are "mere symptoms" of a deeper malaise that the government, the island's elites, and "even the mainstream (sic) Moro revolutionary organizations" have failed to recognize: "[n]amely, the highly skewed distribution of ownership and control over land resources…and the lack of state-regularized and state-guaranteed property security".[20] They argue that the Mindanao conflict will end only with the implementation of a comprehensive agrarian policy centered on land redistribution and "ancestral domain resolution", and when the state (not the MILF or the MNLF) destroys the networks set up by private "entrepreneurs of violence" (the authors' allusion to the political clans and strongmen who exercise legal and extra-legal authority in many Mindanao areas).[21]

Jubair's revisionist portrait of the Muslim elite plays down yet another enduring characteristic of Muslim elite politics — the violent clan wars called *rido*.[22] *Rido* has always been a stumbling block to any lasting peace in southeastern Mindanao and at present it threatens to undermine the separatist cause as MILF and MNLF fighters get drawn into the family wars. The Cotabato columnist Patricio Diaz warns:

> Today, such rivalry for power and prestige is still a major part of the Mindanao Problem. We see this in the elections in Sulu that need army battalions to keep order and prevent bloodshed; in the power rivalry among the Maguindanao, Maranao and Tausug ethnic groups; and in the splintering of the Moro Front movement in 1977 and, again in 2001, of the Moro National Liberation Front. The feuds among the clans in the Datu Piang-Maganoy area boosted by the MILF and MNLF relatives taking sides, triggered armed encounters and mass evacuations in the mid-1990s.[23]

Thus, for an Islamic rebellion to succeed, it must necessarily become a revolt against the old ruling class as well. In continuing to defer to the authority of these elites, Muslim separatists have simply postponed dealing with a major problem that the public intellectual Alunan Glang warned about roughly thirty-two years ago: "The real problem in the country is not economic, political or social, but the Muslim leadership itself."[24] What Glang did not say was that to do battle against both the state and against the elites would be tantamount to political suicide. Thomas McKenna describes this predicament:

> Although both Misuari and Salamat...had held as top priority the reform or elimination of datu leadership, the official ideology of the MNLF hardly addressed issues of internal social transformation...The existence of aristocratic, autocratic leadership was retained, at least implicitly, as an intrinsic component of Moro political culture... [A] call for the abolition of the datu system would have undercut the rebellion's symbolic claims to continuity with past anticolonial struggles...[25]

The picture becomes more complicated once we descend from the elite to the level of the "masses". McKenna discovers that diverse motives led Muslims to join the rebellions: "it was striking...how rarely any of the insurgents, in expressing their motivations for taking up arms or fighting against great odds, made spontaneous mention of either the Moro nation (Bangsamoro) or Islamic renewal, the two central components of Muslim nationalist ideology."[26] Rank-and-file insurgents also displayed an ambivalent attitude to those who surrendered during the MNLF war, in contrast to the leadership's outright censure:

> They were even sparing in their criticism of those commanders and followers who surrendered early to the government and received compensation, remarking only that they "lacked determination". This remarkably tolerant stance toward early rebel defectors contrasts with official pronouncements by the separatist leadership and *indicates both a divergence from official attitudes and an appreciation for the political (and moral) complexities of a largely defensive insurgency.*[27]

Why Mindanao's Muslims rebelled still needs closer examination. It is a topic that scholars, policymakers and activists sympathetic to the MNLF and the MILF have side-stepped or ignored completely. But as the MNLF war waned, other stories have emerged: the role and responses of Muslim women, the war's impact on cleavages within Muslim communities, the consequences of dying languages and dialects. All these will surely complicate the social portrait of an already fragmented *umma.*[28] The failure of the MNLF and the MILF to recognize the importance of issues like gender relations will have a profound impact in the post-war rehabilitation period.[29]

Divergent motivations, of course, reflect a broader mix of sentiments, including an unwillingness to back the rebellions all the way and consistently. Table 12.1 shows, with one exception, community support for the MILF rebellion in provinces with substantial Muslim populations has never exceeded 50 per cent.[30] In fact, in the 6,474 *barangays* (villages) where MILF troops supposedly operate, their presence is noticeable in only 1,463 (22.5 per cent).

TABLE 12.1
MILF Affected Barangays (Last Quarter 2005)

Region/Province	*Number of Barangays*	*Influenced*	*Less Influenced*	*Total*
Region 9				
Basilan	261	11	63	74
Zamboanga del Sur	681	10	5	15
Zamboanga Sibugay	389	30	0	30
Zamboanga del Norte	699	1	22	23
Sub-Total	2,030	52	90	142
Region 11				
Davao del Norte	224	0	5	5
Davao Oriental	183	3	15	18
Davao del Sur	523	0	20	20
South Cotabato	228	5	36	41
Sarangani	142	15	39	54
Sub-Total	1,535	23	116	139
Region 12				
Lanao del Norte	506	52	80	132
Lanao del Sur	1,124	314	100	414
North Cotabato	544	61	121	182
Sultan Kudarat	228	22	76	98
Maguindanao	507	186	170	356
Sub-Total	2,909	635	547	1,182
Grand Total	6,474	710	753	1,463

Source: Armed Forces of the Philippines, J-2, as reprinted in Carolyn O. Arguillas, "Racing Against Time", *Newsbreak* (2 and 16 January 2006), p. 15.

And the MILF is popular in only 710 (11 per cent) *barangays*. Since the Armed Forces of the Philippines (AFP) compiled these statistics, there is reason to suspect their accuracy. But when we factor in additional variables, such as the geography of the war, discussed below, this set of government statistics assumes a new significance: it shows the inadequate support the MNLF and MILF have been receiving from their respective mass bases.[31]

A UNIFIED TRI-PEOPLE?

The fragility of the resistance myth is likewise evident in the absence of solidarity between the Muslim and non-Muslim communities. Religious and ethnic friction between Christians and Muslims is already well documented, but only recently has scholarly and activist attention been directed at the relations between Muslims and the other minorities collectively referred to as *lumad*. This is a much longer relationship, antedating the Spanish era, when Muslim sultanates traded with *lumad* communities for forest goods. It was an economic relationship that was not always trouble-free: when the demand for manpower was high in the maritime Southeast Asia region (and beyond) or when traditional sources of slaves were blocked by rival powers like Spain, the *lumad* became the alternative sources of slaves.[32] These "raids" resulted in tensions that persisted way into the post-colonial periods and explain why the *lumad* often ally themselves with Christian settlers against the Muslims.[33]

The MNLF ignored *lumad* concerns in its negotiations with the government, prompting *lumad* leaders to question the separatist organization's claim to represent the interests of all people in Mindanao. Ramon Moambing, executive director of the Lumad Development Center, an NGO based in Cotabato City, protested that when *lumad* representatives asked the MNLF to consult them, "They [the MNLF] said, 'The MNLF cannot bring or support any agenda of the indigenous peoples. It is the indigenous peoples themselves who will defend their rights.' "[34] There is no record of any response by the MNLF to his complaint. The MILF has shown greater sensitivity to the problematic relations between Muslims and *lumad*, recently recognizing the need to include the latter's concerns in the peace negotiations.[35] Yet, *lumad* leaders remain suspicious of these MILF overtures. As Moambing explains:

> MILF are also collecting revolutionary taxes. The MILF leaders say this should not be going on, but the indigenous people are afraid to refuse, because the collectors are armed. People are afraid to complain. The

> MILF are also exploiting us. The indigenous people have no arms; they are not learned, so the MILF can force them away.[36]

A *lumad* coalition expressed strong concerns about being left out in the negotiations over the ancestral domain issue. The manifesto of the Mindanao Indigenous Peoples Peace Forum warned the MILF and the government "the *Lumad* who are encompassed within the Autonomous Region of Muslim Mindanao (ARMM) are aware that we are not free to claim our ancestral domains and to implement our cultures and traditions." The manifesto also admits that *lumad* communities have joined groups "with varying ideologies even if such were inconsistent with indigenous desires, dreams and aspirations in accord with our lifestyle".[37] This was an indirect way of admitting participating in anti-Muslim warfare in the past.

But recent statements by the so-called "United Indigenous Nations of Mindanao" have become more strident. The coalition, formed after eighteen "tribes" and eight "sub-tribes" met in an "Indigenous People's Summit" on 24 July 2006, declared its "strong opposition for the inclusion of Our Ancestral Domains/Ancestral Lands in the Bangsamoro homeland". It cited ten reasons for its opposition, underscoring the *lumads'* distinct and older relationship with their ancestral domains, which accordingly gives them exclusive right to "utilize the natural resources inside our territories based on our customary laws". These rights and privileges will be negated if a Bangsamoro homeland is created, for the new order "will destruct (sic) our customary use of natural resources inside our territories". Moreover, whatever agreements the government and the MILF will reach over the issue of ancestral domain will simply "violate the traditional agreements" between the *lumads'* gods and ancestors and the existing communities. The MILF avoided a direct response but invoked its right to "draw first the mechanics" of the ancestral domain issue with the government.[38]

These kinds of tensions indirectly feed the strong anti-Muslim bias of Christian groups in Mindanao. Fierce opposition to any state project that appears to give Muslims considerable influence in Mindanao persists.[39] Christian leaders can maintain this belligerent posturing since anti-Muslim biases are still prevalent nationwide. A 2005 survey of Filipino perceptions of Muslims showed that

> A majority of Filipinos (still) think that Muslims are probably more prone to run amok (55 per cent) although probably not oppressive to women (59 per cent). A plurality believes that Muslims are probably terrorists or extremists (47 per cent) and that they probably consider

> themselves as Filipinos (49 per cent). There are equal percentages (44 per cent) of those who believe that Muslims probably secretly hate all non-Muslims and those who do not.[40]

This bigotry also endures because the MNLF and MILF have done very little to reach out to Christians. Neither have special units devoted to "united front" work as does the communist party's National Democratic Front (NDF). This organizational oversight is costing both movements dearly in lost opportunities. For the same pro-autonomy (and often separatist) and anti-Manila sentiments are becoming strong in the Christian provinces of Mindanao, creating the possibility of an actual tri-people's political alliance against "imperial Manila".[41]

If we place these present-day complexities alongside an anti-mythical reading of the past, the portrait of a unified, single-minded, history-inspired *umma* fighting a war against an intrusive Filipino state unravels. Replacing it are a fractured past and a present story anchored in modern-day factors. Even the MNLF was aware of being too bound to the myth. Its first manifesto was permeated by modern themes with very little mention of "traditional sources of authority" or the MNLF's links to the past. The *Bangsamoro Republik* would be "a democratic system of government" that would respect the basic rights of peoples in the same manner as any other democratic, modern nation-state. It would not revive the sultanate but rather transcend it, becoming "one of the members of the family of independent and sovereign nations in the world".[42] What does this make the MNLF rebellion if not modern?

In part because it is more aware of the problematic connections between "traditional" and "modern" forms of authorities, the MILF has distanced itself from the MNLF's republicanism and proposed a modified restoration of the sultanates. Its top ideologue, Jubair, argues that it is difficult to separate "the formation of *Moro* nationalism [from] the survival of the *Moro* people through the centuries".[43] He adds that had the Muslims been "[l]eft to themselves, they might have developed into unified and constitutional sultanates or evolved into a political system of the Malaysian pattern, where the different princely states are federated and headed by a paramount ruler, although he is not the repository of the powers and functions."[44] This is a bizarre musing — the disempowered sultans were retained on their thrones to help legitimize British colonial rule. Much like the Americans restoring the Japanese emperor as they ruled over postwar Japan, or the Thai oligarchy returning symbolic power to the king in order to consolidate their rule, the British gave back the sultanates their lost pomp and glory — *sans* the power — to make colonial rule palatable.[45] In the post-colonial period none of these have ever governed. It goes without saying that these overlords were/are representatives of modern power, albeit wrapped in traditional garb. If this is the model the MILF has in mind, then it is really no different from the MNLF's *Bangsamoro Republik* — which simply brings us back to the issue of modernity.

THE GEOGRAPHY OF THE WAR

The *Bangsamoro Republik* is meant to be comprised of Mindanao, the Sulu archipelago and Palawan island in western central Philippines. Giving this geo-body some corporeality is, however, easier said than done. For one, plebiscite after plebiscite has demonstrated that the majority of the people of these areas do not support separatism. It has not helped that within the Muslim provinces themselves divisions persist. Moreover, the footprint of the *Bangsamoro* territory is modern. This point appears to elude the MNLF and MILF leaders who imagined what the future republic would look like. But it is a lapse that is not entirely unique to them; they share it with nationalist predecessors who unquestioningly adopted the juridical frame crafted by former colonizers, and only later on would embellish it with a history that predates the colonial period and hence deny the state's real origins.[46] In the *Bangsamoro* geo-body's case, it was first visualized by the Spaniards to describe areas over which they had only limited control. It was under the Americans that Mindanao (or more specifically southern Mindanao), Sulu and Palawan were eventually pacified and integrated into the Philippine colonial state.

What makes this future republic most surreal is the discrepancy between the hype surrounding its eventual realization and the actual daily military effort to make the dream come true. A preliminary mapping of the areas of conflict based on available newspaper data shows that the war has been confined to the provinces of southwestern Mindanao and affects, on the average, less than 50 per cent of their populations.[47] The data show that MNLF-AFP (1977–2001) conflicts occurred mainly in the provinces of Basilan, Lanao del Sur, Zamboanga del Sur and Maguindanao (Table 12.2). But breaking down the data further shows that clashes have been clustered in specific communities. In only two areas in Lanao del Sur province (Ramain municipality and in the outskirts of Marawi City), for example, were there repeated military encounters; other places reported only single confrontations. The MNLF tried to open up new battle zones in the non-Muslim provinces, but this offensive came late in the game. Negotiations were winding down and a peace agreement was soon to be signed.[48] AFP-MILF skirmishes have been more frequent, with the MILF showing more initiative than its

TABLE 12.2
Preliminary Data on AFP-MNLF Battles and Locations, 1977–2001

Province/City	*Year*	*Municipality*	*Municipality Population*	*Total Municipalities*	*Provincial Population*	*Population plus cities*	*Municipality/ Provincial Population (percentage)*	*Municipality/ Provincial Population (percentage plus cities)*
Basilan	1973	Basilan City	48,092		171,027	171,027	28.12	28.12
	1980	Isabela	49,891		201,407	201,407	24.77	24.77
Davao del Norte	1984	Mawalo		10	590,015	590,015		
	1987	Tagum			590,015	590,015	22.96	22.96
		Pantulan						
Davao del Sur	2001	Don Marcelino	33,403	15	758,801		4.40	
Lanao del Norte	1989	Bukidnon border		23				
Lanao del Sur	1983	Piagapo	12,108	37	351,159	404,971	3.45	2.99
		Ramain (4)	11,024		351,159	404,971	3.14	2.72
		Lumba-a-Bayabao	17,031		351,159	404,971	4.85	4.21
		Maguing	6,784		351,159	404,971	1.93	1.68
	1984	Ramain	13,332		508,081	599,982	2.62	2.22
	1986	Marawi City	91,901		508,081	599,982	18.09	15.32
	2001	Marawi City	131,090		669,072	599,982	806304	21.85
Maguindanao	1989	Upi	51,141		801,102	801,102	6.38	6.38
	1990	Buldon	26,903		806,304	806,304	3.34	3.34
	2002	Datu Piang	67,303		806,304	806,304	8.35	8.35
North Cotabato	1988	Alamada			862,666	862,666		
Zamboanga del Norte	1972	Sibuco	19,357		490,515	490,515	3.95	3.95
	1973	Sibuco-Siraway	19,357		490,515	490,515	3.95	3.95
Zamboanga del Sur	1973	Labangan	16,257		737,829	1,002,852	2.20	1.62
	1987	Olutangan	16,378		1,102,779	1,446,521	1.49	1.13
		Zamboanga City	343,722		1,102,779	1,446,521	31.17	23.76
	2001	Zamboanga City	601,794		1,333,456	1,935,250	45.13	31.10
	2002	Zamboanga City	601,794		1,333,456	1,935,250	45.13	31.10

Sources: Database collection, Patricio N. Abinales and Edmund Ramos (2005); and Republic of the Philippines. National Census and Statistics Office (Manila, 2000). Henceforth NCSO.

predecessor. Its forces have fought the government in more municipalities and, in 2001, it made a daring attempt to bring the war to the Christian provinces and even to the northern island of Luzon (Table 12.3). But, in the main, its zone of operations remains within the Muslim areas of Mindanao.

The most obvious explanation behind this constricted space is military: the AFP has superior firepower and faces no manpower problems. The MNLF and the MILF could match the AFP in terms of the quantity and quality of their firearms, but they lack the more strategic weaponry — tanks, artillery, air power — necessary to even the match. American military assistance to the Philippine government has varied in amount through the years, but not once has it been cut off. Material support to the MNLF and the MILF from abroad however has been inconsistent. The MNLF received extensive military aid from Libya and Malaysia in the early days of the war, but this declined once the negotiations were opened. It is unclear where the MILF derives it military support, but with Malaysia and Indonesia pushing for the negotiations, the southern routes through which guns and other munitions are smuggled to the MILF may eventually be sealed.[49]

An ancillary reason has been mentioned above — the limited if not absent support for the separatist cause from the non-Muslim Mindanao communities. The anti-Muslim bias of the Christian groups and the persistent suspicions of the *lumad* communities effectively create a political wall that impedes separatist expansion and isolates the MNLF and MILF from the rest of Mindanao. The warning of government negotiator Simeon Datumanong to Misuari when they met in the 1970s captured this dilemma quite well:

> I explained to [Misuari] that Mindanao up to Palawan consisted of about 12 million people [of which] only 3.5 million are Muslims. I said that the Muslims are in the minority and since this is only going to be [an] autonomy [issue] the mode of selecting a leader shall be by election. It is always the situation that the majority will win over the minority. And on top of the fact that Muslims are minorities, there are also three major tribes who have political rivalries. The Tausug, his tribe will put up a candidate; the Maguindanawons, my tribe will put up a candidate, the Maranao tribe of Ambassador Pangandaman will also put up a candidate. All the three candidates together against the majority, the Muslims will lose. And I said if the Muslims will lose, the leadership of the region will be taken away from the Muslims. What are you going to do? Go back to the hills and fight again? Our exchange was candid.[50]

But this handicap suggests something more: while the MNLF and MILF claim to be revolutionary organizations, their military actions show them to

TABLE 12.3
Preliminary Data on AFP-MILF Number of Battles and Locations, 1987–2004

Province/City	*Year*	*Municipality*	*Municipality Population*	*Total Municipalities*	*Provincial Population*	*Population plus cities*	*Municipality/ Provincial Population (percentage)*	*Municipality/ Provincial Population (percentage plus cities)*
Basilan	1999	Tipo-Tipo	48,284	6	259,796	259,796	18.6	18.6
	2001	unspecified		1 city				
	2003	Lamitan						
Davao Oriental	2000	Tarragona	22,848	11	446,191	446,191	5.12	5.12
Davao del Sur	2000	Kiblawan (3)	41,275	16	758,801	1,905,917	5.4	2.2
		Davao City	1,147,116	(including				
		Toril (2)	41,275	Davao City)			5.44	2.17
	2003	Sta. Cruz	67,317				8.87	3.53
Lanao del Norte	2000	Bacolod	17,020	23	473,062	758,123	3.6	2.25
		Baloi	38,534	(including			8.15	5.08
		Inundaran (2)		Iligan City)				
		Kauswagan (3)	15,364				3.25	2.03
		Matungao	9,226				1.95	1.22
		Munai	15,972				3.38	2.11
		Pacalundo						
		Tagoloan	8,223					
	2001	Iligan City	285,061		473,062	758,123	60.26	37.60
		Kauswagan						
	2003	Bacolod			473,062	758,123		
		Baloi (2)						
		Kauswagan (2)						
		Maigo	17,826				3.77	2.35
		Pantao-Ragat	16,474				3.48	2.17

Lanao del Sur	1999	Calanugas	9,989	37	669,072	800,162	1.49	1.25
	2000	Calanugas	9,989		669,072	800,162	1.49	1.25
		Dagupan						
		Malabang (2)	33,177				4.96	4.15
		Marawi City	131,090				19.59	16.38
	2001	Marawi City			669,072	800,162		
	2002	Calanugas	9,989		669,072	800,162	1.49	1.49
		Marawi City	131,090				19.59	16.38
		Piagpao	23,903				3.57	2.99
	2004	Masiu	24,105		669,072	800,162	3.60	3.01
Maguindanao	1987	Buluan	58,785		801,102		7.34	
	1994–96	Sultan sa barongis	34,709		801,102		4.33	
	1997	Raja Muda						
	1999	Buluan	58,785		806,934		7.28	
		Datu Paglas	20,014				2.48	
		Datu Piang	67,303				8.34	
		Matanog (2)	19,006				2.36	
		Pagalungan	25,908				3.21	
	2000	Ampatuan	32,907		806,934		4.08	
		Camp Abu Bakr						
		Buldon	26,903				3.33	
		Gayunga						
		Ginibon						
		Mamasapano	20,059				2.49	
		Matanog (4)	19,006				2.36	
		N. Ramos Highway						
		Oring						
		Shariff Aguak (3)						
		Talayan (6)	33,129				4.11	

continued on next page

TABLE 12.3 — *continued*

Province/City	*Year*	*Municipality*	*Municipality Population*	*Total Municipalities*	*Provincial Population*	*Population plus cities*	*Municipality/ Provincial Population (percentage)*	*Municipality/ Provincial Population (percentage plus cities)*
	2001	Ampatuan	32,907		806,934	964,951	4.08	3.41
		Bagan						
		Barira (2)	18,296				2.27	1.90
		Buldon (2)	26,903				3.33	2.79
		Cotabato City	163,849				20.31	16.98
		Datu Paglas	20,014				2.48	2.07
		Datu Piang (2)	67,303				8.34	6.97
		Matanog (2)	19,006				2.36	1.97
		Pagalungan	25,908				3.21	2.68
		Parang	60,935				7.55	6.31
		Shariff Aguak						
		Sultan sa Barongis	34,709				4.30	3.60
	2002	Barira	18,296		806,934	964,951	2.27	1.90
		Datu Piang	67,303				8.34	6.97
	2003	Barira (3)	18,296		806,934	964,951	2.27	1.90
		Buldon	26,903				3.33	2.79
		Datu Paglas	20,014				2.48	2.07
		Datu Piang (4)	67,303				8.34	6.97
		Datu Odin Sinsuat	71,569				8.87	7.42
		Pagalungan (2)	25,908				3.21	2.68
		South Upi	51,141				6.34	5.30
		Sultan sa Barongis	34,709				4.30	3.60

		Talayan	33,129			4.11	3.43
		Talitay	17,026			2.11	1.76
	2004	Matanog	19,006	806,934	964,951	2.36	1.97
Cotabato (formerly north Cotabato)	1994	Carmen (2)	35,895	862,666	862,666	4.16	4.16
	1996	Carmen (2)					
	1997	Pikit	57,909	862.666	862,666	6.71	6.71
	1999	Banisilan	35,539	958,643	958,643	3.7	4.30
		Kabacan	61,998			6.5	6.5
		Kidapawan	101,205			10.6	10.6
		Matalam	60,146			6.3	6.3
		Mlang	78,170			8.2	8.2
	2000	Aleosan	26,164	958,643	958,643	2.7	2.73
		Carmen	45,909			4.8	4.79
		Kabacan (3)	61,998			6.5	6.47
		Magpet	38,973			4.1	4.07
		Midsayap (2)	105,760			11.0	11.03
		Mlang	78,170			8.2	8.15
		Tulunan	41,756			4.4	4.36
	2001	Bukidnon border		958,643	958,643		
		Carmen (2)	45,909			4.8	4.8
		Kabacan (2)	61,998			6.5	6.5
		Tulunan	41,756			4.4	4.4
	2003	Buliok (2)		958,643	958,643		
		Carmen (2)	45,909			4.8	4.8
		Kabacan	61,998			6.5	6.5
		Midsayap	105,760			11.0	11.0
		Mlang (3)	78,170			8.2	8.2
		Pikit (11)	68,455			7.1	7.1

continued on next page

TABLE 12.3 — *continued*

Province/City	*Year*	*Municipality*	*Municipality Population*	*Total Municipalities*	*Provincial Population*	*Population plus cities*	*Municipality/ Provincial Population (percentage)*	*Municipality/ Provincial Population (percentage plus cities)*
Sultan Kudarat	1999	Unspecified (3)		12	586,595	586,595		
	2000	Unspecified (2)						
	2002	unspecified						
	2003	Columbio	21,698				3.70	3.70
Sulu	2000	Patikul	34,396	24	619,668	619,668	5.55	5.55
	2001	Parang	54,994				8.87	8.87
	2002	Jolo	87,998				14.20	14.20
Zambales (Luzon)	2001	Dagupan City						
Zamboanga del Norte	1999	Sibuoco-Sirawai	23,243	28	770,697	770,697	3.02	3.02
	2000	Sibuoco-Sirawai	23,243	28	823,130	823,130	2.82	2.82
	2001	Siocon	32,699	28	823,130	823,130	3.97	3.97
Zamboanga del Sur	2001	Zamboanga City (2)	601,794		1,333,456		45.13	45.13
		Zamboanga City						
	2002	Pagadian City	142,515		1,333,456	1,333,456	10.69	10.69
	2003	Zamboang City	601,794		1,333,456	1,333,456	45.13	45.13

Sources: Database collection, Patricio N. Abinales and Edmund Ramos (2005); and NCSO 2000.

constantly err on the side of caution. Battles like the burning of Jolo in February 1974 and the first MNLF assaults on AFP positions soon after martial law was declared were epic; they were also the exception. The majority of the engagements between the AFP and the MNLF were unplanned, and while the MILF has been more daring, chance encounters were still at par with planned assaults and ambuscades (Tables 12.4 and 12.5). Moreover,

TABLE 12.4
Types of Military Encounters, MNLF-AFP, 1972–2002

Year	*AFP-initiated*	*MNLF-initiated*	*Chance Encounters*
1972	2	2	1
1973	6		8
1983		1	1
1984	3	1	2
1986	2		2
1987	2	1	3
1988		1	1
1989		3	1
1990		3	
1993	1	2	
2001	1	2	4
2002			1
Total	17	16	22

Source: Abinales and Ramos datafile (2004).

TABLE 12.5
Types of Military Encounters, MILF-AFP, 1987–2003

Year	*AFP-initiated*	*MNLF-initiated*	*Chance Encounters*
1987			1
1994	1	1	
1995		1	
1996	1	2	1
1997	1		
1999	4	1	15
2000	23	29	26
2001	1	12	14
2002	1	5	4
2003	6	37	48
2004	1		1
Total	39	97	110

Source: Abinales and Ramos datafile (2004).

when it does take the initiative against the AFP, MILF losses have been relatively high (Table 12.6). MILF manpower has been in decline since the AFP captured its headquarters, Camp Abu Bakr, in Pikit, North Cotabato, in 2000.[51] The peace talks and arrival of monitoring teams from Muslim countries have also put a damper on its military operations.

Those familiar with Maoist military strategy will know, however, that this relative weakness also creates tactical opportunities for a smaller revolutionary force. The Communist Party of the Philippines (CPP) has overcome this disadvantage by being selective in its military operations (hence always having the initiative) and using its mobility to cover the wide expanse of a guerrilla front. The CPP's New People's Army (NPA) also operated mini-school and health units aimed at capturing the hearts and minds of peasants.[52] This strategy has enabled the CPP to build guerrilla zones nationwide and become the most serious threat to the Marcos dictatorship in the 1970s and 1980s. After a brief internal crisis, which splintered the party in the post-Marcos period, the victorious faction has successfully recovered the majority of guerilla zones it had to abandon in the immediate past.[53] Nothing comparable has happened with the MNLF and

TABLE 12.6
Combatants Killed and Injured in Armed Encounters, AFP, MNLF, MILF, by Administration, 1986–2004

Casualties	*Aquino*	*Ramos*	*Estrada*	*Arroyo*	*Total*
MNLF-AFP					
MNLF killed	66	0	139	2	207
MNLF injured	12	0	0	0	12
AFP killed	55	50	21	5	131
AFP injured	18	1	8	0	27
Sub-Total	151	51	168	7	377
MILF-AFP					
MILF killed	2	213	471	492	1,178
MILF injured	0	7	92	108	207
AFP killed	5	26	222	222	475
AFP injured	0	11	270	218	499
Sub-Total	7	257	1,055	1,040	2,359

Source: Maria Cynthia Rose Banzon Bautista, "Ideologically Motivated Conflicts in the Philippines: Exploring the Possibility of an Early Warning System", a background paper submitted to the Human Development Network Foundation, Inc, for the Philippine Human Development Report 2005, p. 4.

the MILF. Despite the claims of MILF deputy information head Khaled Musa that his organization is "capable and experienced in the art of revolution", the MILF and the MNLF are defensive military organizations, worried primarily about how to maintain physical control of certain towns, municipalities and city outskirts.[54] When they sent battle teams to operate beyond their comfort zones, their effectiveness is limited: after one or two encounters these units disappear or are eliminated. How can one begin to realize the *Bangsamoro* homeland if one's military and political priorities are simply to defend Pikit, Buldon, Matanog and the Buliok complex?

While narrow and limited, this war has nevertheless done extensive collateral damage to the communities affected and the surrounding areas. The exceptional synthesis by the NGO Human Development Network of the social cost of the conflict shows a relatively high and oddly uniform number of casualties among combatants and civilians caught in the crossfire as well as individuals and families displaced by the war since skirmishes began in 1969: 60,000 dead, 54,000 wounded, and 350,000 displaced from their homes (Table 12.7).[55] Congressman Eduardo Ermita, now President Arroyo's executive secretary, gave a higher total in a 1996 speech delivered in the House of Representatives:

> [AFP data] indicate that over a period of 26 years since 1970, more than 100,000 persons were killed in the conflict in southern Philippines. The government suffered about 30 per cent of casualties; the rebels more than 50 percent; while civilians caught in the crossfire came to about 20 per cent of total casualties. About 55,000 persons were wounded, not counting those from the rebel side. From 1970 to 1975 alone, an average of 18 people was slain every day.[56]

TABLE 12.7
Counting the Cost of the Protracted War in Southern Philippines, 1969–1996

Area	*Dead*	*Wounded*	*Displaced*
Cotabato	20,000	8,000	100, 000
Lanao	10,000	20,000	70,000
Sulu, Tawi-Tawi	10,000	8,000	100,000
Zamboanga	10,000	10,000	40,000
Basilan	10,000	8,000	40,000
Total	60,000	54,000	350,000

Source: Philippine Human Development Report 2005, p. 72.

The leftwing research institute Ibon Foundation estimates the total cost of the war since 1973 to be about P73 billion, or P7.1 million per day in fighting, a figure that the anti-communist and former military man Ermita has also used.[57]

These statistics are the most crucial element in understanding why, despite its limited support and area of conflict, the separatist war perpetuates the image of an unstable "Mindanao" and a perpetually rebellious *umma*. It is not the scale or breadth of the confrontations *per se*, but the reverberations in the battle zones and in the adjoining areas. The apprehension that conflict could recur in these areas aggravates the instability and sustains the reluctance of displaced families to return and start the process of recovery; instead they maintain a nomadic existence as internal refugees.[58] This "fear of war", in turn, sustains the premise of a Muslim Mindanao history defined by repression and resistance. Minimizing this fear may be one of the keys to resolving the conflict.

WAR FATIGUE AND THE LURE OF *CACIQUE* DEMOCRACY

The current problems faced by Muslim separatism may pale in comparison to one larger strategic dilemma: the absence of any concrete vision of an alternative society articulated by the separatist group. The MNLF was never able to present specific policies based on a systematic evaluation of the potentials and problems of winning power. Lacking a blueprint for the *Bangsamoro Republik*, its leadership became vulnerable in the peace negotiations, completely dependent on Libya until the peace talks were moved to Southeast Asia. It was inconsistent in defending its positions and in generating proposals, and kept off-balance by a better-prepared Philippine team.[59] According to one Marcos official: "[T]he MNLF panel did not seem prepared to discuss any social or economic plan for the rehabilitation and development of the Muslim peoples; they were not even prepared to discuss anything having to do with the political and administrative aspects of greater local autonomy for these areas."[60] Nur Misuari and his comrades also had nothing to say about what a future society would look like in the Christian and *lumad* areas.

After signing the peace agreement, President Fidel Ramos worked to ensure that Misuari won the ARMM governorship.[61] Yet, it was a coming to power not to his liking; and one that ultimately proved the undoing of this exhausted rebel leader.[62] An organization already suffering from internal splits, wholesale capitulation of local commands, weak ideological unity, declining resources, and a leadership inexperienced in governance, the MNLF became mired in the inefficiency and corruption of the ARMM.[63] By the time of the signing, it was also clearly an exhausted and aging army. Despite initial fears by the AFP senior leadership that the integration of certain units of the MNLF would be divisive to the military, it turned out that of the 5,750 MNLF fighters who would join the military, only 140 qualified. The rest were either too sick or too old to continue combat duty.[64]

The MNLF may have also produced good fighters, but when it came to running offices or development programmes, the same manpower was hobbled by immaturity and inexperience. Misuari symbolized this predicament. As governor, he was unable to end ARMM's insidious spoils system and failed to stop the haemorrhage of funds due to mismanagement.[65] The MNLF leader himself became enamored with the trappings of power. The simplicity of his lifestyle — a source of attraction and inspiration to his followers — was replaced by that of the traditional politician: bodyguards, convoys, a large entourage renting entire hotel floors, travel junkets, etc., all in the name of the Moro struggle. Critics accused him of "living like an oil sheik", tapping public funds and financial support from international agencies and donor governments to sustain his new lifestyle.[66] When his term ended in 2001, Misuari refused to step down and instigated a mini-revolt among his dwindling band of loyalists. It was easily crushed and Misuari, who escaped to Sabah, was later sent back to the Philippines by a Malaysian government tired of supporting a failed rebellion.

The final nail in Misuari's political coffin was driven in by his own comrades; judged "incompetent" as MNLF chairman by a new council of fifteen, he was "retired" and given the title "chairman emeritus". The council then announced to the public that it was taking over the MNLF leadership.[67] Misuari is now under house arrest, a broken man awaiting trial for his aborted 2001 revolt. Manila has reasserted its control over the ARMM's funds, deepening its fiscal dependence on the national capital.[68] Governance continues to be plagued by corruption and mismanagement, with the Commission on Audit discovering anomalous transactions in the region's education department "involving unreported negotiated checks worth P1.02 billion and erroneous bank debits amounting to P7.6 billion".[69] After two successive terms of former MNLF leaders (Misuari's successor, Dr Parouk Hussein, was a member of the MNLF central committee), President Arroyo returned control of ARMM to the political clans; she oversaw the electoral victory of the Ampatuans, the most powerful Maguindanao political family.[70] The restoration of the traditional elite was easily accomplished.[71] "Feudalism", complained one Muslim leader, has never been exterminated by separatism and the "feudal lords" of the late colonial and immediate postwar periods never disappeared.[72] The Muslim provinces continue to lag behind the rest of the country in terms of economic development, social indicators and health of the population — a despicable situation caused by government neglect, the war and the patrimonial rapaciousness of local elites.[73]

The MILF has chosen to remain aloof from these developments insisting, "the common Bangsamoro folk are not taking the ARMM polls 'seriously' because they do not see any role that they can play in the way it is run."[74] The immediate reason for not participating in "traditional politics" is the MILF's continued commitment to independence.[75] Despite this stance, the MILF has not clarified some of its basic positions. The late Hashim Salamat, the MILF's founding chairman, admitted to a lack of consensus on what an independent Islamic state would look like, other than having the Koran as the basis of its law, "not a man-made constitution."[76] There is no sign that his successors, Al Haj Murad Ebrahim and comrades, have given the future any more substance. They seem content to restate that governance will be based on "the teachings of Islam".

The peace talks are proceeding under a vaguely-defined framework, making them "highly volatile, tenuous, insubstantial, and limited to ceasefire agreements (oftentimes breached rather than respected)". [77] But there are some positive signs that the current negotiation will be different. The Arroyo government and the MILF have agreed to a set of "consensus points", which include more specific powers for whatever "system of government suitable and acceptable to [the Bangsamoro people] as a distinct dominant people".[78] The government has given its support to the MILF's Bangsa Moro Development Agency, established in June 2002 to spearhead rehabilitation and recovery plans, which include skills training for MILF fighters to prepare them for the post-war period.[79] Yet, at a certain point, the two parties will have to address the issue of separatism. And while there is less public sympathy among Muslims and non-Muslims for a return to all-out war, the structural, institutional, and political weaknesses that the government and separatist movements are still unable to solve could trigger another short but intense wave of violence. The only thing definite at this point is that optimism prevails among all parties involved.

CONCLUSION

Today's new crop of writings and opinions on Muslim separatism echoes the arguments raised almost half a century ago: the origins or root causes of the rebellions, the long history of Muslim alienation from the national body politic, and the consistent failure of government efforts to address the pervasive deprivation of the Muslim provinces.[80] And because none attempt to transcend older studies, these works repeat the conspicuous lapses of their elders.[81] This chapter has tried to shake this deeply embedded perspective a bit by highlighting the antinomies of the separatist rebellions. It has argued that the dynamics and failure of separatism can be better understood if it is delinked from the mythology of a long history of Muslim "resistance" and seen as a modern phenomenon in which contradictions co-exist alongside uniting elements. Finally, while viewing the current government-MILF peace talks as a significant development, the chapter also cautions optimists on the perils of placing revolutionaries prematurely in seats of state power and of concluding a peace with little idea of what a reconfigured future Muslim Mindanao political zone would look like.

Pro-separatist academics and public intellectuals will probably have a lot to say in response to these arguments. But in his introduction to the 1999 edition of Jubair's book, the eminent Maguindanao politician, public intellectual, historian and now MILF adviser, Datu Michael Mastura, declared that the value of the book lies "in the documentation of sentiments and aspirations that now invite open debates."[82] For someone who believes strongly in the myth, this was a strange way of closing an introduction to the most comprehensive defence of separatism by far. It is evidently a challenge to anti-separatists to engage Jubair's book. It may also be read as a subtle recognition that the myth is no longer invincible; that some of the criticisms directed against it and its practitioners may need to be taken into consideration. It may also be an indirect admission that separatism may just be too utopian a goal, and that perhaps it might be wiser to fight for a lesser goal: a better version of autonomy perhaps?

We may never know what motivated an exceptional political survivor like Mastura to make this call. All we can do is take him up on his offer and hopefully help initiate a series of dialogues and debates — passionate, lively and empirically grounded — to help clarify the separatist question and continue to expand the spaces of peace and stability that are now spreading all over southeastern Mindanao.

Acknowledgement

I would like to thank Donna J. Amoroso for her comments and criticisms. All shortcomings are mine.

Notes

1 As quoted by Donald Kirk, *Philippines in Crisis: U.S. Power versus Local Revolt* (Pasig City: Anvil Publishing, 2005), p. 132.

2 Edward Said, *Culture and Resistance: Conversations with Edward Said*, edited by David Barsamian (Cambridge, Massachusetts: Southend Press, 2003), p. 62.

3 On the MILF's justification for inviting the Americans, see Abhoud Syed M. Lingga, "The U.S. Role in the Mindanao Peace Process: Bangsamoro Perspective", presentation given at the symposium on The U.S. Role in the Indonesian and Philippine Peace Processes, Asian Center, University of the Philippines, 27 November 2003.

4 I exclude the Abu Sayyaf group (ASG) for the simple reason that it is nothing but a kidnapping enterprise with no interest at all in separatism. The ASG's notorious resume, however, has been upgraded with the addition of the title "Islamic radical", thanks in part to the spin of a bevy of "counter-terrorism" experts. For a critique of this extremely lucrative but intellectually problematic line of work, see Natasha Hamilton-Hart, "Terrorism in Southeast Asia: Expert Analysis, Myopia and Fantasy", *The Pacific Review* 18, no. 3 (September 2005): 303–25.

5 See, for example, Amado Guerrero, *Philippine Society and Revolution* (Hong Kong: Ta Kung Pao, 1971), p. 272; and Romeo Intengan, "Christian Social Ethics and the SPCPD", *Moro Kurier* (October–November 1996): 2–4.

6 Only recently has the OIC warmed up to the MILF.

7 See <http://news.bbc.co.uk/1/hi/world/asia-pacific/1695576.stm> (accessed 12 May 2006). See also "Securing Peace in Mindanao: Resolving the Roots of Conflict", co-sponsored with the Asia Society and the Woodrow Wilson International Center for Scholars, 28 September 2004, <http://www.usip.org/events/2004/0928_wksphillippines.html> (accessed 12 May 2006).

8 For a sense of the intensity of the war, see Fortunato U. Abat, *The Day We Nearly Lost Mindanao: The CEMCOM Story* (Manila: SBA Printers, Inc., 1994). The Huk rebellion — formally communist-led, but exhibiting multifarious ideological threads and political sentiments, including peasant desires to be left alone — was mainly a guerrilla war. On the Huks, the classic book is still Benedict Kerklviet's, *The Huk Rebellion: A Study of Peasant Revolt in the Philippines*. Second edition (Lapham, Maryland: Rowman and Littlefield, 2002).

9 B.R. Rodil, *Kalinaw Mindanaw: The Story of the GRP-MNLF Peace Process, 1975–1996* (Davao: Alternate Forum for Research in Mindanao, 2000), pp. 3–11.

10 The more notable studies on the Muslim Mindanao include Peter Gowing, *Muslim Filipinos: Heritage and Horizon* (Quezon City: New Day Publishers, 1979); Peter Gowing, *Understanding Islam and the Muslims in the Philippines* (New Day Publishers, 1988); Cesar Adib Majul, *Muslims in the Philippines* (Quezon City: University of the Philippines Press, 1973); Michael Mastura, *Muslim-Filipino Experience: A Collection of Essays* (Manila: OCIA Publications, 1984); Samuel K. Tan, *Selected Essays on the Filipino Muslim* (Marawi City: Mindanao State University Research Center, 1982); and, Samuel K. Tan, *Decolonization and Filipino Muslim Identity* (Quezon City: University of the Philippines Department of History, 1989).

11 Madge Kho, "100 Years of Moro Resistance: A Chronology of Historical Events", <http://www.upd.edu.ph/~iis/page2_100years.html> (accessed 16 May 2006). Strangely, Matalam's "movement" is excluded in this recounting.

12 James Francis Warren, *The Sulu Zone, 1768–1898: The Dynamics of External Trade, Slavery, and Ethnicity in the Transformation of a Southeast Asian Maritime State* (Quezon City: New Day Publishers, 1985).

13 Reynaldo Ileto, *Maguindanao 1860–1888: The Career of Datu Uto of Buayan* (Ithaca, New York: Cornell University Southeast Asia Program Data Paper no. 82, 1971).

14 O.W. Wolters, *History, Culture and Region in Southeast Asian Perspectives* (Singapore: Institute of Southeast Asian Studies, 1982).

15 Ruurdje Laarhoven, "From Ship to Shore: Maguindanao in the 17th Century from Dutch Sources", M.A. thesis, Ateneo de Manila University, 1985.

16 Patricio N. Abinales, *Making Mindanao: Cotabato and Davao in the Formation of the Philippine Nation-State* (Quezon City: Ateneo de Manila University Press, 2000), pp. 3, 134–42, 185–88.

17 W.K. Che Man, *Muslim Separatism: The Moros of Southern Philippines and the Malays of Southern Thailand* (Quezon City: Ateneo de Manila University Press, 1990), p. 125.

18 The classic example is congressman Gerry A. Salapuddin, acting chairman of the Basilan MNLF from 1972 to 1984 and presently house deputy speaker for Mindanao, <http://www.iro.ph/downloads/resumes/salapuddin.pdf> (accessed 27 May 2006).

19 Salah Jubair, *Bangsamoro: A Nation Under Endless Tyranny* (Kuala Lumpur: IQ Marin SDN BHD, 1999), p. 144. The book was first published in 1984.

20 Eric Gutierrez and Saturnino Borras, Jr., "The Moro Conflict: Landlessness and Misdirected State Policies", *Policy Studies 9*, East-West Center, Washington, 2004, pp. 2–3.

21 Gutierrez and Borras, "The Moro Conflict", p. 5. Gutierrez elaborates on these "entrepreneurs in violence" in an earlier essay, "In the Battlefields of the Warlord", in *Rebels, Warlords and Ulama: A Reader on Muslim Separatism and the War in Southern Philippines*, edited by Kristina Gaerlan and Mara Stankovich (Quezon City: Institute for Popular Democracy, 1999), pp. 41–84.

22 Samira Gutoc, "In Cold Blood", *Newsbreak*, 22 November 2004, pp. 26–28; and Marites Danguilan Vitug, "The Big Kill — Clan Wars not Terrorists or Rebels — are the Most Common Source of Violence in ARMM", *Newsbreak*, 25 April 2005, pp. 28–29.

23 Patricio P. Diaz, *Understanding Mindanao Conflict* (Davao City: Mindanews Publications, 2003), pp. 24–25.

24 Alunan Glang, *Muslim Secession or Integration?* (Quezon City: R.P. Garcia, 1969), p. 26.

25 Thomas M. McKenna, *Muslim Rulers and Rebels: Everyday Politics and Armed Separatism in the Southern Philippines* (Berkeley, Los Angeles and London: University of California Press, 1998), p. 186.

26 McKenna, *Muslim Rulers and Rebels*, p. 186.

27 Ibid., p. 185 (italics mine).

28 Rufa Cagoco-Guiam, "Demanding a Voice", *Accord* <http://www.cr.org/accord/min/accord6/cagoco.shtml> (accessed 30 May 2006). On the expanding role of Muslim women, see Masako Ishii, "Muslim Women and Social Change in Sarangani Region of Southern Philippines: Changing Social Norms of Women as Expressed in their Lifestyles", Ph.D. dissertation, Sophia University, Tokyo, 2000.

29 I owe this insight to Professor Rufa Guiam of Mindanao State University.

30 The exception is Maguindanao, home base of the Maguindanao-dominated MILF.

31 The BBC's observation that "the MILF has broad popular support in rural areas, where the lack of economic development has encouraged dissent" should therefore be taken with a grain of salt. *BBC News*, 17 March 2003.

32 Laura Lee Junker, *Raiding, Trading and Feasting: The Political Economy of Philippine Chiefdoms* (Honolulu: University of Hawaii Press, 1999), pp. 342–45. On filling the gap in the slave supply due to Spanish blockage by raiding the Mindanao upland communities, see Warren, *The Sulu Zone*, pp. 200–03.

33 The classic case of a Christian-*lumad* alliance to fight against Muslims is the brutal vigilante band of Feliciano "Kumander Toothpick" Luces. See T.J.S. George, *Revolt in Mindanao* (Kuala Lumpur: Oxford University Press, 1980), pp. 147–48; and Hilarion Gomez, Jr., *The Moro Rebellion and the Search for Peace: A Study on Christian-Muslim Relations in the Philippines* (Zamboanga City: Silsilah Publications, 2000), pp. 164–73.

34 "Lumads and the Peace Process: Interview with Ramon Moambing", *Accord* <http://www.c-r.org/accord/min/accord6/moambing.shtml> (accessed 30 May 2006).

35 See United States Institute of Peace, "Ancestral Domain in Comparative Perspective: A Workshop", <http://www.usip.org/events/2005/0524_philippine workshop.html> (accessed 26 May 2006); and "MILF to Start Advocacy on Ancestral Domain", *Luwaran.Com*, *http://www.luwaran.com/modules.php?name=News&file=article&sid=163* (accessed 26 May 2006). "RP-MILF peace talks in Malaysia make major breakthrough", <http://news.inq7.net/common/print.php?index=1&story_id=50494&site_id=18>, first posted 17 September 2006 (accessed 26 May 2006).

36 Interview with Ramon Moambing.

37 "Agenda for Peace of the Lumad in Mindanao", as quoted by B.R. Rodil, *A Story of Mindanao and Sulu in Question and Answer* (Davao City: MINCODE, 2003), p. 179.

38 Carolyn Arguillas, "Lumad Groups Oppose Inclusion in Bangsamoro Homeland", <http://mindanews.com/index.php?option=com_content&task=view&id=547&Itemid=75> (accessed 1 August 2006).

39 See the Christian response to the creation of a Muslim-controlled Southern Philippines Council for Peace and Development after the signing of the peace treaty with the MNLF, in "Peace Deal Reached to End Muslim Revolt in the Philippines", *CNN World News*, <http://www.cnn.com/WORLD/9608/30/philippines.peace/> (accessed 27 May 2006); and Tim Healy and Antonio Lopez, "The Anatomy of a Deal", *Asiaweek Magazine*, 13 September 1996, <http://www.pathfinder.com/Asiaweek/96/0913/nat1.html> (accessed 27 May 2006).

40 "Appendix 1.1. Measuring the Bias against Muslims", *Philippine Human Development Report 2005: Peace, Human Security and Human Development in the Philippines* (Manila: Human Development Network, 2005), p. 56.

41 See, for example, Reuben Canoy, *The Quest for Mindanao Independence* (Cagayan de Oro City: Mindanao Post Publishing, 1989). Among the prominent critics of "imperial Manila" is Davao City mayor Rodrigo Duterte who, in 2005, declared, "Let us establish an independent nation in Mindanao!" Rene Ezpeleta Bartolo, "Mindanao State of Mind", *The Filipino Reporter*, Year 33, no. 33, 29 July–4 August 2005 <http://www.filipinoreporter.com/archive/3333/headline04.htm> (accessed 27 June 2006).

42 "1974 Manifesto of the Moro National Liberation Front [on the] Establishment of the Bangsa Moro Republik", as reprinted in W.K. Che Man, *Muslim Separatism: The Moros of Southern Philippines and the Malays of Southern Thailand* (Quezon City: Ateneo de Manila University Press, 1974), pp. 189–90.

43 Jubair, *Bangsamoro*, p. 26.

44 Ibid., p. 127.

45 On the instrumentalization of the traditional Malay sultanates, see Anthony Milner, *The Invention of Politics in Colonial Malaya: Contesting Nationalism and the Expansion of the Public Sphere* (Cambridge: Cambridge University Press, 1994), and Donna J. Amoroso, "Traditionalism and the Ascendancy of the Malay Ruling Class in Colonial Malaya", Ph.D. dissertation, Cornell University, 1996. On Japan, see John W. Dower, *Embracing Defeat: Japan in the Wake of World War II* (New York: W.W. Norton and Company, Inc., 1999), pp. 280–301; and on Thailand, see Chris Baker and Pasuk Phongpaichit, *A History of Thailand* (Cambridge: Cambridge University Press, 2005), pp. 175–80.

46 On the mapping of nation-states, see Thongchai Winichakul, *Siam Mapped: A History of the Geo-Body of a Nation* (Honolulu: University of Hawaii Press, 1997).

47 The data are based on a compilation of news reports of MNLF-AFP and MILF-AFP encounters, collected by Ateneo de Manila University instructor Professor Edmund Ramos and myself.

48 Fighting were reported in one municipality in Palawan and Bukidnon provinces in 1986 and 1987, respectively; three municipalities in Davao del Norte in 1984 and 1987; one municipality in Davao del Sur in 2001; and two in the new province of Zamboanga Siraway in 1988. But there were no repeats.

49 Military assistance to the MNLF and MILF is an area that is still generally unexplored.

50 Simeon Datumanong (December 1976) as told to Rodil, *Kalinaw Mindanaw*, p. 43.

51 MILF forces reached 15,690 in 1999 but declined to 12,080 in 2003, and to 11,099 in 2004. See the statistics in Carolina G. Hernandez, "Institutional Responses to Armed Conflict: The Armed Forces of the Philippines", a background paper submitted to the Human Development Network Foundation, Inc, for the Philippine Human Development Report 2005, p. 26.

52 Francisco Nemenzo, Rectification Process in the Philippine Communist Movement", in *Armed Communist Movements in Southeast Asia*, edited by Lim Joo-Jock and Vani S. (Singapore: Institute for Southeast Asian Studies, 1984), pp. 90–99.

53 Patricio N. Abinales, "Asia's Last People's War: The Communist Insurgency in the Post-Marcos Philippines", paper presented at the Regional Workshop on Political Violence in Southeast Asia, sponsored by the Friedrich Ebert Stiftung, 14–15 March 2005, Bangkok, Thailand.

54 As quoted by Donna Pazibugan, "Gov't Troops Going Full Blast against NPA Rebels", *Philippine Daily Inquirer website* <http://newsinfo.inq7.net/inquirerheadlines/nation/view_article.php?article_id=5776> (accessed 21 June 2006).

55 *Philippine Human Development Report 2005*, p. 72. The authors of the report cited this estimate of Dr Inamullah Khan, the secretary-general of the World Muslim Congress, but do not explain why Khan's statistics on the deaths seemed to be stuck at 10,000. And if they are rounded figures, it becomes more puzzling why the authors decided to simplify these.

56 Eduardo Ermita, vice-chair of the GRP negotiating panel and representative, first district of Batangas, "To Win the Peace, to Build the Nation", speech at the House of Representatives, 23 July 1996. As quoted by Rodil, *Kalinaw Mindanaw*, pp. 8–9.

57 As cited by Miriam Coronel-Ferrer, "Costly Wars, Elusive Peace", *UP Forum* (March–April 2006) <http://www.up.edu.ph/forum/2006/Mar-Apr06/ferrer.htm> (accessed 1 May 2006). Ermita warned: "All in all, the AFP spent about 73 billion pesos in connection with the Mindanao conflict since 1970; or an average of 40 per cent of its annual budget. If this figure could be multiplied by the inflation rate over the years, it is truly a gargantuan expense." As quoted by Rodil, *Kalinaw Mindanaw*, p. 9.

58 In the case of the diaspora of Muslims from Lanao del Sur province, see *Philippine Human Development Report 2005*, pp. 22–23.

59 Marites Dañguilan Vitug and Glenda M. Gloria, *Under the Crescent Moon: Rebellion in Mindanao* (Quezon City: Ateneo Center for Social Policy and Public Affairs and the Institute for Popular Democracy, 2000), pp. 33–59.

60 Under-secretary of Defence Carmelo Z. Barbero, as quoted by Rodil, *Kalinaw*

Mindanaw, pp. 45–46. The split with the MILF served only to weaken further its position.

61 Vitug and Gloria, *Under the Crescent Moon*, pp. 43, 47–48.

62 According to Vitug and Gloria, Misuari was "simply tired of it all, [who] saw the peace process as the only way to retire gracefully from the battlefield". Vitug and Gloria, *Under the Crescent Moon*, p. 44.

63 Vitug and Gloria, *Under the Crescent Moon*, pp. 277–79, 285–86. Vitug and Gloria do cite examples of successful re-integration and recovery at the local level, but how many of these economic cooperatives succeeded and how many failed at the hands of the former guerillas remain unknown.

64 Comments made by Professor Alexander R. Magno at the conference, Whither the Philippines in the 21st Century?, Institute of Southeast Asian Studies, 14 July 2006. Magno was one of the government's consultants during the negotiations.

65 Carolyn Arguillas, "ARMM had P76.3 billion from 2001 to 2005 but…", *Mindanews* <http://www.mindanews.com/2006/05/06nws-armm.htm> (accessed 12 May 2005). See also "Peace in Mindanao: No Breakthrough yet", *University of the Philippines Forum*, 2 August 2002 <http://www.up.edu.ph/forum/2002/Aug02/peace.html> (accessed 30 May 2006).

66 "Philippine troops hunt for rebel governor in S. Philippines", *Asian Political News*, <http://findarticles.com/p/articles/mi_m0WDQ/is_2001_Nov_26/ai_81828061/> (accessed 30 May 2006).

67 Rizal G. Buendia."The GRP-MILF Peace Talks: Quo Vadis?" *Southeast Asian Affairs* (2004): 205.

68 "Amina Rasul-Bernardo, "Assessment of the Situation in Mindanao", *Public Perception of U.S.-Philippine Relations*, Asian Perspectives Seminar Series, The Asia Foundation, Washington, D.C., 14 September 2004, pp. 19–20.

69 Gemma Bagayaua, "Systems Breakdown", *Newsbreak*, 2 and 16 January 2006, pp. 49–50.

70 Jowel Canuday, "A Clan Rules ARMM", *Newsbreak*, 12 September 2005, p. 13.

71 These "feudal lords" played critical roles when the time came to pad Arroyo's "lead" in the last presidential elections. See Carolyn Arguillas, "Cheating Fields: The ARMM Votes can Make or Unmake a President", *Newsbreak*, 15 August 2005, pp. 17–19.

72 Rasul-Bernardo, "Assessment of the Situation in Mindanao", p. 10.

73 On the state of Muslim Mindanao's local economy and social conditions, see *Philippine Human Development Report 2005*, pp. 19–24, 1122–51.

74 Canuday, "A Clan Rules ARMM", p. 13.

75 Carolyn Arguillas, "Racing against Time", pp. 14–15.

76 Vitug and Gloria, *Under the Crescent Moon*, pp. 114–15.

77 Buendia, "The GRP-MILF Peace Talks: Quo Vadis?" p. 205.

78 Carolyn Arguillas, "The Road to the Final Agreement", p. 18.

79 "A view from the MILF: Interview with Mohagher Iqbal, Chair of the Committee

on Information of the MILF Central Committee", *Accord* <http://www.c-r.org/accord/min/accord6/cagoco.shtml> (accessed 30 May 2006). Rufa Cagoco-Guiam, "Negotiations and Detours: The Rocky Road to Peace in Mindanao", *Accord* <http://www.c-r.org/accord/min/accord6/cagoco.shtml> (accessed 30 May 2006).

80 Among the more recent accounts are *The Road to Peace and Reconciliation: Muslim Perspective on the Mindanao Conflict*, ed. Amina Rasul (Manila: Asian Institute of Management Policy Center, 2003); Macapado Anton Muslim, *The Moro Armed Struggle in the Philippines: the Non-Violence Alternative* (Marawi City: Mindanao State University, 1994); and Abhoud Syed M. Lingga, "Understanding Bangsamoro Independence as a Mode (sic) of Self-Determination", paper delivered at the Forum on Mindanao Peace, sponsored by the University of the Philippines Mindanao, the Philippine Development Assistance Program and the Association of Mindanao State University Alumni, Davao City, 28 February 2002.

81 Soliman Santos describes the MILF's negotiating strategy as "deliberate, well-thought-through, and sophisticated". He says very little about Malaysian pressure and MILF's defeats on the battlefield. Soliman M. Santos, Jr. *Dynamics and Directions of the GRP-MILF Peace Negotiations* (Davao: Alternate Forum for Research in Mindanao, Inc., 2005), p. 15.

82 Michael Mastura, Foreword to Jubair, *Bangsamoro*, p. x (italics mine).

References

Abat, Fortunato U. *The Day We Nearly Lost Mindanao: The CEMCOM Story*. Manila: SBA Printers, Inc., 1994.

Abinales, Patricio N. *Making Mindanao: Cotabato and Davao in the Formation of the Philippine Nation-State*. Quezon City: Ateneo de Manila University Press, 2000.

———. "Asia's Last People's War: The Communist Insurgency in the Post-Marcos Philippines." Paper presented at the Regional Workshop on Political Violence in Southeast Asia, sponsored by the Friedrich Ebert Stiftung, 14–15 March 2005, Bangkok, Thailand.

Amoroso, Donna J. "Traditionalism and the Ascendancy of the Malay Ruling Class in Colonial Malaya", Ph.D. dissertation, Cornell University, 1996.

Arguillas, Carolyn. "Cheating Fields: The ARMM votes can make or unmake a president", *Newsbreak*, 15 August 2005.

———. "The Road to the Final Agreement". *Newsbreak*, 2 and 16 January 2006.

———. "Racing against Time". *Newsbreak*, 2 and 16 January 2006.

Bagayaua, Gemma. "Systems Breakdown". *Newsbreak*, 2 and 16 January.

Baker, Chris and Pasuk Phongpaichit. *A History of Thailand*. Cambridge: Cambridge University Press, 2005.

Bautista, Maria Cynthia Rose Banzon. "Ideologically Motivated Conflicts in the

Philippines: Exploring the Possibility of an Early Warning System". A background paper submitted to the Human Development Network Foundation, Inc, for the Philippine Human Development Report 2005.

Buendia, Rizal G. "The GRP-MILF Peace Talks: Quo Vadis?" *Southeast Asian Affairs* (2004).

Canoy, Reuben. *The Quest for Mindanao Independence*. Cagayan de Oro City: Mindanao Post Publishing, 1989.

Canuday, Jowel. "A Clan Rules ARMM". *Newsbreak*, 12 September 2005.

Che Man, W.K. *Muslim Separatism: The Moros of Southern Philippines and the Malays of Southern Thailand*. Quezon City: Ateneo de Manila University Press, 1990.

Diaz, Patricio P. *Understanding Mindanao Conflict*. Davao City: Mindanews Publications, 2003.

Dower, John W. *Embracing Defeat: Japan in the Wake of World War II*. New York: W.W. Norton and Company, Inc., 1999.

George, T.J.S. *Revolt in Mindanao*, pp. 147–48; and 164–73. Kuala Lumpur: Oxford University Press, 1980.

Glang, Alunan. *Muslim Secession or Integration?* Quezon City: R.P. Garcia, 1969.

Gomez, Jr., Hilarion. *The Moro Rebellion and the Search for Peace: A Study on Christian-Muslim Relations in the Philippines*. Zamboanga City: Silsilah Publications, 2000.

Gowing, Peter. *Muslim Filipinos: Heritage and Horizon*. Quezon City: New Day Publishers, 1979.

———. *Understanding Islam and the Muslims in the Philippines*. Quezon City: New Day Publishers, 1988.

Guerrero, Amado. *Philippine Society and Revolution*. Hong Kong: Ta Kung Pao, 1971.

Guiam, Rufa Cagoco. "Negotiations and detours: the rocky road to peace in Mindanao". *Accord* <http://www.c-r.org/accord/min/accord6/cagoco.shtml> (accessed 30 May 2006).

Gutierrez, Eric. "In the Battlefields of the Warlord". *Rebels, Warlords and Ulama: A Reader on Muslim Separatism and the War in Southern Philippines*, edited by Kristina Gaerlan and Mara Stankovich. Quezon City: Institute for Popular Democracy, 1999.

——— and Saturnino Borras, Jr. "The Moro Conflict: Landlessness and Misdirected State Policies". *Policy Studies 9*. Washington: East-West Center, 2004.

Gutoc, Samira. "In Cold Blood". *Newsbreak*, 22 November 2004.

Hamilton-Hart, Natasha. "Terrorism in Southeast Asia: Expert Analysis, Myopia and Fantasy". *The Pacific Review* 18, no. 3 (September 2005).

Hernandez, Carolina G. "Institutional Responses to Armed Conflict: The Armed Forces of the Philippines". A background paper submitted to the Human Development Network Foundation, Inc, for the Philippine Human Development Report, 2005.

Ileto, Reynaldo. *Maguindanao 1860–1888: The Career of Datu Uto of Buayan* (Ithaca, New York: Cornell University Southeast Asia Program Data Paper no. 82, 1971).
Intengan, Romeo. "Christian Social Ethics and the SPCPD". *Moro Kurier* (October–November 1996).
Iqbal, Mohagher, interview with. "A View from the MILF". *Accord* <http://www.c-r.org/accord/min/accord6/cagoco.shtml> (accessed 30 May 2006).
Ishii, Masako. "Muslim Women and Social Change in Sarangani Region of Southern Philippines: Changing Social Norms of Women as Expressed in their Lifestyles". Ph.D. dissertation, Sophia University, Tokyo, 2000.
Junker, Laura Lee. *Raiding, Trading and Feasting: The Political Economy of Philippine Chiefdoms*. Honolulu: University of Hawaii Press, 1999.
Jubair, Salah. *Bangsamoro: A Nation Under Endless Tyranny*. Kuala Lumpur: IQ Marin Sdn Bhd, 1999.
Kirk, Donald. *Philippine in Crisis: U.S. Power versus Local Revolt*. Pasig City: Anvil Publishing, 2005.
Laarhoven, Ruurdje. "From Ship to Shore: Maguindanao in the 17th Century from Dutch Sources". M.A. thesis, Ateneo de Manila University, 1985.
Lingga, Abhoud Syed M. "Understanding Bangsamoro Independence as a Mode (sic) of Self-Determination". Paper delivered at the Forum on Mindanao Peace, sponsored by the University of the Philippines Mindanao, the Philippine Development Assistance Program and the Association of Mindanao State University Alumni, Davao City, 28 February 2002.
———. "The U.S. Role in the Mindanao Peace Process: Bangsamoro Perspective". Presentation given at the symposium on the U.S. Role in the Indonesian and Philippine Peace Processes. Asian Center, University of the Philippines, 27 November 2003.
Majul, Cesar Adib. *Muslims in the Philippines*. Quezon City: University of the Philippines Press, 1973.
Mastura, Michael. *Muslim-Filipino Experience: A Collection of Essays*. Manila: OCIA Publications, 1984.
McKenna, Thomas M. *Muslim Rulers and Rebels: Everyday Politics and Armed Separatism in the Southern Philippines*. Berkeley, Los Angeles and London: University of California Press, 1998.
Milner, Anthony. *The Invention of Politics in Colonial Malaya: Contesting Nationalism and the Expansion of the Public Sphere*. Cambridge: Cambridge University Press, 1994.
Muslim, Macapado Anton. *The Moro Armed Struggle in the Philippines: the Non-Violence Alternative*. Marawi City: Mindanao State University, 1994.
Nemenzo, Francisco. Rectification Process in the Philippine Communist Movement". In *Armed Communist Movements in Southeast Asia*, edited by Lim Joo-Jock and Vani S. Singapore: Institute for Southeast Asian Studies, 1984.
Philippine Human Development Report 2005: Peace, Human Security and Human Development in the Philippines. Manila: Human Development Network, 2005.

Rasul, Amina, ed. *The Road to Peace and Reconciliation: Muslim Perspective on the Mindanao Conflict*. Manila: Asian Institute of Management Policy Center, 2003.

———. "Assessment of the Situation in Mindanao". *Public Perception of U.S.-Philippine Relations*, Asian Perspectives Seminar Series, The Asia Foundation, Washington, D.C., 14 September 2004.

Republic of the Philippines. National Census and Statistics Office. Manila: NCSO, 2000.

Rodil, B.R. *Kalinaw Mindanaw: The Story of the GRP-MNLF Peace Process, 1975–1996*. Davao: Alternate Forum for Research in Mindanao, 2000.

———. *A Story of Mindanao and Sulu in Question and Answer*. Davao City: MINCODE, 2003.

Said, Edward. *Culture and Resistance: Conversations with Edward Said*, edited by David Barsamian. Cambridge, Massachusetts: Southend Press, 2003.

Santos, Soliman M. Jr. *Dynamics and Directions of the GRP-MILF Peace Negotiations*. Davao: Alternate Forum for Research in Mindanao, Inc., 2005.

Tan, Samuel K. *Selected Essays on the Filipino Muslim*. Marawi City: Mindanao State University Research Center, 1982.

———. *Decolonization and Filipino Muslim Identity*. Quezon City: University of the Philippines Department of History, 1989.

Thongchai Winichakul. *Siam Mapped: A History of the Geo-Body of a Nation*. Honolulu: University of Hawaii Press, 1997.

Vitug, Marites Danguilan and Glenda M. Gloria. *Under the Crescent Moon: Rebellion in Mindanao*. Quezon City: Ateneo Center for Social Policy and Public Affairs and the Institute for Popular Democracym, 2000.

———. "The Big Kill — Clan Wars not Terrorists or Rebels — are the Most Common Source of Violence in ARMM". *Newsbreak*, 25 April 2005.

Warren, James Francis. *The Sulu Zone, 1768–1898: The Dynamics of External Trade, Slavery, and Ethnicity in the Transformation of a Southeast Asian Maritime State*. Quezon City: New Day Publishers, 1985.

Wolters, O.W. *History, Culture and Region in Southeast Asian Perspectives*. Singapore: Institute of Southeast Asian Studies, 1982.

Websites

Accord <http://www.cr.org/accord/min/accord6/cagoco.shtml>.

Asiaweek Magazine. *Asiaweek Magazine*, 13 September 1996, <http://www.pathfinder.com/Asiaweek/96/0913/nat1.html>.

British Broadcasting Corporation <http://news.bbc.co.uk/1/hi/world/asia-pacific/1695576.stm>.

CNN World News <http://www.cnn.com/WORLD/9608/30/philippines.peace/>.

The Filipino Reporter, Year 33, no. 33, 29 July–4 August 2005, <http://www.filipinoreporter.com/archive/3333/headline04.htm> (accessed 27 June 2006).

House of Representative, Republic of the Philippines <http://www.iro.ph/downloads/resumes/salapuddin.pdf>.

Madge Kho, "100 Years of Moro Resistance: A Chronology of Historical Events" <http://www.upd.edu.ph/~iis/page2_100years.html>.

Mindanews <http://www.mindanews.com/2006/05/06nws-armm.htm>.

Philippine Daily Inquirer <www.inq7.net>.

University of the Philippines Forum (March–April 2006) <http://www.up.edu.ph/forum/2006/Mar-Apr06/ferrer.htm>.

University of the Philippines Forum, 2 August 2002 <http://www.up.edu.ph/forum/2002/Aug02/peace.html>.

United States Institute of Peace <http://www.usip.org/events/2004/0928_wksphillippines.html>.

13

THE INSURGENCY THAT WOULD NOT GO AWAY

Alexander R. Magno

President Gloria Macapagal Arroyo, in July 2006, broke from what was accepted as the "politically correct" post-1986 policy regarding the Maoist insurgency in the country.[1] She asked the Armed Forces of the Philippines (AFP) to conduct a total effort to eradicate the insurgency by the end of her term of office and requested businessmen to refuse to pay "revolutionary taxes" demanded by the rebel group. To underscore her determination, she ordered the budget secretary to immediately make available an additional P1 billion to purchase the equipment required by the intensified counter-insurgency effort. The military immediately responded by transferring three combat battalions from Mindanao to the three pilot areas of the effort in the main island of Luzon.[2]

The communist insurgency remains, without doubt, a military problem. There has been constant debate, however, over whether this is a problem with a principally military solution.

Over many years, those critical of a principally military approach to the lingering insurgency argued that the rebellion is based on valid social discontent. A "lasting" approach to the problem of insurgency should be based on addressing the social discontent. Government should, according to this position, approach the insurgency as a development question by attacking the poverty in those communities where the insurgency breeds.

This "development-based" approach to the insurgency has, in fact, been the dominant, politically-correct paradigm observed over the past two decades.

The results have not been particularly impressive. Most frequently, this approach produced chicken-and-egg situations where all the best effort to bring investments into the most depressed provinces failed precisely because of the inhospitable business conditions caused by the presence of insurgents. Hundreds of business ventures have failed because of onerous "revolutionary taxation" enforced by the New People's Army (NPA). Hundreds of entrepreneurs who could have led in liberating the poorest communities have either fled because of threats from the rebels or have been killed.[3]

The purpose of this chapter is exploratory, proposing to analyse the communist insurgency in the Philippines in the same manner as business enterprises are understood. Political movements, including those that profess anti-market ideologies, can only be sustainable if they are well-run enterprises — with well-managed ways.

By adopting this approach, this chapter argues that we may better explain the movement's disposition, anticipate decisions it will make, explain some of the more perplexing activities it undertakes, understand how it adjusts to changes in the economic environment and, perhaps, enable the entire counter-insurgency effort to be re-imagined. It is proposed that this approach promises greater explanatory value than the analysis of ideological polemics that constitutes the bulk of existing literature on the communist movement in the Philippines.

An enterprise sustainability analysis of the insurgent movement will, understandably, be challenged by limitations on the availability of financial information. The Communist Party of the Philippines — New People's Army (CPP-NPA) does not publish financial statements as normal businesses do. It is doubtful if this clandestine movement maintains anything that resembles a central accounting system. Thus, analysis will have to rely on anecdotal information and general calculations. However, as will be shown in this chapter, such an approach provides deep insights in understanding this long-running insurgency.

ELUSIVE PEACE

Since the democratic uprising of February 1986 that overthrew the Marcos dictatorship, the standing policy towards the insurgency accorded primacy to achieving a peaceful political settlement with the armed movements. Immediately after Corazon Aquino took over as president, she ordered the release of detained leaders of the Communist Party of the Philippines (CPP), the New People's Army (NPA) and the various components groups of the National Democratic Front (NDF). This was a gesture of goodwill and a measure of the prevailing optimism at that time.

Among those released at this time were CPP founder Jose Ma. Sison and NDF chair Satur Ocampo. Sison has, since 1987, moved to the Netherlands and there, as a self-proclaimed political exile, tried to lead the communist movement towards a more rigid Maoist orthodoxy.[4] That reaffirmation of orthodoxy led to a series of organizational splits within the communist movement. Ocampo led the NDF negotiating panel in 1986 and today sits in the Philippine Congress as a representative of the party-list group *Bayan Muna* (Country First), which is generally understood as the above-ground representation of the NDF.[5]

Through the past two decades since the 1986 Uprising, the CPP-led movement has been racked by often antagonistic debates between the so-called "reaffirmists" (pro-Sison) wing and the so-called "rejectionists".[6] To date, the most important leaders of the "rejectionists" — Felimon "Popoy" Lagman (formerly head of the Manila Commission of the CPP), Arturo Tabara (formerly head of the CPP Visayas Commission) and Romulo Kintanar (formerly head of the NPA) — have been assassinated in a nearly uniform pattern by suspected NPA hitmen.[7]

From the late eighties to the early nineties, the CPP likewise conducted bloody purges within its own ranks. Thousands of loyal party cadres and guerrillas were tortured and killed by their own comrades.[8] One of the key leaders of the CPP responsible for these purges, Jose Luneta, has joined Sison in the Netherlands using a "safe-conduct pass" issued by the Philippine government as one of the confidence-building measures to encourage progress of the peace negotiations. In April 2006, assassins gunned down former NPA leader for Southern Luzon Sotero Llamas in almost the exact manner Lagman, Tabara, and Kintanar were eliminated.

The "rejectionists" have established separate organizations since they split from the main CPP grouping. The followers of Lagman established the Revolutionary Workers Party and the Revolutionary Proletarian Army from party and guerrilla units they mustered to their side. They have likewise established distinct mass organizations and a party-list grouping called *Sanlakas*. But they have never managed to attract the major portion of the CPP-NPA-NDF, which remained firmly under Sison's leadership and administered on the ground by the couple Benito and Wilma Austria Tiamzon (as vice-chairman and secretary-general of the CPP respectively).

The splits and the purges seriously decimated the ranks of CPP-NPA. Once a robust political movement manned by a highly talented cadre during the Marcos dictatorship, the Maoist movement in the Philippines has lost much of its *élan* since 1986.

The strategic political errors committed by the communist movement that caused it to be excluded from the 1986 Uprising produced much disillusionment in the party ranks. Many of the highly educated party activists simply deserted the movement. A number of them began referring to themselves as "popular democrats" rather than as communists and moved above ground, clustered around non-government organizations and cause-oriented groups. The strategic errors precipitated intense internal debates on ideology and strategy that resulted in the spin-off of factional groups. These groups expressed themselves as separate revolutionary parties and armed movements. The most significant of these was the Revolutionary Proletarian Army-Alex Boncayao Brigade (RPA-ABB).

In the confusion that followed the 1986 Uprising the CPP mainstream led by Jose Ma. Sison decided to "reaffirm" the Maoist ideological principles around which the party was organized in 1968.[9] The innovative strategic approaches developed by the CPP leadership during the late seventies and the first half of the eighties was rejected. During this period, when Sison was imprisoned, Rodolfo Salas held the chairmanship of the CPP, Romulo Kintanar directed the NPA and Felimon Lagman led the powerful Manila-Rizal Regional Commission. All were talented, highly sophisticated cadres originating from the student movement of the late sixties.

The re-assertion of the basic principles of Maoist strategy and the rejection of the innovations introduced during the period when the CPP was led by the likes of Salas, Kintanar, Lagman and Tabara (head of the Visayas Commission of the CPP) was accompanied by purges, desertions and, in some instances, bloody clashes among rival insurgent armed units.

The new approaches encouraged during the early eighties involved decentralization of the movement, the formation of large guerrilla formations where this was sustainable, greater flexibility in tactics (including variants of "politico-military strategy" that involved a wide range of combinations of armed action with mass mobilization in the cities), greater leeway for internal political debate and openness to genuine united front activities. The encouragement of innovative approaches produced a wealth of theoretical discourses, including those that explored insurrectionary strategies and those that diminished the primacy of the armed struggle in achieving the political goals of the revolutionary movement.

All these ideological and strategic explorations were, from the point of view of the Maoist hardliners, absolutely heretical. All the complex analytical calculations and the permutations of theory threatened to confuse the grassroots of the party and undermine the hegemony of the central party leadership. It threatened to devolve too much authority to the regional commissions of the CPP and allow too much inner-party democracy than the first generation of party leaders could tolerate.

In this sense, the "rectification" campaign led by Sison and his cohorts was a conservative reaction — as well as a means for the "old guard" to retain their control over the movement. It was a retreat to the certainty of a highly simplified ideological platform and strategic format. That retreat was suffocating to most of the movement's intellectuals. But it was appealing to the rank-and-file, particularly to the peasant base of the guerrilla movement. The party might have lost the likes of Lagman, Tabara and Kintanar along with the spirit of innovation and experimentation their period of leadership represented. But it restored a sense of coherent ideological identity, comprehensible schematics and a uniform — albeit simplistic — "analysis" of the revolutionary project.[10]

The triumph of the "rectification campaign" restored a highly centralized, hierarchical and personality-centered organizational principle. The decentralized, highly flexible and "flattened" organizational format represented by the Salas-Kintanar phase was defeated in the internal party struggle.

Today, Gregorio "Ka Roger" Rosal, spokesman of the NPA, best personifies this retreat to the basic simplifications of Maoism. Rosal is of entirely peasant origin, exhibits very little literacy and speaks no language other than that of his locality.

ALTERED CONTEXT

While the CPP-NPA was conducting its "rectification" campaign, the world was changing dramatically.

Throughout the seventies, the insurgency's main source of logistical support was the Communist Party of China.[11] This was supplemented by support from a wide range of Western European parties and foundations, channeled either clandestinely on a party-to-party basis or through a network of non-governmental organizations, including human rights, environmentalist, and feminist groups.

This explains the sharp pro-China position maintained by the CPP through most of the seventies. When the Tiananmen Massacre happened, only the CPP-controlled Kilusang Mayo Uno publicly endorsed Beijing's action.

Support from China dramatically diminished, however, as the Maoist radicals lost power to a new generation of pragmatists following the ideological inclinations of Deng Xiaopeng. From exporting revolution, China decided to export manufactures — producing record economic growth and liberating more of its people from poverty than the decades of Maoism managed to.[12]

As the support line from China withered, CPP leaders began relying more on European radical groups for finances. A major portion of these financing channels was coursed through non-governmental organizations (NGOs) — especially during the immediate post-EDSA period when a large burst of international goodwill brought immense support for "people's organizations" that were ostensibly experimenting with alternative forms of human development. Up until the nineties, there was a great proliferation of such "people's organizations", a golden age of sorts. During this period, the standard practice was to side-stream resources from the NGOs by having party cadres and activists "employed" in above-ground institutions that, in turn, supported livelihood projects in impoverished (and ideologically-influenced) communities.

Eventually, this channel of externally generated logistical flow began to dry up as well. More and more, the insurgent movement found itself having to generate its logistical needs entirely on its own.

In 1995, the Moro National Liberation Front (MNLF) entered into a political settlement with the Philippine government. During the peak of the MNLF's military capacity, the movement tied down the bulk of the troop strength of the AFP, created a rear base of the communist insurgents in Mindanao and functioned as a source of firearms for them. The Government of the Republic of the Philippines (GRP)-MNLF political settlement added to the diminution of the CPP-NPA's logistical sources.

The problem was compounded by the dissipation of the urban mass movement that had been highly supportive of the insurgent movement during the period of the anti-Marcos struggles. The urban mass movement supplied the insurgency with highly educated, well-connected cadres of middle class origin. It likewise functioned as a source for financial and logistical support for the countryside forces.

Coupled with the purges of the late eighties, the factional struggles within the CPP-NPA, and the altered international environment, the decline of the urban mass movements was reflected in the demographics of the insurgency. The CPP's "cosmopolitanism ratio" declined dramatically through the nineties. The supply of educated and articulate cadres sourced from the urban mass movement was seriously depleted. More and more, the rural movement relied on cadres originating in the peasant communities. This trend had clear organizational implications.

While the rectification campaign asserted the CPP's centralized authority, the declining quality of the party cadre undermined the capacity of the party to rotate talented cadres across the ethnolinguistic regions and assert their authority over the local guerrilla commanders. With less of the educated, multilingual, and cosmopolitan cadres the movement once had in large supply, rotation of personnel among the regions became less and less possible. Local cadres remained largely in the localities they were born in, encouraging a diminished strategic and tactical horizon. The diminished space for "inner-party democracy" and the paranoia over "revisionism" abetted this even more. The virus of parochialism could not be checked.

Eventually, all decisions that had strategic and ideological bearings were left to the cabal of CPP leaders based in the city of Utrecht in Holland. Their issuances trickled down through a highly centralized and uncreative organization — very much as they do through a highly bureaucratized and inflexible corporate organization typical of the machine age. In fact, very much as they did in the Catholic hierarchy during the medieval period in Europe — with Jose Ma. Sison acting much like the Pope, dispensing his wisdom derived from eternal Maoist truths far from the scene of daily political struggles.

While, in principle, the CPP restored centralized leadership and the unchallenged hegemony of the Sison faction over ideological, strategic, and political issuances, the inability of the communist organization to prevent the erosion of its cadre base produces a contrary tendency. Unable to rotate sophisticated and independently decisive cadres nationwide, the CPP's ability to exercise political command over its far-flung armed units appears to be declining. With diminished party control, the local commanders of the NPA appear to be, in fact, exercising greater autonomy — putting, not politics on a national scale, but parochial contingencies in command.

The law of unintended consequences now appears to be in play.

The rectification campaign broke up the once powerful regional commissions and the large formations of the NPA.[13] Both, it was feared, could become alternative centres of power within the movement, challenging the Sison faction's grip on orthodoxy and decision-making. That fear was well placed, considering the extent to which Sison's control over the movement was challenged by the likes of Tabara and Lagman.

In their place, the CPP strengthened the functional commissions of the central organization — such as the united front commission and the trade unions commission. These agencies of the central leadership in turn supervise parallel bureaucracies running down to the district party branches and the small guerrilla fronts.

However, because of the changed circumstances — the disappearance of significant resource inflow from abroad and the diminution of the urban mass movement — the CPP has become dependent on the NPA for resource-generation. In fact, the guerrilla army has become the major source of financial resources for the movement.[14] An army general at the forefront of the counter-insurgency campaign quotes P4 billion as the amount annually funnelled to the insurgency movement from money taken from skimming off NGOs sympathetic to the Left, the funds available to leftist legislators elected to Congress through the party-list system, and criminal activities such as extortion, kidnapping, drug trafficking, dollar counterfeiting, illegal logging, protection money from public officials and money siphoned from foreign-funded projects.[15]

Money has, quite understandably, become an issue between the guerrillas who raise them using their capacity to intimidate and the party leaders who spend them. Reports indicate numerous internal debates have erupted over spending decisions — such as using funds to get party-list representatives elected over providing the same scarce resource to ragtag guerrilla bands who need better equipment or using funds to mount large demonstrations in the metropolitan area over using the same for socially beneficial projects in rebel-controlled communities.[16]

Understandably, the communist movement does not discuss its internal money problems in its publications. The persistent word in the grapevine, however, suggests that some of the high-profile communist personalities such as Tabara and Lagman were assassinated not so much for dissenting ideas they represented as for "financial opportunism" — squirrelling away funds from the central party organs.[17] For a resource-starved movement, especially a movement that now insists on centralizing control, it could indeed be more than a misdemeanour.[18]

FINANCIAL SUSTAINABILITY

Given the larger circumstances that force the communist movement in the Philippines to be almost entirely self-reliant, the aspect of financial sustainability becomes of magnified importance in analysing the behaviour of components of the movement.

In an environment where ideology has become vastly less compelling as a means for attracting support, the communist movement has had to rely on its armed units, with their capacity to inflict violence, as the principal means for generating resources to support the large political infrastructure necessary for the party to control the army as well as for the mass movement to support the armed struggle.

In the romantic notions of national liberation movements during the mid-twentieth century, revolutionary fighters are enthusiastically supported by the "masses" in the areas where they operate. Such romantic notions hardly work in the bitter reality of a society where 70 per cent of the population reside in highly urbanized areas, where the sites of the "protracted people's war" are rural areas characterized by weak agricultural production, where the communist movement is largely distrusted by the wealthier classes and where the guerrilla army operates precisely where the communities are poorest — unable to support their own subsistence, much less adopt an orphaned revolutionary army.

The consistent challenge facing the NPA is to develop a certain functionality in the environment in which they operate in order to raise the logistics required not only for their operational needs but also to support the logistical needs of an urban mass movement that is now bereft of external support.

That functionality requires deploying the NPA's only asset — its armed capability — to perform tasks that will yield financial resources for the movement. Achieving that functionality requires a large dose of pragmatism — a dose that is, fortunately, justifiable by a superficial application of the Maoist dictum that the people's army must constantly maintain a "mass line". It likewise inclines the guerrilla force towards populism.

In abiding by the "mass line", the NPA performs certain "services" for the communities in its areas of operation. They warn philandering husbands to mend their ways, summarily execute rustlers and rapists, return stolen items, intimidate landlords until they are convinced to bring down their rents or terrorize them so that they abandon their estates, freeing the land for cultivation by landless farmers. Aside from the public relations gains won by performing these tasks, the NPA also collects "revolutionary taxation" from the communities under their sway.

The capacity to use swift "revolutionary justice" no doubt produces a tax effort that is probably better than the national government's. But given the poverty of the communities under the influence of insurgent forces, it is likely that funds generated by this effort would not suffice to meet the needs of the whole movement, especially considering its bloated party bureaucracy and its financially inept mass movements. The effort needs to be supplemented by more insidious fund-raising from entities that are better able to yield larger financing volumes.

From its earliest days, the NPA raised a significant amount of money by protecting the activities of illegal loggers. These activities are naturally vulnerable to guerrilla pressure when they take place where the guerrillas operate. They have capital equipment vulnerable to destruction by the guerrilla units should they fail to comply with guerrilla demands.[19] In one famous incident during the eighties, NPA guerrillas raided the Negros Occidental farm of businessman Eduardo Cojuangco and massacred several hundred fighting cocks, apparently for the businessman's failure to pay up protection money more than making any political statement either about Cojuangco's cronyism or the morality of cockfighting as a common form of gambling.

Illegal logging is an unsustainable activity in itself. Over time, as the forests ran out, guerrilla income from protecting logging activities ran out as well. A "market shift" was subsequently required. Eventually, the NPA gained notoriety for burning down equipment of mining companies and plantations that refuse demands for "revolutionary taxes". Their targets soon included bus companies and mobile telephone firms — obviously because of the vulnerability of their assets to attack. On a fairly regular basis, the NPA burns down provincial buses and bombs cell sites of the phone companies.[20]

The regularity suggests that the NPA guerrillas spend a great deal of their time extorting money or punishing non-compliance. Because of the apparent profitability of extortion activities, numerous criminal gangs have attempted to conduct extortion themselves, guised as the NPA. This has become an added problem for the victims since it produces double-taxation. Imaginably, it has become a problem for the NPA itself, since it now has the additional duty of cracking down on pretenders poaching on its turf.

With deforestation killing off logging activities and with the plantation sector basically in its death throes, the NPA's extortion industry could be running out of targets fat enough to be worth the risk. Anecdotal evidence suggests that the NPA demands a 20 per cent rate for "revolutionary taxes" from civilian contractors building roads for the government. That is on top of the same rate demanded by local politicians as kickbacks for the same publicly funded projects. As a result, fewer and fewer contractors are willing to build roads in the inaccessible areas that need them direly, leaving the impoverished provincial economies cut off from the mainstream of the national economy.

Since that, too, is a self-limiting source of revenue for the insurgent movement, recent evidence indicates that the NPA protection racket now extends its coverage to illegal gambling and drug syndicates. Illegal drugs, with most of the ingredients smuggled in from China, are now estimated to be a P200 billion-a-year "industry" despite government's best efforts to crack down on drug use. That is a fairly liquid sector that has also become a major source of campaign financing. Here the protection racket is imaginably profitable — a China connection in an entirely unanticipated way.

There is, as well, a seasonal source of revenue for the armed insurgents. During election years, the NPA has taken to issuing "safe conduct passes" to politicians for a fee. The passes entitle politicians to campaign in rebel-influenced areas without incident. In an increasing number of cases, the guerrillas have demanded guns in place of money — suggesting a serious shortage of this vital instrument of war. Guns, after all, have become a capital resource for the extortion industry to prosper. A number of bank heists have, similarly, been attributed to NPA guerrillas under increasingly severe pressure to produce revenues for the movement.

By poaching on illegal gambling as well as the drug trade, and by demanding protection money from individuals standing for elections, the NPA's revenue generation effort aggravates the crisis of electoral financing that already severely distorts the practice of democracy in the Philippines.

The modernization of the Philippine economy, under pressure from globalization, has seen growth centred on economic sectors that require little political brokerage in the conduct of business. That has diminished the incentive for businessmen to "invest" in candidates, narrowing the sources of electoral financing. Given that context, the insurgent movement has had to resort to "bartering" the votes of the communities it controls in exchange for support from traditional politicians for leftist party-list groupings. But this non-cash transaction does little to alleviate the financing crisis besetting the insurgent movement.

If it is the guerrilla army that raises the bulk of the financial needs of the political movement, this should sooner or later result in increasing the leverage of the largely peasant guerrilla groups over the largely petit-bourgeois party cadre. Or else, this trend will result in greater possibilities for the guerrilla units to descend into plain brigandage — although they might routinely mouth Maoist slogans.[21]

VOLUMES

The P4 billion annually generated revenues by the communist movement's extortion and sidestreaming activities, quoted earlier in this chapter, might be an under-estimation of the financing needs of an insurgency forced into self-sufficiency by adverse macroeconomic conditions.

The AFP estimates current NPA strength at 7,470 people. That represents a 70 per cent decline from the group's peak strength of 25,200 in 1987, although it also represents a significant increase from the insurgency's lowest point in 1995, when the NPA had a personnel complement of 6,020. In terms of firearms, the NPA remains close to its lowest point: presently estimated at 5,950, just slightly above its lowest point of 5,300 firearms in 1995.[22]

The NPA is currently active in 107 guerrilla fronts compared to 41 in 1992.[23] But this ought not to be alarming on closer scrutiny. In 1992, before the "rectification campaign" took full effect, the NPA maintained large formations. Those formations have been sub-divided into smaller territorial units, mostly composed of *Sandatahang Yunit Pampropaganda* (Armed Propaganda Units). These smaller units are designed to be highly mobile and self-contained. They are supposed to be engaged in "educational and propaganda" work to support the movement. Given all that has been mentioned above, these units are very likely engaged in extortion activities most of the time.

The smaller guerrilla units are not suited to engage government troops unless several units are temporarily combined for a "tactical offensive" (most frequently against undermanned and outgunned police outposts). The redistribution of the NPA into smaller units explains the serious drop in armed encounters with government forces over the last decade. The guerrillas' preoccupation with raising the financing needs of the whole movement further reinforces that trend.

On the basis of anecdotal evidence, each NPA full-timer receives a truly spartan allowance of P5,000 a month to cover his personal needs and allow him to help sustain his family. Assuming (conservatively) an operational cost (for food, clothing, transport and communications) of another P5,000 per full-timer per month, then the guerrilla movement should require financing in the amount of about P74 million a month or something in the vicinity of just under a billion pesos annually.

The figure excludes "capital expenditure", which in this case involves the procurement of arms, ammunition, and related pieces of equipment necessary to make a guerrilla unit operational.

There is no official estimate of the number of CPP full-timers. If we assume a cadre strength that roughly equals NPA strength, then that at least doubles the annual budget required by the CPP-NPA combined. Anecdotal evidence indicates that an urban-based cadre receives a P15,000 monthly allowance as his operational costs should be larger than the P5,000 estimated for a peasant guerrilla. Party cadres need to maintain safe houses, procure office supplies and sustain an efficient communications network.

In addition, the CPP-NPA needs to raise funds for the mass movements that are crucial to asserting their political presence in the streets. There is little indication, given the dramatic decline of funding sources for highly politicized "people's organizations", that the mass movements are financially self-reliant — much less a revenue source for the armed movement. The greater likelihood is that the activists of the open mass movements are substantially subsidized from the revenue-generation activities of the NPA.

The operational costs of mounting mass protests in the metropolitan area require a large amount of financing. Over the past few years, the pro-

NDF mass organizations have mounted numerous protest actions in the Manila area. Close observation of the patterns of these demonstrations indicates that full mobilization of pro-NDF groups in the Metro Manila area normally involves about 4,000 people. Any demonstration larger than that will require the pro-NDF groups to bus in their people from the outlying provinces.

In order to bring, say, 12,000 people from Central Luzon and the Southern Tagalog provinces for important demonstration dates such as the President's State of the Nation Address will require hiring about 1,000 jeepneys. At P2,500 per day, that will amount to a tidy sum, especially since the warm bodies bused require feeding and bringing back to their communities afterwards. The rule of thumb is that a large demonstration with elaborate effigies will cost the CPP-NPA-NDF about P10 million.

Again, anecdotal information indicates that the pro-NDF mass organizations often "charge" political partners for bringing their protest manpower to the streets. The recent linkages between the most reactionary political blocs and the leftist mass organizations could not be explained either by ideological affinities or by intersecting strategic interests. They are more easily explained by the usual symbiosis of political convenience: the politicians provide the cash, the leftist groups supply the manpower for undertaking spectacles of protest.[24]

Given these, the AFP's ballpark figure of an annual budget of P4 billion to keep the insurgency — and its concomitant mass movements — going is acceptable as a working figure. Yet, the limitations on financial resource generation will effectively prevent the insurgency from growing any larger. The parameters of revenue generation mentioned in the preceding discussion militate against that. After all, even the most rabid Maoist movement cannot run on ideology alone.

POLITICAL ECONOMY

Much of the publicly available literature on the communist movement in the Philippines focuses on the theoretical debates, the pronouncements of communist leaders and voluminous historical material. Although political economy has been a preferred approach of many radical intellectuals in the Philippines, that approach has not been applied to the analysis of the communist movement itself.

Behind the screen of revolutionary rhetoric, the CPP-NPA is a corporate entity. Thus, it could be analysed like all corporate entities: in terms of its extractive business model, identifying its core competencies, evaluating its market, assessing its revenue stream, and calculating the extent of demand for the "products" it delivers.

Putting aside the vacuous polemics about "social revolution" being the final product of this insurgent enterprise, the CPP-NPA on a day-to-day basis delivers the following "products": the capacity to deliver a disciplined and respectably-sized mass to mount political campaigns; the guerrilla army's ability to inflict violence on demand; the ability of its mass organizations to deliver votes for traditional politicians for a price; and its rather successful branding of itself as both the voice and the instrument of the oppressed.

Strategically, the "market" for these products should be receding. The modernization of the Philippine economy under the aegis of globalization shatters the cohesiveness, self-consciousness, and homogeneity of the "revolutionary classes". The rapid urbanization of Philippine society reduces the "market" for armed groups mediating land rents, chasing cattle rustlers, and punishing miscreants in the villages. The expansion of the market economy and competitive corporate entities reduces the "demand" for organized violence supplanting impersonal market forces.

The only marginally improving "demand" segment for the "products" deliverable by the leftist groups are the various factions of conventional political opposition toying with the possibility of extra-institutional means for altering the set of power-wielders. This "demand" segment, however, is seasonal: the appetite for establishing linkages with the Left diminishes as the real possibility of pre-terminating a presidential term diminishes.

It is, of course, impossible to acquire an accurate financial statement emanating from the CPP-NPA as a distinct corporate entity. However, ballpark calculations, such as the one attempted in the preceding discussion, could be made. On that basis, the health of the insurgent enterprise might be evaluated in terms of its financial sustainability.

The "rectification" of the CPP-NPA's ideological and political lines might have benefited the first generation of this enterprise's leadership, ensuring that the doddering Maoists will have something to do as they near retirement age. But the same "rectification" movement has also added to the movement's rigidities in its decreasing capacity to adjust to a changing political market and its increased vulnerability to "opportunity costs", such as missing out on new constituencies that may be drawn to revolutionary engagement only by an innovative programme and a flexible organization capable of marketing that new programme.

The roaring success of this enterprise in advancing the dynamics of united front politics ranged against a rigid authoritarian regime during the Marcos period has been historically transcended. It is now the revolutionary enterprise itself that has become sclerotic, unable to evolve a new business model that could thrive in dramatically changed circumstances.

An aborted coup conspiracy timed for the twentieth anniversary of the EDSA uprising in February 2006 featured a strange alliance between military adventurers funded by displaced politicians and the forces of the CPP-NPA.[25] This is more than a flirtation. It is indicative of the increasing financial dependence of the "revolutionary movement" on desperate factions of the elite willing and able to raise the finances that the leftist groups need desperately to maintain their own mobilization activities.

Notes

1 Since the Marcos dictatorship was deposed, the Philippine government has maintained continuing dialogue with the three main armed insurgent groups, namely: the CPP-NPA, the Moro National Liberation Front and the Moro Islamic Liberation Front. In 1995, a political settlement was achieved with the MNLF. The former president himself provides the best documentation of this process. See: Ramos, Fidel, *Break Not the Peace: The Story of the GRP-MNLF Peace Negotiations 1992–1996* (Manila: Friends of Steady Eddie, 1996).

2 Jaime Laude, "Ka Roger makes Himself Scarce", in *The Philippine Star*, 24 June 2006, p. 1.

3 More and more, NPA activities have concentrated on attacking vulnerable assets of mining firms, telephone companies, and provincial bus lines. This indicates the increasing role played by the guerrilla unit as fund-raiser for the wider movement. Apart from undertaking destructive attacks in order to enforce extortion demands, the NPA has likewise attacked assets of cooperatives set up by former cadres. See, for instance, a report on one recent attack on a cooperative of former leftists in Negros Occidental in Carla P. Gomez, "NPAs Burn Ex-comrades' Cargo Truck" in *Philippine Daily Inquirer*, 16 August 2006, p. A17.

4 For a comprehensive coverage of the events of this heady period, mainly from a left-wing perspective, see *Dictatorship and Revolution: Roots of People Power*, edited by Aurora Javate-de Dios, Petronilo Bn. Daroy and Lorna Kalaw-Tirol (Manila: Conspectus, 1988). For a discussion of the early indications of serious ideological stirrings within the communist movement, see Alexander R. Magno, "The Filipino Left at the Crossroads: Current Debates on Strategy and Revolution", in Third World Studies Center, *Marxism in the Philippines* (Quezon City: Bede's Publishing House, 1988).

5 Military spokesmen continue to maintain that Ocampo remains a member of the Central Committee of the CPP. In February 2006, shortly after President Arroyo declared a state of emergency after a foiled coup attempt, Ocampo and five other congressmen representing pro-NDF party-list groups were charged with rebellion before Philippine courts.

6 For a compendium of contending position papers from the various schools of

thought within the Philippine communist movement, see *Kasarinlan: A Philippine Quarterly of Third World Studies.* Special Issue on the Philippine Left (Third Quarter, 1992).

7 All three were shot and killed by a single gunman, apparently familiar to the victims. In June 2006, the Philippine National Police arrested an NPA gunman accused of these killings.

8 For a moving, personal account of torture and survival during these purges, see Robert Francis Garcia. *To suffer Thy Comrades: How the Revolution Decimated Its Own* (Pasig City: Anvil Publishing, 2001).

9 The CPP was itself a breakaway group from the traditional, pro-Soviet Partido Komunista ng Pilipinas.

10 For an insight into Jose Ma. Sison's thinking, see Kathleen Weekly, "Jose Ma. Sison: Talks on Parliamentary Struggle, Revisionism, Inner Party Rectification, Peace Talks, Gorbachevism in the Philippines and the Future of the National Democratic Movement", in *Kasarinlan* (Fourth Quarter, 1992).

11 Gregg Jones, *Red Revolution: Inside the Philippine Guerrilla Movement* (Boulder, CO: Westview Press, 1989).

12 Trade between China and the Philippines had been expanding exponentially from the late nineties. The Philippines, in 2005, enjoyed a US$1 billion trade surplus with China and Beijing has offered the Philippines a free trade arrangement sweetened by a generous package of loans and grants for a number of key infrastructure projects. Beijing, obviously playing the "Philippine card", has offered weaponry, although Washington vehemently objected to this.

13 "Reaffirm our Basic Principles and Carry the Revolution Forward", CPP Statement on its 23rd Anniversary, 26 December 1991, in *Rebolusyon*, no. 1 (January–March 1992): 11

14 Loretta Ann P. Rosales, "The NPA as the New Mafia". *Newsbreak*, 1 March 2004, p. 24.

15 Cecil Morella, "Military Uses New Tactics on and off the Battlefield", in *Businessworld*, 3 February 2006, p. 1.

16 There has been increasing talk, of late, about growing tensions between the Sison leadership and "militarists" in the CPP-NPA hierarchy. The "militarists" prefer that both strategy and resources flow primarily to building up the NPA. According to the leftwing grapevine, one of the leading "militarists" is veteran CPP cadre Caridad Magpantay who oversees the insurgent organization in the Central Luzon area.

17 Interview with Army intelligence officers, May 2006.

18 According to data compiled by the National Security Council, the CPP-NPA is responsible for 1,130 "liquidation missions" from January 2000 to May 2006. These missions resulted in the deaths of 1,227 individuals, most of them civilians and a great number ostensibly for failure to pay "revolutionary taxes". See Katherine Adraneda, "CPP-NPA killed 1,227 people in past six years, says Gonzales", in *Philippine Daily Inquirer*, 8 August 2006, p. 5.

19 Marites Danguilan Vitug, *Power from the Forest: The Politics of Logging* (Manila: Philippine Center for Investigative Journalism, 1993).

20 Although there has been no systematic effort to categorize the "tactical offensives" mounted by the NPA over the past five years, there is a marked trend towards avoidance of confrontation with the military and the police and a greater focus on enforcing extortion demands.

21 The bloody purges conducted by the CPP-NPA over the past two decades were, in the main, functions of the effort to reintroduce doctrinaire Maoism. Many of these purges were carried out, ostensibly, to rid the movement of "deep-penetration agents" inserted by military intelligence. There is another sociological dimension to this phenomenon, however. It could also indicate the assertion of authority by local peasant cadres over *petit-bourgeois* party workers sent to the localities by the central party leadership. That could become more evident in the current purge that military intelligence reports to be in progress. See Jaime Laude, "AFP bares purge sanctioned by NPA" *The Philippine Star*, 13 August 2006, p. 11. See also Charlie Lagasca, "2 Reds Indicted in Bayan Muna Leader's Slay", *The Philippine Star*, 13 August 2006, p. A-24.

22 Information from the Office of the Deputy Chief of Staff for Intelligence, Armed Forces of the Philippines (undated).

23 Ibid.

24 In the first week of July 2006, opposition senator Jamby Madrigal, heiress to one of the largest landowning families in the country, visited CPP leaders in Utrecht, Holland and signed a "communiqué" calling for the resumption of peace talks. She admitted that she paid for the travel of Bayan Muna representative Satur Ocampo to Europe during the same period. During the months of agitation calling for President Gloria Arroyo's resignation, Madrigal appeared in several street demonstrations organized by the Left-wing groups. That allowed her to engineer media events and project herself to the public. Presumably, she contributed more than her actual participation in making the demonstrations possible.

25 See "Mahahalagang Punto ng Mga Kaisahan at Unawaan sa Pagitan ng Partido Komunista ng Pilipinas at Kalipunan ng mga Anak ng Bayan" (Photocopy of document captured 21 February 2006 summarizing the main points of agreement between representatives of the CPP-NPA and those of the groups involved in plotting a coup attempt. Circulated by the Intelligence and Security Group, Philippine Army.)

14

WHITHER THE PHILIPPINES IN THE 21ST CENTURY?: SUMMARY, CONCLUSIONS, AND ADDITIONAL THOUGHTS

Rodolfo C. Severino

Over 2006, financial analysts were positively optimistic about the Philippines. A Royal Bank of Scotland report in February declared, "We arrived in Manila cautiously bullish. We left Manila bullish."[1] In April, UBS Investment Research announced, "In the past months of marketing, we've picked up something … that we haven't seen in a very long time indeed: a palpable sense of interest and even excitement about the Philippines."[2] Also in April, Merrill Lynch reported,

> The fiscal performance has been quite robust since the beginning of the year. We think that the fiscal outlook is strong for 2006 and is likely to translate into declining borrowing needs. Based on its strong fiscal program, the government is likely to cut the public debt substantially this year. Meanwhile, we think that the prospects for economic growth are favorable, the inflation outlook is not a source of concern, and the external sector will remain strong.[3]

In September, the same Merrill Lynch strategist wrote, "We expect a strong fiscal story this year, with a sharply reduced fiscal deficit. We maintain our overweight recommendation on the Philippines in our model portfolio."[4]

What are the sources of the analysts' optimism? Generally, as the quotes above make clear, they are the macroeconomic indicators that are the normal grist for financial analysts' mill. In 2006, the gross domestic product grew at a respectable rate of 5.4 per cent. The growth is attributed largely to good weather (that is, adequate rainfall), which boosted agricultural production, foreign investments in the electronics sector, the rise in exports in that sector, the expansion of call centres, and the increase in tourism. Merrill Lynch thinks that the GDP growth figure may even be understated, because it does not take sufficient account of the growth in services as well as of the large informal sector.

The analysts applaud the government's improved fiscal performance, which is partly due to the implementation of the expanded value added tax, despite doubts about the efficiency of the revenue collecting agencies. The government deficit narrowed to 1.4 per cent of the GDP in 2006. Inflation is slowing down and the peso is stable.

SLOW REDUCTION OF POVERTY

These are good macroeconomic signs that are encouraging for portfolio investors, who are the financial analysts' principal clients and whose main interests are fairly short-term. The picture becomes less cheery, however, when viewed from a longer-term perspective and in the regional context of Southeast Asia.

In their chapter for this book, Hal Hill and Sharon Faye A. Piza recall that in the mid-1970s Thailand's per capita income caught up with that of the Philippines, once Southeast Asia's fastest-growing economy. From 1960 to 2004, the Philippines' per capita income did not quite double, while those of the other four original members of the Association of Southeast Asian Nations (ASEAN) grew at least five times, with Singapore's expanding 11 times. The other original ASEAN members and Vietnam, which entered the association in 1995, have outstripped the Philippines' growth rate since the 1980s. Poverty incidence in the Philippines is "considerably higher" than even in Indonesia and Vietnam. Hill and Piza cite the abnormally large share of services in the Philippines' gross domestic product at the expense of manufacturing, the small share of investments, the low savings rate, the wide income inequality, the slow generation of jobs, the relatively sluggish rate of poverty reduction, and the slippage in the country's lead in higher education.

They attribute this comparatively dismal record partly to the Philippines' "complicated political history".

In his chapter Gerardo Sicat, former National Economic and Development Authority minister and professor emeritus of economics at the University of the Philippines, is quite specific on the political roots of the Philippines' economic sluggishness. Making observations similar to those of Hill and Piza, he points a finger at the state's political inability to adopt and carry out the necessary policies, the country's rapid population growth, the long period of protectionism, rigidities in the labour market, and constitutional restrictions on foreign direct investments. He also blames corruption, political interference in the management of state-owned enterprises, and pork-barrel considerations in the construction of infrastructure. Indeed, in another chapter, the business consultant and long-time Philippine resident Peter Wallace observes that overall expenditures on education and infrastructure, particularly on power generation and distribution, have gone down, while corruption and policy inconsistency have deterred investments.

The problems that Sicat mentions are ultimately rooted in politics. Restrictions on foreign ownership preserve the monopolies enjoyed by favoured Filipino industrialists or offer influential Filipinos opportunities for rent. Rigid labour costs result from pressure from powerful labour organizations and politicians' tendency to appear "populist". So-called sin taxes cannot be raised sufficiently because of the inordinate influence of tobacco and liquor interests. Bad infrastructure is often the result of corruption.

Nevertheless, Hill and Piza, Sicat, and Wallace all see some bright spots in recent developments. They welcome the approval of the value added tax as a measure of fiscal reform and stabilization. They are cheered by the rapid growth of exports, although Hill and Piza note that the increase in exports, as well as investments, has been too narrowly based on electronics. They laud the lowering of protection and the opening of the economy to competition, late though these may be in coming. Hill and Piza cite the Philippine economy's ability to ride out the 1997–98 financial crisis. According to them, this was due to the relatively thin flow of private short-term capital into the Philippines, the sharp depreciation of the peso, the strong connection to the U.S. market, and the effective regulation of the financial sector. Reform of the Central Bank has also contributed to the Philippines' recent good record of controlling inflation.

Wallace refers to the results of his survey of business executives, who had high opinions of the qualities of people in the Philippines — as distinct from their government. He stresses that the country has pronounced advantages in some sectors and that business can succeed in it although with greater effort than would otherwise be required.

For the vast majority of the people of the Philippines, the question is when — or whether — the benefits of economic growth will filter down to them, a question that is not only economic but political and social as well.

While the good macroeconomic news was coming out, there was other news. According to the Labour Force Survey of the Philippine National Statistics Office (NSO) released on 15 September 2006, the number of employed people in the Philippines increased by only 2.3 per cent from July 2005 to July 2006, a rate less than half of the economic growth rate, while the unemployment rate rose from 7.7 to 8 per cent over the same period. The rate of under-employment increased from 20.5 to 23.5 per cent. Unable to find full-time or any kind of jobs at home or seeking better ones elsewhere, Filipinos officially "deployed" overseas, according to the Philippine Overseas Employment Administration, increased from 933,588 in 2004 to 981,677 in 2005. These figures do not include the hundreds of thousands of workers who have gone out to work abroad through "unofficial" channels. According to the Central Bank, overseas workers remitted to the Philippines US$8.6 billion in 2004 and US$10.7 billion in 2005 through banks alone. This does not include money sent through informal channels. Worker remittances have vitally helped the Philippine economy to stay afloat. They are also a measure of the magnitude of the Philippine exodus and the lack of opportunities at home.

According to the Asia Regional Information Centre of the Asian Development Bank, the percentage of Filipinos living on less than US$2 a day was 43.2 in 2002, as compared to 4.0 for Malaysia and 26.7 for Thailand. Joel Rocamora, in his chapter for this book, notes that while, according to official statistics, poverty incidence declined from 49.2 per cent in 1985 to 39.4 per cent in 2000, the absolute number of poor people rose from 26.5 million to 30.4 million. Whereas the average annual reduction in poverty incidence in the Philippines over those years was 0.7 per cent, the rates in Indonesia and Thailand over more or less the same period were 1.6 and 1.7 per cent, respectively.

In this book, Arsenio N. Balisacan declares with startling directness, "Addressing the widespread poverty problem is the single most important policy challenge facing the Philippines. Not only is poverty high compared with other countries in East Asia, but also its reduction is so slow that the country has become the basket case in the region."

Not surprisingly, Balisacan points to the slow growth of the agricultural sector and the low level of rural productivity as the reasons behind the country's deep-seated poverty. Accordingly, he calls for investments in rural infrastructure and in human capital in the rural areas, specifically in health and educational services, and for improved access by rural folk to land and technology. He urges the removal of "public-spending biases favouring large farmers and agribusiness enterprises" and the "promotion of small-scale enterprises". He stresses that, contrary to the claims of some "civil society" groups, economic growth is essential for poverty reduction, but it is not enough, a point that Rocamora also makes. The weakness, Balisacan says, lies in the inability to transform income growth into poverty reduction.

RAPID POPULATION GROWTH

A basic problem is that economic growth is offset to a significant extent by a high population growth rate — 2.3 per cent a year in the 1990s, well above Thailand's 1.4 per cent and Indonesia's 1.6 per cent. According to the NSO, the country had 76.5 million people in 2000. This was 15 million more than Thailand's, whereas in 1965 the two countries had had about the same number of people. In 2004, the Philippines' population growth rate was 1.79 per cent, an improvement over the average growth rate in the 1990s, but still high compared to its neighbours. The NSO estimates that, by 2005, the Philippine population had soared to 85.3 million. In this light, the Philippine economy needs to grow much faster than at 5.5 per cent and its fruits spread out more widely if Filipinos are to find jobs at home and get out of poverty in substantial numbers. One analyst writes, "Even 6% GDP growth is not enough to make any meaningful dent in the Philippines' widespread poverty… . For the current economic recovery to resonate in the lives of more Filipinos, the GDP growth needs to be driven further upward to between 7% to (sic) 8%."[5] Hill and Piza, Sicat, and Balisacan point to the Philippines' rapid population expansion as a key reason why its economy's growth rate is not enough and why the reduction of its people's poverty is so slow.

THE FILIPINO EXODUS

One outstanding manifestation of the country's shortfall in economic growth and poverty reduction, as well as a measure of both the abundance and the quality of Filipino manpower, is the massive and accelerating exodus of Filipinos seeking work in other countries. Sicat attributes the exodus partly to the low level of investments in the Philippine economy. Filipino labour, he points out, combines with foreign capital to develop other countries, whereas a larger inflow of capital into the country in combination with stay-at-home Filipino labour could be developing the Philippines.

In another chapter, Ernesto M. Pernia analyses the phenomenon of Filipino workers' out-migration and their remittance of funds back home. From 1995 to 2001, among Asian labour exporters, Philippine remittances were next only to India's in absolute terms and the highest relative to population and GDP. From 1995 to 2004, the recorded average annual growth rate of remittances was 12.1 per cent — three times the rate of increase in the number of Filipinos going overseas for work. This might be attributed to the growing use of official remittance channels because of their improved efficiency.

Pernia found that remittances helped lift Philippine households out of poverty and contributed to increased spending for consumption and larger investments in human capital and housing. At the same time, he cautions that the substantial contribution that remittances make in keeping the Philippine economy afloat may be easing the pressure on the government to undertake the necessary policy reforms. To this basic disadvantage, one might add the exploitative "commissions" or fees that Philippine and foreign labour recruiters skim off a worker's earnings (often the first eight months of a Filipino maid's salary), the opportunities for money-laundering that the remittance system presents, and the social costs of breaking up families, often at crucial stages in children's lives. Finally, the exodus of Filipino teachers and health workers cannot but have an impact on the quality of education and healthcare in the country.

As Balisacan points out, the Philippine problem is a matter both of accelerating economic growth and of transforming that growth into the reduction of poverty. If this is the case, the issues and prescriptions are apparent:

- a clear population policy;
- investments in rural infrastructure and technology;
- investments in public education and public health;
- a significant reduction in corruption, inefficiency and waste; and
- the removal of constitutional restrictions on the mobilization of foreign capital in key sectors of the economy.

All these reforms entail a re-arrangement of priorities and a re-allocation of resources — from the rich to the poor, from the urban to the rural, from the powerful to the powerless, from the rent-seekers to the workers and entrepreneurs. There reforms have to do with distribution, as well as growth, which is to say with political power and political pressure.

NO REAL POLITICAL PARTIES

A significant problem is that, in the Philippines, there are no political parties through which people can articulate their preferences, priorities and grievances. There are no political parties in the real sense, with certain broad policies, political leanings, ideologies and overall image. In countries with parties contending for political leadership and power, the parties proffer policies and programs and represent a certain image to the electorates. If a party wins an election, the electorate can hold it to its programmes and promises under pain of losing the next elections to a rival party. In states where single parties are dominant, such as China and Vietnam, the party in power has to deliver and perform under pain of being overthrown or at the risk of social chaos — unless it resorts to outright dictatorship, which would bring on its own problems.

In the Philippines, no such identifiable parties exist. Party labels are attached to candidates at election time only because the law requires it. Before Marcos, the Nacionalista and Liberal parties were merely labels appropriated by candidates running for office in order to entitle them to election inspectors. The parties were indistinguishable in terms of policy stances. Until today, there is no identifiable set of leaders whom voters can reward or punish — or protest against — for the impact of state policies and actions on their lives or for the behaviour of its members.

THE CASE FOR CONSTITUTIONAL CHANGE

Some of the more sincere advocates of constitutional change in the Philippines aim to develop real political parties. José V. Abueva, eminent political scientist and educator, was at the forefront of the most recent attempt to revise the Philippine constitution. In his chapter in this book, Abueva characterizes Philippine political parties:

- Filipino political parties are personal factions and alliances united mainly for elections and patronage. In the present unitary-presidential system, most political parties are loose personal factions/organizations that exist mainly to elect their candidates and distribute patronage. They are organizations of politicians and have no mass memberships.
- Political parties have no serious platform or programme of government

to offer the people. They do not have a serious programme of government to campaign for and to implement when they are in power.

- They are largely undemocratic, undisciplined and opportunistic. Their opportunistic members change parties for their personal convenience. They are not bound by party loyalty or democratic rules in selecting the party candidates and building party unity and cohesiveness.
- They are not responsible and accountable to the people for their performance in or out of office. And the people do not take seriously the statements and promises of party leaders. Not surprisingly very few leaders and citizens in business or civil society join the political parties.

It was partly to promote the creation of genuine political parties that Abueva and others of like mind pushed for a "people's initiative" to revise or amend the 1987 Constitution. In 2005, President Arroyo appointed Abueva to head the Consultative Commission on Constitutional Change, which proposed three major changes to the constitution: the shift from the presidential system with two houses of Congress to a unicameral parliamentary set-up, the switch from a unitary to a federal republic, and the liberalization of the conditions governing the participation of foreign capital in the economy. The Consultative Commission proposed several provisions designed to encourage the development of real political parties. In his chapter, Abueva explains in detail how constitutional change would do this.

Unfortunately, the debate on constitutional change became preoccupied with the motivations of the politicians supporting it — President Gloria Macapagal-Arroyo, Speaker of the House José de Venecia, other members of the House of Representatives, and local government officials. These people, critics claimed, were interested only in staying in power indefinitely and controlling the process of constitutional revision. Meanwhile, senators opposed the proposed changes in the face of the Senate's projected abolition.

On 25 October 2006, the Supreme Court, through a split 8–7 decision, struck down the campaign to use "people's initiative" to amend the Constitution The majority cited flaws in the gathering of the signatures and claimed that the signatories had not been shown the proposals that they were approving. The Supreme Court decision also contended that the constitutional changes being proposed amounted to a revision rather than mere amendments — a revision not being subject to the "people's initiative" mode of changing the constitution. On the other hand, the seven dissenting justices argued that it was for the Commission on Elections to pass judgement on the validity of the signatures and that the proposed changes, going by precedents, could, in fact, be considered as amendments.

Joel Rocamora, writing about charter change, declares, "It is not just President Arroyo who is being challenged; it is the capacity of the whole political system to select leaders capable of responding to the needs of the Philippines in the twenty-first century." Rocamora argues:

> While competing proponents of chacha ("charter change") all publicly support a shift from a presidential to parliamentary form of government and from a unitary to federal system, there is a deep divide between the two sides. At the root of this division is the difference between one side which wants to transform the political system to ensure the reproduction of the political class which has controlled Philippine politics for most of the last century and the side which wants to transform the distribution of political and social power in the society. In the end, substantive reform happens only when the balance of political power has shifted.

The question is how the balance will shift and who is to lead the effort to tip it. Rocamora quotes Mario Taguiwalo, a leading advocate of reform, as saying, "We must begin by accepting that this is about the capture and exercise of political power and we need leaders who can gain credibility and following on the basis of what we stand for and who can then become our reliable champions as well as faithful agents in the execution of our agenda for reform."

Rocamora and Taguiwalo are key members of Akbayan, a political party with seats in the House of Representatives through the party-list mode. However, the constitution limits party-list representatives, who generally espouse identifiable programmes, to at most 20 per cent of all members of the House. A law restricts each party-list to three representatives. These clearly are meant to ensure that parties with alternative programs do not gain a majority in the House. Akbayan members have filed some bills providing for reforms, although none, it seems, have gotten anywhere.

RELIGIOUS ORGANIZATIONS IN POLITICS

In the absence of real political parties, elements of organized religion have stepped into the vacuum. Grace Jamon and Mary Grace Mirandilla trace the growth of churches and religious sects in the Philippines and, specifically, the roles that they play in Philippine politics. The Roman Catholic Church has been most prominent in this, being the most widespread and most active of all the religious organizations. It helps, of course, that 80 per cent of Filipinos adhere to Roman Catholicism. Leaders of the Catholic clergy have involved themselves actively in efforts at regime change by extraordinary means, which have led to the removal of Ferdinand Marcos and Joseph Estrada from the presidency. While no one takes issue with the bishops' condemnation of violations of human rights, their assumption of positions on specific political issues is more questionable. These issues, as Jamon and Mirandilla recount them, include constitutional change, mining, the legalization of the popular numbers game called *jeuteng*, the death penalty, and the use of contraception as a birth control method. Jamon and Mirandilla quote Archbishop Angel Lagdameo as saying, "Concretely, the bishops, clergy, and laity must be involved in the area of politics when moral and gospel values are at stake." The question is: who decides in what political issues "moral and gospel values are at stake"? After all, constitutional change, mining policies, the legalization of certain forms of gambling, the death penalty, population policy, and the impeachment of a president are all political issues on which morally upright people can honestly and in good conscience disagree.

The point is that, in the absence of political parties, unelected religious leaders have found it necessary — or have seized the opportunity — to articulate the views of certain segments of the population that would otherwise have no channels for politically conveying those views. Yet, the problem is that religious leaders perceived to be powerful by virtue of their large followings exert pressure on government decisions without bearing the responsibility for the consequences of those decisions. For example, religious leaders do not assume responsibility for the economic impact of rapid population growth or for the crime and corruption surrounding illegal gambling even as they block the government from effectively promoting family planning and legalizing popular forms of gambling. Leaders of the religious organizations Iglesia ni Kristo and El Shaddai are said to influence appointments even to minor posts in the government. This is what happens when no political parties present the people with policy choices.

THE MILITARY IN POLITICS

Sporadically, disgruntled elements of the Philippine military have tried to manifest their opposition to the system through displays of force — coup attempts, mutinies, and rebellious capers. However, their demands are invariably vague except when it concerns their personal or institutional interests. Twice, in 1986 and 2001, the military establishment, or a major part of it, withdrew its support from an incumbent leader, causing his downfall and replacement. Although it immediately ceded formal power to civilian authorities, the military or a significant element thereof showed what a critical force it can be. This demonstration has not been lost on civilian politicians. In this regard, the Philippine situation is different from those in Laos, Malaysia, Singapore, and Vietnam, or in China and Japan, where political power in military hands is all but unthinkable today.

Carolina G. Hernandez lays the blame for the Philippine armed forces' "interventionist tendency" squarely at the door of the politicians and civilian authorities. She cites the military's assumption of civilian functions as an important factor in "interventionism". The military's role in Marcos' martial law and in the political successions of 1986 and 2001 gave it, in some people's eyes and, not least, in its own perception, an image of being a force for political stability and regime survival. Civilian politicians have, accordingly, sought to enlist the military in the pursuit of their political agendas.

Hernandez contends that civilian control and oversight of the military is key to its proper functioning and role. However, she points out that the weakness of civilian political institutions is a big challenge to democratic civilian control over the military:

> Political parties and political leaders have remained unable to move beyond personalities to principled structural and behavioural reforms… . Oversight powers are often misused or abused. Some use their office in oversight bodies as rent-seeking avenues exacting tolls from officers being considered for promotion or high-ranking appointments. Politicians and private persons continue to enlist military support for their private agenda.

Hernandez, who was a member of the Feliciano Commission that recommended reforms in the Philippine military, asserts that many substantial reforms in military institutions, as proposed by the Feliciano Commission and the earlier Davide Commission, have been carried out. However, she stresses that the problems in the Philippine military, including its "interventionist tendency", cannot be effectively addressed in isolation from reforms in the broader political environment. Indeed, she argues that undertaking reforms solely in the military would not reduce the military's tendency to intervene in politics if only "out of frustration with abusive, corrupt, and non-performing civilian officials".

THE ROLE OF THE MEDIA

The Philippine media, being formally free of government control or influence, could partially fill the vacuum created by the absence of political parties by explaining issues, advocating positions, exposing crimes and misdemeanours, and so on. However, in this, the Philippine media have fallen short. In her chapter, Melinda de Jesus argues, "The free press in the Philippines has shown that it is not up to the challenge of nurturing … a community of free citizens." Although the media are supposed to be free of direct state interference, most media outlets are owned by big business concerns, whose control of editorial policy and content varies widely. De Jesus contends that media content about public affairs is remarkably shallow, continuing to focus on "leaders" and prominent personalities rather than articulating the viewpoints of the poor and marginalized. Politicians hardly talk of issues or platforms in media interviews. De Jesus observes, "Investigative reports have singular rather than regular impact and effect on the quality of governance." By this she means that the exposure of corruption may result in an individual being fired but does not lead to any change in the culture of corruption. Media practitioners themselves often succumb to corruption, with columnists, broadcasters, and "talking heads" doubling as lawyers or public relations operatives and using their media platforms to promote their clients' interests or damage those of their competitors. At the other end of the spectrum, many journalists have been killed in the line of duty. According to international media watchdogs, the Philippines is one of the most dangerous places in the world in which to practise journalism. In any case, newspaper readership in the Philippines is tiny and shrinking. This may be partly due to the fact that all nationally circulated newspapers are in English, which indicates that in the Philippines public affairs are debated only within a small, English-speaking elite.

THE INSURGENCIES AS POLITICAL FORCES

The outside world, including some Filipinos, has regarded two movements as being potential political forces in opposition to the Manila-centred establishment — the communist and the Muslim insurgencies. Alexander Magno and Patricio Abinales, in their chapters, arrive separately and in their own ways at the conclusion that these insurgencies are nothing of the sort.

Magno asserts that, from being an ideologically driven, mass-based revolutionary force, the New People's Army has been reduced basically to raising funds in support of the activities of the Communist Party of the Philippines (CPP) and its above-ground fronts. This situation has come about because of the drying up of the party's former sources of financing: the Chinese Communist Party and European non-governmental organizations. Moreover, the end of anti-Marcos mass mobilization deprived the CPP of a source of cadres. Meanwhile, the diminution of conventional conflict in Mindanao has constricted an important source of arms. What remains by way of fund-raising has been essentially extortion operations targeted at logging, telecommunications and transportation companies, plantations, and public works contractors. Yet, Magno points out that even these activities as sources of funding have become less lucrative. The large-scale deforestation of the Philippines has diminished logging, legal or illegal, as a profitable activity. The economic importance of plantations is reduced by urbanization and industrialization. Squeezed between "revolutionary taxation" and kickbacks to politicians, contractors and other businesses are less able to cough up the extorted amounts. Thus, to raise funds, the NPA has had to resort to drug dealing, counterfeiting, kidnapping, and the issuance of "safe conduct" passes to politicians campaigning for election in NPA-controlled areas — activities that do not make the NPA very popular. Meanwhile, costs are increasing for the sustenance of urban cadres and countryside workers, the procurement of arms and ammunition, and the mobilization of large numbers of people for urban protests. The CPP has also resorted to forming operational alliances with wealthy politicians, whatever the latter's ideological leanings, if any, in exchange for votes in areas that the NPA controls or for warm bodies needed for urban political rallies.

Meanwhile, Abinales shatters the romantic myth of a united Muslim community defending its "homeland" in Mindanao in pre-colonial, colonial and post-colonial times. He points out that, in pre-colonial times, Muslim leaders kept themselves busy not fighting against foreign invaders in defence of a Muslim "homeland" but operating in port cities largely for economic purposes. He stresses that the Muslim community has long been divided between clans and between factions of the Muslim elite, citing the persisting hierarchical structure of Mindanao society. In this sense, Muslim politics reflects the feudal structure of Philippine society. Abinales notes that the Muslims have not sought to team up with the indigenous, non-Muslim *lumad* or with the Christian inhabitants of Mindanao on behalf of Mindanao interests. He points out that separatism enjoys little public support, even among Muslims.

Finally, Abinales invites attention to the fact that neither the Moro National Liberation Front (MNLF) nor the Moro Islamic Liberation Front (MILF) has a coherent vision of an "alternative society" for the putative Muslim homeland. The MNLF hierarchy has sunk into corruption once handed the leadership of the Autonomous Region of Muslim Mindanao, while the MILF has been placed on the defensive by the militarily superior Philippine armed forces and the better-prepared peace negotiators from Manila. Abinales highlights the Muslim leaders' deficiencies in vision and governance.

Thus, Magno and Abinales argue that neither the Communist Party of the Philippines and the New People's Army nor the MNLF or the MILF offer an alternative vision of society.

DEMOCRATIC FAILURE

In the introductory chapter, Mely Caballero-Anthony neatly summarizes many of the points made in the book's subsequent chapters, focusing on the political roots of the Philippine malaise. Calling Philippine democracy "dysfunctional", Caballero-Anthony states baldly that "the democratic system of the Philippines has failed in its duty to deliver the basic goods", a failure that has resulted in high unemployment and poverty levels and a massive brain drain. She attributes the failure to weak political institutions, a weakness characterized by the elite's and the political clans' dominance of the political system and by "patronage-infested" political parties serving merely as vehicles for entrenching themselves in power. Another characteristic is the frailty of the Philippine state, which has induced institutions like the Catholic Church and the military to try to step into the gaping political spaces and led the alienated to resort to "people power" or to outright rebellion. However, Caballero-Anthony cites several factors that mitigate the consequences of the country's "democratic deficit" — the "vibrant civil society", which has some political impact, the "deep pool of talent" that remains in the country, the "excellent" universities, the lively service industry, the resourceful entrepreneurs, and the flourishing arts scene.

THE PHILIPPINES — AWAITING BASIC REFORMS[6]

Given the seemingly insurmountable problems and challenges discussed above, what can be done? Economies can grow despite poor governance and bad politics, as demonstrated by some countries in South Asia and Latin America. Today this is made possible partly by information technology and other technological innovations. However, in most cases, the private sector cannot drive development by itself. Government must devise the strategy, set national priorities, lay down policies, and provide public goods. For example, in developing tourism, the state must do its part by putting up physical infrastructure, liberalizing air services, and ensuring personal security.

Despite the dysfunctional nature of the Philippine political system, some reform is possible. It may be recalled that foreign trade, telecommunications, domestic air and sea transport, and banking were liberalized during the Fidel Ramos administration. However, such reforms were partial at best and required extraordinary leadership. Similar reforms are needed in areas such as population, health, education, and savings and investment policies. In mature democracies, these issues are subjected to political debate between contending political parties, in which professional politicians, experienced in governance at various levels, rise through the ranks, as in Germany and other countries in Europe and elsewhere. Pending the emergence of such parties — or of extraordinary leadership at the top — Filipinos who care about their country must engage in "informed advocacy" and political education on their own, an enterprise of uncertain efficacy.

Meanwhile, short of the necessary fundamental reforms, periodic elections, in response to shifts in economic and social conditions, should produce more enlightened and dedicated members of the legislature and local government leaders operating in their limited jurisdictions. The economy will probably continue to plod along at respectable growth rates. Inflation should continue to be manageable unless energy prices shoot through the roof. Unfortunately, the workers and the poor will continue to suffer from deteriorating social services. In desperation, more and more Filipinos will seek greener pastures overseas. The exodus will ease pressures for fundamental reform, with the disaffected and hope-deprived middle class viewing migration as an option in the absence of alternative leaderships. Yet, basic changes are essential — changes in the way that Filipinos govern themselves and share their country's wealth and resources — if Filipinos are to experience substantial and long-term improvements in their lives. Whether, when, and how such changes take place hold the key to the Philippines' future.

As Hill and Piza put it:

> (T)here is a possible way forward: maintaining the hard-won fiscal reform measures, continuing the microeconomic reforms, addressing the social inequities, resolving the deep-seated Mindanao insurrections, and avoiding debilitating coup attempts and military disaffection. A decade of accelerating growth would lift living standards substantially and develop a constituency for further, deeper reform. The next few years will determine whether the current political leadership is up to the challenge.

Notes

1 Gene Frieda and Craig Chan, "Philippines Trip Notes: On a Wing and a Prayer", *The Royal Bank of Scotland Global Emerging Markets Strategic Research*, 6 February 2006.

2 Jonathan Anderson, "The Buzz About the Philippines", *UBS Investment Research Asian Focus*, 24 April 2006.

3 Benoit Anne, "Philippines: Solid Fundamental Story", *Merrill Lynch Emerging Markets*, 20 April 2006.

4 Benoit Anne, "Philippines: Success Story in 2006, but Mounting Risks Next Year", *Merrill Lynch Emerging Markets*, 28 September 2006.

5 John Stuermer, "Philippines Update: GDP Growth in 1H06 Exceeds Expectation but will It Build Support for Arroyo Allies in the May 2007 Election", *Bear Stearns Emerging Markets Sovereign Research Asia, Pacific*, 7 September 2006.

6 Ideas in this section arose from a panel discussion during the 13–14 July 2006 Conference on the Philippines at the Institute of Southeast Asian Studies in Singapore. The panel was made up of Manu Bhaskaran, a Singapore-based international consultant; Frank Cibulka, a Philippines expert and professor at Zayed University in Abu Dhabi; Grace Padaca, the remarkable governor of Isabela Province; and Klaus Preschle, Philippine country representative of the Konrad Adenauer Foundation.

INDEX

A
ABC-5, 133
Abinales, Patricio 29
ABS-CBN radio and television, 43, 69, 133
Abueva, Jose V., 45, 46, 55, 72
accountability, 49
activists
  killing of, 184
ad valorem tax base, 157
Afghanistan, 22
aggregate demand, 142, 149, 150
aggregate supply, 142
Aglipay, Gregorio, 103
Aglipayan Church, 103, 104
agrarian reform programme, 274
agribusiness enterprises
  public-spending bias, 212
agricultural employment, 209
agricultural growth
  effect on rural poverty, 212
agricultural terms of trade, 208
agriculture, 146
  decline in, 150
  low productivity growth, 211
  output, 150
  shifting from, 253
Aguinaldo, Emilio, 54
Al Qaeda, 279
Albania, 224
alienation of masses, 7
Almeda, Wilde, 110
Almonte, Jose, 10
Alunan Glang, 282
American colonial regime, democratic institutions created during, 2
American Christianity, 117
American educators, 103
American period, 129, 130
Ampatuans, 299
Ang, Dante, 133
anitos (spirit of ancestors), 102
annual exchange rate
  per U.S. dollar, 262
annual fiscal balances, 264
annual GDP growth, 250
anti-Arroyo struggle, 20, 21
anti-chacha camps, 26
anti-poverty programmes, 219
anti-smuggling, 192
Apostol, Eugenia, 133
Aquino administration
  failed coup attempt against, 80
  low infrastructure expenditure, 188
Aquino, Benigno, 85, 131
  assassination, 131
Aquino, Corazon, 8, 20, 21, 44, 85, 113, 132, 314

backing of armed forces, 10
restoration of pre-martial law political system, 26, 28
Arab merchants, 102
Araneta, Salvador, 55
Armed Forces of the Philippines (AFP), 31, 78, 116, 277
AFP-MILF skirmishes, 287, 290–94
AFP-MNLF battles, 288
compilation of statistics, 284
deactivation of RSBS, 90
Intelligence Services of, *see* Intelligence Services of the Armed Forces of the Philippines (ISAFP)
interventionist tendency, 79
politicization of, 81
superiority over rebels, 289
Arroyo, 8, 13, 18, 19, 20, 21, 22, 23, 25, 55, 87, 88, *see also* President Arroyo
agreement with MILF, 300
backing of armed forces, 10
call for resignation, 96
constitutional change via people's initiative, 114
deadline for military to end Maoist insurgency, 31
difficulties, 30
effort to remain in power, 31
situation confronted in elections (2004), 29
strong-arm tactics, 115
supporters of, 24
undermining efforts to improve civil service, 32
wooing of INC, 113
Arroyo administration
on survival mode, 21
Arroyo, Gloria, 15, 171
ASEAN, 12
economic cooperation, 145
ASEAN countries, 152
complementation in car parts manufacturing, 164
high growth, 142
investments in, 188
ASEAN economies
summary, 248
ASEAN Five, 248
quantitative examination of growth in, 271
ASEAN Free Trade Area (AFTA), 165
ASEAN Six, 12, 253
Asia
net foreign direct investment into, 188
Asia Regional Information Centre, 333
Asian developing countries (ADCs), 225
Asian Development Bank (ADB)
key indicators, 170
view on Arroyo's "Ponzi game", 34
Asian financial crisis, 151, 152, 164, 180
effect in Indonesia, 210
exchange rates, 241
improvement of tourism since, 198
Asian religiosity, 101
Association of Major Religious Superiors of the Philippines (AMRSP), 21, 105, 116
Ateneo de Manila University, 69
Atienza, Lito, 21, 44
Augustinians, 105
Australia, 65
substantial investments, 188
Autonomous Region of Muslim Mindanao (ARMM), 205, 206, 285
mismanagement of, 299
average years of schooling, 257

B

babaylan, 102
Bacani, Teodoro, 104
back-office operations, 168

Balisacan, Arsenio M., 207
banking and financial reforms, 167
Bangko Sentral, 170
Bangladesh, 229
  independent central bank, 259, 273
Bangon Pilipinas, 110
Bangsa Moro Development Agency, 300
Bangsamoro, 58, 277, 285
Bangsamoro Republik, 278, 286, 287
Basilan, 110, 287
barangays (village), 283
battle of institutions, 11
Bayan Muna, 315
  killings of leaders of, 31
Bellah, Robert, 100
Belmonte, Betty Go, 133
Benedictines, 105
Berger, Peter, 100
bicameral Congress, 44
  obstructive and ineffective, 48
Bicol
  high rate of poverty, 205
  OFWs from, 231
Bids and Awards Committees, 89
big business, 21
big tent politics, 29
Bills
  critical to business, 192
Black and White Movement, 39
Bohlin, Thomas, 106
Boncodin, Emy, 21
Borras Jr., Saturnino, 281
borrowing
  massive, 35
bossism, 4, 7
Botswana, 272
brain drain, 225
Brunei Darussalam, 12
build-operate-transfer (BOT)
    investment arrangements, 168
build-operate-transfer scheme
  privately financed projects, 191
Buldon, 297
Buliok, defence of, 297
Bulletin Today, 131
Bunye, Ignacio, 34
Bureau of Internal Revenue,
    resignations, 35
bureaucracy
  huge increase in number of
      personnel, 33
  weak and dysfunctional, 48, 272
Burgos, Jose, 131
Business Day, 132, 133
business groups, 47
business performance (2006), 186
Business Process Outsourcing (BPO),
    196, 197
Business World, 133
businessmen's perceptions
  (2006) survey, 194

C
cacique democracy, 4, 7
Cagayan Valley
  OFWs from, 231
Calibrated Pre-emptive Response,
    Supreme Court objection, 182
call centres, 168, 196, 197
Camp Abu Bakr
  capture by AFP, 296
Canada, 65
Canoy, Reuben, 55
capital
  lack of, 61
  policies relating use of, 145
capital deregulation, 167
capital formation, 151
  low rate of, 152
Cardinal Sin, 109
Career Executive Service Officer
    (CESO), 33
Career Service Executive Board
    (CESB), 32
  accusations against Malacanang and
      Cabinet for transgressions, 32

Carpio, Antonio, 66
Catholic Bishops' Conference of the Philippines (CBCP), 8, 22, 71, 105, 111, 114, 115, 116
Catholic Church, 2, 7, 8, 9, 21, 28, 65, 105, 109, 113, 196
  advocate for protection of environment, 116
  backing impeachment of Estrada, 114
  divisions in, 22
  natural family planning methods, 117
  opposed to charter change, 115
  opposition to mining, 201
  progressive sections of, 21
  view on population growth, 214
Catholic friars, 103
Catholic hierarchy, 22
Catholicism
  spread of, 102
ceasefire, 92
Cebu, 164
Center for Media Freedom and Responsibility (CMFR), 135
  promotion of culture of ethics and self-regulation, 140
central bank, 259
central development puzzle, 246
Central Luzon
  OFWs from, 231
charter change, 19
  option, 13
Charter Change Advocacy Commission, 44
Chief Justice, 66
children, underweight and under height, 37
Chile, 272
  role of mining, 196
China, 12, 62, 152
  agricultural growth, 210
  economic growth, 252
  FDIs into, 240
  growth elasticity, 209
  growth rates, 268
  high growth rate, 188
  high TFP growth rate, 211
  inflow of foreign direct investment, 168
  production sites shifted to, 165
Chinese Buddhism, 101
Christian groups, 102
Christianity, 101
  American, 117
  Iberian, 117
chromite
  rich deposits of, 196
citizen press councils, 140
Citizens' Movement for a Federal Philippines (CMFP), 55, 62
  Draft Constitution, 50, 51
civic journalism, 138
civil-military relations, 10
  democratizing, 86
civil service
  steps for improvement undermined, 32
Civil Service Eligibility Exam
  effort to terminate, 32
civil society, 14
civil society coalition, 20
civil society groups, 85, 203
civil society organizations (CSOs), 14, 47
civilian authority
  supremacy of, 78
civilian control
  personalization of, 82
civilian oversight institutions, 79
Clark
  ecozone, 192
  export zone, 186
class distinction, 28
class interest, 28
clientelism, 28–29
CODE-NGO, 20
Cojuanco Jr., Antonio, 133

Collas-Monsod, Solita, 34
collective interest, 28
collective responsibility, 49
combatants
numbers killed in armed encounters, 296
commercial uncertainty, 272
Commission on Appointments, 47
Commission on Audit, 299
Commission on Elections (Comelec), 19, 27, 31, 44, 45, 46, 50, 72, 112
reverification of signatures for constitutional amendment petition, 67
Commission on Human Rights of the Philippines, 87, 96
communist insurgency, 79, 91, 313
problem of, 2
Communist Party of China, 317
Communist Party of the Philippines (CPP), 22, 82, 296, 313
CPP/NPA, 13, 317
centralized authority, 318
financial resources, 320
Manila Commission, 315
Comprehensive Agrarian Reform Program (CARP)
implementation of, 208
source of provincial income, 218
Confucianism, 100
Congress, 157
acts of, 19
responsiveness to Bills, 192
"congressional horse trading", 27
consolidating democracy, 13
Constantino, Renato, 4
Constitution (1935), 55, 62, 117
change to convert unicameral legislature to bicameral, 68
Constitution (1987), 25, 43, 55, 62, 63, 64, 108
comprehensive set of proposed amendments, 45
failure of effort to amend, 66
participatory process proposed, 57
proposal to amend, 43, 44
Constitutional Convention (1971), 63
constitutional reform, 25
need for, 38, 337, 338
Consultative Commission (2005), 44, 50, 62
Chairman, 45, 46
proposals for political parties, 53, 54
consumer companies
downgrading size of products, 194
consumption expenditure, 236
conventional growth explanations, 270
copper
deposits of, 196
corruption, 299
discouraging investments, 184
major problem of, 183
tolerance towards, 30
cosmopolitanism ratio, 318
costs of production
reducing, 170
coup attempts, 274
coup d'etat
criminalized, 80
Couples for Christ, 108, 109
criminal activities, 320
crisis of confidence, 23
crisis of representation, 18
Crisostomo, Manuel
termination of, 32
crony debt, 263
Cruz, Jr., Avenlino, 89
Cruz, Oscar, 116
current account balances, 264, 265
current account deficit, 254, 263

D

Datu Ali of Kudarangan, 279
Datu Michael Mastura, 301
Datu Udtog Matalam, 279
Datumanong, Simeon, 289

David, Randy, 30
Davide Commission, 83, 84
  coup attempts investigated by, 85
Davide Commission Report, 85
Dayrit, Manuel, 118
de Mesa, Max, 116
de la Salle University, 69
de Venecia, Jose, 25, 44, 55, 70
  "chacha" agenda, 27
debt
  external, 265
  source of vulnerability, 35
debt consolidations, 161
debt service burden, 168
debt/GDP ration, highest of ASEAN Four, 263
debt-driven growth, 252
defence reform, 79
  measures, 86, 87
Defence Secretary, 99
definitions
  people power, 98
demobilizing, effect of Philippine populism, 29
democracy
  failure of, 343
  low quality, 4
democratic consolidation, 3
  as a process, 3
democratic deficit, 4
democratic Left, 20
democratic system
  well entrenched, 182
democratization, 2
demographic dividend, 219
Deng Xiaopeng, 317
Department of Education
  Culture and Sports (DECS), Undersecretary, 32
  presentation of results to Cabinet, 37
Department of Finance, 192
  resignations, 35
Department of Information and Communication Technology (DICT), 192
Department of Interior and Local Governments, 44
Department of National Defence (DND), 87
Department of Trade and Industry, 192
development economics literature, 246
development record, 273
development-based approach to insurgency, 313
developmental journalism, 130
developmental power, 7
Diaz, Patricio, 281
domestic banking
  internationalizing of outlook, 167
domestic investment, 152
  (1960s to 2000), 254
dominant institutions, 7
dominant social bloc, 21
Dominicans, 105
double taxation, 322

E

East Asia, 146, 154, 167
  comparison with, 142
  high growth economies, 143
  poverty reduction, 205
  trade competition with, 165
  working-age population, 213
East Asia region, 152
East Asian miracle, 213
  demographic dividend, contribution of, 213
economic competitiveness, 12
economic forecast, 200
economic growth, 226
  poor performance of, 204
  required for reduction of poverty, 203
economic liberalization, 154, 163

economic performance
  accentuated booms and busts, 143
  poor, 149
  sluggishness, 332
economic reforms
  need for, 170
economic zones
  granting investment incentives in, 186
economy
  consumption driven, 149
  growth performance, 142
  key indicators, 249
  payments position, 142
EDSA, 23
EDSA (1), 21, 117
  role of church, 22
EDSA (2), 1, 21, 26
  role of church, 22
EDSA (3), 1, 26
EDSA "people power", 63
Edsa-like "revolution", 2
educated migrant outflows, 223
education, 203
  falling standards, 35
  investments in, 209
  journalism school, 139
  language medium of, 196
  shortage of classrooms, 37
  spending on, 183
El Shaddai Prayer Movement, 108, 109, 110, 115
elections, 19
  cheating in, 29
  legitimacy of, 18
  May, 38, 2007
elections (2004), 29
Electric Power Industry Act (EPIRA), amendments, 192
electricity
  access to, 205
electronics, 164
  performance of, 268
elite factions, 18
elite military units, 22
elites, domination of politics and economics, 11
elitist, 28
emigration
  effect on quality of goods and services, 225
employment
  opportunities, 212
  sluggish growth, 258
empowering the marginalized, failure to, 7
endemic corruption, 159
English language proficiency, 168, 184, 257
"entrepreneurs of violence", 281
envelopmental journalism, 130
Erap, *see* Estrada, Joseph
Ermita, Eduardo, 297
Escriva, Jose Maria, 106
Estanislao, Dr Jesus, 107
Estrada government, 19
Estrada, Joseph, 4, 6, 7, 19, 20, 21, 26, 28, 171
  actor-turned-politician, 113
  extravagant lifestyle, 135
  military breakaway from, 84
  ousting of, 8
  uprising against, 10
ethnic separatism, 82
European radicals
  support for communists, 318
Evangelical Church, 103, 108
Evangelicals, 104
exchange rate, 163
  annual, 262
  long-tern movements, 261
executive branch
  members prohibited from testifying in Senate, 31
Executive Order (EO)(464)
  deemed illegal by Supreme Court, 32

members of executive branch prohibited from testifying in Senate, 31
objection of Supreme Court, 182
expenditures
health and education, cutting back on, 36
exports
performance, 163, 164
external debt, 161, 168, 265
external trade, 142
extra-constitutional ascension, 19
extra-judicial killings, 31
extracting rents
Philippines political system, 29

F
Fababaer, Zaldy M., 116
Family Income and Expenditure Survey (FIES), 236
Fareed Zakaria, 3
federal republic
expected advantages in changing to, 58
federalism
broaden and deepen democracy, 59
Federalistas, 54
Feliciano Commission, 83, 84, 88, 90, 93, 98
recommendations, 99
feudal lords, 299
feudalism, 299
Filipino diaspora, 222
remittances from, 15
Filipino expatriates
publishing of *La Solidaridad*, 129
Filipino revolution, 54
Filipino revolutionaries, 103
financial crisis, 165, 269, 270
financial sector
access to world capital market, 166
financial-technical assistance agreements (FTAA), 115
"firewall"
between economy and politics, 33
fiscal account balances, 265
fiscal borrowing
solution through massive borrowing, 35
fiscal deficit, 154, 155, 161
fiscal incentives
rationalization, 192
fiscal measures, 156
fiscal performance
methods to improve, 155
fiscal problems
other solutions, 36
fiscal sector
deficit reduction, 142
flash memory
production, 275
food insecurity
effect of agricultural growth, 212
food prices
domestic, 210
food processing, 199
foreign capital
dependency on, 153
liberalization of, 169
foreign direct investment, 146, 164, 167, 222
average shares of, 266
downward trend, 226
into Asia, 188
Japan, 225
foreign exchange
remittances as source of, 229
foreign exchange earnings
diversification of sources, 161
foreign exchange inflows
impact of, 229
foreign investments
evaluation of, 194

foreign-owned companies
mining, 147
Fort Bonifacio, 88, 90
"fourth estate", 129
fragile democracy, 82
Franciscans, 105
fraud
tolerance towards, 30
free expression
tradition of, 128, 129
free press, 10
free trade agreements (FTAs)
United States of America, 246
freedom of press, 10
French Revolution
ideals of, 129

G
Garci tapes scandal, 29, 31
Garcillano, Virgilio, 19
Gawad Kalinga, 109
General Court-Martial (GCM), 87
General Council of the Union, 103
Germany, 24, 62, 65
Glang, Alunan, 282
Gloriagate scandal, 113
gold
rich deposits of, 196
goods and services
deterioration of quality, 225
governance
crisis of, 127
issue of, 7
governance vacuum, 23
Government of the Republic of the Philippines (GRP), 92
government consumption expenditure, 149
government expenditure, 158
(1960s to 2000), 254
government spending
poverty programme, 213
Gozon, Felipe, 133
Great Britain, 24
GMA-7, 133
gross capital formation, 149
gross domestic product (GDP), 11, 61
annual growth rate, 250
average growth (1961–2004), 181
growth of selected Asian countries, 181
low per capita growth, 217
manufacturing, 253
per capita, 180
services, 253
widening disparity with GNP, 147, 148
gross national expenditure, 254
widening disparity with GDP, 147, 148
gross national product (GNP), 143
gross regional domestic product (GRDP)
data on remittances, 236
growth elasticity
poverty reduction, of, 208
growth rates, 143
discrepancies in, 148
Gutierrez, Eric, 281

H
Hadji Kamlon, 279
Harberger, A.C., 272
Hashim Salamat, 300
health and education, 212
healthcare, 199
investments in, 209
Hidalgo, Fe, 36
Honasan, Gregorio, 83, 99
Hong Kong, 143, 196
hotels
insufficiency of, 197
House of Representatives, 20, 27, 31, 44, 45, 46, 114

dismissal of impeachment motion against Arroyo, 114
final push for charter change, 70
support for constitutional amendments, 66
House Speaker, 25
Huk insurgency, 78, 97
Huks
counter-insurgency against, 81
human capital, 208
Human Development Index (HDI)
Metro Manila, of, 218
Human Development Network, 297
human rights violations, 31
hunger
high rate of, 183
Huntington, Samuel, 100
Hyatt 10
cabinet ministers who resigned, 20
call for elections, 38, 39

I
IBC-13, 133
Iberian Christianity, 117
Iglesia Filipina Indpendiente (IFI), 103, 116
Iglesia ni Cristo (INC), 103, 104, 112
support of El Shaddai's position on people's initiative, 115
Ileto, Reynaldo, 4
illegal loggers, 321, 322
Ilocos
OFWs from, 231
Iloilo
revolutionary leaders in, 54
impeachment attempts, 23
impeachment cases, 8
import substitution, 266
income
long-term growth, 203
income inequality, 228
income growth
not able to sustain population growth, 217
income transfers, 229
independent central bank, 259
independent public broadcasting
need for, 139
India, 65, 222
call centres, 197
FDIs into, 240
weak economic growth, 223
Indian Buddhism, 101
Indigenous People's Summit, 285
Indonesia, 12, 143, 252
agricultural growth, 210
coefficient of variation, 274
decline in poverty, 33
emigration, 223
exchange rate movements, 261
growth elasticity, 209
inequality levels, 257
inflow of foreign direct investment, 168
influence of military, 22
low level of investments, 188
massive inflow of capital, 165
population growth, 213
rate of domestic investment, 152
TFP growth, 211
industrial cronyism, 151
industrial development, 166
industrial performance, 163
industrial sector
access to international credit, 166
industrial upgrading prospects, 275
industry
decline in output, 150
inflation, 259
annual, 260
average, 261
coefficient of variation, 261
information technology (IT), 193
potential of, 196
information technology enabled services (ITES), 196
infrastructure
access to, 204, 208

economic zones, in, 186
expansion of, 146
low rate of spending on, 183
role in attracting private investment, 189
rural, 212
structural policy reforms affecting, 169
infrastructure expenditure
Aquino administration, during, 188
infrastructure facilities
insufficient, 197
infrastructure investment
importance of, 187, 188
infrastructure projects
Arroyo administration, 191
infrastructure spending
as percentage of GDP, 190
Iniguez, Deogracias, 114, 118
initial human capital stock, 208
Initiative and Referendum Act, 67
Inspector-General, 87
Institute for Strategic and Development Studies, 91
Institute for Studies in Asian Church Culture, 107
institutional barriers, 272
institutional crisis, 5
institutionalized civilian oversight, 81
Institute of Peace, United States, 278
institutions
damage to, 30–33
dominant, 7
weak, 5
insurgencies
development based approach to, 313
political forces, as, 341, 342
Intelligence Services of the Armed Forces of the Philippines (ISAFP)
virtual takeover of, 31
Intel
flash memory production, 275
interest groups, 47
internal debt, 161
internal security operations, 91
international capital markets
exclusion from, 269
international credit
access to, 161, 166
international migration, 224, 225
international reserves, 184
interventionist, 94
inward foreign capital
restrictions placed upon, 148
investment
trend in, 190
investment in health, 203
investment incentives, 156
investment opportunities, 195–99
investment policies, 145
investment rates, 151, 254
investments
barriers to, 184
information technology, in, 193
not broad-based, 193
Islam, 101, 102
Islamic missionaries, 102
Israel, 62
Italy, 65

J

Japan, 24, 62, 65, 143, 278
FDI from, 225
long-term recession, 270
substantial investments, 188
Japanese emperor
restoration after post-war Japan, 286
Japanese religions, 101
Jaraula, Constantino G., 46
Jemaah Islamiyah (JI), 91, 279
Jesuits, 105
Jesus is Lord (JIL) Fellowship, 110, 119
Jesus Miracle Crusade, 110
Joint Defence Assessment (JDA), 88
Joint U.S. Military Advisory Group—Southside Homeowners Association, Inc., 90
Jollibee, 199

Jolo, 295
journalism
civic, 138
education, 139
journalists
celebrities, 136
integrity of, 135, 136
murder of, 136, 137, 184
Judaism, 101
Justice, Peace and Integrity of Creation Commission, 106

K
Karaos, Anna Marie, 28
KEPCO, 189
Keppel, Gilles, 101
key social indicators, 256
Khaled Musa, 297
Kilusang Mayo Uno, 317
kinship network, 224
Kintanar, Romulo, 315
Konrad Adenauer Foundation, 55
Korea, 62
tax effort ratio, 35
tourists from, 198
Korean shipbuilding enterprise, 164
Krusadang Bayan Laban sa Jueteng (National Crusade Against Jueteng), 116
Kusog Mindanao (Mindanao Force), 55

L
La Solidaridad, 129
labour
availability, 184
policies affecting use of, 145
Labour Force Survey, 333
labour market policies
restrictive, 258
labour policy
minimum wage setting, 145
Laban ng Masa, 20
Lagdameo, Angel, 70, 114
Lagman, Felimon, 315, 316
Lakas Christian-Muslim Democrats Party, 44
Lakas-NUCD-UMDP, 55
Lamas, Sotero, 315
Lanao de Sur, 287
land
policies affecting use of, 145
structural policy reforms affecting, 169
land reform, 11
large farmers
public spending bias, 212
large-scale mining
lack of capital, 61
Lasallians, 105
Latin American populists, 29
Latin-American-style hyper-inflation, 247
Left group, 20, 21, 23, 24, 28
to provide major change in perspective, 40
Leftist groups
distrust of police, 22, 24, 31
legislative oversight committees, 79
legislature
disbanding during martial law, 78
strong, 272
Liberal Party, 20, 21
LIBOR, 161
Libya, 278
military aid to MNLF, 289
life expectancy, 248
Lihok Pideral Mindanao (Mindanao Federalist Movement), 55
Lim, Danilo, 83, 84
literacy rate
adult, 208
Locsin Jr., Teodoro, 133
Locsin, Raul, 133
London inter-bank rate, 162
Lorenzana Lito, 55

lumad (indigenous peoples), 58, 284, 289
coalition, 285
Lumad Development Center, 284
Luneta, Jose, 315
Luz, Juan Miguel, 37
sacking of, 32
Luzon, 189, 204, 298
blackouts in, 191

M

macro balances
long term, 263
macroeconomic data
external sector, 175, 176
output and expenditure, 172
prices and interest rates, 174
public finance, 177
savings, investment and revenue, 178, 179
selected, 172
macroeconomic management
lag in, 258, 259
macroeconomic performance, 169
macroeconomic problems, 142, 143
Magdalo leaders, 84, 88
Oakwood Mutiny, 98
Maguindanao, 281, 287
Maguidanaoans, 289
Makati Business Club, 20, 21, 69
Malacanang Palace, 1, 104
Malawi, 224
Malaya, 132
Malaysia, 12, 65, 143, 223, 272
agricultural growth, 210
coefficient of variation, 274
domestic investment rate, 152
elimination of absolute poverty, 204
Employees Provident Fund, 263
exchange rate movements, 261
exports, 164
inflow of foreign direct investment, 168
infrastructure spending, 183
massive inflow of capital, 165
population growth, 258
self-sufficiency in capital, 153
tax effort ratio, 35
Malolos Constitution, 54, 128
Malolos Republic, 2
Manalo, Felix, 103
Manila
new international airport, 158
Manila International Airport, 131
Manila Standard, 133
Manila Times, 133
manufactured exports, 164
growth, 268
manufacturing output, 150
manufacturing sector
export markets, 166
Maoists, 20, 40
Insurgency, 31, 82
Movement, 316
Maranao, 281, 289
Marawi City, 287
Marcos, Ferdinand, 6, 9, 8, 20, 21, 28, 81, 94, 101
"entrepreneurial" supporters, 263
overthrow of, 4, 314
sequestration of political opponents' property, 78
success into second term, 130
uprisings against, 10
Marcos, Imelda, 130
Marcos loyalist officers, 84
Marine Base, 84
Marines, 22
market-friendly institutions, 212
martial law, 8, 78, 79, 279
killings during, 115
lifting of, 131
position of press, 130, 131
September (1972), 78
martial law period, 111
Marxists, 105

Mastura, Michael, 55
Matalam, Udtog, 55
Matanog, 297
maximalist view, 3
McKenna, Thomas, 282
mean consumption expenditure, 236
Medalla, Felipe, 247
media, 8
  celebrity, 136
  centre of countervailing power, 47
  interference from owners, 133
  role of media in politics, 340, 341
medium-term outlook, 200
Menzi, Hans, 131
Merrill Lynch
  report, 330, 331
Metro Manila
  lowest poverty, 205
  vibrant retail sector, 149
Mexico, 222
  effect of remittances in, 241
  tax effort ratio, 35
  upward pressure on wages, 224
middle class
  political expressions of, 21
middle class frustration, 20
Middle East
  volatility of situation in, 166
middle management
  quality of, 185
migrant determinants, 224
migrant stock, 224
migration, 335
military, 8, 9, 10
  breakaway from Estrada, 84
  corruption, 81
  establishment of investment corporations, 81
  influence of, 22
  interference with politics, 339, 340
  interventionist tendency, 82, 84
military bases
  hosting of, 128
military disaffection, 274
military interventionism, 83
  in politics, 80
military modernization, 88
millenarian movements, 103
Mindanao, 22, 55, 91, 204, 289
  insurrections, 274
  leaders in, 72
  reasons as to Muslim rebellion, 282, 283
  settlers in, 57
  whether military obstructing peace in, 79
Mindanao Independence Movement (MIM), 279
Mindanao Indigenous People's Peace Forum, 285
mineral exploitation, *see also* mining
  expansion of, 146
  foreign-owned companies, 147
minimalist view, 3
minimum wages, 145
mining
  effort by Church to ban, 196
  foreign-owned companies, 147
missionaries
  Islam, 102
Misuari, Nur, 289
  abandoned by allies, 280
Moambing, Ramon, 284
modernization, 100
monetary reform, 155
monopolies
  public utilities, 159
Moro Islamic Liberation Front (MILF), 55, 91, 277
  inferior to AFP, 289
  not reaching out to Christians, 286
  peace talk with government, 301
  Salah Jubair, 281
  support of community, 283
Moro National Liberation Front (MNLF), 55, 82, 277, 281

first assaults on AFP, 295
inferior to AFP, 289
military aid from Libya, 289
negotiation with government, 278
not reaching out to Christians, 286
rebellion, 279
settlement with government, 318
Moro nationalism, 286
Moro rebellions, 71
Moro separatism, 79, 92, 94
Moros, 58
marginalization of, 57
mortality rates, 213
movie personalities
in politics, 6
Mozambique
upward pressure on wages, 224
Mr. & Ms. Special Edition, 132
multinational corporations
view on Philippine situation, 187
Muslim elite politics, 280
Muslim minority, 56
Muslim separatism, 13, 278
Muslims, 104
mutiny
criminalized, 80
Myanmar
power of military in, 22

N
National Capital Region
OFW from, 231
National Council of Churches in the Philippines (NCCP), 107, 111, 115
National Democratic Front (NDF), 82, 314
national emergency, 1
National Recovery Program, 88
national saving rate, 152
National Statistics Office, 104
natural advantage, 195
natural resources
exploitation of, 146
policies affecting use of, 145
structural policy reforms affecting, 169
NBN-4, 133
Negros Occidental, 327
net foreign demand, 149
New Bill of Duties and Obligations
proposal for, 62
New National Defence Act, 90
New People's Army (NPA), 82, 296, 314
consistent challenge, 321
hitmen, 315
revolutionary taxation, 321
safe conduct passes, 322
New Procurement Reform Law (Republic Ac 9184), 88
New York Times, 135, 180, 187
NGOs
opposed to mining, 201
nominal tariff rates
reforms reducing, 163
non-government organizations (NGOs), 196, 203
non-tax revenues, 155
North Korea, 199
Norway, 65
Nur Misuari, 278, 289, 298
see also Misuari

O
Oakwood Mutiny, 84, 85
perpetrators, 97
obtructionist Senate, 13
off-budget government activities, 263
Office of Ethical Standards and Professional Accountability, 87
Office of the Presidential Adviser for the Peace Process, 90
Office of the Presidential Adviser to Implement the Feliciano Commission Recommendations (OPAIFCR), 89

official development assistance (ODA), 222
oil drilling
  lack of capital, 61
oligarchic democracy, 11
Ombudsman, 31
One Voice alliance, 69
open economy, 166
Oplan Bantay Laya (Operation Freedom Watch), 116
Oplan Hackle, 83, 84, 96
opposition senators, 20
Opus Dei, 106
orang besar, 280
Organization of Islamic Conference (OIC), 278
  recognition of MNLF, 279
Osama bin Laden, 279
Osmena, John H., 55
output
  growth, 144
outsourcing, 168
Overseas Contract Workers (OCWs), 230
overseas Filipino workers (OFWs), 148, 230
  regional distribution of, 231
  remittances, 34, 149, 168, 169, 184
overseas workers, 232
Overseas Workers Welfare Administration (OWWA)
  lack of funds to repatriate Filipinos from Lebanon, 32

P

Pakistan, 224
Panganiban, Artemio, 186
  Chief Justice, 66
Parish Pastoral Council for Responsible Voting (PPCRV), 112
Parliament
  acts of, 19
parliamentary government
  broadening and deepening of democracy, 59
  encourage development of two-party system, 49
  expected advantages over presidential government, 48, 49, 50
Parouk Hussein, 299
partisan politics, 19
parts and components
  exports of, 267
Party of the Global Filipino Nation, 71
party politics, 20
party system
  weak and dysfunctional, 48
Pascual, Maitet Diokno, 34
Pastoral Letter, 114
patrimonial state, 11
patronage
  tolerance towards, 30
pay incentives
  introduction of, 157
PDP-Laban political party, 55
peace talks
  government-MILF, 301
Pedrosa, Carmen N., 69
pension systems, 154
Pentecostal, 108
People Power, 1, 9, 15, 64
  definition of, 98
  method of political succession, 83
  ouster of Marcos, 82
  revolts, 49
  revolution waged on EDSA, 101
  twentieth anniversary, 1
People Power (1986), 4, 8
People Power, demonstration, 7
"people power" movements, EDSA, 1, 2
"people power" revolt, 19
people's initiative, 38

per capita GDP, 215, 247, 248, 251
average growth, 251
per capita income, 208
Peron, 29
personalitic politics, 6
peso
depreciation, 263
exchange rate policy, 167
Philippine Alliance of Human Rights Advocates, 116
Philippine Center for Investigative Journalism, 6, 116
Philippine Commission on Human Rights, 138
Philippine Constabulary, 86
Philippine Council of Evangelical Churches (PCEC), 107
Philippine Daily Inquirer, 69, 133
influential media establishment, 43
Philippine Defence Forum, 90
Philippine Defence Reform, 10
Philippine Fact Book (2003), 134
Philippine Human Development Report (2005), 92, 205
Philippine Human Rights Commission, 80
Philippine Independent Church, 103, 112
Philippine Military Academy (PMA), 93
Philippine Mining Act (1995), 115
Philippine National Police, 32, 116
Philippine National Statistics Office, 333
Philippine Overseas Employment Administration, 333
Philippine populism
effect of, 29
Philippine Star, 69, 133
Philippines
incidence of poverty, 206, 207
income growth, 206, 207
investment opportunities in, 195–99
lowest growth among major Asian countries, 180
negative image overseas, 182
perception as in investment site, 193
upward pressure on wages, 224
Pikit
defence of, 297
Pimentel, Aquilino Q., 55
PJR Report, 140
Plaza Accord, 225
Poe Jr., Fernando, 6, 7, 19, 26, 28
police
functional separation from military, 80
Police Special Action Force, 22
political barriers, 272
political bossism
tolerance towards, 30
political clans, 281
political class, 26
political crisis, 23
aspects of, 127
political disturbance
certain countries more prone to, 248
political instability, 55
political interference
operations of public corporations, 159
political Islam
rise of, 279
political parties, 6, 27, 64, 85, 93
early 1990s, 132
lack of, 336
members chosen by, 47
poor state since independence, 51
proposed reforms to strengthen, 51
strengthening of, 13, 51
weak institutions, 5
weak state of, 29
political society, 3
political stability, 79

political structure, 7
political system
  corrupt and patronage-ridden, 27
  rapid degeneration, 19
political system (1935)
  as restored by Aquino, 26
political system
  problems derived from, 19
political transition, 2
political will
  common good, for, 59
politics
  control of, 26
  personalistic, 272
"Ponzi game"
  borrowing to repay maturing loans, 34
Pope Benedict XVI, 117
Pope John Paul II, 106
popular democrats, 316
population growth, 144, 203, 209, 258
  contentious issue, 214
  high, 334
  need to address, 218
  Philippines, 215
  rapid, 212–16
  rate of growth, 203
  Thailand, 215
  young dependants, 149
populism, 29
pork-barrel system, 159
post-Enlightenment religion, 117
post-Marcos populism, 28
post-martial law, 9
poverty, 255
  East Asia, 205
  factors influencing reduction of, 208
  high level of, 60
  incidence of, 33, 248, 331
  persistence of, 217
  problem of, 202
  proposal to reduce, 61
  rates, 209
poverty reduction, 64, 204, 216, 273
  advocates of, 203
  growth elasticity, 208
  international remittances, 226
  poor performance in, 204
  remittances contribution, 222
  slow rate of, 202
  slower, 256, 257
  sluggish rate of, 209
  sustained, 209
power
  developmental, 7
  infrastructural, 7
power plants, 189
prayer rallies, 118, 119
pre-martial law
  position of press, 130
President Arroyo, 4, 7, 214
  acceptance of Supreme Court decision, 68
  coup attempt against, 1
  impeachment attempt, 70
Presidential Commission on Good Government (PCGG), 32
Presidential Council on Moral Values, 108
presidential government
  separation of powers, 49
Presidential Regional Officers for Development, 81
presidential system, 128
  inefficient and obstructive, 48
Presidential Task Force for Military Reform, 94
President's Social Fund for Zambales Congressman Antonio Diaz, 32
press
  adversarial relationship with government, 128
  "champion of the underdog", 129

clampdown on freedom of, 130
government action against, 137, 138
independence, 128
integrity of, 135, 136
political institution, 127
power and influence of, 135
power of, 134
reform of, 139, 140
as "watchdog", 128
press freedom, 10, 128, 129
price controls, 167
focus on "breaking news", 138
price stabilization, 159
Pritchett, L.
growth explanation, 270
private consumption expenditure, 149
private investment
attraction of, 189
private sector management, 160
privatization
competing with corporate governance, 160
pro-Arroyo chacha camp, 26
Proclamation No. 1017
objections of Supreme Court, 182
Proclamation No. 1081, 130
productivity
growth of, 144
rapid, 209
professionals, young, 168
property rights security
lack of, 255
proportional representation, 50
Proposed Revision of the 1987 Constitution, 52
Consultative Commission, 72
protected industries, 151
protectionist policies, 145
Protestant Church, 107
Protestantism, 103
protracted people's war, 321
"protracted struggle", decades of, 40
public broadcasting
independent *see* independent public broadcasting
public corporations
fiscal problems, 159
political interference in, 160
public debt
financing of, 161, 162
management of, 142
public expenditure
efficiency of, 158, 159
public utilities, 146, 159
structural policy reforms affecting, 169
evolution of, 146
public utility services, 169
public works contracts
corruption in, 159
Pulse Asia survey, 23
Puno, Reynato S., 67
Puno, Ronaldo, 44
Purisima, Cesar, 21

Q
Querubin, Ariel, 83, 84
Quezon, Manuel L., 44

R
Radio Veritas, 111
Ramos, Fidel V., 15, 113
amnesty extended to coup plotters, 86
ensuring Misuari's governorship, 298
macroeconomic management improvement, 259
Ramos administration
budget deficit during, 34
Ramos years
enthusiasm sensed during, 186
rate of hunger, 183
Razon Jr., Enrique, 133
reaffirmists, 315
recession, 269

Reform the Armed Forces of the Philippines Movement (RAM), 83, 84
regime survival, 79
regression equations
effect of remittances on development, 235
rejectionists, 315
religion
interference with politics, 339
religious groups
convergence of views regarding Arroyo's election, 118
religious institutions, 7
religious motivation, 101
de-activation, 90
remittance recipient country, 22
remittance system, 226
remittance windfall
moral hazard effect, 229
remittances
consequences of, 228
effect on regional development, 235
for consumption and investment, 227
from Filipino diaspora, 15
impact on poverty reduction, 239
international migration, 222
motivation to send, 227
overseas Filipino workers, 34, 149, 168, 169, 184
regional distribution of, 231, 232, 233
source of foreign exchange, 22
third largest recipient, 258
reproductive health advocates, 118
Republic Act No. 6735, Initiative and Referendum Act, 67
Resolution 619
list of personnel actions by Arroyo administration, 33
retirement homes, 199
Retirement Service and Benefits System (RSBS), 81, 84, 89
revenue administration
need for reform, 35
Revolutionary Proletarian Army, 315
Revolutionary Proletarian Army-Alex Boncayao Brigade, 316
Revolutionary Workers Party, 315
Reyes, Angelo, 88
Reyes, Isabelo de los Reyes, 103
RFM, 199
rido
violent clan wars, 281
Rizal Park
massive rally at, 71
Roman Catholic, 104
Roman Catholic Association of Major Religious Superiors, 20
Roman Catholic Church, 104, 106
Roman Catholic Renewal Movement, 109
RORO ports, 191
Roxas, Mar, 23
RPN-9, television network, 133
rule of law, 3
Runo, Ronald
explanations for killings, 31
rural development, 209
rural non-farm areas, 212

S
Sachs-Warner indicator of openness, 275
Sacred Heart Novitiate, 111
Said, Edward, 277
Salah Jubair, 281
Salceda, Joey, 33, 34
Salesians, 105
San Miguel Corporation, 199
Saudi Arabia, 196
savings
low rate of, 61, 142, 152, 254
saving-investment gap, 151, 152
savings and investment issues, 142
scandals
Garci tapes, 31

Scandinavian, 62
schooling years, 257
Scout Rangers, 22
secessionism
  discouragement of, 58
Second Plenary Council of the Philippines (PCP-II), 111
Second Vatican Council, 109
secular values, 101
security sector reform (SSR), 94, 95, 96
Security Sector Reform Index (SSRI), 90
Self-Reliant Military Defence Programme, 81
semiconductors, 164
Senate, 20
  constitutional change, 46
  intransigence of, 26
  objections to proposed Constitutional amendments, 44
  power of, 25
Senate investigations
  Overseas Workers Welfare Administration (OWWA) lack of funds, 32
separation of church and state, 103, 117
separation of powers, 182
separatism
  Muslim South, 2
  support, 287
services
  cutting back on, 36
  growth of sector, 253
  output, 150
  rise in output, 150
Shleifer-Vishny
  view on corruption, 270
"showbiz democracy", 4, 6
Sigaw ng Bayan (Cry of the People), 27, 44, 65, 69
  appeal against dismissal of petition, 67
  petition dismissed, 66
Sin, Jaime Cardinal, 8, 22
Singapore, 12, 62, 65, 143, 195
  capital exporting, 153
  coefficient of variation, 274
  domestic investment rate, 152
  exchange rate against U.S. dollar, 261
  highest score for TIMSS, 37
  inflow of foreign direct investment, 168
  substantial investments, 188
simplified net income taxation system (SNITS), 192
Sison, Jose Maria, 315, 316, 319
slaves, 284
social capital, 224
social inequities
Social Security System, 153
social services
  access to, 204
  investments in, 209, 218
  manifestation of, 202
Social Weather Stations, 183
Society of Jesus, 106
socio-economic fault lines, 11
socio-economic issues, 11, 12
Soliven, Jr. Maximo, 133
Sosmena Jr., Gaudencio, 55
South Korea, 24, 143, 152, 167
  emigration from, 223
Southeast Asia, 2, 154
  remarkable economic growth, 203
Southern Tagalog
  OFW from, 231
Southridge School for boys, 107
Spain, 65
  dictatorial regime, 106
  revolution against, 54
Spanish-American war, 128
Spanish Catholicism, 117
Spanish colonial period, 117

Spanish colonizers, 102
  conquistadores, 8, 102
Spanish friars, 102
Spanish sovereignty, 103
Sri Lanka, 224
stable societies, 19
stagnation, 252
state of emergency
  proclamation by Arroyo, 23
strong institutions, 3, 7
structural policy reforms, 169
structural problems, 146
struggle for constitutional reform, 27
Struggle of the Masses, 20
sub-national data, 226
Subic Bay, 186
  area, 164
subsidies, 219
Suharto, 152
Sultan Kudarat, 279
sultanates
  destruction of, 102
Sunday homilies, 105
Supreme Court, 23, 65, 67, 96
  cancelling measures of Arroyo administration, 182
  rejecting proposed amendments to 1987 Constitution, 44
  rejection of people's initiative petition, 66
Survey of Overseas Filipinos (SOF), 230, 231
Sweden, 65
  tax effort ratio, 34
system change, 18
systemic change, 21
  orientation, 20
systemic crisis, 18
systemic inertia, 24

T
Tabara, Arturo, 315
Tagaytay, 117
Taiwan, 62, 143
tariff protection
  structural distortions caused by, 163
Tausug, 281, 289
tax administration, 157, 158
tax collection agencies
  improving administration of, 157
tax effort, 155
  raising of, 157
tax effort ratio, 35
  OECD countries, of, 34
tax evasion cases, 157
tax incentives system, 193
tax performance
  improvement needed in, 155
tax revenues, 155, 156
tax system
  reform of, 185
television networks, 133
Tendero, Efraim, 108
tertiary educations institutions, 257
Teves, Rey Magno, 55
Thai oligarchy, 286
Thailand, 12, 65, 167, 223
  agricultural growth, 210
  coefficient of variation, 274
  comparison with, 214
  decline in poverty, 33
  domestic investment rate, 152
  elimination of absolute poverty, 204
  exports, 164
  GDP, 215
  growth elasticity, 209
  inequality level, 257
  inflow of foreign direct investment, 168
  influence of military, 22
  infrastructure spending, 183
  massive inflow of capital, 165
  population growth, 213, 215
  similarities with, 247
  TFP growth, 211
theology of liberation, 108

Third world
church's view on situation, 108
Today, 133
total consumption, 149
total factor productivity (TFP) growth, 211
total government revenues, 155
total public debt, 161
total saving to finance investment
sources of, 153
tourism
expansion of, 146
importance of, 198
potential of, 197
tourists
Asian countries, from, 198
trade
average shares of, 266
growth of, 166
liberalization of, 268
trade openness, 224
trade policy interventions, 266
traditional patron, 28
traditional politics, 28
training schools
journalism, 139
Transco
privatization, 191
Transparency International survey, 183
trapos, 29
traditional politician, 5, 19
Trends in Math and Science Survey (TIMMS)
national average score, 37
turncoatism, 5

U

umma
fragmented, 283
unemployment
high rate of, 183
"unfinished revolution", 3, 4
unicameral parliamentary government
proposals for, 44
Union of Local Authorities of the Philippines (ULAP), 27, 44, 46, 55, 65, 66, 69
appeal against rejection of petition, 67
United Church of Christ in the Philippines, 107
United Indigenous Nations of Mindanao, 285
United Kingdom, 62, 65
United Methodist Church, 107
United States of America, 22, 24, 54, 62, 278
federal republic, to, 54
free trade agreement with, 246
influence of, 21
shift to federal republic, 56
since, 55, 1946
tourists from, 198
unitary republic
University of Asia and the Pacific, 107
University of Philippines, School of Economics, 156
Unlad Pilipinas (Party of the Global Filipino Nation), 71
upper class
political expressions of, 21
urban "people power", 71

V

value added tax (VAT), 185
Velarde, Mike, 108, 109, 117, 119
Veritas Newsweekly, 132
Vietnam, 12
agricultural growth, 210
coefficient of variation, 274
inequality level, 257
population growth, 213
production sites shifted to, 165
refugee-type migration, 223

Vietnam war, 223
Visayas, 204
  poverty, 205
Villanueva, Eddie, 110, 119
Villar, Manuel, 71

W
wage effect, 224
Wald, Kenneth, 101
Wallace Business Forum, 184
war fatigue
  MNLF, 298
Washington Post, 135
water supply
  access to, 205
weak state, 4
wealth
  redistribution of, 202
Western businesses
  characteristics of, 184
Western colonizers, 102
Western culture and management practices
  adaptability to, 184, 185
Western Mindanao
  high rate of poverty, 205
Western Visayas
  OFWs from, 231
Woodrose School for girls, 107
World Trade Organization, 145, 210

Y
Yap, Emilio, 133
young societies, 19

Z
Zamboanga del Sur, 287

www.ingramcontent.com/pod-product-compliance
Lightning Source LLC
Chambersburg PA
CBHW021544260326
41914CB00001B/161
* 9 7 8 9 8 1 2 3 0 4 9 9 5 *